Aircraft for the Few

Patrick Stephens Limited, a member of the Haynes Publishing Group, has published authoritative, quality books for enthusiasts for more than 20 years. During that time the company has established a reputation as one of the world's leading publishers of books on aviation, maritime, military, model-making, motor cycling, motoring, motor racing, railway and railway modelling subjects. Readers or authors with suggestions for books they would like to see published are invited to write to: The Editorial Director, Patrick Stephens Limited, Sparkford, near Yeovil, Somerset, BA22 7JJ.

Aircraft for the Few

The RAF's Fighters and Bombers of 1940

Michael J.F. Bowyer

Patrick Stephens Limited

First published in 1991

British Library Cataloguing in Publication Data
Bowyer, Michael J.F. (Michael John Frederick) *1928-*
   Aircraft for the few.
   1. Great Britain. Royal Air Force. Fighter aeroplanes, history
   I. Title
   623.74640941

   ISBN 1-85260-040-3

Patrick Stephens Limited is a member of the Haynes Publishing Group P.L.C., Sparkford, Nr Yeovil, Somerset BA22 7JJ.

Typeset by Burns and Smith Ltd

Printed in Great Britain

10   9   8   7   6   5   4   3   2   1

Contents

Abbreviations and terms used

'A/210'	Aircraft 'A Apple' of No 210 Sqn; standard Coastal Command recording style
A&AEE	Aeroplane and Armament Experimental Establishment
ACAS	Assistant Chief of the Air Staff
AFDE/AFDU	Air Fighting Development Establishment/Unit
AP	Armour Piercing
ASU	Aircraft Storage Unit
BDST	British Double Summer Time (times quoted)
CFS	Central Flying School
CRO	Civilian Repair Organisation
CRU	Civilian Repair Unit
DIA	Damaged (slightly) in action
DGRD	Director General Research and Development
DR	Destroyer
DTD	Directorate of Technical Development
EAO	Aircraft Category E (write-off) on the ground following enemy bombing, etc.
EAO2	As above, but requiring contractor's attention
EATS	Empire Air Training Scheme
EFA	Aircraft Category E (write-off) due to flying accident
EFAO	As above, but happening during the course of operational flying or during operations air test
EFB	Aircraft Category E (write-off), due to 'flying battle' — directly as a result of battle damage sustained, possibly crashing as a result
FAO2	Aircraft damaged in flying accident during operations and requiring contractor's attention (The latter shown by suffix '2')
FAT	Flying accident during training
FBO2	As above (FAO2) but aircraft suffering battle damage
FH	Flying hours/minutes (total)
FN	Forth/North convoy
FS	Full Supercharger
FS	Forth/South convoy
FTR	Failed to return
GR	General Reconnaissance
IE	Initial or Immediate Equipment
IR	Immediate Reserve
MFS	Marshall's Flying School, Cambridge
MU	Maintenance Unit

MV	*Merchant Vessel*
NPL	*National Physical Laboratory*
OTU	*Operational Training Unit*
PDU	*Photographic Development Unit*
PRU	*Photographic Reconnaissance Unit*
RAE	*Royal Aircraft Establishment*
RIW	*Repair in works — i.e. repair by contractor at factory or CRU*
s/d	*Known to have been shot down*
SOC	*Struck Off Charge*
TAS	*True air speed*
"270° Bishop's Rock 78 miles"	*Incident 78 miles from Bishop's Rock on compass bearing 270° (generally magnetic)*

Parameters

It seems doubtful whether any aircraft will achieve greater adulation than that afforded to those used during the Battle of Britain. Surveyed here are origins, operations, and individual examples of operational home-based aircraft types which served with the Royal Air Force in 1940. Hurricane and Spitfire are well known, but they fought not alone. Fighter Command relied upon others, and the nation also upon the Commands, with heaviest losses being proportionally sustained by two Coastal Command squadrons.

Within the section entitled 'The Fighters' may be found the home defence Lysanders of No. 22 Group, large numerically and providing perhaps one of a number of interesting surprises relating to 1940s aircraft. Such transport aircraft as existed were also under Fighter Command control, but I have listed them separately, along with potentially operational American aircraft which reached Britain in surprisingly large numbers during the Battle period. Since there was no precise start or ending to the Battle I have concentrated upon the period 1 July to 15 October, the latter date being that upon which German invasion of Britain was postponed.

Dates alongside the listings of individual aircraft show the period of availability to the squadron, ceasing if they sustained major damage although aircraft often remained with a squadron for some time after such an event while awaiting categorization and attention. The main sources for individual aircraft histories are the Air Ministry's wartime Form 78s which may now be viewed at the RAF Museum. Raised for accounting and statistical purposes, they do not have Historical Document status. Theoretically they record movement dates between units and often carry dates of allocation, but compiled in critical times they must be viewed as giving only probably accurate information, albeit the best available. Additionally, bad weather, operational conditions, etc., interfered with movements as much as recording. Unless I have found proof that listed items are wrong I have accepted Form 78 data.

Individual aircraft are listed within squadron groups, allowing them to be more readily related to particular engagements although there were frequent occasions when aircraft were manned, and operated, by squadrons other than those to which they were assigned. For that reason some entries in RAF Form 541s (Squadron Operations Record Books) — legal documents — should not be too hastily dismissed as inaccurate. Correlations between RAF Command Operations Record Books and their Appendices, Air Ministry War Room and Intelligence reviews, Station ORBs, Group records and relevant files (many now available for consultation at the Public Record Office, Kew) almost inevitably produce anomalies, some of which defy unravelling. If you do consult any please treat them with great care, for too many which arrived at Kew in immaculate condition are already much damaged. A tendency to 'tamper' with the evidence they present in order to fit supposed 'facts' half a century later is something which should not be lightly undertaken.

I have worked from Official documents during almost all of the half-century since the Battle, and hereby acknowledge the Crown Copyright which exists within them. I have supplemented it with items from the RAF Museum and the Imperial War Museum to whom I extend my thanks. Also included is much material from private sources — including my own recording of aircraft seen that fateful summer. To this is added items gathered during many hours spent with fellow enthusiasts.

Michael J.F. Bowyer
Cambridge

The Fighters

Prime task of the fighters was the air defence of the United Kingdom. Most of Fighter Command's aircraft combined high speed with fixed armament, rapid climb and a duration of about 1 hr 20 min, judged sufficient for the task if radar early warning was effectively employed. Elaborate identification and tracking systems backed the fighters in their actions.

It was to Fighter Command, its personnel, its aircraft, that the nation looked most for protection. Before furious fighting developed the Command was called upon to protect shipping which task, until 1943, absorbed a very considerable part of its effort. Despite lack of suitable aerodromes it became forced to protect Britain's western flank, which promoted a need for longer duration fighters than it possessed. By autumn 1940 Fighter Command also required night fighters, of little use without airborne interception radar. Luckily the Beaufighter was then to hand.

Each type of aircraft in the Command was designed for a specific task. Hurricanes which replaced the traditional Bristol Bulldog were intended to repel bomber formations, while Spitfires carried out more specialized point defence, protecting particularly vital places. That is the real reason for the disparity in their numbers. Sir Hugh Dowding was content to field just these two types of superb fighters, but he was presented with other types to deploy. One was the Defiant intended to support Field Force, its late delivery forcing precious Hurricane squadrons to be diverted to Army protection. Aged Demon two-seat 'turret' fighters having to be replaced, a scheme was devised whereby surplus Blenheim 1 bombers were hurriedly converted into interim fighters with a prime role of ground strafing. Their subsequent vulnerability forced them to be employed at night in a role for which they were never intended. One squadron of Gladiators defended Devonport because Plymouth's airport was initially unsuitable for fast monoplane fighters. The Whirlwind cannon fighters never went into the fight and Spitfire cannon fighters proved too troublesome to maintain in the front line.

At first glance the inclusion of the strange-looking Lysander army-co-operation aircraft within this section may seem incongruous, but large numbers served within 22 Group controlled by Fighter Command. Lysanders had an Army support and home defence role both on the mainland and in Northern Ireland.

Complexities arising from fighter losses are considerable. Basically, aircraft were written off as a result of damage sustained during operational flying or training flights, with seriously damaged machines being repaired by contractors on-site or at a Civilian Repair Unit within the Civilian Repair Organisation. A surprisingly small number were destroyed or seriously damaged on the

Fighter Command — Strength and Serviceability

Date/time		Blenheim A	B	C	Defiant A	B	C	Gladiator A	B	C	Hurricane A	B	C	Spitfire A	B	C	Serviceable/establishment
JULY																	
1	09:00	7	16	68	2	16	25	–	–	–	23	16	282	19	16	243	618/816
12	09:00	6	16	64	2	16	27	–	–	–	25	16	316	19	16	228	635/832
18	09:00	6	16	62	2	16	23	–	–	–	27	20	323	13 / 6	16 / 20	232	640/996
22	09:00	6	16	63	2	16	21	–	–	–	27	20	357	13 / 6	16 / 20	228	669/996
30	09:00	6	16	74	2	16	23	–	–	–	27	20	333	13 / 6	16 / 20	232	662/996
AUG																	
8	09:00	6	16	66	2	16	20	–	–	–	28	20 / 16	}370	13 / 6	16 / 20	257	713/1,024
12	09:00	6	16	60	2	16	24	–	–	–	28	20 / 16	}363	13 / 6	16 / 20	248	699/1,032
15	08:00	6	16	61	2	16	25		16	2	28	20 / 16	}351	13 / 6	16 / 20	233	672/1,032
21	08:00	6	16	58	2	16	25		16	7	30	20 / 16	}400	13 / 6	16 / 20	239	729/1,082
24	08:00	6	16	63	2	16	23		16	8	30 / 1	20 / 16	}408	13 / 6	16 / 20	238	740/1,098
26	18:00	6	16	56	2	16	18		16	8	30 / 1	20 / 16	}408	13 / 6	16 / 20	240	728/1,098
30	18:00	6	16	52	2	16	14		16	7	31	20 / 16	}410	13 / 6	16 / 20	234	717/1,102
31	18:00	6	16	54	2	16	13		16	4	31	20 / 16	}417	13 / 6	16 / 20	212	700/1,102
SEPT																	
3	18:00	6	16	53	2	16	25		16	8	31	20 / 16	}400	13 / 6	16 / 20	221	707/1,102
7	18:00	6	16	44	2	16	20		16	9	32	16	398	19	16	223	694/952
12	18:00	6	16	50	2	16	21		16	8	33	16	392	19	16	208	679/968
15	18:00	6	16	47	2	16	24		16	8	33	26	389	19	16	192	660/698
16	18:00	6	16	60	2	16	19		16	8	33	16	356	19	16	218	659/968
18	18:00	6	16	51	2	16	25		16	5	33	16	362	19	16	212	655/968
26	18:00	6	16	56	2	16	15		16	7	33	16	392	19	16	203	673/968
OCT																	
15	18:00	6	16	53	2	16	18		16	8	33	16	405	19	16	208	692/976
31	18:00	6	16	40	2	16	10		16	8	34	16	399	19	16	227	684/984
DEC																	
31	19:00	6* + 21 Beau'	16	32	3	16	38		16	8	36	16	471	19	16	242	810/1,040

Notes:
'A' columns = number of squadrons, 'B' columns = theoretical/established squadron strength, 'C' = total number of aircraft serviceable within squadrons
Squadron generally established with 16 aircraft (12 + 4 reserves) sometimes equipped over laid down strength.
'Half squadrons' had established strength of 16 aircraft although normally held 8.
December 31 return included for comparison.
*Squadrons equipped with both Beaufighters and Blenheim Is

12

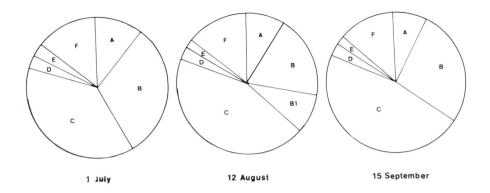

| 1 July | 12 August | 15 September |

The composition of Fighter Command, July to September 1940

Pie charts showing the squadron percentage proportions of Fighter Command.

LEGEND:

Letter	Identity	1 July	12 August	15 September
A	Blenheim 1(f)	11	9	8
B	Spitfire	31	19 + 9	27
C	Hurricane	38	43	47
D	Defiant	3	3.75	3
E	Blenheim (22 Grp)	3	–	–
E	Gladiator*	–	2.25	2
F	Lysander	14	14	13

*includes Gladiators at half-squadron strength

These and the accompanying aircraft strength figures reveal a Fighter Command remarkably intact at the end of its gruelling fight.

ground as a result of air attack.

I have attempted, despite all the attendant difficulties, to classify losses within four groups. Aircraft which failed to return (FTR) could equally have done so due to being quickly shot down, crashing as a result of battle damage, suffering mechanical problems, or be missing due to a pilot suffering misfortune. Aircraft shot down were sometimes repairable, damage category often being decided some time after the event — this made recording difficult and some Official records appear to contain errors when they were in fact accurate.

What is very clear is the enormous contribution to the Battle of Britain made by the Hurricanes, although examination of computerized statistics provides some surprises. 'Computerized' — what effect upon the Battle would such magic machines have produced?

13

The Boulton Paul P.82 Defiant

'Had it shed its turret, acquired wing guns and an AI operator instead of a gunner, what a useful aeroplane it could have become.' That was Fighter Command's verdict on a somewhat traditional type of aircraft, traversing gun two-man fighters having been part of the RAF's inventory since its inception. Many served in the RFC on the basis that their gunner's wide field of fire increased operational flexibility whereas fixed guns in fighters appeared to possess serious limitations. Although the Hurricane and Spitfire were clearly brilliant performers, revival of the two-seat fighter found favour especially since the squadrons it was to equip were to be assigned to the mobile Field Force.

During a 1934 Continental sales drive, Boulton & Paul of Norwich was approached by French manufacturer Société Anonyme Machines Matrices, who suggested that the British company might like to purchase British Empire Rights to their advanced gun turret, designed by M. de Boisson, despite its rejection by the French Air Ministry.

Mr J.D. North, Boulton & Paul's Chief Designer, and Flt Lt Cecil Feather, the company's Chief Test Pilot, upon their return tried to persuade the Air Ministry to buy two examples and a further two incorporating the company's ideas. Failing in both intentions, Boulton & Paul purchased one turret then floated the idea of a turret fighter to replace the biplane Hawker Demon which the company was producing. Fighter Command, about to be dragged into a scheme it neither wished for nor approved of, later decided to switch the aircraft to its Field Force.

Relying upon traversing guns, a pack of such fighters could engage an enemy bomber from below, behind, and with a beam onslaught, making speed and stability more important than fast climb and good manoeuvrability. To avoid crew confusion when in action these fighters — which would need to be of clean design to compensate for the drag and weight of the turret — would forgo forward firing guns. Fuel for about 3 hours' cruise would be needed, allowing for half an hour at a top speed of about 280 mph. A ceiling of about 30,000 ft was required, and eight 20-lb anti-personnel bombs would be carried for use against troops.

Air Ministry attention successfully aroused led to the F.9/35 turret fighter needing a top speed of about 298 mph compared with the equivalent single-seater's 315 mph.

Approved on 20 May 1935, the specification was circulated on 26 June 1935 to 15 firms. Six responded — Armstrong Whitworth, Bristol, Fairey, Hawker, Supermarine and Boulton & Paul. They were considered at a conference on 12 September 1935. Preference was for the Hawker design which became the Hotspur, with favourable comment greeting Boulton & Paul's layout. Two prototypes of both designs were ordered, and two examples of the Fairey contender (loosely based upon the Battle bomber), along with one expensive Armstrong Siddeley Terrier-powered Armstrong Whitworth twin-engined fighter, soon cancelled.

Late February 1936 the Boulton & Paul fighter mock-up became available for Official viewing, and prototype construction was well under way. When in June 1936 the project was reviewed in detail there seemed little chance of it entering production, because a Hawker Hotspur order was being prepared.

Boulton & Paul rightly believed Official interest lay in its turret and not their aircraft. In September 1936 the first turret arrived from France and the Director of Technical Development hurried to Norwich to view it. He saw far more than he expected. Of the turret he wrote that it was 'a very high-class piece of design'. Although built largely from

Fine lines of the Defiant displayed by K8620, *the second prototype.*

magnesium casting and thus encroaching upon scarce materials, Official opinion was that it must be put into production in Britain.

But it was not just the turret that pleased the Ministry man, for construction of the Boulton & Paul fighter was fast advancing, its very appealing lines clear to view. DTD was greatly impressed, especially with its very advanced all-metal construction and widespread sub-assembly. Every part of the structure was bench-made in small components then bolted together. Top and bottom wing skins would be fastened to ribs before the front and rear spars were fixed, then the leading and trailing edges would be positioned. The Rolls-Royce engine mounting was already in hand, the tailplane partly complete and the retractable Dowty undercarriage eagerly awaited. Not surprisingly DTD reported that Boulton & Paul 'could become a good production unit', but his recommendation that a small production order now be placed was turned down on the grounds that the firm had 'still to prove themselves an acceptable production unit'. Boulton & Paul decided to move from Norwich to Wolverhampton early in 1937, delaying the F.9/35 prototype by three months, but increasing its workforce and impressing the authorities.

Tests of the aircraft's advanced wing structure undertaken at Farnborough in January 1937 confirmed its strength and quality. By mid-April the fuselage was complete, day and night work shifts being introduced in May.

With all going well the company (now named Boulton Paul) was faced with a highly disturbing challenge. The Air Ministry informed the industry that future fighter armament must include cannon. Since the Boulton Paul P.82 could never carry that in a turret, Official interest switched to ideas for a large three-seat twin-engined 375 mph fighter, the F.11/37, armed with a twin 20 mm cannon turret, and carrying 250-lb bombs intended to be dropped into bomber formations to split them apart. Boulton Paul promptly designed an impressive twin-Vulture fighter.

On 25 February 1937, although firmly favouring cannon, Air Ministry placed a production order, after all, for the promising Boulton Paul P.82. Ignoring late delivery of the prototype, *K8310* (due on 4 March 1937), the company on 28 April received an order for 87 examples, to Specification 5/37P, soon named Defiant. Fairey's competitor was cancelled, but Hawker's design, its wings interchangeable with the Hurricane's eight-gun variety, was an attractive proposition. July 1937 saw Hawker ordered to fully develop their machine, now named Hotspur. On 11 August 1937 Cecil Feather took *K8310* on its first flight. No turret was yet

15

installed, in which state the Defiant certainly outshone the Hurricane. With wing guns only it would have developed into a very effective fighter.

Undercarriage retraction problems occurred in September 1937. Boulton Paul decided to replace the Dowty gear with a Lockheed type before *K8310* went to Martlesham for trials extending from 7 to 31 December.

A top speed of 320 mph was recorded there, 10,500 ft reached in 7.5 min, and the service ceiling was 33,500 ft — but no turret had been installed. Wind tunnel tests suggested that performance with turret in situ would be good, and official test pilots wrote that 'The Defiant is the finest built aircraft that has come to Martlesham Heath'. Air Ministry, less elated, told the company that they had 'put on a really bad show' by not having the turret installed in time. *K8310* must, they said, be available fully armed for tests not later than February 1939. Doubt that there was sufficient power to rotate the turret at high speed made flight tests essential.

Nash & Thompson had not even assembled the Hotspur's cramped turret, and with Hawker's attention focused on the Hurricane and Henley bomber, Hotspur production was cancelled on 11 January 1939. Another 389 Defiants were quickly prescribed, 202 more in February 1938 and an extra 161 three months later. By mid-February 1938 a Boulton Paul built turret had been fitted in *K8310* which, on the 18th, commenced 10 days of intensive trials at Martlesham.

Although its loaded weight was now 7,500 lb, *K8310*'s top speed had only fallen to 302 mph. The 1,030 hp Rolls-Royce Merlin I exhibited severe cutting in dives while extended aileron trailing edges reduced aerodynamic balance. Cockpit glazing had recently been modified, and telescopic radio masts fitted. A novel feature was a rectractable fairing forward of the turret allowing the guns 360° traverse. It reverted to its normal position automatically. Consensus nevertheless was that it should be controlled by the gunner!

The Hawker Hotspur first flew on 14 June 1938. With a wooden mock-up turret and ballast, it already weighed 7,650 lb loaded, reached 316 mph at 15,800 ft and had a ceiling of 28,000 ft. *K8620*, the second Defiant and with a 1,500 hp Merlin III, closely resembled a production aircraft. Not until 18 May 1939 did it fly, by which time hastily converted Blenheims and not Defiants were replacing Demons.

Initiated at Wolverhampton in January 1939, production to 'Defiant 1/P1/5/37' was planned to provide the first Defiant 1 in April 1939, the ACAS now certain that when it entered service Defiant performance would fall short of that expected. Indeed, on 17 April 1939 he said that because of likely slower speed he hoped to see Defiants serve only until the large F.11/37 was ready. He suggested fitting Merlin XIIs or the forthcoming RR-37 Griffon in Defiants (optimism indeed), and clipping wing tips to reduce weight and increase manoeuvrability. Nothing came of these suggestions, but in June 1939 it was decided to fit a Merlin X in the Defiant Mk II intended to enter production in mid-1940. Extra speed was not vital.

The first production aircraft *L6950*, first flown on 30 July 1939, was delivered to A & AEE on 19 September 1939. The second, *L6951*, reached CFS Upavon on 5 September for preparation of pilot's notes, then on 17 September joined *L6952* at Northolt's AFDE for tactical trials. Five production examples were delivered during September by which time Belgium was showing a keen desire for Defiants which could not be met because of the slow production rate. Although Air Ministry and Fighter Command thought such disposal of the Defiant a good idea, they were already considering its night fighter possibilities.

Highest speeds attained during tests of *L6950* were 297 mph TAS at 15,000 ft with + 6½ lb boost; 303 mph with + 12 lb boost. It took 10.1 min to reach 15,000 ft, 15.1 min to 20,000 ft where the top speed was 295 mph.

L7012, *an early production Defiant 1.*

Within three weeks of the delivery of the first Defiant a long list of complaints was compiled. The company did well to rectify many in a few days, but could do nothing to increase speed. By the end of December 1939 only 15 out of 650 on order (an additional 363 had been contracted for in September 1939) had reached the RAF. Nevertheless two more orders, for 150 and 50, were placed.

No. 264 Squadron, Martlesham Heath, received its first three Defiants (*L6959, '60, '61*) on 9 December. Engine failures and hydraulic problems were encountered and the Defiants were grounded on 28 January. Further speed and dive-bombing trials followed resumption of flying in February. One aircraft reached its top speed of 260 mph TAS at 3,000 ft while another peaked at 286 mph. A third, performing on 2,770 engine revs, made 291 mph at 5,000 ft, another attaining 282 mph TAS by flying on 2,950 revs and + 12 lb boost!

Traditionally the pilot captained an aircraft, but control of the Defiant was vested in the gunner, making it essential that the pair fought as a team — none too easy for a fighter pilot trained to be individualistic. To Sqn Ldr P.A. Hunter fell the task of turning No. 264 Squadron into a fighting team.

When the Defiants first went into action only 56 of the 563 on order had been delivered, and all with two pitch DH propellers. The superior constant speed DH propeller, first fitted to *L6954* in April, equipped the 87th and later examples. This increased the top speed — usually to about 302 mph at 20,000 ft — took the service ceiling to 30,000 ft and reduced take-off run.

Nothing came of April 1940 ideas to lighten and convert some Defiants into PR aircraft, but in June 1940 go-ahead was given for the night fighter and completion of two Mk IIs, one with a Merlin RM2SM, the second with an RM3SM. A further 300 Defiants (in the AA serial range) were ordered in July 1940. Rapidly the company undertook Mk II development, *N1550* with a Merlin XX giving 1,260 hp at 12,500 ft and first flying on 20 July 1940, the second Mk II later that summer. The Mk II was only about 12 mph faster than its predecessor.

Operationally, the Defiant was a disappointment due to rules for tactical employment taking no account of fighter-escorted bombers flying higher than expected. When such misfortunes loomed large thought was given to fitting eight guns

K8310 *modified to single-seat fighter configuration. Fitted with eight wing guns it would have been a very useful fighter.*

in the Defiant wings, removing the turret and keeping the second cockpit for an AI radar operator. Such a scheme was discussed at a DGRD/ACAS(T) Liaison Meeting on 4 September 1940, along with results of Boulton Paul's trials with *K8310* fitted with streamlining combing in place of a turret. Twelve Browning guns could have been wing mounted, alternatively cannon. The company claimed a top speed of 345 mph for a Merlin XX version, but the Air Staff had already decided to use Defiants as night fighters to supplement slow Beaufighter delivery and poor performance of the Blenheim 1(f).

Operations

Defiants of 264 Squadron first went into action on 12 May 1940, and by the end of that month fourteen had been either lost or put out of action during 164 sorties. The squadron's claim of 65 enemy aircraft destroyed was much inflated; a dozen is a more realistic total. If the enemy mistook Defiants for Hurricanes and made stern attacks, then he quickly discovered his error and found the Defiant's limited manoeuvrability and unsuitability for individual combat.

No. 141 Squadron, the second with Defiants, became operational from 3 June 1940. On 28 June it moved from

A trio of 264 Squadron Defiants, L7026:V, N1535:A *and* L6967:T. (IWM)

Prestwick to Grangemouth and Turnhouse, from where L6983, L6988 and L7016 flew the first operational sorties the following day, and on 1 July L6997 made the Defiant's first operational night patrol. On 10 July No. 141 left Turnhouse to replace 79 Squadron in the Biggin Hill Sector, placing its 16 operational aircraft at West Malling where the squadron arrived on 12 July.

The Defiant's unsuitability for fighter-versus-fighter combat was cruelly proven on 19 July. At 12:15 hrs Raids H47 and H49 — 30 bombers (mainly Do 17s) flying at 12,000 ft with a few Ju 87s and coming from the south-west — were heading for two convoys converging in the Straits of Dover. There they dive-bombed a destroyer. Although between 12:22 and 12:39 hrs all Dover's AA guns fired, producing a barrage comprising 129 ARBT, 18 ABT and 17 AEB shells along with 71 20 mm Hispano rounds and small arms fire, they failed to deter the enemy. A dozen Defiants of 141 Squadron earlier sent forward to stand by at Hawkinge were at 12:23 ordered to cover at 5,000 ft one of the convoys south of Folkestone. Only nine Defiants managed to take off to patrol in vics closely packed line astern in the practised manner. Barely had they adopted their box formation in cloudless weather when they were bounced out of the sun by Bf 109Es of experienced II/JG2. Two Defiants were picked off during the first fast diving onslaught, another two when attacked from below. L6974 (Plt Off J.R. Kemp/Sgt R. Crombie), L6995 (Plt Off R.A. Howley/Sgt A.G. Curley), L7015 (Plt Off R. Kidson/Sgt F.P.J. Atkins) and L7016 (Plt Off J.R. Gardner/Plt Off D.M. Slatter) were all shot down at sea, only Gardner surviving. A further Defiant, L7009 (Flt Lt I.D.G. Donald/Plt Off A.C. Hamilton), was shot up and crashed outside Dover, and L7001 (Flt Lt M.J. Louden/Plt Off E. Farnes) was forced to land 200 yd from Hawkinge. L6983 (Plt Off I.N.M. MacDonald) also made base, but without his gunner Sgt J.F. Wise who

had baled out. L6999 and L7014 were the only two Defiants to survive. Pilots of 111 Squadron, called too late to give support, reckoned Defiant gunners destroyed four enemy fighters, in exchange for which the Luftwaffe virtually wiped out 141 Squadron during its first engagement.

Fearing another massacre, 12 Group ordered 264 Squadron from Duxford to Turnhouse to where on 21 July 141 Squadron flew, taking with it seven new aircraft as it headed for Grangemouth to re-establish its HQ. On 21 July 141 Squadron arrived at Prestwick and next day reorganized itself, placing 'A' Flight at Montrose and 'B' Flight at Dyce. There, on 28 July No. 141 commenced convoy escorts off Scotland and on the 29th L7011 flew the second night patrol by the Squadron. Before '264' had a chance to move serious fighting over the south and east caused its diversion to Kirton-in-Lindsey, Lincolnshire. Fighter Command had rightly deduced that since Lincolnshire ports and airfields were beyond the range of Bf 109s, Defiants could safely engage bomber formations. 'B' Flight of 264 Squadron was placed at Coleby Grange on 2 August, further dispersal following on 5 August when 'A' Flight moved to Ringway to protect Manchester. Within a few days the squadron reassembled at Kirton to defend Hull upon which attacks were forecast.

Eleven Defiants (L6973, L7003, L7006, L7018, L7021, L7024, L7026, L7027, L7028, N1535 and N1536) of 264 Squadron were taking off from Kirton just after 13:00 hrs on 15 August to escort convoy 'Arena' 30 miles east of North Coates when news was flashed that formations of He 111s of KG26 and Ju 88s of KG 30 (among them a handful of Ju 88C heavy fighters) were approaching. Although a classic opportunity presented itself, orders were for the squadron to remain with and to protect the convoy. Next night Plt Off Whitley (L6985) sighted a He 111 which his gunner engaged in the first such event, but the Defiant's day

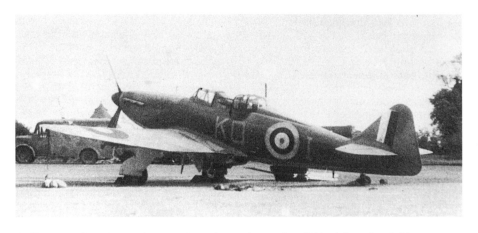

Defiant N1572, 'KO:I', of 2 Squadron, during September 1940 trials at Cambridge to assess its army co-operation potential. (W. Shearman, via A.S. Thomas)

fighting career was far from over.

Dowding decided that, to give other squadrons a brief rest, No. 264 must move south, and to Hornchurch on 22 August. At 05:10 hrs on the 24th came instructions to advance to Manston and into the extreme front line.

Enemy activity off Kent commenced around 08:00 hrs, and 264 Squadron patrolled over Manston. Engine starter problems delayed Flt Lt E.W. Campbell-Colquhoun/Plt Off G. Robinson (*L7013*) who took off late and in misty conditions formated upon two aircraft they thought were Defiants but turned out to be Bf 109s. These rapidly turned upon them, their shots igniting Verey cartridges. Skilfully evading his attackers, Plt Off Robinson landed at Manston. Other 109s inconclusively engaged the remaining Defiants (*L6967*, *L7003*, *L7005*, *L7006*, *L7018*, *L7025* and *N1536*) which touched down at Hornchurch around 11:30.

Respite was brief, midday bringing the next battle. A dozen Defiants orbited Manston for an hour then, with the enemy absent, nine landed to refuel, leaving Yellow Section on guard. At 12:40 hrs the nine were scrambled and as they took off at 12:46 hrs Manston was attacked by at least a score of Ju 88s of KG76 escorted by Bf 109s. The bombers came in at 13,200 ft and dived to 4,000

ft to release their bombs during three minutes of bombing. Lucky to get airborne, the Defiants were soon embroiled in individual combats as the diving bombers began levelling out. Sqn Ldr Garvin, Plt Off Whitley (*L7021*), and Sgt Thorn (*L7003*) each claimed a Ju 88 and Plt Off Barwell a Bf 109, enemy records suggesting that five Ju 88s were lost or irreparably damaged. But 264 Squadron lost Sqn Ldr Philip Hunter with Plt Off F.H. King (*N1535*), who had taken part in every one of the squadron's major engagements and were last seen by Red Section following a Ju 88 towards France. Plt Off I.G. Shaw/Sgt A. Berry (*L7027*) and Plt Off J.T. Jones/Plt Off W.A. Ponting (*L6966*) were all missing when the squadron landed at Hornchurch.

Led by Sqn Ldr G.D. Garvin, the new Commanding Officer, in *L7025*, 264 Sqn was yet again ordered up. At 15:30 hrs Raid H8, comprising 15 He 111s of KG53 flying at 15,000 ft with Bf 109s escorting, turned from north Medway over the Thames Estuary obviously making for Hornchurch, so at 15:40 hrs 264 Squadron was scrambled. Two Defiants collided on the ground, leaving only seven (*L6967*, *L6985*, *L7003*, *L7005*, *L7024*, *L7025* and *N1536*) to proceed. Take-off had been ordered so late that bombs were bursting on the airfield as the last two fighters got away. Local AA gunners were firing before the fighters took off, the fourth salvo from battery N11 at 15:41 hrs tearing out the port engine from an He 111 which crashed at North Ockendon. The Defiants climbed away too fast to get into formation before contacting the raiders north-east of the aerodrome. Sqn Ldr Garvin tackled the main formation, strafing two bombers during overtaking and converging passes, and Walsh (*L7003*) tackled a straggler 400 yds behind the main formation, blasting it during a crossover attack. A Bf 109 was fired upon by three Defiants and Plt Off Young (*L7005*) claimed a He 111 with an overtaking run. Flt Lt Banham/Plt Off Goodall (*L6985*) damaged another bomber which flew off towards London. But Plt Off R.S. Gaskell (*L6967*), shot down by a 109, had leg injuries and Sgt W.H. Machin, his gunner, was wounded. No. 264 Squadron had acquitted itself well, but at tragic cost. On the 25th seven new Defiants reached Hornchurch all needing modifications which took about 48 hours per aircraft. Some had no self-sealing fuel tanks, incorrect fuel and the wrong type of plugs, and all guns needed harmonizing. Night work was impossible for no lights were permitted in the hangars.

The first scramble on the 26th resulted in five Defiants fruitlessly patrolling over Thameshaven. Then at 11:40 seven Defiants, this time led by Flt Lt Banham (*L6985*) and flying in vics line astern between Herne Bay and Deal, engaged 12 Do 17s strongly escorted by two *Gruppen* of Bf 109s intending to attack West Malling. As the Defiants tackled the Dorniers from below they were immediately set upon by Bf 109s. Flt Lt A.J. Banham/Sgt B. Baker (*L6985*) claimed a Do 17 before an explosive shell burst in the cockpit setting the Defiant ablaze. Banham told his gunner to bale out, and was then picked up after 1½ hours in the sea off Herne Bay. Baker was not found. Plt Off Goodall (*L7024*) was also

attacked by a '109 before he set fire to a Do 17 from which two of the crew baled out. Plt Off Hughes (*L7028*), making converging attacks, claimed two Dornier 17s. Sgt E.R. Thorn and Sgt F.J. Baker put up a fine show and claimed two Dorniers but while attacking a third were themselves shot up by a Bf 109. They took evasive action and spun away with oil and glycol leaking and made a crash landing at Marshside, near Herne Bay. As they did so the Bf 109 made another pass at a mere 500 ft and set *L7005* on fire. Before it crashed Baker fired his remaining rounds at the enemy, bringing it down a few fields away from the Defiant. Another fight had taken place between Flt Lt Campbell-Colquhoun (*L7026*) who, after leaving a Do 17 smoking, was attacked by 109s before he could confirm his prize. Flg Off I.R. Stephenson's *L7025* was set on fire by another Bf 109. He baled out and was later rescued from the sea but his gunner Sgt W. Maxwell was posted missing. For any Defiant gunner the chance of getting out in an emergency was indeed slim. The squadron had done well, three Dornier 17Zs of KG3 being certainly shot down in the sea. Another two crash-landed on the Continent.

In the mist of 27 August 264 Squadron proceeded to Rochford, Hornchurch's satellite, and managed only one uneventful patrol over the Thames Estuary before the next day's major tragedy. At 08:30 12 crews flying *L6957*, *L6963*, *L7018*, *L7021*, *L7026*, *L7028*, *N1556*, *N1569*, *N1574*, *N1576*, *N1672* and *N1673* were ordered to patrol Dover at 12,000 ft. Near Folkestone they tackled 20 escorted He 111s of KG53 facing Bf 109s of JG26 and the bombers' cross-fire. Plt Off Carnaby/Plt Off C.C. Ellery (*N1576*) in their first engagement claimed hits on a He 111, which was further damaged by Sgt A.J. Lauder/Sgt V.R. Chapman (*L6957*). A fuse blew in the turret of Sqn Ldr Garvin's aircraft *L7021* and as Flt Lt R.C.V. Ash was replacing it the Defiant was set ablaze by a cannon shell, then crashed near Faversham. Both men had baled out but Ash was dead when found. *N1574*, manned by Plt Off D. Whitley/Sgt R.C. Turner, was brought down and one of the most successful crews died in flames at Kingswood. Plt Off J.R.A. Bailey (*N1569*) had to force land after being strafed by a Bf 109, he and Sgt O.A. Hardy his gunner surviving the crash at Petham. Of the eight Defiants which landed at base only three remained serviceable — and the day's fighting was not yet over.

At 12:45 a large enemy force was approaching Rochford, authority for those three remaining Defiants to do battle being strongly refused. By 13:00 the raiders were overhead at 18,000 ft and only then was permission given to engage. The section comprising *N1556*, *N1576* and *N1672* was just airborne when a stick of bombs fell across Rochford slightly damaging one of the fighters, all of which left too late to engage. Five more sorties over Rochford and Hornchurch remained to be flown before the brave, badly battered remnants of 264 Sqn retired to Kirton-in-Lindsey and tasks less hazardous. During its August spell with 11 Group the squadron had flown 78 sorties and lost nine aircraft.

September 1940 saw 264 Squadron flying convoy protection patrols and practising night flying — and not without tragedy. On the 4th *N1628* crashed on take-off, killing its crew, Flg Off O'Malley and Sgt Rassmussen. To avoid lighting Kirton, all 264's night fighting activity was switched to the Caistor satellite from 10 September, from where 'A' Flight operated. Two days later 'B' Flight moved to Northolt to share in London's night defence. Night patrols began on the 13th, five sorties being flown during one of which Flg Off Barwell and Plt Off Goodall briefly contacted a raider. Night flying at Caistor on the 14th attracted an intruding He 111 which put 12 bullets into the Chance light but none in the Defiants.

During the big raids over the south on 15 September six Defiants were, at 12:25 and again at 14:45, ordered up to guard Northolt but did not take part in the fighting. 'B' Flight nightly patrolled without success and on the 19th moved to Luton to continue the task. On 20 September 'A' Flight placed three aircraft at Ringway for night defence of Liverpool. Luton's element meanwhile maintained patrol lines over Halton, Maidenhead and Guildford, but flying at under 2,000 ft and fast using fuel they could not hear the controller at Northolt. Although sorties at the rate of about six a night were usual it was 16 October before Plt Off Hughes and Sgt Gash (*N1621* shot down a He 111 of 2./KGr 126 at 01:30 hrs near Brentwood.

No. 141 Squadron had also been active at night. It reassembled at Turnhouse on 30 August, 'B' Flight moving to Biggin Hill on 13 September and dispersing to Gatwick on the 18th. Night operations commenced on 15 September, eight sorties being flown. Next night, flying *N1552*, Plt Off Waddingham and Sgt Cumbers claimed two He 111s and on the 17 there was no doubt about the success of Sgt Laurence/Sgt Chard (*L6988*) whose victim, a Ju 88A-1 of I/KG54, smashed into a Maidstone housing estate. No. 307 (Polish) Squadron, the third to have Defiants and which formed at Kirton on 5 September, did not commence operations until 8 December 1940.

As a night fighter the AI Mk IV equipped Defiant proved too slow, had insufficient duration and again suffered from lack of forward firing guns. Fighter Command later pressed strongly for more powerful Merlin XX, even Mk XLV engined Defiants, for as crews gained experience the Defiant's night effectiveness clearly improved. On 15 March 1941 the Command commented, 'Defiants have done well recently and Fighter Command thinks it is a useful night fighter.' Within the Defiant saga was an ironic twist — it might have proven ideal in enemy hands for his night fighters frequently had batteries of upward firing guns.

Ultimately the Defiant operated with some success as a night-fighter, an example of which is depicted here in 256 Squadron markings. (RAF Museum)

Individual aircraft

No. 264 Sqn

L6955	12.12.39–22.12.40
L6957	21.11.39–3.9.40
L6963	5.3.40–5.7.40, 19.7.40–1.11.40
L6964	4.3.40–13.7.40
L6966	18.1.40–3.9.40
L6973	24.4.40–9.11.40
L6974	11.3.40–13.7.40
L6979	27.8.40–4.12.40
L6985	13.6.40–shot down nr Herne Bay 26.8.40
L6996	4.6.40–FTR 24.8.40
L7003	31.5.40–FA 25.8.40 (overshot Hornchurch)
L7006	31.5.40–FTR 26.8.40
L7007	20.5.40–FTR 25.8.40
L7013	1.6.40–5.9.40
L7017	27.8.40–1.11.40
L7018	31.5.40–EFB 7.10.40
L7021	4.6.40–FTR 28.8.40 off Dover
L7024	30.5.40–FA 26.8.40
L7025	30.5.40–FTR 26.8.40 off Dover
L7026	1.6.40–FTR 28.8.40 off Dover
L7027	1.6.40–FTR 24.8.40
L7028	4.6.40–13.11.40
L7033	27.8.40–28.11.40
N1535	14.6.40–FTR 24.8.40 in Channel
N1548	28.9.40–18.1.41
N1556	25.8.40–17.12.40
N1558	28.8.40–12.12.40
N1562	28.8.40–27.12.40
N1569	25.8.40–FA 18.9.40 (force landed Petham)
N1574	25.8.40–FTR 28.8.40
N1576	25.8.40–27.12.40
N1578	23.8.40–FTR 7.10.40
N1581	27.8.40–2.2.41
N1621	9.10.40–13.10.41

N1623	11.10.40–4.2.41
N1626	9.10.40–26.11.40
N1627	29.8.40–EFB 8.10.40 (crashed nr Marlow)
N1628	27.8.40–EFB 4.9.40 (crashed nr Kirton-in-Lindsey)
N1630	27.8.40–30.9.40
N1672	21.8.40–1.10.41
N1673	25.8.40–4.9.40

No. 141 Sqn

L6964	13.7.40–26.11.40
L69083	4.4.40–FAO 19.7.40, RIW
L6984	16.4.40–4.11.40
L6988	3.5.40–22.2.41
L6989	3.6.40–22.2.41
L6992	3.5.40–22.2.41
L6994	8.4.40–26.2.41
L6995	8.4.40–FTR 19.7.40
L6997	6.5.40–12.8.40
L6998	6.5.40–EFAO 8.7.40 (ground accident)
L6999	24.5.40–21.10.40
L7000	20.7.40–9.4.41
L7001	20.7.40–9.4.41
L7009	25.5.40–FTR 19.7.40
L7011	25.5.40–6.9.40, RIW
L7013	1.6.40–5.9.40, RIW
L7014	24.5.40–FA 28.9.40, RIW
L7015	6.7.40–FTR 19.7.40
L7016	25.5.40–FTR 19.7.40
N1537*	20.7.40–27.4.41
N1546	8.8.40–17.4.41
N1549	25.6.40–20.7.40
N1552	20.7.40–19.7.40
N1554	27.8.40–12.4.41
N1561	5.8.40–8.11.40
N1563*	20.7.40–4.11.40
N1564	20.7.40–13.12.40
N1566	20.7.40–EFAO 30.10.40 (stalled during night approach, Biggin Hill)

N1568	29.9.40-9.12.40
N1622*	27.8.40-21.11.40
N1688	11.10.40-12.1.41
N1706	2.10.40-12.8.41
N1725	11.10.40-19.7.41

No. 307 (Polish) Sqn

L7035	14.9.40-6.12.40
N1559*	14.9.40-5.3.41
N1560	14.9.40-11.11.40
N1624	17.9.40-8.12.40
N1640*	14.9.40-3.2.41
N1641	14.9.40-23.12.40
N1642*	14.9.40-3.2.41
N1643*	14.9.40-5.3.41
N1671	17.9.40-14.1.41
N1675	18.9.40-14.1.41
N1683	18.9.40-14.1.41
N1684	18.9.40-29.1.41
N1686	14.9.40-2.1.41
N1688	11.10.40-12.1.41
N1695*	17.9.40-3.2.41
N1696*	17.9.40-17.1.41

* Later converted to Defiant TT Mk III, a version which saw mainly naval use.

From 9 September Defiants were delivered (three on the 15th) direct to ASUs, and none of these were issued to squadrons before 15 October 1940. Final deliveries in the period were of *N1808–N1812* inclusive plus *N3307*, all delivered on 29 October 1940.

Summary

By 30 June the RAF had received 108 Defiants, of which 72 remained on charge. Examples up to and including *N1792* had been delivered by 15 October 1940. By then 267 had been received, 223 remained on charge and 96 had seen active service in squadrons or other units. Eighty-seven served into 1944, 47 into 1945 and nine remained on charge in 1946, the last four being SOC in October 1946. The only Defiants with squadron service during the Battle to survive the war were *N1563*, *N1581*, *N1544* and *N1546*. The only Defiant remaining is *N1671*, initially delivered to 6 MU on 7.8.40 and then to 307 Sqn 17.9.40-14.1.41 and again 13.7.41-10.6.41, to 153 Sqn 30.10.41, to 285 Sqn 22.6.42-23.2.43, to 10 MU 16.5.43, to 52 MU 8.9.44, subsequently stored for museum use and now displayed in the Battle of Britain Museum, Hendon.

The Bristol Beaufighter

Within days of the Beaufort's first flight in October 1938 Bristol told the Air Ministry of a feasible cannon fighter version of their GR bomber. It was not the company's first try at such a machine for they had proposed two schemes to the requirement that produced the Westland Whirlwind, but this 'conversion' quickly aroused Official interest. On 29 November 1938 the Air Council discussed the proposal and a week later the Air Staff decided that Fighter Command should have cannon-armed fighters (none of which yet existed in Britain). That made Bristol's Type 156 of even greater interest.

By having two Hercules VISM engines with high-speed super-chargers, this 16,000 lb fighter would have a top speed of about 370 mph, the firm claimed. Mainplanes needed few changes, but the after fuselage would be slimmed and a wider floor would allow for the two-paired guns between which would be the crew novel entry doors. Necessary larger propellers meant a taller under-carriage and having the engine mid-set in place of the Beaufort's underslung type. The pilot would sit in the extreme nose and have a good view forward. Aft would be the cannon loader who could observe ongoing events from beneath a teardrop dome.

The Air Staff pressed for more details which were passed to Air Marshal Sir Wilfrid Freeman on 23

December 1938. According to the company 'Beaufighters' could be available for testing about six months after an order was placed. Reassessment of the likely performance indicated a top speed of 361 mph at 15,000 ft and good duration, and a further Air Council meeting, on 2 January 1939, discussed the project with enthusiasm. On 24 February 1939 a £3.3m order for 300 Beaufighters was placed. To speed production early examples would have lower rated Hercules III engines which meant reduced performance. But the RAF would be getting a fast and very roomy cannon fighter with good development potential, as events were to prove.

April 1939 brought the detailed official specification for the aircraft which it referred to as 'an interim replacement for F.37/35' (i.e. the Westland Whirlwind). It went ahead on the basis of being Hercules VI powered and having a top speed of 'not less than 350 mph' below 15,000 ft, climbing to 20,000 ft in 10 min and being able to cruise for 3 hours. But problems with the Hercules were surfacing and in April 1939 Bristol informed the Ministry that many early aircraft would need to have Hercules III engines. Worse still, the first 30 Beaufighters would have Hercules IIs, poorly rated above 10,000 ft, which news prompted the Air Staff on 22 June 1939 to dilute the specification and call for a top speed of 336 mph at 15,000 ft from the Hercules III aircraft. Bristol expressed 'no real concern' and again claimed that 361 mph would be met with later aircraft. Despite deep concern and the realization that it would be inferior to the Hurricane, Air Ministry never contemplated cancellation for they needed this cannon fighter even though on 24 May 1939 the first cannon-armed Hurricane, L1750, flew.

Bristol certainly did well to get the prototype Beaufighter R2052 flying on 20 July 1939, for much redesigning of the fuselage had proven necessary and only the outer mainplanes, tail unit and undercarriage were similar to the Beaufort's. But not until January 1940 did R2052 (Hercules 1-SM similar to the III) venture to Boscombe Down for official trials which showed a top speed of 335 mph at 16,800 ft. R2053 (Hercules 1-M like a Mk II) reached only 310 mph, and at 4,000 ft, and when a Hercules III machine was tested it could only reach 309 mph at 15,000 ft. Fitting a camera blister and locking down its troublesome tailwheel gave R2054 a top speed of 300 mph at 14,060 ft. Six early Beaufighters would now have Hercules II engines, others Mk IIIs. As a reserve item Rolls-Royce was soon ordered to build 100 Merlin XXs as power eggs to be fitted to Beaufighters should Hercules production fail. As for the standard Beaufighter, Lord Beaverbrook selected it in May 1940 as sixth priority type.

On 26 July 1940, with the Air Staff already planning superior cannon-armed fighters, the Beaufighter was declared fit for operational service and 25 Squadron was initially chosen to equip. Hasty decision forced by urgent need could not overcome problems with feeding the ammunition from the drums into the cannon. Weak gun mountings led to inaccurate firing. Pilots expressed dislike of the heavy cockpit framing and huge engine cowlings spoiling their view. Beaufighter production amounted to two in June, five in July, 23 in August, 15 in September and another 65 before 1940 ended.

Operations

The first Beaufighter to serve in an RAF unit was R2066 which joined the Tangmere Special Flight (alias the Fighter Interception Unit) on 12 August 1940. AFDU Northolt received R2055 next day and the first deliveries to squadrons took place on 2 September with R2072 reaching 29 Squadron at Digby and R2073 joining No. 604 at Middle Wallop. Next day R2057 reached 25 Squadron at North

R2069, *an early Beaufighter I of 25 Squadron, wearing Sky under surfaces because it was intended for day fighting.*

Weald and on the 8th Nos. 23 at Ford and 600 Squadrons each received one so that snags could be explored by various units.

On 18 September Sqn Ldr S.C. Widdows on 29 Squadron in *R2072* made from Digby the first operational sortie (day) in a Beaufighter. As with the Blenheim, there had never been any intention to operate the Beaufighter primarily at night. Its ample internal space allowing early bulky AI radar to be carried brought that about, also a top speed below that originally expected. Squadron flying suggested the Hercules III version could attain between 312 and 325 mph at 15,000 ft — and enemy night bombers were coming in at 18,000 ft which gave little cause for comfort. No successful engagement had taken place by the end of September.

By the end of October the Beaufighter's future looked increasingly likely to be within Coastal Command, for whom two special versions were devised. Fighter Command retained priority delivery of the first 100 examples and on 12 October 219 Squadron, Redhill, inherited all 600 Squadron's aircraft. Nos. 25 and 604 would, however, become the first to be fully equipped and operational.

General and operations summary

2.9.40	*R2072* to 29 Sqn, Digby
2.9.40	*R2073* to 604 Sqn, flying that evening
17.9.40	*R2077* left Satellite L1 for 23 Sqn, Ford
18.9.40	29 Sqn: Sqn Ldr Widdows & Plt Off Watson (*R2072*) first patrol — over Hoylake, 17,000 ft
2.10.40	604 Sqn: first operational patrol by Sqn Ldr Anderson in *R2073* over Worth Matravers
9.10.40	25 Squadron: first operation, by *R2080*
25.10.40	219 Sqn: Sgt Hodgkinson (*R2126*?) engaged a Do 17Z which subsequently crashed at Cormeilles

Bristol Beaufighters in Squadron and trials unit hands 1 July–15 October 1940

R2055	FIU Tangmere 2.9.40 to 604 Sqn 28.1.41
R2056	AFDU 13.8.40 to 25 Sqn 2.9.40–28.2.41
R2057	25 Sqn 3.9.40 to A&AEE 25.7.41–1.1.44
R2059	FIU 1.9.40–24.9.40
(*R2062*	Merlin RM 2SM prototype — destroyed during bombing of Filton 13.10.40)
R2065	600 Sqn 11.9.40 to 219 Sqn 12.10.40–4.11.40
R2066	FIU 12.8.40 to Special Flight, Christchurch 26.8.40 to RAE 11.10.40
R2067	25 Sqn 8.9.40–EFA 15.9.40

R2068	25 Sqn 8.9.40–FTR 21.11.40 (in the sea)	R2078	A&AEE 8.9.40 to FIU 12.9.40–12.10.42	
R2069	25 Sqn 8.9.40–24.8.41	R2079	600 Sqn 12.9.40 to 219 Sqn 12.10.40–EFA 14.10.40	
R2070	219 Sqn 2.9.40 to 600 Sqn 12.10.40–23.11.40	R2080	25 Sqn 8.9.40–15.3.41	
R2071	600 Sqn 11.9.40 to 219 Sqn 12.10.40–EFA 13.11.40	E2081	25 Sqn 13.9.40–13.10.40	
R2072	29 Sqn 2.9.40 to 600 Sqn 26.9.40 to 219 Sqn 12.10.40–FA02 15.10.40	R2082	25 Sqn 20.9.40–16.8.41	
		R2083	600 Sqn 1.10.40 to 219 Sqn 12.10.40–EFAO 30.4.41	
R2073	604 Sqn 2.9.40–EFA 29.8.41	R2090	600 Sqn 20.9.40 to 219 Sqn 12.10.40–21.5.41	
R2074	600 Sqn 11.9.40 to 219 Sqn 12.10.40–16.1.41	R2091	25 Sqn 2.10.40 to 604 Sqn 8.12.40	
R2075	600 Sqn 11.9.40 to 219 Sqn 12.10.40–14.11.40	R2092	25 Sqn 17.9.40–8.12.40	
R2076	600 Sqn 8.9.40 to 219 Sqn 12.10.40–1.8.41	R2098	25 Sqn 1.10.40 to 604 Sqn 29.10.40	
R2077	23 Sqn 8.9.40 to 29 Sqn 13.9.40 to 23 Sqn 17.9.40 to 604 Sqn 1.11.40			

Delivery reached *R2142* by 28 October 1940, Hercules X engines fitted in *R2139 et seq.*

The Blenheim 1(f) two-seat fighter

September 1938, and the word throughout the land is 'Munich'. With the crisis at its height the RAF stood mobilized. Making ready to defend the land, armourers were loading live ammunition into the belts of the latest fighters — Hurricanes, a handful of Spitfires, and Gladiators. Four other squadrons were also preparing, all with one thing in common — they had quite outdated Hawker Demon two-seat fighters.

A First World War anachronism, the two-seat fighter was something that Fighter Command's brilliant leader, Air Chief Marshal Hugh Dowding, had inherited. He saw no tactical virtue in such a machine, yet he was to have a more advanced version (the Defiant) introduced into his Command — when it was ready which, in September 1938, was far from the case. Indeed, moving the Defiant's place of manufacture at a critical time meant that delivery was unlikely in under another year. Had nothing been done, four squadrons would have gone to war with Demons.

As the 1938 crisis receded Air Ministry reviewed 'the Demon question', hitting upon a seemingly bright idea. With a new version of the Bristol Blenheim entering production, many short-nosed Mk 1s would be cast aside by bomber squadrons. Since the Blenheim bomber was rated faster than opposing fighters, surely here was the ideal gap filler to hold the fort until the Defiant sallied forth? In October 1938 a proposal came — convert Blenheims into multi-gun fighters with probably a battery of four fixed forward-firing Browning guns placed in a tray fitted into the bomb bay and supplementing the usual wing gun.

Any decision to go ahead needed to be taken rapidly and was discussed in the first week of November 1938. Dowding suggested converting the concept into a single-seat fighter, but others favoured a crew of two and an all-round view. Certainly a Blenheim pilot had an extremely restricted view and no possibility of seeing aft. A rear lookout at least was needed. Yet a turret was a heavy, highly restrictive item, so should it be removed, adding 8-10 mph to top speed?

On 7 November 1938 interested parties met in the knowledge that the Blenheim fighter was going ahead in view of the 'late delivery of modern fighters'. Up for questioning were the number to become 'intermediate fighters', the fitting of four guns in the bombing compartment, possibility of some forward protective armour and the extent of equipment to be carried along with any possibility of rapid return to bomber configuration. By the end of the day the decision had been made; to provide Nos. 23, 29, 64 and 25 Squadrons, in that order, each with 14 IE + 5 IR Blenheim 'auxiliary fighters'. As if to emphasize that designation, Nos. 600, 601 and 604 Auxiliary Air Force Squadrons were to re-equip with Blenheim 1 fighters at Hendon. Long-range Blenheims, still officially called Mk II but soon renamed Mk IV and about to join Nos. 53 and 59 Squadrons of No. 22 Army Co-operation Group, were also reckoned suitable for fighter conversion. As to the one or two-man crew, C-in-C Fighter Command would investigate that question.

No. 11 Group backed Dowding's idea for a single-seat turretless fighter; No. 12 Group supported the Air Ministry view — turret gun and gunner providing all-round lookout. Guess who won?

The speed with which the plan went ahead remains amazing. By 24 November firm plans were laid to re-equip the Regulars by the end of January 1939, the others by mid-February. Allied AAF adjustments resulted in four squadrons being listed to have Gladiators, four with either Hurricanes and Spitfires and 611 Squadron to have Hurricanes in May 1939. Perhaps most interesting of all were three others which were to receive Gauntlets, Nos. 615, 616 — and the County of Leicester Squadron, when it formed, bearing the future hallowed title, No. 617 Squadron!

With a prototype conversion already undergoing trials and development at Martlesham, Fighter Command signalled Wittering on 28 November 1938 that No. 23 Squadron was 'temporarily' to have Blenheims until the Defiant was ready, apologizing for the 'short notice' and adding that they 'will later get a temporary conversion set suiting them to be fighters', the four-gun set on a date uncertain. The Station Commander was told that dual control aircraft were presently being prepared to allow flying training to start with the help of Blenheim bomber pilots. Demons were to be quickly despatched to 8 MU Little Rissington to make room for 21

Blenheim I(f) fighters of 601 Squadron (unit identity letters YN) at Hendon in summer 1939. (RAF Museum)

Some Blenheim Is reached fighter squadrons prior to having gun packs fitted in order to speed conversion training, as can be seen from this early wartime illustration of 601 Squadron aircraft.

Blenheims being prepared by Bristol at Filton. An additional 72 NCOs and airmen would be posted in to service the new, more exacting and temperamental aircraft, leaving Wittering to find space for all these new occupants. Gladiator/Mercury IX experienced men were chosen to service the newcomers although the Blenheim's Mk VIII had a different reduction gear ratio.

By 2 December 1938 five Blenheims at 26 MU Cardington and 16 at 27 MU Shawbury had been chosen for 25 Squadron, and later that month a further 42 were earmarked for Nos. 29 and 64 Squadrons. A census taken on 31 December 1938 revealed a further 38 examples suitable for conversion in ASUs. To ease conversion problems each auxiliary squadron would have an Oxford trainer. No. 25 Squadron's Gladiators were soon on their way to 607 Squadron. No. 23 Squadron had five Blenheims by 12 December, No. 64 holding 11 by 6 January 1939. Lack of accommodation at Church Fenton prompted the idea of supplying Bellman hangars.

Delivery of Blenheim bombers was one thing, but what of the general conversion programme and the equipment? At a time of increasing production problems Bristol and the Ministry turned to an unexpected source by ordering from the Southern Railway's Eastleigh workshops an initial batch of 150 gun packs for the new fighters, to be fitted at ASUs and stations by contractors and Service personnel — and fast.

A further conference to discuss the whole problem was convened for 16 January 1939 by which time 'permanent fighters' and bombers and GR Blenheims convertible into fighters were available. Sufficient Blenheim 1s would be converted to arm and back seven squadrons each of 21 aircraft. The permanent ones were now designated 'Blenheim 1(f)' (*sic*), others listed as 'Bleinheim AC' or 'Blenheim Bmr'. Compliance with the C-in-C's wish for a cupola to replace the turret was agreed, thus providing a lookout for the pilot, Beaufighter style. Adding another wing gun was too complicated, but a ring and bead and GM 2 gunsight were to be fitted, and each gun would have 500 rounds available.

Within a short time the question of removing and replacing turrets arose. Because it would be time-consuming the plan was reversed, and on 25 January 1939 AVM Sholto-Douglas, ACAS, informed Fighter Command that the turrets must stay, certainly in the Regular squadron aircraft which were now allocated to Field Force wherein rear defence was necessary. Incidentally, at no time in the initial thinking was the term 'Blenheim night fighter' mentioned, although the Mk 1(f) Blenheim, despite the poor view, had full night flying gear.

On 26 January 1939 *L1512* was chosen for full trial conversion into a fighter and *L1525* on 9 February, some two months after No. 23 Squadron had received its first Blenheim 1s, to serve at Filton as the development aircraft. Suggestions that the pilot was very vulnerable to return fire had prompted provision of armour. This idea was rejected because of its weight.

By Spring 1939 all the squadrons were equipped or equipping with their far from ideal interceptors. Fighter Command realized that in wartime it would inevitably have to patrol over coastal shipping and coastal areas, for which the Blenheim's duration made it suitable. Already a new use for the aircraft came when a trainer for Bawdsey-based airborne interception radar operators was needed. A Blenheim was sent to Martlesham and

at once seen to be sufficiently capacious to carry the bulky radar gear. More by chance than design was born a new role for the aircraft. But by the time the fighters were in service their limitations were well appreciated, the major failing being that the aircraft was too slow.

Late 1939 saw attempts at Bristol and PDU Heston to increase the Blenheim's performance. *L1348* was polished, skin cracks were filled and smooth paint were all tried. In 1940 the machine, after conversion into a fighter, was used in various attempts at further improvement.

The most obvious was to fit more powerful Mercury XVs in place of Mk VIIIs, and switch to de Havilland CS 10° pitch propellers in order to improve the climb rate. Trials at Boscombe Down and Farnborough showed that *L1348* weighing 11,250 lb had, when cleaned and with wing tips clipped by 3 ft, a top speed of about 276 mph TAS at 13,000 ft. Adding the gun pack and raising the rear turret for action in a standard aircraft reduced the top speed to 227 mph. Removal of any unnecessary equipment was worthwhile, but not until autumn 1940 was *L1290* tested with a Beaufighter-type canopy in place of the turret, a suggestion Dowding had made in 1938.

An early wartime photograph of a 604 Squadron Blenheim 1(f), the serial number of which has been painted over for security reasons.

30

The drag-producing turret in operation position on a Blenheim I(f) whose forward hatch, where Blenheim guns were later sited, is open.

To be effective, AI radar was essential, but any additional weight was bound to reduce the already poor pursuit performance. Assessment in March 1940 had shown that fitting AI Mk IV aerials cut the speed by 10 mph, making the removal of the turret and the 100 lb of rear fuselage armour essential. No. 32 MU Colerne did just that, the aircraft's fully loaded weight then becoming 12,566 lb, still well above that of the cleaned-up example.

Results of RAE trials with Mk 1(f) *L1290* with various gun tray/turret/AI combinations showed top speeds at 18,000 ft (at which altitude German night bombers frequently operated) to be:

no AI, or guns	280 mph (at 11,700 ft)
turret, but no belly guns	261.5 mph
AI IV, no turret, or gun ring	245 mph
AI, turret up	229.5 mph
AI, no turret, gun ring fitted	233 mph

Fitted with a DH CS propeller an AI-equipped, fully armed Blenheim 1(f) at 14,500 lb showed it to take 6 min to reach 10,000 ft, 18 mins to 20,000 and 24 to 20,050 climbing at 2,550 revs.

Further trials followed with Mercury XV engines and DH CS propellers in *L6671* and rear armament removed, providing these results:

Ft	Time to... (mins)	top speed (mps)
10,000	4.5	259
15,000	8.5	252
20,000	14.5	245
25,000	25	232

Removing the Blenheim's dorsal armament did not meet with general approval so Frazer Nash produced a two-Browning gun ring, first fitted in place of the turret. Later it was installed in place of the forward hatch and preceded by a small wind shield. Trials with these features and specially rounded AI aerials were undertaken using *K7033*, but there was no way of converting the Blenheim 1(f) into a very desirable fighter. Rough gun pack workmanship was often blamed, along with the heavy turret's high drag.

On 2 October 1940 Fighter Command decreed that the 64 aircraft in its four Blenheim 1(f) squadrons should all have their turrets removed, the well being covered with a plywood panel. A speed increase of up to 80 mph was gained and 100 modification sets were ordered. First to convert would be Middle Wallop's 604

Blenheim I(f) K7090:ZK-V *of 25 Squadron at North Weald in early 1940.*

Squadron to whom nine sets of parts were delivered on 6 October 1940, with Nos. 25, 219 and 23 Squadrons following in that order. By then a better solution, the Beaufighter, was becoming available. Conversion work was barely underway before November.

Operations

The extent of RAF activity on the day that the war commenced was more than is generally appreciated. As well as bombers and coastal aircraft, Fighter Command operated too. From Wittering a dozen Blenheims of 29 Squadron and 604 Squadron (*L6740, L6645, L1502, L8661, L6741* and *L8373*) set forth to search over the North Sea for an approaching enemy. None being found, the event made no headlines. They came when, after proceeding to Bircham Newton on 28 November, a dozen Blenheim 1(f)s (*L1406, L1408, L1433, L1437, L1440* and another of 25 Squadron with six of 601 Squadron) set off mid-afternoon to strafe at dusk German mine-laying seaplanes at Borkum.

Interception and convoy protection patrols were supplemented by much practice flying until the May 1940 *Blitzkrieg*. As early as 03:40 on 10 May Sqn Ldr Anderson of 600 Squadron engaged several He 111s whose return fire crippled his Blenheim. Turret disabled, flaps and undercarriage useless, he had to crash land at Manston. Around noon six Blenheims of 600 Squadron set out to strafe Ju 52s on an airfield near Rotterdam. A dozen Bf 110s bore down upon them in a fierce fight in which Bf 109s joined and four Blenheims were destroyed. Undaunted, four more took off at 13:30 and damaged a He 111 off Holland before 25 Squadron took over the patrol. Martlesham based, that squadron had been busy of late co-operating in radar development and training with the Bawdsey station.

Despite its losses on that fateful Tuesday, No. 600 Squadron mounted a bomber escort in the evening, with No. 604 Squadron, but heavy losses discouraged much further commitment. On 14–15 May No. 600 withdrew to Northolt, No. 604 Squadron having arrived on 13 May to replace it. No. 604 had also operated on 10 May, twice providing escort for Wattisham's Blenheim IVs attacking Ju 52s on beaches north of the Hague. After the bombers first struck, in went '604', guns blazing during low-level strafing to claim four Ju 52s destroyed and three damaged. *L1517* (Flg Off I.K.S. Joll) was brought down on the shore.

Ground strafing by Blenheim formations — clearly too costly — again aroused the problem of this

Blenheim I(f) L8740:NG-Q of 604 Squadron airborne from Manston and photographed in August 1940 wearing day fighter colours.

fighter's employment. If not safely by day, what possibility of night activities? On 18 May Flg Off Hunter of 604 Squadron patrolling over France fired at a He 111 which he was sure fell into the sea off Dunkirk. More night patrols were flown on 22/23 May when three pilots fired at raiders. Night operations were practicable.

Early June 1940 brought a great increase in enemy activity over Britain and in the moonlight of 18/19 June when over 70 He 111s raided England, Blenheims of 23 and 29 Squadrons tackled them. The results remain quite amazing for, mainly relying upon searchlight glare and eyesight, seven crews of 23 Squadron found raiders. Upon opening fire any Blenheim position was betrayed, S-Sugar (*L1458*) being shot down by return fire. But the enemy lost out too when *YP-L* shot down a He 111 near Sheringham and *YP-X* destroyed another near Newark before that Blenheim entered an unrecoverable spin. Plt Off J.S. Barnwell (*L6636*) of 29 Squadron was also successful, but a Heinkel gunner badly crippled the Blenheim which crashed in the sea drowning its pilot. Not for many months was such success repeated by British fighters at night. With poor view to the flanks, no radar aid, a gunner giving limited help, it remains surprising that the night's activity

proved so successful.

By late June No. 29 Squadron was using Wellingore(F1), where in mid-July the proposed FN twin-Browning gun mount was fitted to one aircraft, the rest to be modified soon after. Self-sealing fuel tanks were also applied. Frequent night patrols were flown and on 29 July two Blenheims were detached to Tern Hill for the defence of Liverpool.

By that time No. 600 Squadron was operating at night from Hornchurch and trying out the early AI radar recently installed in its Blenheims, Flt Lt Clarkson in 'R' being, on 19 July, the first squadron pilot to have an 'enemy blip' on his set. Next night under Foreness Radar Plt Off Boyde engaged a night flying He 59 and on 25 July tried for another. August found No. 600 using Manston as an advance base from where on the 8th Flg Off Boyde and Flg Off Grice took off to practise AI interceptions. Barely were they airborne when enemy aircraft were reported overhead. Boyde hurried home, but Grice's aircraft, an engine blazing, dived over Ramsgate then plunged into the sea. Courageously he had avoided the town, but it cost Grice his life and those of Sgt Keast and Aircraftsman Warren, his AI operator. Manston was bombed on 12 August and on the 14th when a hangar and three aircraft were hit. On the 16th eight Bf 109s

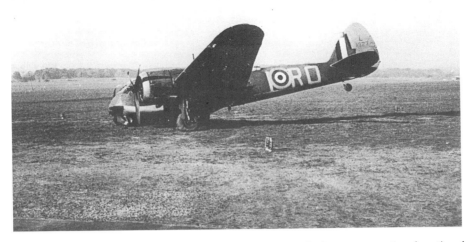

Another Blenheim I(f) wearing day fighter colours and also unconventional national markings, L1327:RO-1 of 29 Squadron. (R. North)

strafed the aerodrome setting a Blenheim and a Spitfire on fire. Airfield defence was attempted by three Blenheims (D,M,R) on the 20th, but Bofors firing impeded the effort when the squadron bravely tackled 10 Bf 109s. By 24 August, 600 Squadron had fully vacated Manston.

From Tern Hill the 29 Squadron detachment was successful early on 18 August. Plt Off R.A. Rhodes and Sgt Gregory took off in *L6741* and at 02:28 south-west of Chester came upon a He 111. This they followed across England, opening fire some 25 miles off Spurn Head. The raider fell into the sea 10 miles west of Cromer Knoll LV. Two nights later Flt Lt J.S. Adam with Plt Off Watson up from 'L1' in *L1237* at 03:10 began chasing a raider, but it was too fast for them. Then it circled, they caught up, Adam fired and the bomber was last seen diving away off the Isle of Wight. No. 29 Squadron was again in action on 24 August. Plt Off Braham (*L1463*) saw a raider held by searchlights in the Humber area, and both aircraft exchanged fire. Soon after, searchlight crews reported an aircraft burning on the sea. Meanwhile the Tern Hill detachment, doubled from 10 September, maintained night patrols defending Liverpool.

No. 219 Squadron had been operational since 21 February 1940, flew frequent night training sorties particularly from West Hartlepool, and saw no action — until 15 August. At 13:10 12 Blenheims (*K7118, L113, L1128, L1229, L1236, L1240, L1261, L1374, L6624, L8698, L8699* and *L8724*) were ordered to engage enemy bombers making their only major day raid on the Driffield–Scarborough area. Although the battle was inconclusive it brought high drama for Sgt Dube (*L6624*) who was wounded. His air gunner, Sgt Bannister, came to his aid and between them they flew the damaged Blenheim to Driffield, there making a wheels-up landing. Each was awarded a Distinguished Flying Medal.

Active since the start of the German night bombing campaign, No. 604 Squadron fielded many sorties and gave night protection to the Dunkirk evacuation. The squadron moved from Manston on 20 June to Northolt and to Gravesend on 3 July and then, aided by 271 Squadron, settled at Middle Wallop on 26 July. Midday 11 August brought a special operation, two Blenheims (*L6774* Sqn Ldr Anderson and *L6728* Plt Off Crew) escorted by three Spitfires of 152 Squadron being ordered to investigate a He 59 floatplane which had alighted 30 miles off France and was surrounded by small vessels. This was an ideal target and 604 Squadron soon had it blazing. As the Blenheims departed six Bf 109s tackled the

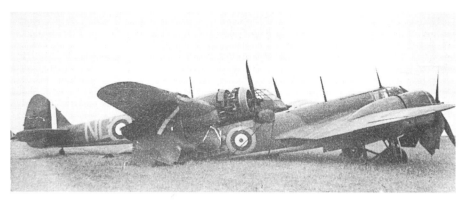
Two Blenheims of 604 Squadron at Middle Wallop after involvement in a ground accident.

British contingent, all of whom escaped. After dark No. 604 resumed more normal activity, making four patrols of 6 hr 25 min total duration. Led by Sqn Ldr Anderson five Blenheims flew a daylight air–sea rescue search on 13 August, and on the 15th operated six daylight interception sorties. These items all show how wrong it is to class the Blenheim as just a night fighter. Indeed, 604's aircraft and most of the others long wore day fighter colours.

The end for the Blenheim fighter began when on 2 September Beaufighters began reaching the squadrons. Making the massive replacement into a going concern proved far more lengthy than expected and several interim measures were applied to the Blenheim. No. 604 Squadron experimentally added more guns to one of theirs and, making the most of their main equipment, Anderson and Crew on 11 September flew another 152 Squadron-escorted daylight operation, this time setting fire to a Do 18 being towed in the Channel by E-Boats. Blenheim sorties by the squadrons were averaging about five per night.

Blenheim night operations were not entirely devoid of success. On 4 September Plt Off Rofe of 25 Squadron attacked three raiders, and in the face of 'friendly' AA fire which damaged the tail of *ZK:J*. More

successful was Plt Off M.J. Herrick, also of 25 Squadron, who around 01:00 shot down He 111 H-3 *V4 + AB* of *Stab* 1/KG1 which crashed at Rendlesham, near Bentwaters, and possibly destroyed another bomber. Early on 14 September Herrick scored again, bringing down a He 111 H-4, *5J + BL* of 3./KG4, near Sheering, Essex. On 16 September it was 600 Squadron's turn, Flt Lt Pritchard claiming to shoot down in flames a He 111 which crashed off Bexhill. Rofe damaged another raider on 18 September.

Blenheim 1(f) used by operational squadrons 1 July–15 October 1940

No. 23 Sqn **Wittering/Collyweston; to Ford 13.9.40 (det. to Middle Wallop 12–25.9.40)**

K7092	10.8.40-FBO2 17.8.40
K7156	3.6.40-EFAO 5.7.40 (crashed nr Digby)
L1178	10.3.40-31.8.40
L1265	18.12.38-EFA 2.7.40 (crashed Seland)
L1320	16.5.40-25.3.41
L1356	16.5.40-FAO2 4.8.40 (damaged landing base)
L1360	8.11.39-20.2.41
L1438	22.8.40-23.4.41
L1451	6.12.38-7.3.41
L1453	7.12.38-FTR 4.3.41
L1454	9.12.38-19.10.40
L6605	6.3.40-14.1.41
L6611	19.6.40-26.2.41
L6646	30.8.39-29.7.40

L6686 15.9.39-EFB 22.12.40
L6721 6.3.40-EFB 30.10.40 (crashed Bognor)
L6737 5.3.40-2.10.41
L6739 3.9.39-31.12.40
L6743 5.3.40-4.5.41
L6781 31.7.40-?
L6841 31.7.40-EFB 23.11.40
L6855 10.10.39-EFAO 16.1.41
L8684 3.9.40-16.1.41
L8694 23.6.40-2.6.41
L8722 6.3.40-EFB 8.10.40 (overshot
       Tangmere)
L8728 6.3.40-14.7.40

No. 25 Sqn, Martlesham Heath, and from 1.9.40 North Weald also (used earlier with Debden)

K7048 20.3.40-31.7.40
K7090 22.2.40-21.11.40
K7123 18.8.40-16.1.41
K7125 18.8.40-23.10.40
L1172 13.9.40-17.9.40
L1207 3.6.40-4.3.41
L1235 11.6.40-EFAO 7.12.40
L1291 12.3.40-25.6.40, 9.7.40-16.1.41
L1418 30.11.39-EFAO 14.8.40
L1440 15.12.39-22.9.40
L1512 1.2.39-EFB 3.9.40 (shot down by
       Hurricane nr Hatfield)
L1523 4.9.40-17.12.40
L6602 3.8.40-5.3.41
L6676 26.5.39-15.1.41
L6677 26.5.39-4.2.41
L6679 25.11.39-FBO2 19.9.
L6710 10.3.40-11.12.40
L6726 22.8.40-19.1.41
L6727 18.8.40-10.10.41
L6736 28.8.39-31.7.40
L8656 10.12.39-24.9.40.
L8657 10.12.39-16.1.41
L8659 29.8.40-3.9.41

No. 29 Sqn, Digby, also using Wellingore, Lincs, from 8.7.40

K7135 15.2.40-EFB 13.9.40 (shot down by
       Hurricanes S. of Liverpool)
K7172 6.6.40-EFAO 3.12.40 (crashed E. of
       Stockport)
L1169 5.8.40-5.3.41
L1237 20.3.40-EFA 18.4.42
L1292 12.6.40-6.2.41
L1327 9.3.40-1.1.41
L1330 18.6.40-EFB 25.8.40 (crashed nr
       Wainfleet)
L1371 25.10.39-20.9.39
L1375 25.10.39-3.3.41
L1376 6.11.39-EFAO 1.7.40
L1377 6.11.39-EFAO 9.8.40 (belly landed
       Wittering)
L1463 19.12.39-3.3.41
L1472 11.7.40-EFAO 12.10.40
L1503 27.1.39-FAO2 9.11.40
L1505 27.1.39-EFAO 29.11.40
L1507 30.1.39-EFB 19.11.40
L1508 4.2.39-1.1.41

L6612 14.8.40-EFAO 19.12.40
L6637 9.3.40-s/d 13.10.40 NW of Liverpool
L6722 27.3.40-EFAO 31.7.40
L6741 8.9.40-22.2.41
L8509 28.3.40-EFAO 1.8.40 (crashed nr
       Wellingore)

No. 219 Sqn, Catterick, to Redhill 12.10.40

K7118 6.6.40-12.10.40
L1006 29.12.39-22.7.40
L1109 18.6.40-17.1.41
L1113 19.3.40-EFA 12.10.40 (crashed nr
       Ewhurst, Sussex)
L1128 19.3.40-20.11.40
L1168 15.6.40-12.8.40
L1170 23.8.40-18.10.40
L1229 18.5.40-21.2.41
L1236 11.5.40-27.10.40
L1240 20.11.39-23.11.40
L1248 18.5.40-24.7.40
L1261 19.3.40-EFB 30.9.40 (crashed taking
       off at Catterick)
L1374 19.11.39-21.8.40
L1511 8.1.40-22.8.40 (became 2180M)
L1518 16.5.40-23.7.40
L1522 7.5.40-24.7.40
L1524 22.4.40-FAO2 27.8.40
L6642 27.3.40-15.11.40
L6712 2.4.40-5.1.41
L6732 3.11.39-16.10.40
L6733 5.11.39-24.7.40
L6839 18.8.40-4.3.41
L6843 18.8.40-16.11.40
L8685 6.6.40-13.10.40
L8698 20.11.39-13.10.40
L8699 15.11.39-21.8.40

No. 600 (City of London) Sqn, Manston, main base Hornchurch, retired there 22.8.40; Redhill 12.9.40, Catterick 12.10.40

K7118 12.10.40-7.1.41
K7124 15.9.40-27.5.41
K7126 6.6.40-19.5.41
L1115 16.8.40-3.5.41
L1117 16.8.40-28.9.40
L1170 13.10.40-10.1.41
L1256 16.8.40-11.4.41
L1272 22.8.40-13.10.40
L1277 26.8.40-10.4.41
L1289 28.8.40-27.11.40
L1494 6.9.40-14.10.40
L1513 30.1.40-14.10.40
L1521 5.5.40-EAO 14.8.40 (bombed at
       Biggin Hill)
L6599 16.3.40-26.10.40
L6608 15.5.40-26.8.40
L6626 15.5.40-14.10.40
L6646 29.7.40-11.10.40
L6684 12.6.39-EFAO 7.9.40 (force landed
       Rainham)
L6732 12.10.40-15.6.41
L6786 21.5.40-8.1.41
L6791 5.5.40-FBO2 25.9.40
L8451 19.9.39-FAT2 27.7.40

36

L8665	20.5.40–FTR 8.8.40 (shot down off Ramsgate)		L6681	15.4.40–19.9.40
L8669	22.8.40–7.6.41		L6723	10.3.40–FTR 1.8 or 15.8.40?
L8670	21.5.40–27.8.40		L6728	5.11.39–EFB 26.11.40
L8679	19.9.39–EFB 9.8.40 (crashed nr Westgate)		L6774	10.3.40–30.11.40
L8685	13.10.40–3.5.41		L6777	16.5.40–6.8.40
L8698	13.10.40–7.5.41		L6782	10.3.40–EFAO 25.8.40 (crashed Witheridge, Devon)
L8723	3.10.40–19.2.41		L6802	8.6.40–11.12.40
L8729	12.10.40–10.3.41		L6803	8.6.40–EAO 30.7.40
L8730	5.5.40–FBO2 29.9.40		L6807	22.3.40–EAO 12.5.41
			L8676	17.5.40–EAO 14.8.40 (Middle Wallop)
			L8680	8.9.39–5.2.41
			L8681	8.9.39–25.2.41

No. 604 (County of Middlesex) Sqn, Manston; to Gravesend 3.7.40, to Middle Wallop 26.7.40

K7044	23.7.40–27.9.40		L8693	6.3.40–27.10.40
K7083	19.8.40–25.8.40		L8715	8.9.39–14.5.41
K7117	24.6.40–14.8.40			
L1178	31.8.40–11.12.40			
L1179	15.5.40–16.7.40			

Blenheim 1(f) of units with operational capability

L1222	5.8.40–31.8.40
L1281	27.9.40–10.12.40
L1285	18.8.40–30.11.40

Fighter Interception Unit

L1186, L1340, L1404, L6688, L6788, L6805, L6835, L6836, L6837, L6838

L1422	10.12.39–2.41
L4908	14.4.39–EFB 6.9.40
L6609	18.6.40–24.11.40

Martlesham Heath Radar Development & Training Flight

L6610	20.1.39–EFB 15.8.40 (attacked by Spitfire, belly landed Middle Wallop)		L6622	2.1.40–25.2.41
L6617	15.5.40–8.9.40		L6624	2.1.40–EFA 6.10.40
L6640	6.3.40–10.12.40		L6627	7.3.39–23.12.40
L6671	15.5.40–12.5.41			

The Gloster Gladiator

It may come as a surprise to discover that Gladiator biplane fighters remained in front line service with Fighter Command during the Battle of Britain. The end of a line originating in the 1914–18 war, the Gladiator emerged from Specification F.7/30 which indirectly also sired the Spitfire. In the Gladiator the biplane fighter came near to perfection.

A Bristol Mercury IX powered the Gloster SS 37 Gladiator prototype K5200, tested at Martlesham Heath in July 1935. By then 23 of a production version had been ordered. Later in 1935, with a three-bladed propeller absorbing more engine power, K5200 weighing 4,456 lb showed a creditable top speed of 253 mph TAS at 14,500 ft. Yet it was already obsolete for on 30 October 1935 the prototype Hurricane first flew.

Nevertheless the Gladiator was to give a good and famous account of itself. A total of 210 Mk 1s were ordered, this version attaining about 240 mph around 15,000 ft. Of the refined Mk II another 252 were acquired. By the outbreak of war all the Mk 1s had been delivered of which 38 were by then off charge. All of the 224 Mk IIs which the RAF had received remained in fine fettle. By then 52 Mk 1 and 20 Mk IIs were serving at home within five Auxiliary Air Force squadrons. Of these Nos. 607 and 615 (designated Hurricane Squadrons) were soon in France where their Gladiators did their best in May 1940 against overwhelming odds.

No. 263 Squadron greatly distinguished itself by operating Gladiators from a frozen lake during the campaign in Norway. Once home and reformed No. 263 Squadron re-equipped with Hurricanes. That left in Britain only the Shetland defence flight, an offshoot of 152 Squadron, formed in January 1940 with Gladiators for front line fighting purposes.

Although not truly operational, additional Gladiators played a special part in the Battle of Britain by serving in two Meteorological Flights — at Aldergrove in Northern Ireland within No. 25 Group (e.g. *N5590, N5591, N5592, N5593*) and in 3 Group at Mildenhall, Suffolk (e.g. *N5582, N5594*). Twice daily each flight would despatch one of its Gladiators to climb high, its pilot recording temperatures and humidity during his time aloft. Back home the data would go to the Central Meteorological Office to form the basis of weather forecasts upon which operational flying was based.

There were in 1940 sundry other active Gladiators in Britain, at No. 6 Fighter OTU and also with 18 Squadron which rescued a handful from France and held several into August 1940. These included *N2300, N2310, N5580, N5583* and *N5717*. Repair and major servicing for British based Gladiators between 1940 and the end of the war was provided by Marshall's Flying School at Cambridge.

Gladiator N2306 *airborne in August 1940.*

Operations

Only once engaged in combat during the Battle, the Gladiator equipped just 247 Squadron. Initially this was produced by hiving off on 22 November 1939 a part of 13 Group's 152 Squadron, Acklington. On 25 November the unit reached bleak Sumburgh in the Shetlands and was initially known as Fighter Flight, Shetlands whose Gladiators on 4 January 1940 became part of Fighter Flight RAF Sumburgh. Operational work consisted of convoy and interception patrols and the protection of Sullom Voe flying-boat station. An attack upon that base by two He 111s on 1 January 1940 had brought the Flight its first combat, and the Luftwaffe the loss of a bomber. On 12 January the Flight became part of 18 Group, Coastal Command. A second success came on 5 June when Flg Off Gillen shot down a Do 17 off Lerwick. After 498 operational patrols the Flight was on 14 July 1940 ordered to move to Roborough, Plymouth, its northern task being taken over by a Flight of Hurricanes from 3 Squadron, Wick. On 21 July the Gladiators set off on the long transit south, the unit finally assembling there on 1 August on which day it became 247 Squadron, a designated night fighter squadron of St Eval Fighter Sector, 10 Group. Roborough was a primitive station, in naval hands, where on 13 August the

squadron was declared operational, the intention being to extend the aerodrome to allow for night defence of Devonport. Meanwhile night flying took place at St Eval from where operational patrols were undertaken.

At Roborough airmen slept on palliasses in bell tents without even one locker among them. Rough conditions for sure. Two Gladiators were maintained at Readiness and two available by day at the base. Six flew to St Eval each evening — two for training — and returned to Roborough in the morning. Not until 28 October did the first and only Gladiator night interception take place, when Plt Off Winter (*N5622*) attacked a He 111 over Plymouth.

Gloster Gladiators in Fighter Command hands 1 July–15 October 1940

K7918	Stn Flt Northolt 24.3.40–21.6.41
K8026	13 Grp 30.7.40–19.4.41
K8049	247 Sqn 15.8.40–20.2.41
L7609	?–8.8.40
N2308	247 Sqn 15.8.40–3.3.41
N5585	247 Sqn 27.7.40–MFS 5.9.40
N5622	Fighter Flight Shetlands 14.7.40, 247 Sqn, to 8 MU 3.3.41
N5575	247 Sqn 27.7.40–5.9.40
N5576	247 Sqn 27.7.40–MFS 19.2.41
N5644	Fighter Flight Shetlands 14.7.40, 247 Sqn, EFAO 21.11.40 (Okehampton)
N5648	247 Sqn 27.7.40–20.2.41
N5649	247 Sqn 27.7.40–EFAO 22.11.40
N5682	Fighter Flight Shetlands 23.1.40 to 247 Sqn 11.8.40–3.3.41
N5684	247 Sqn 10.8.40–25.4.41
N5702	Fighter Flight Shetlands 23.1.40, 247 Sqn, to MFS 6.6.41
N5716	Fighter Flight Shetlands 18.4.40–EFA 21.6.40
N5897	247 Sqn 10.8.40–20.2.41
N5901	Fighter Flight Shetlands 29.2.40, 247 Sqn, EFB 27.8.40

Hawker's Hurricane

The Hurricane was the most numerous RAF aircraft in operational use during the Battle of Britain. Hurricanes destroyed more enemy machines than other types, and their rugged qualities allowed them to accept heavy punishment and survive. To the Hurricane victory in the Battle must be largely attributed. How strange that the Spitfire snatched the glory, the glamour and the adulation!

On almost every count those were quite different aircraft. Ironically the Hurricane was born of the Hawker Fury whose concept sired the Spitfire. Looking for an advanced monoplane fighter Sydney Camm, Hawker's brilliant designer, in the closing weeks of 1933 devised the Rolls-Royce Goshawk Fury Monoplane. Discussion at Air Ministry on 18 December led to the Rolls-Royce PV-12 ethylene glycol engine (based upon the Kestrel and which became

the Merlin) replacing the steam-cooled Goshawk in a revised design entitled 'Interceptor Fury Monopolane'. First drawings of this reached Hawker's Experimental Section at Kingston in May 1934, and wind tunnel model testing followed at NPL in June, of a design reckoned likely to weigh 4,600 lb and fly in a year's time.

June 1934 found the Air Staff out of favour with specialized fighters, and believing that the Fury had little value. Fast climb, high speed, rapid acceleration then the delivery of a short massive punch was what was needed. Cannon being remote, heavy .50 in guns firing too slowly, the Vickers gun outdated, new guns costly to develop, they chose the American Colt Browning .303 in machine gun and, to ensure rapid *coup de grace*, opted for eight fixed guns able to fire 734 rounds per second between them.

The fighter to carry these needed to

The Hurricane began life as the Hawker Fury Monoplane. Just how clearly these two were related can be seen by comparing this view of Fury K2071 with that of P2617 below. (RAF Museum)

fly at over 275 mph at 15,000 ft, have a ceiling of 33,000 ft, a normal endurance of 1.25 hrs then land within 600 yd. A 10° view over the nose, retractable undercarriage, R/T, oxygen supply and a vital good all-round view were necessary basic features.

Some officials still wanting traversing guns pointed to gun firing, heating and stoppage problems in wing-mounted armament — which eight guns implied. But these could all be overcome — although in five years' time the proposed 275 mph fighter just about available would then be obsolete. Speed therefore became a new No. 1 priority, 300 and even 350 mph being needed in a fighter engaging a foe at maybe 25,000 ft —

Hurricane P2617, painted to represent an aircraft of 607 Squadron, shows lines similar to those of the Hawker Fury.

accurate forecasting indeed.

Between 27 July and 23 August 1934 the question of armament was thrashed out at Air Ministry with Sqn Ldr Ralph Sorley pressing the idea of using eight guns for a two-second fatal punch. Such guns wing-mounted demanded rigid structure, complex feed, firing and heating systems. Nevertheless, against fast bombers the concept became favoured and was enshrined in a new fighter Specification, the 310 mph/15,000 ft F.10/35.

Similar ideas were also found in the proposed F.5/34 Fury replacement, and both became overtaken by events when Camm's latest plans for his Monoplane reached Air Ministry on 4 September 1934 — based upon a 310 mph at 15,000 ft formula. Following lengthy, complex discussion of fighter policy (see *Interceptor Fighters*/PSL) the Air Ministry on 21 February 1935 ordered a Hawker prototype to Specification F.36/34 which, all-up weight 4,900 lb, was forecast to attain 330 mph at 15,000 ft. Not until 20 July 1935 was the fitting of eight guns agreed — too late for them to be featured by the prototype and also delaying the general development of the aircraft. A trials eight-gun wing was built, firing from which started on 23 August 1935.

The Merlin 'C' prototype *K5083*, fitted with a hefty two-bladed Watts propeller, reached Brooklands in October 1935, its loaded weight listed as 5,416 lb. On 6 November P.G. Bullman made the first flight and on 7 February 1936 trials began at Martlesham where pilots found it 'Simple and easy to fly...with no landing problems...able to reach 30,000 feet in 8.1 minutes; 430 yards take off to clear 50 ft...'—here indeed was a winner. In June 1936 600 examples were ordered and on 27 June the name Hurricane was officially bestowed. Delivery was ordered to begin in October 1937, with 500 in service by March 1939. These would replace the Bristol Bulldog and Gloster interim fighters, making the Hurricane the prime general purpose home defender.

A building specification 15/36 for the Hurricane I (Merlin II) was agreed on 20 July 1936. December saw it compromised when metal wings were approved for Hawker's Henley bomber — interchangeable with the Hurricane's. This occurred when spin problems were being encountered on the fighter, Hawker stating that entering a spin was unlikely, to which the Director of Training retorted that 'the problem must be cured'. RAE Farnborough acting as go-between devised a solution — an enlarged rudder and ventral fillet — although

First for the Few, the Hurricane prototype K5083. (Rolls-Royce)

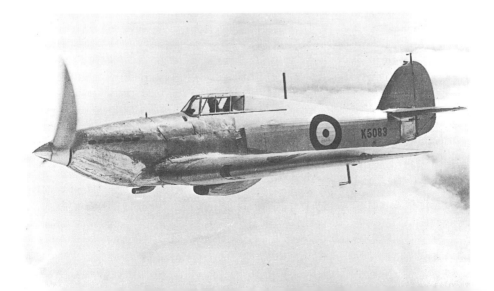

101 production aircraft had been completed by the time the modifications were introduced to the production lines in February 1938. Fitting the Merlin II — which produced 880 hp for take-off and 1,030 hp at 16,250 ft and had a revised cylinder block — meant a modified cowling was necessary. A variety of small modifications further delayed the aircraft and increased its weight.

L1547, the first production Hurricane, flew on 12 October 1937 and on 15 December 1937 when *L1548* joined No. 111 Squadron at Northolt the first of the monoplanes entered front line service. Six were in use by the end of the year. In February 1938 Sqn Ldr John Gillam amazed the nation by flying a Hurricane from Edinburgh to Northolt at an 'average speed of 408 mph'. That was his indicated air speed helped by a strong tail wind. The true air speed at 17,000 ft was 325 mph.

By the end of 1938 195 Hurricanes were in squadron hands. August 1938 had seen trials underway using *L1562* fitted with a three-bladed DH two-pitch propeller on a Hurricane whose all-up weight had risen to 6,300 lb.

But the fighter was an excellent advance and in November 1938 1,000 more Hurricanes were ordered and armour plating was being added. This new weight rise prompted Hawker to try improving performance by fitting a Merlin III in a 'private' Hurricane, *G-AFKX*, first flown on 24 January 1939. Another helpful advance came with the decision to use leaded 100 octane fuel. In a world now shunning such petrol it is perhaps worth pointing out that, although expensive, it made a very considerable contribution to the winning of the Battle of Britain and indeed the whole outcome of the war. Along with the constant speed propeller it altered performance dramatically — viz:

Fixed wooden propeller and 87 octane petrol — take-off run 563 yd CS propeller and 100 octane petrol — take-off run 310 yd

The latter greatly improved climb away and rapid reaction, and a three-bladed propeller helped further by readjusting the cg forward after equipment had shifted it aft. A pair of metal stressed skin wings fitted to

Hurricane L1822 *depicted pre-war as* TM:K *of 111 Squadron served with 312 Squadron in 1940 and with No. 9 Service Flying Training School (SFTS) in 1941.*

Hurricane L1662:SD-V *of 501 Squadron typifies the early wartime markings of fighters and features the Watts propeller of the first Hurricanes.*

L1877 and first flown on 28 April showed a further advance.

What could not easily be increased was the top speed. Indeed, when Fighter Command carried out speed trials in July 1939 it rated the ever heavier Hurricane as attaining 288.6 mph at 10,000 ft, 302.21 mph at 15,000 ft and 302.8 mph at 18,000 ft. Against the Bf 109 it would clearly be at a disadvantage speedwise and, there being no easy way to improve the situation, the Air Staff decided on 12 December 1939 to recommend that Hurricane development should be phased out.

By 3 September 1939 475 Hurricanes had been delivered of which 75 had been struck off charge. Sixteen squadrons had Hurricanes, and two half squadrons. On 12 January 1940 Hawker presented plans for fitting 12 guns to the fighter and received an order to try the idea although it increased the fighter's weight to 6,300 lb, about the acceptable limit. Air Ministry approved such armament only for a Merlin XX engined Hurricane Mk II. A trial installation of the Mk XX version — which after some modifications Hawker claimed could attain 360 mph — was ordered on 12 March 1940. Ever adding to the weight produced a Mk II little better than a Mk 1, the first production

eight-gun Mk II series 1 being delivered to No. 111 Squadron at Croydon on 2 September and rapidly withdrawn due to fuel flow problems.

An average number of 1,326 Hurricanes were in hand in various states during the Battle of Britain. On 4 January 1939 a Hurricane production order had been placed with the Canadian Car and Foundry Company. The first of these arrived in Britain in June 1940, Merlin IIIs being fitted on arrival in the 25th and subsequent airframes, 42 of which were here by the end of October 1940. Battle of Britain Hurricanes featured a top speed of around 310 mph at 17,000 ft and a wide assortment of detail differences, the major advance coming when engine boost was lifted from $6\frac{1}{4}$ lb to 12 lb which, for brief periods, increased the speed by 25 mph.

Despite the official preference for Spitfire development the Hurricane held a major advantage — the relative ease with which its thicker section wings could accept a variety of weapons, not least 20 mm cannon. *L1750*, first flown with 20 mm Hispanos on 24 May 1939, had its guns underslung — which the Air Ministry rated 'ingenious'.

They had also played off Vickers and Hawker, telling each of the other's intention to fit such guns in its fighters, and they were determined the prime contractor should not be left out. Slow fire and the small ammunition load were criticized when Martlesham tested *L1750*. Weighing 6,169 lb loaded, its top speed was 302 mph at 16,800 ft, the cannon reducing it by 8 mph. After lengthy development work *L1750* was assigned to 151 Squadron on 27 March, modified at 10 MU in April and re-issued on 3 June 1940 to No. 151 for squadron trials. Flt Lt R.L. Smith flew it operationally from Rochford and North Weald, and also the next cannon Hurricane, *V7360*.

Into a pair of battle-damaged wings four cannon had been installed during June 1940 and these wedded to *V7360* produced the Hawker P.1002. Learning from experience the aircraft was first tested at Boscombe Down between 3 and 15 August, then sent to 151 Squadron and Flt Lt Smith for operational assessment. On 22 August he flew the first of ten prescribed patrols and early on 31 August claimed a probable Bf 109. Briefly held by 56 Squadron, the aircraft then spent two more weeks with No. 151. Its success was such that on 2 September orders were given for 30 Hurricanes to have cannon likewise fitted and by 15 September eight Mk IIs were getting them. Like the Mk II itself the RAF cannon fighter was not ready in time for the big Battle.

Summary

Between 1 July and 15 October 1940 1,994 Hurricanes saw service in Fighter Command squadrons, 523 being written off during operational flying. As Britain's most numerous 1940 combat aircraft the Hurricane surely merits additional review. Its operations, during the course of about 35,000 legendary sorties, are incidentally outlined in *The Battle of Britain — 50 Years On* (PSL).

By September 1939 482 Hurricanes had reached the RAF, delivery reaching *L2102*. During the Battle the numbers used monthly by squadrons were 792 in July, 1,055 in August,

1,036 in September and 871 to mid-October. Of Hurricanes used in the period 125 eventually joined the Royal Navy, 66 became Mk IIs and 45 were passed to the USSR.

Repair, servicing and salvaging by civilian and RAF organizations provided essential back-up for the Battle. Total numbers of Hurricanes monthly attended to by such units follow, some having weeks of attention and others a matter of hours, were as shown in the table opposite.

The 870 Hurricanes delivered to the RAF during the Battle of Britain included 49 Mk II srs i eight-gun fighters. The remainder were Mk 1s variously modified and wearing widely assorted paint schemes. Some had long lives, but few survived the war.

Of the much used 'L' series batch a dozen were stored throughout the 1940 fight. Increasing numbers joined Nos. 5 and 6 OTUs, 39 in August' and 58 by October 1940. Three (*L1581*, *L1807*, *L1824*) were shipped to the Mediterranean area, three (*L1831*, *L1989*, *L2099*) to the USSR. Seven were converted into Mk II (*L1581*, *L1658*, *L1807*, *L1824*, *L1836*, *L1989* and *L2099*) and renumbered. During 1943 58 'L' aircraft remained in active use, 33 in 1944 and one in 1945. The last surviving airframes were *L1798/3576M* used by 5 and 7 OTUs in 1940 and disposed of in November 1946, *L1592* (museum aircraft), *L1750* (SOC 3.5.45), *L1796*, *L1814*, *L2052* and *L1824* (SOC 31.5.45 overseas).

Of the 'N' range the six that survived into 1945 and their 1940/41 operators were *N2325* (stored), *N2344* (6 OTU, 1 RCAF Sqn, 213 Sqn), *N2398* (6 OTU), *N2435* (601 Sqn, later *4577M* used by RN; SOC 13.2.45), *N2477* (79 and 85 Sqns, to India, SOC 6.4.45, brought back on charge and despatched to Rhodesia where it was SOC 5.9.46) and *N2453* (615 and 253 Sqns, *4693M* of RN and SOC 30.12.46).

Service details of *N2548* remain uncertain, also for *P2881*, *P2904*, *P3042*, *P3048* and *P2557*. Long

Hurricanes repaired, serviced or salvaged by civilian and RAF organisations

Unit/CRU	July	August	September	October
Airtraining, Oxford	40	59	67	64
DH Witney	36	32	43	45
Hawker	5	16	28	29
Rolls-Royce	33	28	35	62
Gloster	1	1	18	19
Rollason, Croydon	4	6	3	7
Austin Motors	-	1	10	13
Scottish Aviation	-	-	7	9
Cunliffe Owen	-	-	4	5
Air Service Training	-	1	2	1
Southern Aviation	-	-	1	1
Maintenance Units (No.)				
5 Kemble ASU	72	82	78	67
10 Hullavington ASU	77	58	44	53
13 Henlow, repair depot	59	100	102	78
15 Wroughton ASU	34	60	33	58
18 Dumfries ASU	-	-	21	17
19 St Athan ASU	74	52	43	54
20 Aston Down ASU	21	74	80	82
22 Silloth ASU	72	65	36	25
27 Shawbury ASU	122	86	69	64
44 Edzell ASU	-	-	1	-
45 Kinloss ASU	-	-	1	-
46 Lossiemouth ASU	-	7	14	13
48 Hawarden ASU	24	53	38	21
49 Horsham, salvage centre	4	18	6	-
50 Oxford, salvage centre	7	6	4	7
51 Lichfield, ASU	1	15	20	20
54 Cambridge, salvage centre	3	5	8	6
71 Slough, salvage centre	-	-	4	9

surviving 'P' Hurricanes included *P3929* (SOC at Morrison's Whittlesey works on 3.1.45) and *P5170* (the first Canadian, written off at 22 MU on 4.7.45). *R2685* was written off on 24.2.45 at No. 1 Air Armament School, and *R4231* on 12.3.45. Many of the 'Vs' served long into the war, notable survivors and their official dates of demise being *V7246* (24.8.45), *V7480* (30.11.45), *V7508* (16.11.45) and *V7653* (17.2.45). *V6787* (with 501 Sqn, then 112 Sqn RCAF, and later used by both HQ 12 and 10 Groups) was shipped to Bombay in November 1943 on SS *Clan*. After use as a trainer it was sent to Rhodesia in April 1945 and there struck off charge on 31 March 1946. *V6846*, used by 312 Sqn in October 1940 and subsequently in front line use with Nos. 3 and 17 Squadrons in Scotland and then with 247 and 87 Squadrons into 1943, also went to India in November 1934 and now resides in Patna. Two 1940 survivors are *L1592* in the Kensington Science Museum and *P2617* in the Hendon Battle of Britain Museum.

Hurricanes which saw squadron service 1 July–15 October 1940

Aircraft losses form a highly complex subject, some aircraft being written off only to become repairable after all. Many with slight damage received not even a Category 1 rating, and the official classification of the nature of damage seems not always correct. Some aircraft remained a while on squadron strength after receiving battle damage, and prior to being taken to repair centres. Generally the loss of a fuselage resulted in an aircraft being struck off charge. Further complications arise when aircraft are used by a squadron either on brief loan or before the necessary 'paper work' is produced — if, indeed, it ever was. As for the sites of accidents, anomalies frequently occur particularly when a pilot bales out and lands some way from the impact place of his aircraft. Any listing, due to the many factors bearing upon it, is likely to be incomplete.

No. 1 Sqn

L1731	9.9.40–20.10.40
L1934	30.8.40–2.10.40
L1973	18.8.40–25.8.40
N2607	2.10.40–8.10.40
N2618	19.9.40–6.2.41
P2678	6.4.40–FTR 1.9.40?
P2686	? (DIA 16.8)–EFB 6.9.40
P2751	? (DIA 16.8)–EFA 3.11.40
P2877	19.9.40 to 14.3.41
P2890	6.40–EFAO 23.8.40 (crashed at Withyam)
P3043	? –s/d 15.8.40
P3044	7.40–FTR 3.9.40
P3047	7.40–s/d 15.8.40 (nr Harwich)
P3048	12.6.40–6.12.40
P3169	11.7.40–1.1.41
P3170	11.7.40–28.8.40
P3172	11.7.40–s/d 11.8.40 (Sandown)
P3173	11.7.40–s/d 16.8.40 (nr Portsmouth)
P3229	23.7.40–14.3.41
P3276	14.5.40–EFB 1.9.40 (Ruckinge)
P3318	1.9.40–13.11.40
P3395	6.40–8.11.40
P3470	20.8.40–30.8.40
P3471	11.6.40–s/d 19.7.40 (nr Brighton)
P3653	6.40–FA 16.8.40
P3678	3.6.40–FBO2 15.8.40
P3684	6.6.40–13.7.40
P3782	6.40–FTR 3.9.40 (FH 49.40)
P3897	12.8.40–EFAO 27.8.40 (Lacey Green, Bucks)
P5187	5.10.40–EFAO 30.10.40
P5197	30.8.40–EFB 6.9.40
P5199	28.8.40–6.2.41
R4075	23.7.40–s/d 15.8.40 (nr Harwich)
V7256	17.8.40–5.2.41
V7258	17.8.40–3.3.41
V7301	17.8.40–FBO2 8.9.40
V7302	17.8.40–11.10.40?
V7375	21.8.40–s/d 31.8.40 (Halstead)
V7376	20.8.40–EFAO 9.10.40 (FH 61.40)
V7377	21.8.40–5.3.41
V7379	20.8.40–12.12.40
V7464	17.9.40–24.3.41

No. 3 Sqn

L1583	25.7.40–12.8.40
L1723	8.6.40–21.9.40
L1846	12.9.39–2.2.41
P2693	22.5.40–9.5.41
P2859	31.5.40–19.11.40
P2860	31.5.40–4.1.41
P2861	31.5.40–21.7.40
P2862	31.5.40–EFA 23.7.40 (crashed taking off at Wick, hit 269 Sqn Hudson)
P2863	? to ? and possibly used by 56 and 249 Squadrons
P2864	30.5.40 to 2.2.41
P2909	11.6.40 to 21.7.40
P2911	8.6.40 to 21.7.40
P3020	3.7.40–FAO2 16.9.40
P3021	12.7.40 to 14.7.40
P3095	25.7.40 to 7.3.41
P3255	23.7.40 to 6.4.41
P3256	23.7.40 to 3.4.41
P3260	23.7.40–EFA 19.10.40 (Castletown)
P3261	23.7.40–FAO2 1.10.40
P3318	10.4.40 to 6.7.40
P3410	24.5.40 to 10.10.41
P3413	24.5.40 to 21.7.40
P3429	31.5.40–FAO2 11.9.40
P3454	18.5.40 to 6.4.41
P3607	11.6.40 to 28.2.41
P3608	12.7.40 to 13.10.40
P3664	23.6.40 to 21.7.40
P3770	11.7.40 to 16.8.40
P3771	11.7.40 to 20.7.40
P3772	12.7.40 to 14.7.40
P3773	11.7.40 to 6.4.41
P3774	12.7.40 to 14.7.40
P3982	22.8.40–FAT2 18.11.40
R4076	23.7.40–6.4.41
R4077	23.7.40–2.2.41
R4078	23.7.40–2.2.41
R4079	23.7.40–27.10.40
V7311	27.8.40–6.4.41

No. 17 Sqn

L1727	25.8.40–21.9.40
L1808	11.9.40–20.9.40
L1836	25.8.40–8.9.40
L1921	28.5.40–s/d 18.8.40 (at sea)
N2359	6.6.40–25.8.40
N2438	24.2.40–21.8.40
N2456	29.2.40–EFA 7.8.40 (crashed Debden Park, Essex)
N2526	29.2.40–21.8.40
N2662	24.2.40–30.10.40
N2666	12.5.40–21.8.40
P2557	21.5.40–FTR 12.7.40 (on 85 Sqn; off Felixstowe)
P2558	6.6.40–25.8.40
P2559	6.6.40–FTR 1.7.40
P2674	31.7.40–30.10.40
P2794	24.8.40–EFA 11.11.40
P2874	29.6.40–8.7.41
P2905	21.5.40–FTR 6.7.40
P2972	24.8.40–3.3.41
P2994	9.9.40–FBO2 5.9.40
P3023	6.6.40–FAO2 11.12.40
P3025	23.6.40–FAO2 15.7.40
P3027	23.6.40–EFB 24.9.40 (crashed taking off, Debden)
P3033	25.6.40–11.10.40
P3061	20.9.40–2.3.41
P3168	13.7.40–FBO2 24.9.40 (crash landed Debden)
P3176	17.9.40–3.3.41
P3209	21.7.40–DIA 18.8, to 22.8.40
P3482	30.6.40–EFAO 15.7.40 (Elsenham)
P3536	28.5.40–s/d by AA fire 13.10.40 (Chatham; FH 107.10)
P3539	28.5.40 (FBO2 11.8.40)–15.8.40
P3623	26.9.40–EFA ? 11.40?
P3673	6.6.40–s/d 3.9.40 (Ingrave, Essex)

46

P3878:YB-V *of 17 Squadron.*
(RAF Museum)

P3701	22.8.40-FBO2 5.9.40
P3760	6.40-FTR 11.8.40
P3788	6.40-FAO2 14.7.40
P3868	21.9.40-13.3.41
P3878	1.7.40-EFB 24.9.40 (Chatham)
P3891	13.7.40-FBO2 15.8.40
P3892	13.7.40 (DIA 11.8, 3.9, 11.9)-12.9.40
P3894	17.7.40-3.3.41
R4091	20.8.40-FBO2 31.8.40
R4174	17.8.40-s/d 3.9.40
R4199	22.8.40-s/d 25.8.40
R4224	28.8.40-FBO2 31.9.40 (s/d nr North Weald)
V6743	19.9.40-3.3.41
V6759	26.9.40-EFB 28.12.40 (crashed Debach)
V6553	30.8.40-3.3.41
V6561	18.8.40-26.8.40
V6600	26.8.40-30.8.40
V7241	28.8.40-2.3.41
V7407	13.8.40 (DIA 18.8)-s/d 25.8.40 (off Bognor)
V7408	13.8.40-19.8.40
V7416	20.8.40-25.9.40
V7500	25.9.40-FTR 17.11.40 (FH 73.05)
V7542	5.10.40-3.3.41
V7568	5.10.40-3.3.41
V7570	5.10.40-s/d 11.11.40 (FH 57.40)

No. 32 Sqn

L1747	11.6.40-20.10.40
L1831	20.5.40-19.8.40
L2062	12.7.40-s/d 1.9.40 in use by 79 Sqn (Chelsfield)
L2075	7.7.40-17.7.40
L2086	19.8.40-21.9.40
N2342	11.6.40-FAO 2.7.40
N2345	28.8.40-EFB 31.8.40 (with 79 Sqn)
N2409	13.2.40-7.9.40
N2433	18.8.40-FTR 24.8.40
N2458	7.7.40-SOC 1.9.40
C/N2459	12.1.40-FTR 15.8.40 (off Harwich; FH 130.15)
N2460	12.2.40-EFB 8.7.40
F/N2461	12.2.40-s/d 18.8.40 (nr Detling)
N2462	12.2.40-7.7.40
N2524	10.2.40-14.2.41
H/N2532	12.2.40-EFB 20.7.40 (crashed nr Hawkinge)
N2540	27.8.40-EAO 30.8.40 (destroyed by bombing, Biggin Hill)
N2587	23.9.40-22.11.40
N2588	5.4.40-FBO2 17.7.40
N2596	11.7.40-s/d 12.8.40 (nr Hawkinge)
N2670	23.5.40-s/d 20.7.40 (N. Foreland ?)
N2671	23.5.40-FBO2 15.8.40
P2724	18.5.40-4.7.40
P2795	20.8.40 (DIA 23.8)-8.9.40
P2921	11.6.40-21.2.41
P3036	4.9.40-4.7.41
P3112	13.7.40-18.11.40
P3144	12.7.40-s/d 19.7.40 (nr Dover; FH 8.15)
P3146	12.7.40-FBO2 14.8.40
P3147	21.7.40-s/d 18.8.40 (Herne Bay)
P3171	13.8.40-EFB 14.8.40
P3205	21.7.40 (DIA 22.8)-13.8.40
P3351	6.9.40-21.12.40
P3411	4.5.40-21.7.40
P3460	25.8.40-FAO2 5.11.40
P3461	20.5.40-s/d in error 8.7.40
P3481	1.6.40-EFB 24.8.40 (nr Hawkinge)
P3522	20.5.40, damaged by bombing 15.8, FBO2 23.8.40
P3534	22.5.40-3.7.40
P3677	4.6.40-FBO2 25.7.40

47

N2359:YB-J *served with 17 Squadron during the Battle, and at 6 OTU from August 1940 to 11 June 1941 when it crashed.*

P3679	4.6.40 (DIA 20.7)–FAO2 24.10.40		L1955	18.5.39–EFAO 29.7.40 (crashed Brabourne Lees, Kent)
P3900	14.8.40–FAO2 23.8.40		L1963	27.8.40–28.10.40
P3936	12.7.40–21.2.41		L1968	9.9.40–4.2.41
P3981	25.8.40–7.2.41		L2143	7.9.40–2.9.41
P5203	28.8.40–FBO2 31.8.40		N2621	9.6.40–s/d 16.8.40 (crashed nr Parkhurst, Isle of Wight)
R4081	23.7.40–EAO2 18.8.40			
R4106	7.8.40–s/d 18.3.8.40		N2665	11.4.40–8.12.40
R4122	8.9.40–21.2.41		P2684	29.8.40–27.9.40
R4200	25.8.40–21.2.41		P3140	11.7.40–s/d 19.7.40 (off Felpham, W. Sussex)
R4216	25.8.40–7.1.41			
V6535	15.8.40–s/d 18.8.40		P3179	9.8.40–s/d 30.8.40 (in Hove)
V6536	15.8.40–29.9.40		P3202	3?.7.40–EFB 26.8.40 (crashed Tangmere)
V6540	19.8.40–s/d 31.8.40			
V6545	19.8.40–22.12.40		P3214	22.7.40 (DIA 8.8)–15.8.40
V6546	19.8.40–4.4.41		P3216	22.7.40 (DIA 16.8)–24.8.40
V6547	19.8.40–s/d 25.8.40		P3220	22.7.40–s/d 26.8.40 (nr West Wittering)
V6551	26.8.40–28.3.41			
V6552	26.8.40–7.1.41		P3267	16.6.40–FBO2 8.8.40
V6565	18.8.40–27.8.40		P3357	25.10.40–FBO2 31.10.40
V6568	20.8.40–s/d 24.8.40		P3386	19.5.40–FAO2 26.1.41
V6572	20.8.40–s/d 24.8.40		P3464	9.6.40–EFB 9.7.40 (crashed nr Tangmere)
V6602	26.8.40–FAO2 29.9.40			
V6616	26.8.40–s/d 15.9.40 ??		P3466	9.6.40 (DIA 13.7 and 8.8)–15.5.41
V6724	21.9.40–EFAO 18.11.40			
V7205	24.7.40–EFAO 6.8.40 (Biggin Hill)		P3468	9.6.40 (DIA 19.7)–s/d 8.8.40 (nr Isle of Wight)
V7223	23.7.40 (DIA 14.8)–FBO2 24.8.40		P3527	9.6.40–26.11.40
			P3531	9.6.40–s/d 19.7.40 (off Selsey)
V7363	15.8.40–s/d 18.8.40 (Edenbridge)		P3665	16.9.40–20.1.41
V7425	24.8.40–27.3.40		P3757	2.10.40–15.2.41
			P3776	7.9.40–20.1.41
No. 43 Sqn			P3781	9.6.40–s/dl 8.8.40 (Isle of Wight)
L1577	5.10.40–8.10.40			
L1594	28.9.40–5.10.40		P3784	9.6.40–FBO2 20.7.40
L1727	29.11.38–25.8.40		P3786	9.6.40–s/d 2.9.40 (nr Ashford)
L1728	30.9.40–2.10.40		P3809	30.10.40–11.2.41
H/L1736	30.12.38–EFAO 16.8.40, (crashed nr Tangmere)		P3903	14.8.40 (DIA 26.8)–s/d 2.9.40
			P3964	12.7.40–FTR 20.7.40 (S of Isle of Wight)
L1739	15.12.38–s/d 14.8.40 (Channel)			
L1742	16.10.39–22.8.40		P3971	11.7.40–FBO2 15.8.40 (destroyed by bombing, 16.8.40)
L1758	11.4.40–EFB 26.7.40 (crashed in sea)			
			P3972	11.7.40–EFAO 13.8.40 (Cocking Down, W Sussex)
L1824	?–FAO2 9.7.40			
L1836	11.4.40 (DIA 17.8)–25.8.40		P3973	11.7.40–s/d 21.7.40
L1849	30.11.39–EFAO 7.7.40, (crashed SE of Tangmere)		P5188	27.8.40–8.12.40
			P5191	27.8.40–FAO2 25.9.40

P5196	27.8.40-FBO2 6.9.40	P5209	16.9.40-1.1.41
R4102	9.8.40-s/d 13.8.40	R4074	6.9.40-FTR 22.10.40
B/R4107	9.8.40 (DIA 15.8)-1.10.40	V6549	8.9.40-s/d 11.9.40 (Sandhurst, Kent)
R4108	9.8.40-FAO2 12.8.40 (destroyed by bombing, 16.8.40)	V6550	8.9.40-FTR 15.10.40 (Gravesend)
R4109	9.8.40-26.8.40	V6554	8.9.40-s/d 18.9.40 (Chatham)
R4110	9.8.40-destroyed by bombing 16.8.40	V6582	5.9.40-FBO2 8.10.40
R4196	2.10.40-21.2.41	V6631	31.8.40-EFB 8.9.40 (FH 7.10)
R4225	29.8.40-EFB 10.11.40	V6748	20.9.40-s/d 30.9.40 (E. Sussex)
R4321	17.8.40 (DIA 26.8)-28.8.40; 10.9.40-16.9.40	V6751	21.9.40-27.9.40
V6533	17.8.40-24.8.40	V6758	21.9.40-FBO2 27.9.40
V6542	17.8.40, DIA 5.9 to 5.9.40	V6785	25.9.40-3.10.40
V6548	17.8.40-s/d 30.8.40	V6788	25.9.40-30.11.40
V6641	1.9.40-s/d 7.9.40 (Purley)	V6789	25.9.40-s/d 15.10.40 (Gravesend)
V6925	28.10.40-EFB 9.2.41	V6790	25.9.40-? (?later became a Mk II)
V7206	23.7.40-9.2.41		
V7221	23.7.40-29.10.40	V6803	29.9.40-FBO2 20.10.40
V7231	23.7.40-29.10.40	V6804	29.9.40-s/d 25.10.40
V7257	19.8.40-s/d 7.9.40 (Blackheath)	V6816	1.10.40-EFA 13.1.41
V7259	19.8.40-s/d 26.8.40 (Birdham, Hants)	V6817	1.10.40-20.10.40
V7303	19.8.40-EFA 24.10.40 (crash landed Usworth)	V6818	1.10.40-15.5.41
V7308	18.8.40-FBO2 26.8.40	V6877	14.10.40-20.5.41
V7309	18.8.40-s/d 7.9.40 (Sutton Valence, Kent)	V6916	16.10.40-FBO2 24.11.40
		V6918	16.10.40-15.5.41
V7364	9.8.40-EAO 16.8.40 (destroyed by bombing, Tangmere)	V6922	16.10.40-EFB 8.11.40
V7366	9.8.40-29.4.41	V6928	24.10.40-EFB 20.11.40
V7420	24.8.40-s/d 2.9.40 (Ivychurch, Kent)	V7201	12.7.40 (DIA 4.9)-10.9.40
		V7202	12.7.40-EFB 30.11.40
		V7232	29.7.40-s/d 11.9.40
		V7409	6.9.40-17.9.40
		V7438	6.9.40-9.5.41
		V7442	10.9.40-s/d 18.9.40 (Chatham)
		V7443	10.9.40-FTR 10.2.41 (ditched, Channel; FH 136.20)
		V7594	24.10.40-s/d 10.2.41 (off Calais)
		V7603	27.10.40-15.5.41
		V7610	9.10.40-EFB 9.4.41 (crashed, Church Fenton)
		V7616	20.10.40-FTR 1.11.40
		V7617	20.10.40-EFB 5.12.40

No. 46 Sqn

L1750	21.9.40-10.10.40
N2345	19.6.40-FA2 28.7.40
N2480	18.6.40-s/d 15.10.40 (Lt Thurrock)
N2497	9.9.40-24.9.40
N2599	7.7.40-13.10.40
P2677	10.9.40-25.9.40
P2685	18.6.40-EFA 24.7.40 (nr Derby)
P2965	6.40-EFA 17.10.40
N2968	10.9.40-2.10.40
P3024	18.6.40-s/d 3.9.40 (Canewdon)
P3026	18.6.40-21.9.40
P3030	18.6.40-FAO2 20.8.40
P3031	18.6.40-FBO2 4.9.40 (damaged landing, Rochford)
P3052	19.6.40-s/d 4.9.40 (Hawkwell)
P3053	19.6.40-FBO2 8.9.40 (shot down)
P3060	19.6.40-FAO2 5.7.40
P3062	19.6.40-1.10.40
P3063	19.6.40-FBO2 3.9.40 (crashed nr Canewdon)
P3064	19.6.40-FTR 3.9.40
P3066	19.6.40-s/d 4.9.40
P3067	19.6.40-s/d 2.9.40 ?
P3096	12.7.40-EFB 11.9.40
P3114	25.7.40-9.9.40
P3201	12.7.40-s/d 8.9.40
P3309	17.9.40-15.5.41
P3429	24.10.40-EFB 30.11.40
P3525	5.9.40-EFB 11.9.40
P3539	19.9.40-19.10.40
P3597	18.6.40-FBO2 2.9.40
P3756	18.6.40-FBO2 27.9.40
P3816	9.9.40-s/d 18.9.40 (nr Chatham)

No. 56 Sqn (NB: considerable interchange of aircraft with 249 Squadron in September 1940)

L1594	3.7.40-20.8.40
L1715	17.8.40-20.8.40
L1748	17.8.40-20.8.40
L1764	20.5.40-21.7.40; 24.9.40-s/d 30.9.40 (Chesil Beach)
N2386	24.9.40-15.2.41
N2400	11.7.40-27.7.40
N2402	1.3.40-EAO2 23.9.40
T/N2429	24.2.40-s/d 13.8.40
N2432	24.2.40-s/d 13.7.40 (off Calais)
N2434	24.9.40-s/d 30.9.40 (nr Portland)
N2440	1.3.40-FBO2 25.7.40
N2523	29.2.40-s/d 28.8.40 (Hawkinge)
N2667	?-FTR 11.8.40 (off Walton-on-Naze) (FH 170.15)
N2668	17.8.40-s/d 30.8.40
N2712	2.10.40-25.2.41
P2692	13.7.40-s/d 13.8.40 (Weymouth Bay)
P2863	29.8.40-8.9.40
P2866	24.9.40-s/d 30.9.40 (East Knighton, Dorset)

49

P2910	24.9.40-EFA 23.11.40
P2922	11.6.40-s/d 13.7.40 (off Calais) (FH 40)
Y/P2970	6.6.40-FTR 12.8.40 (off Margate)
P2985	11.7.40-FBO2 13.7.40
P2988	29.8.40-s/d 2.9.40
P3025	29.8.40-FTR 7.9.40 (on 111 Sqn)
P3028	23.6.40-FBO2 15.7.40
P3043	?-FTR 15.8.40
P3055	24.9.40-21.2.41
N/P3088	24.8.40-s/d 30.9.40 (Portland)
P3153	11.7.40-s/d 21.8.40
P3154	24.9.40-s/d 7.10.40
P3356	24.5.40-22.7.40
P3384	18.5.40-FBO2 2.9.40
P3421	24.9.40-s/d 10.10.40 (Portland; FH 95.05)
P3473	18.5.40-EFB 26.8.40 (crashed Foulness)
P3479	24.5.40-s/d 13.8.40 (crashed Faversham; FH 13.05)
P3525	3.9.40-5.9.40
A/P3547	18.5.40-FTR 16.8.40 (FH 122.25)
P3554	11.7.40-13.8.40
P3579	2.6.40-s/d 10.1.41
P3587	2.6.40-FTR 13.8.40 (FH 89.40)
P3594	2.9.40-s/d 7.9.40 (nr Maidstone; FH 11.55)
P3612	13.6.40-13.8.40
R/P3655	24.9.40-s/d 30.9.40 (Portland; FH 113.10)
P3667	3.9.40-3.10.40
P3702	24.9.40-26.2.41
P3784	24.9.40-25.2.41
P3855	24.9.40-25.2.41
P3862	24.9.40-25.2.41
V/P3866	24.9.40-FBO2 11.10.40
P3870	24.9.40-2.12.40
P3879	17.7.40-s/d 29.7.40 (nr Dover; FH 27.25)
P3902	24.9.40-23.2.41
P3925	27.7.40-15.1.41
P5190	20.8.40-16.9.40
P5206	1.9.40-24.9.40
R2686	28.7.40-18.8.40
R2689	28.7.40-EFB 30.8.40 (FH 57.30)
P/R4093	28.7.40-s/d 13.8.40 (off Sheerness)
R4114	20.8.40-s/d 7.9.40 (on 249 Sqn)
R4117	20.8.40-s/d 28.8.40
R4196	13.8.40-FBO2 16.8.40
R4197	13.8.40-s/d 31.8.40
R4198	13.8.40-s/d 28.8.40
R4229	14.8.40-s/d 6.9.40 (on 249 Sqn)
R4320	14.8.40-FTR 7.9.40 (on 249 Sqn)
R4232	14.8.40-25.8.40
V6534	14.8.40-24.9.40
V6559	30.8.40-24.9.40
V6574	3.9.40-16.9.40
V6610	19.7.40-FBO2 7.9.40
V6614	1.9.40-24.9.40
V6625	29.8.40-s/d 5.9.40 (on 249 Sqn)
V6628	29.8.40-s/d 31.8.40 (nr Colchester)
V6634	1.9.40-2.9.40
V6635	3.9.40-24.9.40
V6636	1.9.40-22.12.40
V6880	14.10.40-26.2.41
V7315	11.10.40-26.2.41
V7340	28.8.40-s/d 26.8.40
V7341	20.8.41-s/d 31.8.40 (Springfield, Essex)
V3742	20.8.40-s/d 28.8.40 ? (classified EFB 3.9.40, SOC 20.9.40)
V7352	14.8.40-FBO2 2.9.40
V7360	31.8.40-3.9.40
V7368	13.8.40-s/d 16.8.40 (Manston)
V7378	20.8.40-s/d 31.8.40 (Osea Is, Essex)
V7382	27.8.40-FBO2 28.8.40
V7401	27.8.40-1.9.40
V7435	1.9.40-22.12.40 (sold to Eire 10.3.44)
V7505	2.10.40-26.2.41
V7508	1.10.40-26.2.41
V7509	2.10.40-25.2.41
V7510	2.10.40-EFAO 20.11.40
V7569	9.10.40-FAO2 20.11.40
V7589	8.10.40-FAO2 24.10.40
V7611	11.10.40-25.2.41

No. 66 Sqn/421 Flight (latter marked*)

Z2311	10.10.40-9.11.40
*Z2317	10.10.40-9.11.40
*Z2318	10.10.40-11.11.40
Z2327	10.10.40-9.11.40
*Z2328	10.10.40-91 Sqn 10.10.40 to 6.3.41
*Z2329	10.10.40-9.11.40
*Z2345	9.10.40-31.10.40
*Z2352	9.10.40-FBO2 19.10.40

No. 73 Sqn

L1766	7.9.40-27.9.40
L1808	20.9.40-25.10.40
L1965	18.6.40-20.7.40
L1968	18.6.40-14.8.40
L1975	2.10.40-25.10.40
B/L1981	7.9.40-26.9.40
F/L2036	18.6.40-s/d 23.9.40 (Thames Estuary)
L2039	7.9.40-s/d 14.9.40 ?
L2047	18.6.40-16.9.40
A/N2337	24.9.40-FBO2 27.9.40
N2386	18.6.40-20.7.40
N2457	15.9.40-9.11.40
N2476	15.9.40-19.11.40
D/P2542	18.6.40-s/d 14.9.40
P2796	27.6.40-s/d 11.9.40 (Detling)
B/P2815	18.6.40-FBO2 5.9.40
P2869	18.6.40-1.10.40
P2875	18.6.40-FTR 6.9.40 (FH 86.10)
P2953	18.6.40-FBO2 21.7.40
P2962	18.6.40-FAO2 5.7.40
A/P2984	18.6.40, DIA 5.9., to 13.9.40
P3034	21.6.40-FAT2 21.7.40
P3060	11.9.40-9.11.40
G/P3110	13.7.40-s/d 5.9.40 (FH 37)
P3204	26.8.40-s/d 5.9.40
P3209	24.9.40-FBO2 27.9.40
L/P3224	23.7.40-s/d 5.9.40 (N.Fambridge)
P3226	23.7.40-s/d 23.9.40

P3234	23.7.40–s/d 7.9.40 (nr Billericay)
P3351	18.6.40–27.7.40
P3398	18.6.40–14.11.40
P3456	18.6.40–FAO2 4.9.40
P3470	18.6.40–FAO2 21.7.40
P3467	18.6.40, FAO2 16,7 held to 23.7.40
P3758	21.6.40–EFB 25.8.40 (AA fire damage, NW of Beverley)
P3785	18.6.40–27.9.40
C/P3863	13.7.40–FBO2 7.9.40
P3864	7.9.40–FBO2 2.10.40
K/P3865	13.7.40–s/d 15.9.40 (Teynham, Kent)
P8812	28.7.40–s/d 23.9.40 (Sheppey)
V6573	15.9.40–9.11.40
V6674	28.9.40–EFB 10.12.40 (crashed at night, Tilbury; FH 42.30)
V6676	29.9.40–s/d 11.10.40 (Frindsbury, Kent)
V6677	29.9.40–14.11.40
V6679	28.9.40–EFB 22.12.40
V6725	13.9.40–5.11.40
V6738	18.9.40–14.11.40
V6857	12.10.40–14.11.40
V6981	28.10.40–14.11.40
V7209	23.7.40 (DIA 14.9)–24.10.40
V7444	8.9.40–FAO2 9.11.40
A/V7445	8.9.40–s/d 23.9.40
E/V7446	11.9.40–FBO2 14.9.40
V7463	11.9.40–9.11.40
V7501	24.9.40–14.11.40
V7502	24.9.40–FBO2 11.10.40
V7571	5.10.40–9.11.40
V7572	5.10.40–14.11.40

No. 79 Sqn

L1617	14.7.40–7.10.40
L1784	9.6.40–6.12.40
L1841	14.7.40–22.7.40
L1942	6.7.40–2.9.40
N2384	21.1.40–s/d 8.7.40 (Temple Ewell, Kent)
N2477	28.5.40–10.8.40
N2609	29.5.40–FA2 12.7.40
N2619	24.5.40–s/d 4.7.40 (St Margaret's Bay)
N2620	7.9.40–FAO2 20.9.40
N2671	1.10.40–7.5.41
N2708	1.10.40–EFB 25.10.40 (crashed on return)
P2630	24.5.40–EAO2 31.8.40
P2718	24.5.40–s/d 28.8.40
P2756	24.5.40–FBO3 7.7.40
P2762	5.40–FAO2 12.7.40
P3035	2.9.40–EFA 15.2.41
P3050	10.7.40–s/d 31.8.40 (Hawkhurst)
P3092	8.9.40–8.4.41
P3100	21.7.40–21.9.40, 8.10.40–2.1.41
P3103	11.8.40–25.9.40
P3121	29.6.40–25.8.40
P3122	29.6.40–EFA 25.2.41 (Pembrey, FH 211.35)
P3170	1.9.40–FAO2 15.11.40
P3203	13.7.40–EFB 30.8.40 (collided with He 111 over Brockham)
P3211	1.9.40–12.9.40
P3216	5.7.40–22.7.40
P3217	1.9.40–10.9.40

P3592	28.5.40–EAO2 31.8.40
P3609	1.9.40–19.9.40
P3640	8.9.40–4.4.41
P3659	23.8.40–7.5.41
P3661	1.9.40–EFB 4.4.41 (FH 212.10)
P3676	1.9.40–s/d 4.9.40 (Biggin Hill)
P3771	1.9.40–17.3.41
P3777	1.9.40–FBO2 6.9.40
P3871	8.9.40–FAT2 10.9.40
P3809	13.7.40–EAO2 31.8.40
P3810	31.8.40–EAO2 31.8.40
P3877	10.7.40–FBO2 31.8.40
P3938	10.7.40–FBO2 28.8.40
P5175	1.9.40–21.11.40
P5177	1.9.40–FTR 29.9.40
P5178	1.9.40–FTR 29.9.40 (force landed in Co Wexford and sold to Eire)
P5204	7.9.40–6.11.40
P5207	1.9.40–FBO2 5.9.40
V7200	13.7.40–FBO2 31.8.40
V7315	22.8.40–EAO2 13.8.40
W6670	17.8.40–s/d 1.9.40 (Biggin Hill)

No. 85 Sqn

L1715	2.9.40–6.11.40
L1796	1.9.40–7.11.40
L1808	20.7.40–11.9.40
L1854	27.5.40–EFAO 25.9.40
L1889	?–damaged, ground accident Debden 13.8.40
L1915	26.5.40–s/d 29.8.40 (Ashburnham, Kent)
L1933	4.7.40–damaged by AA fire 24.8.40 and SOC 11.9.40
L1935	30.8.40–7.11.40
L1989	9.9.40–23.9.40
O/L2071	20.7.40–s/d 1.9.40 (Sanderstead, Kent)
N2351	2.9.40–26.9.40
N2427	1.9.40–7.11.40
N2457	11.6.40–FAO2 10.7.40
N2476	25.5.40–15.9.40
L/N2477	30.8.40–EAO2 1.9.40
G/N2544	25.5.40–FBO2 31.8.40
N2645	8.6.40–21.11.40
N2712	14.5.40–FBO2 2.7.40
P2673	24.5.40–FTR 1.9.40
F/P2716	29.5.40–s/d 11.7.40 off Suffolk
P2722	29.5.40–5.11.40
P2805	20.8.40–25.8.40
P2806	20.8.40–25.8.40
P2827	30.8.40 FA 9.9, to 11.9.40
P2879	18.5.40 (DIA 29.8)–30.8.40
R/P2923	11.6.40–FTR 18.8.40 (FH 110.20)
P2958	3.9.40–7.9.40
P2975	24.5.40–FBO2 1.9.40
P3150	5.7.40–s/d 1.9.40 (Kenley)
Y/P3151	30.8.40–FBO2 1.9.40 (crashed Kenley)
Q/P3166	13.7.40–s/d 3.8.40 (Goudhurst)
P3402	30.5.40 (DIA 25.8)–30.8.40
P3408	30.5.40–FAO2 8.10.40
P3409	29.5.40–GA 13.8.40 (collided with L1889, SOC 19.8.40)
P3459	18.5.40–7.11.40
P3467	30.5.40–FBO2 28.8.40
P3649	18.5.40–FBO2 18.8.40

Hurricanes of 85 Squadron were in action during much of the Battle. P3408:VY-K later served with 306 Squadron from December 1940, then with 257 Squadron from April to June 1941 and later with 55 OTU, 9 SFTS, 247 Squadron, 56 OTU, and Nos 1 and 2 Tactical Exercise Units before being struck off charge on 17 July 1944. (IWM)

P3854	19.5.40–25.11.40
P3895	13.7.40–EFA 22.7.40 (undershot Castle Camps, Cambs)
P3965	13.7.40–13.9.40
P3966	13.7.40–s/d 26.8.40 (Pitsea)
P5171	30.8.40–FBO2 1.9.40
P5192	19.8.40–6.11.40
V6661	2.9.40–21.11.40
V6668	2.9.40–26.9.40
V6760	24.9.40–FBO2 19.11.40
V6761	24.9.40–FAO2 17.11.40
V6580	24.8.40–EAO 26.8.40 (bombed, Croydon)
V6581	24.8.40–s/d 31.8.40 (Newendon)
V6607	30.8.40–8.11.40
L/V6623	27.8.40–s/d 29.8.40 (Rye)
D/V6624	27.8.40–s/d 30.8.40 (Smarden)
V6845	19.10.40–2.11.40
V7248	31.7.40–20.11.40
V7249	31.7.40–s/d 18.8.40 (off Clacton)
V7343	26.8.40–FBO3 1.9.40
V7349	26.8.40–FBO2 22.9.40
V7350	26.8.40–s/d 29.8.40 (Etchingham, Kent)
V7381	25.8.40–EAO2 26.8.40
V7412	25.8.40–26.8.40
V7440	2.9.40–FAO2 22.9.40

No. 87 Sqn

L1627	12.8.38–4.9.40
L1636	16.5.40–3.10.40
L1768	17.8.40–5.11.40
P2548	17.5.40–5.10.40
P2823	13.5.40–13.12.40
P2855	28.5.40–EFB 28.7.40 (crashed into P3225, taking off)
P3093	13.7.40–FBO2 21.10.40
P3118	25.7.40–EFB 1.11.40 (crashed Knaphill, Woking)

P3149	17.8.40–10.4.41(?)
P3215	13.7.40–EFB 15.8.40
P3225	24.7.40–FB02 28.7.40 (collided with P2855)
P3264	12.8.40–19.8.40
P3317	14.5.40–FA02 28.7.40; returned to 87 Sqn
P3380	26.10.40–14.4.41
P3387	? (DIA 11.7)–FTR 13.8.40
P3394	28.5.40–5.5.41
P3404	28.5.40–EFAO 24.10.40 (collision)
P3465	28.5.40–EFB 15.8.40 (became 3213M)
P3525	28.5.40–FAO2 25.7.40
P3593	30.5.40–EFB 1.5.41
P3594	30.5.40–20.8.40
P3596	30.5.40–EFAO 25.7.40 (crashed nr Hullavington, FH 49.50)
P3598	30.5.40 (DIA 11.8)–20.8.40
P3640	8.9.40–4.4.41
P3755	25.6.40–EFB 19.12.40 (crashed Windrush, at night)
P3900	26.10.40–8.11.40
P3979	12.8.40–15.8.40
R2687	28.7.40 (DIA 15.8)–22.8.40
V6960	28.10.40–FAOE 12.5.41
V7204	13.7.40–EFA 23.12.40
V7207	13.7.40–7.1.41
V7231	29.7.40–FTR 11.8.40
V7233	29.7.40–s/d 11.8.40 (off Portland)
V7250	17.8.40–s/d 25.8.40 (Portland)
V7255	17.8.40–9.10.40
V7285	30.7.40–10.8.41
V7307	17.8.40–s/d 3.9.40 (convoy patrol)
V7310	17.8.40–FBO2 10.9.40
V7404	14.10.40–8.11.40
V7569	5.10.40–9.10.40
W6667	12.8.40–FTR 11.9.40 (ditched)

No. 111 Sqn

L1823	16.2.39–22.8.40, damaged, SOC 24.8.40
L1892	20.8.40–EFB 6.9.40 (Kenley)
L2052	7.6.40–3.9.40, 8.9.40–16.9.40
L2055	20.8.40–7.9.40
N2340	16.10.39–EFB 18.8.40 (crashed Oxted)
P3215	13.7.40–EFB 15.8.40
N2482	15.4.40 (DIA 16.8)–18.9.40
N2529	20.8.40–18.9.40
N2648	6.9.40–17.9.40
N2660	6.9.40–18.9.40
P2886	23.5.40–EFAO 14.10.40
P2888	23.5.40–11.7.40 and 19.8.40–s/d 31.8.40
P2924	27.8.40–29.8.40
P2958	8.6.40–FBO2 14.7.40 (crashed on take off, Hawkinge)
P2979	6.9.40–25.4.41
P3025	5.9.40–s/d 7.9.40 (Newchurch)
P3029	23.6.40–s/d 16.8.40 (nr Paddock Wood)
P3046	18.6.40–23.8.40, 13.10.40–FBO2 24.10.40
P3105	14.7.40–s/d 11.8.40
P3106	14.7.40–12.2.41
P3162	17.7.40–16.9.40
P3399	7.6.40–FBO2 18.8.40
P3458	12.8.40–17.9.40
P3459	23.5.40–FBO2 10.7.40
P3470	8.9.40–EFAO 5.12.40
P3515	11.7.40–FAO2 17.7.40
P3524	19.5.40–26.4.41
P3530	19.5.40–FBO2 13.8.40
P3548	23.5.40–EFA 16.8.40 (fuel shortage, crashed Boyton, Suffolk)
P3595	7.6.40–EFB 15.8.40
P3600	13.9.40–22.10.40
P3663	11.6.40–FBO2 10.7.40
P3671	11.6.40–EFB 10.7.40 (collided with DO 17, off Folkestone)
P3676	11.6.40–FBO2 10.7.40
P3875	18.7.40–s/d 2.9.40
P3880	17.7.40–FBO2 13.8.40
P3922	14.7.40–FTR 11.8.40
P3942	11.7.40–FTR 11.8.40
P3943	11.7.40–s/d 18.8.40 (nr Kenley)
P3944	11.7.40–s/d 15.8.40 (Selsey)
P3961	11.7.40 (DIA 15.8)–22.11.40
P5183	6.9.40–FAO2 11.9.40
P5187	8.9.40–17.9.40
R4096	17.8.40–s/d 26.8.40 (nr Martlesham)
R4112	18.8.40–FBO2 30.8.40
R4172	17.8.40–s/d 4.9.40 (off Folkestone)
R4187	12.8.40–s/d 18.8.40 (Kenley)
R4188	13.8.40–22.8.40
R4193	12.8.40–EFB 16.8.40 (collision over Marden, Kent)
R4195	12.8.40–FBO2 15.8.40
R4226	16.8.40–FA2 23.9.40
R4228	16.8.40–FBO2 2.9.40
V6538	16.8.40–22.11.40
V6539	18.8.40–FBO2 25.10.40
V6560	10.9.40–s/d 3.11.40

Without backing from the Civilian Repair Organisation, the Battle of Britain might have been lost. In this late 1939 scene Hurricane L1583 of 111 Squadron is under repair before serving with Nos 263, 3 and 504 Squadrons during the Battle. (via Bruce Robertson)

V6562	20.8.40-EFA 6.2.41
V6606	11.9.40-24.4.41
V6613	11.9.40-25.4.41
V6696	13.9.40-11.5.41
V6701	13.9.40-16.5.41
V7222	14.8.40 (DIA 16.8)-FBO2 26.8.40
V7237	23.10.40-21.3.41
V7361	14.8.40-15.1.41
V7385	27.8.40-11.4.41
V7386	27.8.40-FBO2 6.9.40
V7400	27.8.40-22.2.41
V7461	12.9.40-19.6.41
V7462	12.9.40-10.4.41

Mk II

Z2308	2.9.40 (DIA 4.9.40)
Z2309	2.9.40-s/d 4.9.40 (off Folkestone)
Z2310	2.9.40-7.9.40 (with 421 Flt 9.10.40-11.11.40)
Z2311	2.9.40-7.9.40
Z2312	2.9.40-9.9.40
Z2313	2.9.40-7.9.40
Z2314	2.9.40-5.9.40
E/Z2315	2.9.40-FBO2 4.9.40 (Ewhurst, Surrey)
Z2317	2.9.40-7.9.40
Z2318	2.9.40-7.9.40
Z2319	2.9.40-7.9.40

No. 145 Sqn

L1783	7.6.40-9.9.40
N2487	9.8.40-23.10.40
N2494	28.3.40-FBO2 27.10.40
N2495	28.3.40-15.2.41
N2496	29.3.40-11.2.41
N2497	29.3.40-FBO2 7.7.40
N2703	9.7.40-EFA 12.7.40 (Ringwood)
P2684	9.8.40-29.8.40
P2696	9.7.40-EFB 20.9.40
P2720	17.7.40-EFB 29.10.40
P2770	30.5.40-FBO2 19.7.40
P2918	4.6.40 (DIA 11.8)-23.8.40
P2924	4.6.40-FBO2 2.7.40; 29.8.40-EFB 7.11.40
P2951	30.5.40-s/d 11.8.40 (off Swanage)
P2955	30.5.40-s/d 8.8.40 (off Isle of Wight)
P2957	30.5.40-s/d 8.8.40 (off Isle of Wight)
P3155	17.7.40-s/d 1.8.40 (Hastings)
P3163	12.7.40-s/d 8.8.40 (off Isle of Wight)
P3164	14.7.40 (DIA 11.8)-23.8.40
P3167	12.7.40-s/d 27.10.40 (off Isle of Wight)
P3221	22.7.40-15.2.41
P3381	30.5.40-s/d 8.8.40 (off Isle of Wight)
P3391	17.5.40-s/d 12.8.40 (Isle of Wight)
P3400	18.5.40-s/d 11.7.40 (off Selsey Bill), (FH 99.45)
P3516	25.5.40, FAT2 24.7, to 29.7.40
P3517	18.5.40-FAO 15.7.40 (became 2121M 22.7.40)
P3521	15.5.40-FBO2 8.12.40
P3545	17.5.40-FBO2 8.8.40 (re- classified from EFB)
P3704	17.5.40-EFB 30.11.40 (crashed nr Chichester)
P3896	14.7.40-s/d 12.10.40 (Cranbrook)
P3926	27.7.40-FBO2 25.10.40
P3898	12.8.40-FBO2 27.8.40
P3899	12.8.40-28.8.40
R2683	29.8.40-18.11.40
P8816	28.10.40-FTR 7.11.40
R4176	9.8.40-FTR 12.8.40 (Isle of Wight)
R4177	9.8.40-FBO2 6.11.40
R4180	9.8.40-s/d 12.8.40 (Isle of Wight)
R4191	14.8.40-15.8.40
R4218	14.8.40-15.8.40
R4224	14.8.40-28.8.40
R4225	14.8.40-29.8.40
R4227	14.8.40-3.9.40
V6626	29.8.40-4.2.41
V6627	29.8.40-s/d 6.11.40
V6856	13.10.40-FAO2 18.10.40
V6876	13.10.40-FAO2 18.10.40
V6889	21.10.40-s/d 7.11.40
V6920	19.10.40-FAO2 20.11.40
V6940	20.10.40-4.2.41
V6979	28.10.40-1.3.41
V7237	16.8.40-23.10.40
V7251	12.8.40-FBO2 12.10.40
V7294	3.8.40-s/d 11.8.40 (Swanage)
V7230	28.10.40-EFA 29.12.40
V7337	29.8.40-s/d 15.10.40 (New Milton, Hants)
V7422	29.8.40-FAO2 27.10.40
V7426	29.8.40-EFB 12.10.40 (FH 30.08)
V7592	17.9.40-s/d 27.10.40 (Isle of Wight)
V7675	28.10.40-1.3.41

No. 151 Sqn

L1750	3.6.40-8.9.40, 10.10.40-12.12.40
L1777	7.10.40-3.11.40
L1975	13.7.40 (DIA 15.8)-23.8.40
L2005	14.3.40-s/d 28.8.40 (Godmersham)
L2047	16.9.40-30.10.40
P2826	11.7.40 (DIA 30.9)-1.10.40
G/P3065	7.7.40 (DIA 15.8)-24.8.40
P3119	25.7.40 (DIA 30.8)-5.9.40
P3152	3.7.40-FBO2 12.7.40
P3206	19.7.40-7.8.40
P3273	15.5.40-FBO2 24.8.40
P3275	15.5.40-s/d 12.7.40 (off Orfordness)
P3301	24.5.40-EFB 31.8.40 (later to RN)
P3302	24.5.40-s/d 12.8.40 (off North Foreland)
P3304	24.5.40-FBO2 12.7.40, 28.7.40-s/d 12.8.40
P3305	21.5.40-8.7.40
P3306	21.5.40-FBO2 29.7.40, repaired, EFA 24.9.40 — collided with V7432
P3307	21.5.40-13.8.40
P3309	16.4.40-FBO2 9.7.40

54

P3310	14.4.40-s/d 14.8.40	V7286	3.8.40-22.2.41
P3312	17.4.40-EFB 31.8.40 (crashed Southend)	V7360	19.8.40-31.8.40, 3.9.40-13.9.40
		V7369	20.8.40-s/d 30.8.40 (nr Strood)
P3316	17.4.40-EFB 24.7.40 (crashed, North Weald)	V7380	20.8.40-FBO2 24.8.40
		V7384	25.8.40-11.9.40
P3320	13.5.40-FBO2 28.8.40	V7406	2.9.40-EFAO 4.9.40 (hit crane
P3650	29.10.40-22.12.40		on take off, Stapleford Tawney)
P3780	17.7.40-FBO2 13.8.40	V7409	1.9.40-6.9.40
P3806	21.6.40-s/d 9.7.40	V7410	13.8.40-s/d 15.8.40
P3807	21.6.40-7.9.40	V7411	13.8.40-27.8.40
P3871	11.7.40, DIA 18.8-20.8.40	V7432	1.9.40-FAO2 24.9.40 (forced
P3882	11.7.40-EFB 29.8.40 ?		landing Waddington; collided
P3739	20.8.40-1.5.40		with P3306)
P3813	20.8.40-EFA 16.1.41	V7434	1.9.40-EFAO 20.10.40 (crashed,
P3940	11.7.40-s/d 18.8.40		Digby)
P3941	17.7.40-s/d 15.8.40	V7438	1.9.40-6.9.40
P5182	31.8.40-FAO3 1.10.40	V7439	1.9.40-FA 25.11.40
P5183	31.8.40-2.9.40	V7496	19.9.40-3.7.41
P5186	31.8.40-1.10.40		
P5195	29.8.40-3.11.40		

No. 213 Sqn

R4074	1.9.40-6.9.40	L1777	27.8.40-6.9.40
R4181	14.8.40-s/d 18.8.40	G/N2336	4.6.40-s/d 27.8.40 (Channel)
R4182	14.8.40-SOC 21.9.40	Q/N2401	20.3.40-s/d 27.9.40 (nr
R4183	14.8.40-s/d 24.8.40		Sevenoaks)
R4184	17.8.40-FA 26.10.40 (crashed on	N2479	17.8.40-25.8.40
	take off, Digby)	N2541	2.3.40-FTR 15.7.40 (off
R4185	19.8.40-EFB 16.9.40		Dartmouth)
R4213	21.8.40-s/d 30.8.40 (nr	N2608	7.10.40-EFB 1.11.40
	Rochester)	N2630	4.6.40-11.12.40
		N2631	4.6.40-2.7.40
V6543	1.9.40-FAO2 6.11.40	N2646	4.6.40 (DIA 25.8)-12.9.40
V6634	2.9.40-SOC 31.3.41 (FH 150.10)	O/N2650	4.6.40-s/d 11.8.40 (off Portland)
V6793	26.9.40-25.3.41	H/N2661	1.3.40 (DIA 11.8)-19.8.40
V6796	26.9.40-22.3.41	C/N2708	20.4.40 (DIA 11.8)-23.8.40
V6957	28.10.40-29.10.40	P2731	31.5.40-28.9.40
V6955	28.10.40-22.12.40	P2766	20.5.40-FTR 25.8.40 ?
V7222	2.10.40-22.3.41	R/P2802	20.5.40-s/d 12.8.40
V7234	2.10.40-14.3.41		

Hurricane N2479:US-P of 56 Squadron at North Weald in March 1940. With the squadron until 13 May, it was used by 213 Squadron in August then joined 6 OTU. July 1941 saw it moved to the Middle East and to Iraq in 1943.

55

P2814	26.8.40-1.11.40	W6667	12.8.40-s/d 11.9.40
M/P2854	23.7.40-FTR 12.8.40	W6668	13.8.40-FTR 25.8.40 ?
P3057	17.8.40-FAO2 17.12.40	W6669	13.8.40-21.8.40
P3091	13.7.40-SOC 31.8.40 (FH 17.10)		
P3092	12.7.40-FBO2 3.8.40 ?		

No. 229 Sqn

F/P3113	13.7.40-s/d 15.9.40	L1769	6.3.40-27.9.40
P3174	16.8.40-s/d 16.10.40 ?	L1783	2.10.40-12.10.40
P3200	12.8.40-s/d 25.8.40 (Portland)	L1808	9.5.40-20.7.40
P3267	20.10.40-EFB 3.12.40	L1829	7.3.40-19.8.40
B/P3348	31.5.40-s/d 13.8.40	L2071	24.5.40-20.7.40
P3350	31.5.40-SOC 16.9.40	A/N2436	13.9.40-1.10.40
P3362	20.5.40-16.9.40	N2465	4.6.40-FBO2 17.9.40
P3474	18.5.40-SOC 21.11.40	N2466	2.6.40-s/d 11.9.40
P3480	20.5.40-SOC 26.8.40	N2537	17.5.40-s/d 15.9.40 (Staplehurst,
P3522	19.9.40-10.1.41		Kent)
P3554	27.8.40-s/d 5.10.40 (Swanage)	N2592	2.6.40-FBO2 14.9.40
M/P3585	2.6.40-FBO2 11.8.40	N2631	2.7.40-12.8.40
P3641	26.9.40-1.11.40	N2647	7.9.40-FBO2 30.9.40
A/P3780	27.8.40-s/d 11.9.40 (Selsey)	N2648	2.6.40-6.9.40
P/P3789	13.7.40-s/d 11.8.40	N2652	28.9.40-s/d 3.9.40 (nr
P3979	15.8.40-FBO2 27.9.40		Edenbridge)
P5189	16.8.40-25.8.40	N2660	4.6.40-6.9.40
P5198	27.8.40-15.2.41	P2674	24.5.40-31.7.40
P5202	21.8.40-FBO2 5.11.40	P2815	8.9.40-s/d 30.9.40 (Ightham,
R4086	24.7.40-22.10.40		Kent)
R4099	30.7.40-FBO2 14.8.40	P2877	21.5.40-15.9.40
V6533	16.9.40-FAT2 16.9.40	P2879	16.9.40-s/d 23.9.40 (nr
V6541	16.9.40-FBO2 14.10.40		Westcliff)
V6544	16.9.40-FBO2 15.10.40	P2901	19.5.40-FAO2 29.11.40
V6726	28.9.40-s/d 15.10.40 (Tangmere)	P2979	2.9.40-6.9.40
V6752	26.9.40-15.2.41	P3037	12.7.40-s/d 30.9.40
V6779	29.9.40-21.10.40	P3038	12.7.40-s/d 11.9.40
V2708	13.7.40-15.12.40	P3039	12.7.40-7.10.40
V7224	14.8.40-9.10.40	P3114	2.10.40-5.5.41
V7226	12.8.40-FTR 25.8.40	P3124	28.9.40-s/d 15.10.40 (Stockbury)
V7227	13.8.40-FTR 15.8.40 (off	P3212	12.7.40-7.4.41
	Portland)	P3227	24.7.40-FBO2 30.9.40
V7306	17.8.40-EFA 12.9.40 (missing on	P3265	4.7.40-FBO2 26.9.40
	transit flight)	P3422	18.5.40-FBO2 30.9.40
V7421	24.8.40-FAO2 22.10.40	P3456	9.10.40-FBO2 15.10.40
V7432	31.10.40-14.1.41	P3463	19.5.40-FBO2 11.9.40, and
V7602	22.10.40-FTR 6.11.40		2.10.40-21.2.41
V7605	31.10.40-15.2.41	P3475	19.5.40-1.10.40
V7622	20.10.40-FTR 29.10.40		

P3039:RE-D *of 229 Squadron also flew with 312 Squadron from May to July 1941 and then was briefly used by 56 OTU.*

Battle veteran P3039 served with 55 OTU as 'PA-J' from 21 September 1942 until it was destroyed in an accident on 27 May 1943.

X/P3603	2.6.40–FBO2 27.9.40
P3710	4.6.40–23.2.41
P3712	4.6.40–FAO2 20.11.40
P3716	4.6.40–9.10.40
P3898	1.10.40–8.11.40
P5183	2.9.40–6.9.40
P5207	2.10.40–9.10.40
R4112	28.9.40–FBO2 30.9
V6704	13.9.40–FTR 26.10.40
Y/V6745	15.9.40–s/d 26.9.40
V6780	24.9.40–FBO2 27.9.40
T/V6782	24.9.40–s/d 27.9.40
V6820	1.10.40–EFB 8.10.40
V7245	9.10.40–17.3.41
V7411	16.9.40–EFB 30.9.40
V7465	18.10.40–5.5.41
V7469	13.9.40–FAO2 22.9.40
V7534	28.9.40–17.12.40
V7535	5.10.40–EFB 5.11.40
V7674	27.10.40–19.6.41
W6669	1.10.40–s/d 26.10.40 (Channel)

No. 232 Sqn

L1952	23.9.40–10.10.40
P2861	21.7.40–EFA 23.7.40 (ditched off Sumburgh)
P2909	21.7.40–30.4.41
P2911	21.7.40–25.11.40
P3104	25.7.40, DIA 23.8.40,–10.9.40
P3411	21.7.40–2.3.41
P3413	21.7.40–24.8.40, 2.10.40–21.3.41
P3449	21.7.40–7.5.41
P3608	13.10.40–EFAO 20.3.41
P3664	21.7.40–10.10.40
P3738	21.7.40–EFAO 22.9.40 (crashed Castletown)
P3772	23.9.40–6.5.41
P3928	27.7.40–18.8.41
P8810	15.7.40–4.2.41
R4090	1.8.40–EFA 1.8.40 (on delivery to Sumburgh)

No. 234 Sqn (allocated to, used by 249 Squadron)

P2866	11.6.40–24.9.40
P2910	11.6.40–24.9.40
P3576	11.6.40–s/d 16.8.40 (on 249 Sqn, nr Southampton; FH 95.10)
P3615	11.6.40–19.8.40
P3616	11.6.40–s/d 16.8.40 (FH 49.40)
P3655	11.6.40–24.9.40
P3656	11.6.40–15.9.40

No. 238 Sqn

L1702	27.9.40–EFB 30.9.40 (collided with N2474)
L2089	12.6.40 (DIA 15.9)–1.10.40
L1827	6.7.40–18.8.40
L1998	17.9.40–6.11.40
L2089	12.6.40–1.10.40
N2329	6.7.40–25.7.40
N2400	27.9.40–s/d 28.9.40 (off Isle of Wight)
N2474	27.9.40–EFB 30.9.40 (collided with L1702 over Shaftesbury)
N2546	28.9.40–8.10.40
N2597	11.9.40–EFB 25.9.40 (crashed Charmy Down; became 3577M)
P2769	21.5.40–SOC 30.9.40 (on 79 Sqn; FH 61.35)
P2827	18.6.40–FBO2 11.8.40
P2830	15.8.40–FTR 15.9.40 (nr Tonbridge)
P2836	15.8.40–EFB 15.9.40 (Pembury, Kent)
P2920	1.10.40–30.3.41
P2946	11.6.40–FBO2 19.7.40
P2947	11.6.40–s/d 8.8.40 (off Isle of Wight)
P2948	11.6.40–FBO2 18.7.40
P2950	11.6.40–EFB 13.7.40 (crashed Warmwell)
P2978	12.6.40–s/d 11.8.40 (off Weymouth)
P2983	12.6.40–13.11.40
P2989	13.6.40 (DIA 13.8.40)–21.8.40
P3096	15.8.40–s/d 11.9.40
P3098	15.8.40–s/d 26.9.40 (FH 30.45)
P3123	24.9.40–FBO2 10.10.40
P3124	30.6.40–FBO2 11.8.40
P3176	9.8.40–18.8.40
P3177	9.8.40–FTR 13.8.40 (Portland)
P3178	9.8.40–7.12.40
P3204	21.7.40–16.8.40
P3208	22.7.40–25.7.40
P3214	2.10.40–30.3.41
P3219	22.7.40–2.2.41

VK-A *of 238 Squadron.*

P3222	22.7.40-FTR 11.8.40
P3223	22.7.40 (DIA 25.9)-2.10.40
P3264	18.9.40-1.10.40
P3314	2.10.40-30.3.41
P3349	28.9.40-EFB 28.11.40 (crashed NE of Andover)
P3413	2.10.40-21.3.41
P3462	12.6.40 (DIA 15.9)-1.10.40
P3599	12.6.40-s/d 1.10.40 (off Poole; FH 97.35)
P3611	13.8.40-s/d 5.10.40 (Mere, Shaftesbury)
P3617	12.6.40-s/d 8.8.40 (Isle of Wight)
P3618	12.6.40-EFAO 14.11.40 (crashed Stockbridge)
P3684	13.7.40-EFAP 19.8.40 (collided with balloon cable, Finsbury Park)
P3700	11.6.40-FBO2 3.7.40
P3702	11.6.40-FBO2 26.7.40
P3703	11.6.40-EFAO 6.7.40
P3764	11.7.40-s/d 13.8.40
P3766	11.7.40-s/d 20.7.40 (Lyme Bay, FH 8.45)
P3767	11.7.40-15.7.40
P3805	18.6.40-s/d 13.8.40
P3819	21.7.40-s/d 11.8.40
P3823	11.7.40-s/d 8.8.40 (Isle of Wight)
P3830	13.8.40-s/d 26.9.40
P3833	13.8.40 (DIA 15.9)-1.10.40
P3836	13.8.40-FTR 28.9.40 (FH 41.10)
P3920	13.8.40-19.9.40
P3984	15.8.40-s/d 10.10.40 (nr Poole)
R2680	7.8.40-FAO2 3.9.40
R2681	8.8.40-30.3.41
R2682	15.8.40-s/d 11.9.40
R4097	27.7.40-s/d 11.8.40 (off Weymouth)
R4098	30.7.40-5.5.41
R4099	1.10.40-30.3.41
R4232	18.9.40-30.3.41
V6727	28.9.40-26.11.40
V6754	27.9.40-13.10.40
V6776	27.9.40-s/d 28.9.40 (Isle of Wight)
V6777	27.9.40-s/d 7.10.40 (FH 6.25)
V6778	27.9.40-FBO2 28.9.40
V6792	27.9.40-s/d 26.9.40 ?
V6801	30.9.40-24.12.40
V6814	30.9.40-FTR 6.11.40
V7240	15.8.40-FTR 11.9.40
V7612	11.10.40-EFB 30.11.40
V7613	10.10.40-FAO2 10.11.40
V7619	18.10.40-9.1.41
V7620	18.10.40-FBO2 21.12.40
V7625	31.10.40-15.2.41

No. 242 Sqn

L1638	19.5.40-19.7.40
L1756	26.5.40-?
L1766	17.8.40-7.9.40
L1981	19.5.40-7.9.40
L2039	9.7.40-7.9.40
L2087	26.5.40-4.3.41
N2649	6.6.40-7.9.40
P2769	21.5.40-SOC 30.9.40 (with 79 Sqn; FH 61.35)
P2806	17.9.40-FTR 5.11.40
P2831	4.6.40-s/d 9.9.40 (Kenley, FH 117.30)
V/P2884	23.7.40-s/d 15.9.40 (Udimore, E Sussex)
P2878	19.5.40-4.7.40
P2961	2.6.40-FTR 30.1.41 (FH 263.0)
P2962	3.9.40-s/d 7.9.40 (Theydon Bois?)
X/P2967	31.5.40-FTR 20.8.40
P2983	12.6.40-5.11.40
P/P3034	17.9.40-13.3.41
N/P3054	6.40-?
D/P3061	7.7.40-FBO2 7.9.40
Q/P3087	24.6.40-s/d 9.9.40 (Caterham; FH 120.40)
L/P3088	24.6.40-FAO2 11.7.40
R/P3089	24.6.40-19.7.40
S/P3090	24.6.40-15.9.40
L/P3207	13.7.40-9.4.41
P/P3218	13.7.40-22.12.40
Y/P3485	2.6.40-17.9.40

P3684	13.7.40-EFAO 19.8.40 (collided with balloon cable, Finsbury Park)	P3674	4.6.40-EFA 6.8.41
P3515	11.9.40-7.2.41	P3759	26.6.40-20.7.40
M/P3715	13.7.40-21.9.40	P3761	26.6.40-15.7.40
T/P3718	6.40-?	E/P3762	26.6.40-14.2.41
P3813	24.6.40-15.7.40	P3835	13.7.40-FBO2 13.10.40

P3684 — 13.7.40-EFAO 19.8.40 (collided with balloon cable, Finsbury Park)
P3515 — 11.9.40-7.2.41
M/P3715 — 13.7.40-21.9.40
T/P3718 — 6.40-?
P3813 — 24.6.40-15.7.40
P3814 — 24.6.40-FBO2 30.8.40
P3815 — 24.6.40-FAO2 6.7.40
U/P3864 — 13.7.40-17.8.40 & 25.8.40-7.9.40
R4115 — 3.9.40-13.3.41
V/V6575 — 11.9.40-s/d 17.10.40 (off Gt Yarmouth; FH 48.35)
V6576 — 12.9.40 (DIA 15.9 and 27.9)-30.9.40
V6578 — 12.9.40-6.4.41
V6675 — 30.9.40-9.4.41
V6739 — 18.9.40-14.10.40
V6740 — 18.9.40-9.4.41
T/V7203 — 13.7.40-FTR 12.1.41
V7467 — 11.9.40-13.3.41

No. 245 Sqn

N2486 — 24.5.40-25.11.40
N2558 — 15.3.40-1.6.41
N2594 — 15.3.40-31.12.40
N2707 — 15.3.40-EFA 7.10.40 (FH 191)
P2681 — 4.6.40-19.7.40
P2835 — 13.7.40-FBO2 13.10.40
P2902 — 19.5.40-SOC 10.8.40 (FH 8)
P2906 — 9.6.40-6.2.41
P2913 — 4.6.40-25.2.41
P2914 — 4.6.40-14.2.41
P3097 — 13.7.40-6.10.40
P3099 — 13.7.40-EFAO 9.11.40 (FH 75)
P3101 — 13.7.40-FTR 29.8.40?
P3165 — 23.7.40-FBO2 15.8.40?
P3428 — 19.5.40-EFA 26.6.41 (hit HT cables, Ballymena; FH 336.15)
P3549 — 19.5.40-31.5.41
P3577 — 4.6.40-2.7.40
P3602 — 16.6.40-6.2.41
P3657 — 4.6.40-EFB 21.10.40 (crashed in Lough Neagh; FH 165)

P3674 — 4.6.40-EFA 6.8.41
P3759 — 26.6.40-20.7.40
P3761 — 26.6.40-15.7.40
E/P3762 — 26.6.40-14.2.41
P3835 — 13.7.40-FBO2 13.10.40

No. 249 Sqn (some jointly used with 56 Squadron in 9.40)

L1595 — 12.6.40-EFAO 20.9.40 (crashed Bulford Camp, Amesbury)
L1715 — 12.6.40-FAO2 15.7.40
L1764 — 2.9.40-24.9.40
L1832 — 12.6.40-22.9.40
L1998 — 12.6.40-17.9.40
L2067 — 12.6.40 (DIA 31.8)-10.9.40
N2351 — 19.8.40-21.8.40
N2386 — 20.7.40-24.9.40
N2434 — 12.6.40-24.9.40
N2440 — ?-EFB 7.9.40
N2597 — 23.7.40-11.9.40
P2910 — 11.6.40, (DIA 26.8.40) (possibly with 56 Squadron 24.9.40)-EFB 23.11.40
P2995 — 13.6.40-EFAO 16.7.40 (crashed on take off, Church Fenton)
P3055 — 12.6.40-24.9.40
P3057 — 12.6.40-FAT2 16.7.40
P3088 — 19.8.40-24.8.40
P3123 — 29.6.40-24.9.40
N/P3154 — 11.7.40-FA 24.7.40, 7.9.40 to 24.9.40
P3576 — 11.6.40-s/d 16.8.40 (flown by F/L J B Nicolson, VC)
P3594 — 2.9.40-s/d 7.9.40 (Faversham)
P3616 — 11.6.40-s/d 16.8.40 (crashed nr Lee-on-Solent)
P3660 — 13.6.40-15.9.40
P3667 — 3.9.40-3.10.40
P3834 — 8.9.40-s/d 27.9.40 (Dallington)
P3868 — 13.7.40-21.9.40
P3870 — 13.7.40-24.9.40
P3902 — 21.8.40-24.9.40
P5206 — 24.9.40-22.10.40
V6534 — 24.9.40-25.1.41

Hurricane V6728:GN-Z of 249 Squadron photographed at North Weald in late 1940, Flt Lt Georges Perrin (Free French) is pictured alongside. (Michael Payne)

Hurricane GN-M *of 249 Squadron, its serial number seemingly overpainted.*

V6559	24.9.40–31.10.40	L1965	20.7.40–s/d 30.8.40 (Wrotham)
V6561	4.9.40–20.9.40	N2455	13.9.40–19.10.40
V6566	8.9.40–FBO2 22.10.40	N2588	2.9.40–EAO2 17.10.40
V6574	3.9.40 (DIA 7.9)–16.9.40	X/P2631	15.5.40–s/d 30.8.40 (nr
V6582	4.9.40–5.9.40		Biddendon)
V6610	1.9.40–19.9.40	P2677	25.9.40–s/d 29.9.40 (nr
V6614	24.9.40–20.2.41		Newhaven)
V6615	4.9.40–s/d 6.9.40 (Maidstone)	P2865	31.8.40–EAO2 17.10.40
R/V6617	5.9.40–s/d 28.9.40 (Tonge)	P2883	19.5.40 (DIA 11.9)–13.9.40
V6622	8.9.40–FBO2 27.9.40	P2946	31.8.40–s/d 2.9.40
V6625	29.8.40–s/d 5.9.40	P2958	7.9.40–FTR 26.9.40
V6635	24.9.40–29.2.41	P2960	2.6.40–FBO2 30.8.40
V6680	8.9.40–30.9.40	P3032	23.6.40–EFB 6.9.40
V6682	8.9.40–s/d 11.9.40 (Benenden;	P3115	13.7.40–s/d 31.8.40 (Cudham)
	FH 2.0)	P3162	16.9.40–2.6.41
V6683	8.9.40–FBO3 27.9.40 (collided	P3213	13.7.40–s/d 30.8.40
	with Bf 110; Hailsham)	P3357	28.5.40–25.10.40
V6685	8.9.40–s/d 18.9.40 (Margretting)	P3359	28.5.40–EFB 10.7.40 (crashed
V6692	11.9.40–s/d 29.11.40		Irby, Lincs)
V6693	11.9.40–11.10.40	P3412	28.5.40–FBO2 30.8.40
V6694	11.9.40–27.9.40	P3457	19.5.40–EFB 7.8.40
V6728	16.9.40–FBO2 11.10.40	P3488	20.5.40–EAO 18.8.40 (Kenley)
V6729	16.9.40–FTR 28.11.40	P3511	19.5.40–5.1.41
V6798	29.9.40–20.1.37	P3537	28.5.40–EFAO 17.10.40
V7313	24.9.40–s/d 12.10.40 (nr	P3609	19.9.40 (DIA 29.9)–1.10.40
	Eastchurch)	P3610	16.6.40–EFB 18.9.40 (crashed
V7409	21.10.40–5.11.40		Nonington, Kent)
V7507	29.9.40–FBO2 7.11.40	P3678	6.6.40–s/d 16.8.40
V7536	5.10.40–s/d 30.10.40 (FH 46.10)	P3713	12.6.40–FBO2 31.8.40
V7537	4.10.40–FTR 10.10.40 (FH 3.30)	P3714	12.6.40–FBO2 31.8.40
V7538	5.10.40–21.3.41	P3717	13.7.40–FBO2 30.8.40
V7600	17.10.40–20.1.41	P3802	13.7.40–s/d 30.8.40 (Maidstone)
		P3804	13.7.40–s/d 14.9.40 (nr

No. 253 Sqn

			Faversham)
L1600	23.1.40–30.10.40	P3921	11.8.40–s/d 30.8.40
L1663	19.5.40–19.7.40		(Waldingham)
L1666	24.9.40–24.6.41	P5172	30.8.40–17.12.40
L1712	19.5.40–29.10.40	P5179	30.8.40–FBO2 20.9.40
L1818	28.3.40–29.10.40	P5181	30.8.40–s/d 5.9.40
L1830	23.1.40–s/d 31.8.40 (nr Biggin	P5184	30.8.40–EFB 14.9.40
	Hill)	P5185	30.8.40–s/d 1.9.40
L1928	27.9.40–EFB 10.10.40 (oxygen	R2686	1.9.40–FTR 20.9.40
	failure, crashed at Maidstone)	R4081	30.9.40–5.1.41

V6533	18.10.40–5.1.41
V6570	28.9.40–s/d 11.10.40 (Tunbridge Wells)
V6621	24.9.40–s/d 29.9.40 (Chailey)
V6638	1.9.40–s/d 4.9.40 (Banstead)
V6639	1.9.40 (DIA 9.9)–19.9.40
V6640	1.9.40–EFB 2.9.40 (nr Rye)
V6691	1.6.40–FBO2 27.9.40 (on 213 Sqn)
V6698	14.9.40–FBO2 15.9.40
V6736	16.9.40–s/d 20.9.40
V6756	26.9.40–FBO2 15.10.40
V6757	21.9.40–EAO2 17.10.40
V6813	30.9.40–27.10.40
V7301	15.10.40–FBO2 30.10.40
V7441	6.9.40–EFB 23.9.40 (became 2233M)
V7466	11.9.40–5.1.41
V7470	17.9.40–s/d 26.9.40
V7499	21.9.40–9.1.41
V7606	20.10.40–8.11.40
V7608	11.10.40–5.1.41

No. 257 Sqn

L1585	17.8.40–s/d 3.9.40 (Margretting, Essex)
L1703	11.7.40–EFB 15.8.40 (crashed at Watford Way, Edgware)
L1706	11.7.40–30.10.40
L2101	12.6.40–16.7.40 (Cat FA2 12.7.40)
P2835	3.9.40–FBO2 21.11.40
P2960	13.9.40–s/d 23.9.40 (Eastchurch)
P2981	12.6.40–s/d 8.8.40
D/P3049	17.7.40–s/d 7.9.40 (Sheppey)
P3058	11.7.40–s/d 8.8.40
P3175	9.8.40–s/d 31.8.40 (Walton-on-the-Naze)
P3518	11.7.40–s/d 3.9.40 (Ingatestone, Essex)
P3601	12.6.40–EFB 15.8.40
P3620	12.6.40–12.10.40
P3622	12.6.40–EFB 28.7.40 (written off some time after crashing nr Maidstone)
P3623	12.6.40 (DIA 13.8)–26.8.40
P3641	12.6.40, FA 23.7–27.8.40
P3642	12.6.40–FBO2 16.9.40
P3643	12.6.40–s/d 23.9.40 (Detling)
P3662	13.6.40–s/d 12.8.40 (Portsmouth)
P3704	11.6.40–FBO2 3.9.40
P3705	11.6.40–19.6.41
P3706	11.6.40–29.12.40
P3707	11.6.40–FAO2 12.7.40
P3708	11.6.40–s/d 18.8.40
P3709	11.6.40–FBO2 12.9.40
P3775	11.6.40–FAO2 23.9.40
P3776	11.6.40, FBO2 29.7, FBO2 12.8, off squadron 21.8.40
P3890	9.8.40–10.8.40
P3893	11.7.40–FBO3 29.10.40
R4088	25.7.40–19.6.41
R4094	30.7.40–FTR 8.8.40
R4189	13.8.40–28.8.40
R4190	13.8.40–29.12.40
R4195	24.9.40–s/d by AA fire 22.10.40 (Lydd)
V6555	9.9.40–FBO2 11.10.40

V6557	9.9.40–29.12.40
V6558	9.9.40–FBO2 18.9.40
V6563	20.8.40–EFAO 26.8.40
E/V6601	26.8.40–s/d 31.8.40 (nr Brightlingsea)
V6604	17.9.40–FBO2 17.10.40
V6741	19.9.40–17.11.40
V6794	26.9.40–17.10.40
V6795	26.9.40–FBO2 29.10.40
V6802	27.9.40–16.11.40
V7254	14.8.40–s/d 7.9.40
V7296	9.8.40–19.6.41
V7298	9.8.40–s/d 12.10.40 (Stone, Kent)
V7317	3.9.40 (DIA 7.9)–17.9.40
V7338	31.8.40–FBO2 12.9, to 18.9.40
V7607	29.10.40–4.6.41

No. 263 Sqn

L1583	13.7.40–25.7.40
L1803	7.7.40–EFA 24.8.40 (nr Falkirk)
N2493	17.7.40–5.2.41
P2570	7.7.40–5.12.40
P2857	21.6.40–5.12.40
P2915	18.6.40–5.12.40
P2916	18.6.40–4.9.40
P2917	18.6.40–EFA 21.7.40 (nr Tranent, East Lothian)
P2988	19.6.40–FBO2 2.7.40
P2990	18.6.40–EFAO 6.8.40 (crashed nr Grangemouth)
P2991	18.6.40–EFA 13.7.40 (Carstairs)
P2992	18.6.40–5.12.40
P3145	13.7.40–30.11.40
P3307	1.9.40–5.12.40
P3606	18.6.40–30.11.40
P3658	18.9.40–5.12.40
P3761	15.7.40–5.12.40
P3767	15.7.40–8.10.40
P3881	13.7.40–5.12.40

No. 302 Sqn

R/P2752	20.8.40–s/d 15.10.40
P2918	7.10.40–?
E/P2954	18.8.40–s/d 15.9.40 (Battlebridge; FH 26.20)
A/P3085	19.7.40–EFAO 29.10.40 (Chobham; collided with U/V6923)
Z/P3086	19.7.40–1.10.40
P3120	27.7.40–7.9.40
E/P3205	18.9.40–7.4.41
P3217	19.7.40, FA2 29.7, to 3.8.40
P3538	20.8.40–FTR 8.11.40
R/P3785	22.10.40–7.4.41
L/P3812	19.7.40–FBO2 15.10.40
F/P3867	27.7.40–EFA 14.2.41 (FH 80.60)
P3872	16.10.40–EFA 2.11.40 (FH 80.35)
P3877	17.10.40–19.3.41
P3903	27.7.40–FBO2 19.10.40
Y/P3924	27.7.40–18.10.40
P3927	27.7.40–EFA 17.8.40 (nr Beverley) FH 37
X/P3930	27.7.40–EFB 18.10.40 (collided with P3931)
P3931	27.7.40–EFB 18.10.40 (collided with P3930, Kempton Park, Middx)

O/P3932	27.7.40-FBO2 21.8.40
H/P3934	27.7.40-FBO2 21.8.40 (eventually lost at sea from Camship, in action, 2.6.42; Sea Hurricane Mk 1a)
P3935	27.7.40-FBO2 6.11.40
B/R2684	27.7.40-FAO2 15.10.40
R2685	27.7.40-7.9.40
N,M/R4095	30.7.40-20.9.40
K/V6569	20.8.40-11.40
V6570	22.8.40-26.8.40
U/V6571	22.8.40-FTR 18.10.40
K/V6734	16.9.40-7.4.41
M/V6735	16.9.40-22.10.40
C/V6744	19.9.40-19.3.41
Z/V6753	21.9.40-FBO2 18.10.40
T/V7417	22.8.40-FBO2 17.10.40
V7593	20.10.40-FTR 25.10.40 (FH 6.0)
V7597	17.10.40-FAO2 5.11.40
W6669	16.9.40-24.9.40

No. 303 Sqn

M/L1696	3.9.40-s/d 27.9.40 (Borough Green)
L1769	27.9.40-24.4.41
L2026	9.9.40-1.2.41
L2099	9.9.40-1.2.41
N2460	29.9.40-3.1.41
N2661	29.9.40-3.1.41
P2686	?-s/d 6.9.40 (flying with 1 Sqn)
P2903	12.9.40-FBO2 15.9.40
P2985	20.8.40-s/d 5.9.40 (North Benfleet)
P3089	7.9.40-FBO2 7.10.40
P3120	7.9.40-EAO 6.10.40 (Northolt)
P3206	8.10.40-1.11.40
P3217	27.9.40-EAO2 6.10.40
P3383	1.10.40-3.1.41
P3544	16.9.40-FBO2 26.9.40
P3551	9.40-11.40
P3577	10.9.40-s/d 15.9.40 (Dartford)
P3645	?-E (ground accident) 9.8.40
P3663	29.9.40-FBO2 30.9.40
P3700	8.8.40-s/d 9.9.40 (nr Hove)
P3890	10.8.40-s/d 7.9.40 (nr Loughton)
P3892	2.10.40-s/d 5.10.40
P3901	17.9.40-3.1.41
M/P3939	7.9.40-s/d 15.9.40
P3974	10.8.40-s/d 6.9.40
U/P3975	10.8.40-FBO2 9.9.40
P1580	5.9.40-8.9.40
R2688	8.8.40-FBO2 3.9.40
R4100	1.8.40-FAO2 8.8.40
R4173	8.8.40-s/d 7.9.40
R4175	8.8.40-EFB 8.10.40
R4178	8.8.40-11.9.40
R4179	8.8.40-FBO2 6.9.40
R4217	14.8.40-FBO2 7.9.40
V6665	7.9.40-s/d 11.9.40 (Pembury)
V6667	7.9.40-s/d 11.9.40 (Selsey)
V6673	10.9.40 (DIA 15.9)-FBO2 26.9.40
V6681	12.9.40-FAO2 26.10.40
J/V6684	12.9.40 (DIA 15.9 and 27.9)-FAO2 19.12.40
V7235	10.8.40-3.1.41
V7242	1.8.40-s/d 11.9.40 (Westerham)
V7243	1.8.40-EFB 6.9.40
V7244	1.8.40-1.11.40

V7245	1.8.40-FAO2 8.8.40
V7246	2.8.40-EFB 27.9.40
V7247	1.8.40-FAO2 29.8.40
V7284	1.8.40-FBO2 6.9.40
V7289	8.8.40-s/d 27.9.40 (Stoke D'Abernon, Suffolk)
V7290	8.8.40-s/d 6.9.40
V7245	1.8.40-FA2 2.8.40
V7401	6.10.40-31.10.40
V7465	8.9.40 (DIA 11.9 and 15.9)-26.9.40
V7503	27.9.40-31.1.41
V7504	29.9.40-31.1.41
V7624	28.10.40-3.1.41

No. 306 Sqn

L1687	31.8.40-24.12.40
L1700	31.8.40-30.10.40
L1717	31.8.40-26.11.40
L1771	31.8.40-10.10.40
L1895	31.8.40-14.12.40
L1956	31.8.40-23.2.41
L1969	31.8.40-26.11.40
L2011	31.8.40-14.12.40
P2724	31.8.40-1.4.41
V7533	22.10.40-EFAO 23.11.40

No. 308 Sqn

P2855	11.10.40-8.4.41
P3399	11.10.40-EFAO 16.10.40 (hit balloon cable, Whitley, Coventry)
P3452	11.10.40-30.10.40
P3598	11.10.40-14.6.41
P3891	11.10.40-FAO2 10.11.40
P3939	1.8.40-7.9.40

No. 310 Sqn

L1596	17.8.40-28.8.40
L1842	7.9.40-EFB 2.11.40
P2715	7.9.40-28.10.40
P2953	16.9.40-15.1.41
P3056	19.7.40-7.4.41
P3069	27.9.40-FBO2 10.10.40 ?
P3142	24.7.40-27.9.40 (crash landed Oxted 9.9.40, damaged)
D/P3143	24.7.40-EFA 16.10.40 (nr Ely)
P3148	24.7.40-25.4.41
P3156	24.7.40-FAO2 15.8.40
P3157	24.7.40-20.8.40
P3159	24.7.40-s/d 31.8.40
P3268	28.8.40-FBO2 31.8.40
P3621	7.9.40-30.3.41
P3707	17.9.40-28.10.40
P3887	19.7.40-s/d 26.8.40 (Maldon)
P3888	19.7.40-FBO2 31.8.40
P3889	19.7.40-FBO2 31.8.40
P3960	25.7.40-s/d 26.8.40 (Southminster)
P8809	25.7.40-FBO2 5.9.40, FAO3 1.11.40
P8811	1.8.40-s/d 3.9.40
P8814	1.8.40-s/d 31.8.40
R4084	25.7.40-EFB 9.9.40 (crashed nr Purley)
R4085	25.7.40-s/d 15.9.40 (Billericay)
R4087	25.7.40-s/d 15.9.40
R4089	25.7.40-FBO2 5.11.40
V6573	11.9.40-15.9.40

V6579	11.9.40-6.4.41
V6608	12.9.40-s/d 27.9.40 (Chilham)
V6619	9.9.40-EFB 5.11.40
V6621	28.8.40-FBO2 31.8.40
V6642	2.9.40-6.4.41
Y/V6643	2.9.40-FBO2 7.9.40
V6645	2.9.40-s/d 27.9.40 (Sittingbourne)
V6646	2.9.40-s/d 6.9.40
V7304	17.8.40-22.3.41
V7405	2.9.40-12.9.40
V7412	2.9.40-s/d 9.9.40 (Croydon)
V7436	2.9.40-29.3.41
V7437	2.9.40-s/d 7.9.40 (Sheppey)
V7538	11.10.40-FBO2 1.11.40 (AA fire damage)

No. 312 Sqn

L1926	31.8.40-3.10.40
L1547	31.8.40-EFB 10.10.40
L1644	31.8.40-crashed 10.9.40 (nr Fen Ditton, Cambs)
L1701	31.8.40-16.1.41
L1740	31.8.40-27.11.40
L1748	31.8.40-31.7.41
L1807	31.8.40-11.10.40
L1822	31.8.40-26.11.40
L1841	31.8.40-16.1.41
P2575	10.10.40-14.10.40
P3889	12.9.40-FBO2 31.8.40 (crashed Duxford 29.10.40; FH 109)
P3983	11.10.40-3.5.41
V6846	8.10.40-FAO2 15.10.40

No. 501 Sqn

L1572	3.9.40-21.10.40
L1578	13.8.40-FTR 2.9.40
L1657	13.8.40 (DIA 30.9)-2.10.40
L1659	19.8.40-FBO2 24.8.40
L1864	19.6.40-5.8.40
L1865	14.7.39-s/d 24.8.40
L1868	9.3.39-10.9.40
L2038	19.6.40-30.10.40
L2046	5.9.39-18.8.40
N2329	25.7.40 (DIA 14.9)-15.9.40
N2485	19.6.40-FTR 11.7.40 (off Portland)
N2596	9.7.40-11.7.40
N2617	13.8.40-s/d 18.8.40
P2549	18.5.40-s/d 18.8.40?
P2691	19.6.40-SOC by 4.9.40 (FH 57.15)
P2760	28.5.40-s/d 15.9.40
P2793	30.8.40-s/d 13.9.40
P2986	19.6.40-FAO2 12.8.40
P3040	22.6.40-s/d 15.8.40
P3041	22.6.40-12.8.40
N/P3059	9.7.40-FTR 18.8.40 (Canterbury)
P3082	22.6.40-s/d 20.7.40 (Lyme Bay)
P3083	22.6.40-FAO2 7.8.40
P3084	22.6.40-s/d 12.7.40 (off Portland)
P3102	19.8.40-s/d 29.8.40 (FH 29.53)
P3119	25.7.40-5.9.40. 17.10.40-2.11.40
P3140	7.7.40-s/d 11.7.40
P3141	7.7.40-FTR 24.8.40
T/P3208	25.7.40-s/d 18.8.40 (FH 27.55)
P3270	7.6.40-FTR 18.8.40
P3349	5.6.40-FAO2 31.7.40

P3397	16.6.40-FBO2 12.8.40
W/P3417	6.9.40-s/d 28.9.40 (Deal)
P3429	22.10.40-EFB 30.11.40
P3516	3.9.40-s/d 6.9.40
P3582	13.8.40-s/d 15.8.40 (Folkestone; FH 7.15)
P3605	6.9.40-FBO2 28.9.40
P3646	28.5.40-s/d 31.7.40 (nr Canterbury)
P3651	28.5.40-s/d 15.8.40
P3672	15.10.40-14.12.40
P3767	8.10.40-FBO2 15.10.40
P3803	22.6.40-s/d 12.8.40 (Gravesend)
P3808	22.6.40-s/d 27.7.40 (Dover)
P3815	1.7.40-s/d 18.8.40 (Canterbury; FH 42.35)
P3816	1.7.40-23.8.40
P3819	11.7.40-21.7.40
P3820	11.7.40-s/d 17.9.40 (Ashford)
P3831	16.8.40-18.8.40
P3934	27.7.40-EFB 21.8.40
P3983	11.10.40-3.5.41
P5189	17.9.40-FTR 28.11.40 (FH 88.35)
P5193	25.8.40-FTR 24.10.40
P5194	25.8.40-FAO2 15.10.40
P5200	25.8.40-s/d 11.9.40 (Maidstone)
P8816	7.8.40-6.9.40
R4101	7.8.40-FBO2 15.8.40; 20.9.40-FBO2 10.12.40
R4105	7.8.40-FAO2 27.10.40
R4219	16.8.40-s/d 18.8.40
R4222	16.8.40-FAO2 27.8.40
R4223	16.8.40-s/d 29.8.40 (Acrise)
V6570	6.9.40-18.9.40
V6600	6.9.40-s/d 18.9.40 (Staplehurst)
V6612	3.9.40-s/d 6.9.40 (Eltham)
V6620	6.9.40-s/d 18.9.40 (Charing)
V6644	2.9.40 (DIA 5.9)-s/d 15.9.40 ?
V6645	2.9.40-s/d 27.9.40 (Sittingbourne)
V6646	2.9.40-s/d 6.9.40 (nr Ashford)
V6672	6.9.40-s/d 27.9.40 (Godstone)
V6703	17.9.40-EAO2 17.10.40
V6722	8.10.40-EFB 15.10.40 (FH 19.50)
V6723	17.9.40-15.4.41
V6733	19.9.40-FBO2 4.10.40
V6787	28.9.40-FBO2 15.10.40
V6799	29.9.40-FBO2 7.10.40
V6800	29.7.40-s/d 7.10.40 (Darenth, FH 10.35)
V6840	6.10.40-8.6.41
V6841	7.10.40-EFA 28.3.41
V7229	28.9.40-7.6.41
V7230	3.8.40 (DIA 15.8, 2.9)-23.9.40
V7234	3.8.40-FBO2 2.9.40
V7402	31.8.40-FBO2 2.9.40
V7403	31.8.40-15.9.40
V7404	31.8.40-FBO2 11.9.40
V7433	6.9.40 (DIA 15.9)-22.9.40
V7469	27.10.40-8.6.41
V7497	19.9.40-s/d 28.9.40
V7498	19.9.40 (DIA 22.9)-FBO2 4.10.40
V7595	27.10.40-FBO2 29.10.40
V7596	20.10.40-24.5.41
V7614	15.10.40-22.12.40
V7625	27.10.40-24.11.40

63

No. 504 Sqn

L1583	12.8.40–22.3.41
L1615	28.5.40–s/d 7.9.40 (nr Faversham)
L1913	14.9.39–EFB 29.9.40 (damaged by AA fire, night; crashed nr Nuneaton)
L1945	1.6.40–FAO 2.8.40
L1952	13.5.39–23.9.40
L1957	19.5.40–FAO2 1.8.40 (Wick)
L1999	9.5.40–25.10.40
N2471	1.4.40 (DIA 11.9)–14.9.40
N2481	24.5.40–s/d 15.9.40
N2587	28.5.40–23.9.40
N2669	12.6.40–6.8.40
N2705	28.4.40–s/d 15.9.40 (Dartford)
P2725	5.40–s/d 15.9.40 (Buckingham Palace Road, London)
P2908	27.7.40–5.8.41
P2987	28.6.40–FBO2 30.9.40
P2993	17.6.40 (DIA 18.8)–27.8.40
P3021	14.7.40 (DIA 7.9, 30.9)–5.10.40
P3206	4.10.40–8.10.40
K/P3414	24.5.40–s/d 30.9.40 (off Weymouth)
P3415	24.5.40–FBO2 27.9.40
P3614	5.8.40–1.8.41
P3770	16.8.40–s/d 11.9.40 (Newchurch)
P3772	14.7.40–23.9.40
V/P3774	14.7.40–13.5.41
R4178	2.10.40–29.10.40
V6695	14.9.40–4.1.41
V6698	14.9.40–FBO2 15.9.40
V6700	14.9.40–12.5.41
V6702	12.9.40–1.8.41
V6730	17.9.40–FTR 13.5.41
V6731	17.9.40 (DIA 30.9)–1.10.40
V6732	17.9.40–20.2.41
V6751	20.9.40–28.4.41
V7618	17.10.40–FAO2 26.11.40

No. 601 Sqn

L1670	21.5.40–23.9.40
L1772	1.3.40–EFA 22.7.40 (Pagham, Sussex)
L1819	4.3.40–22.10.40
L1894	16.8.40–EFAO 21.9.40 (crashed taking off, Exeter)
L1917	9.6.40–23.8.40
L1936	9.6.40–force landed 4.7.40 (Lewes)
L1951	12.7.40–26.9.40
L2057	5.8.40–s/d 11.8.40 (off Portland)
L2102	4.3.40–26.10.40
L2143	2.9.40–7.9.40
N2435	21.5.40–9.8.40
N2602	7.6.40–s/d 31.8.40
P2696	10.6.40–9.7.40
T/P2753	18.5.40–s/d 26.7.40 (in sea, off Isle of Wight)
P2920	9.6.40–FBO2 13.8.40
P2949	31.8.40–14.3.41
P3030	27.9.40–10.2.41
P3230	12.8.40–16.1.41
P3232	12.8.40–s/d 15.8.40 (Winchester)
P3358	30.5.40–EFB 16.8.40 (crashed Tangmere)
P3263	12.8.40–FBO2 31.8.40
P3362	25.9.40–15.12.40
W/P3363	24.5.40–s/d 6.9.40 (nr Tunbridge Wells)
P3382	24.5.40–s/d 6.9.40 (Sutton Valence)
P3383	24.5.40 (DIA 13.8)–FBO2 17.8.40
P3393	18.5.40–17.10.40
P3402	27.9.40–4.12.40
P3460	18.5.40–FBO2 11.7.40
P3675	27.8.40–14.3.41
P3681	6.6.40–s/d 11.7.40 (Cranmore, Isle of Wight)

V6630:UF-L *of 601 Squadron flown by Sgt Frank Jensen and photographed at Exeter at the close of the Battle.* (Michael Payne)

P3709	18.10.40–EFAO 25.10.40 (collided with *V6917*, Exmouth)
P3735	18.8.40–s/d 31.8.40 (Colchester)
P3783	14.6.40–s/d 11.8.40 (Portland)
P3831	18.8.40–8.4.41
P3884	12.7.40 (DIA 13.8)–FBO2 16.8.40
P3885	12.7.40–s/d 11.8.40 (Portland)
P3886	12.7.40–9.12.40
P5208	2.9.40–29.11.40
P8818	25.7.40–s/d 6.9.40
R4092	27.7.40–s/d 11.8.40 (off Portland)
R4120	19.8.40–FAO2 24.9.40
R4191	15.8.40–FTR 18.8.40
R4214	19.8.40–FBO2 4.9.40
R4215	19.8.40–FTR 31.8.40
R4218	15.8.40–FAO3 7.10.40
V6647	3.9.40–s/d 6.9.40 (Pembury, Kent)
V6649	3.9.40–19.10.40
V6666	3.9.40–FAO2 15.10.40
V7229	29.7.40–FAO2 10.8.40
V7236	18.8.40–23.9.40
V7238	18.8.40–EAO 26.8.40 (burnt out, bombed?)
V7253	14.8.40–FBO2 15.8.40
V7255	9.10.40–27.10.40
V7260	19.8.40–s/d 31.8.40
V7305	14.8.40–damaged 18.8.40
V7317	18.10.40–EFAO 30.11.40
V7539	20.10.40–EFA 31.3.41
V7601	22.10.40–5.41

No. 605 Sqn

L2012	26.6.39–EFB 15.9.40 (crashed into Do 17; Marden, Kent)
L2014	26.6.39–29.10.40
L2018	3.7.39–29.10.40
L2059	4.8.39–s/d 9.9.40
L2061	20.9.39–s/d 8.9.40 (nr Tunbridge Wells)
L2103	6.10.39–EFB 9.8.40 (in sea off Dunbar)
L2122	30.9.39–s/d 15.9.40 (nr West Malling)
N2546	8.10.40–s/d 15.10.40 (nr Gillingham)
N2557	1.6.40–27.9.40
N2589	27.8.40–FBO2 16.9.40
N2593	30.6.40–EFA 28.7.40
P2717	1.6.40–FBO2 15.8.40
P2765	1.6.40–s/d 9.9.40 (nr Borden, Hants)
P2835	28.5.40–5.7.40
P2994	18.6.40–9.9.40
P3022	1.7.40–s/d 12.10.40
P3107	13.7.40–31.10.40
P3308	11.6.40 (DIA 15.8)–4.1.41
P3385	4.6.40–6.2.41
P3580	1.6.40–23.12.40
P3583	24.5.40–4.1.41
P3588	24.5.40–FBO2 11.9.40
P3650	1.6.40–FBO2 15.9.40
P3677	11.9.40–s/d 7.10.40 (Westerham)
P3737	3.7.40–EFB 26.10.40 (Rutherfield, Sussex)
P3827	13.7.40–FBO2 15.8.40 (crashed nr Usworth)

P3828	13.7.40–s/d 28.9.40 (Lamberhurst)
P3832	13.7.40–s/d 24.9.40
P3965	13.9.40–4.1.41
P5186	24.10.40–3.2.41
R4105	29.9.40–FAO2 27.10.40
R4118	17.8.40–23.10.40
V6699	14.9.40–s/d 28.9.40 (Dallington)
V6722	17.9.40–FBO2 20.9.40
V6755	22.9.40–FBO2 20.10.40
V6783	25.9.40–s/d 23.10.40 (Dorking)
V6784	25.9.40–FBO2 4.10.40
V6786	26.9.40–15.2.41
V7305	29.9.40–s/d 7.10.40 (Bexley)
V7468	17.9.40–4.1.41
V7506	29.9.40–23.12.40
V7540	8.10.40–9.12.40
V7599	17.10.40–EFB 27.10.40
V7609	15.10.40–FTR 1.11.40 (FH 63)

No. 607 Sqn

L1956	4.6.40–13.7.40
L1577	8.10.40–EFA 1.2.41
L1728	2.10.40–EFB 7.10.40 (collided with *P3860*)
L1824	7.10.40–22.3.41
L1968	14.8.40–9.9.40
P2565	15.4.40–10.11.40
P2617	15.4.40–26.10.40 (RAF Museum exhibit)
P2680	4.6.40–s/d 9.9.40 (East Peckham)
P2728	4.6.40–s/d 9.9.40 (Goudhurst)
P2900	30.5.40–s/d 1.10.40 (nr Swanage; FH 157.35)
P2904	30.5.40–4.7.41
P2912	2.7.40–8.10.40
P3108	28.6.40–s/d 28.9.40 (off Selsey)
P3116	1.7.40–12.10.40
P3117	11.7.40–s/d 9.9.40 (Cranbrook)
P3305	4.10.40–EFAO 15.11.40
P3425	30.9.40–EFB 11.4.41
P3458	30.5.40–12.7.40
P3574	1.6.40–s/d 9.9.40
P3665	30.5.40–16.9.40
P3667	30.5.40–13.7.40
P3668	30.5.40–FBO2 5.10.40
P3675	4.6.40–FAO2 1.7.40
P3711	15.6.40–11.9.40
P3759	20.7.40–9.10.40
P3829	13.10.40–5.1.41
P3860	4.7.40–EFA 7.10.40 (collided with *L1728*; Slindon, Sussex)
P3929	11.7.40–FAO2 18.9.40
P3933	11.7.40–EFB 17.9.40
P3937	11.7.40–9.7.41
P3962	11.7.40–FBO2 20.12.40
P5205	10.9.40–s/d 26.9.40 (Isle of Wight)
R4189	12.8.40–FTR 28.9.40 (off Selsey)
V6686	10.9.40–s/d 1.10.40 (FH 31.55)
V6687	10.9.40–EFA 10.3.41
V6688	10.9.40–s/d 15.9.40 (Appledore)
V6689	10.9.40–EFB 28.9.40
V6690	10.9.40–8.9.41
V6742	19.9.40–FBO2 5.10.40
V7223	4.10.40–30.11.40
V7380	6.10.40–18.11.40
V7590	6.10.40–EFA 20.7.41

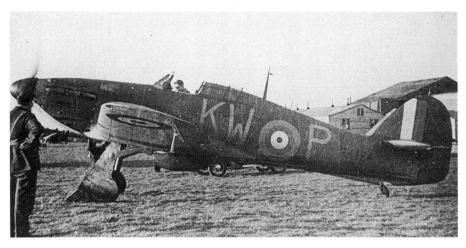

R4194:KW-P *which fought with 615 Squadron for much of the Battle was briefly used by 9 SFTS in 1941.*

No. 615 Sqn

L1584	29.5.40-s/d 14.7.40 (St Margaret's Bay)
L1592	23.7.40-EFB 18.8.40
L1983	27.5.40 (DIA 14.8)-21.8.40
L1992	27.5.40-30.10.40
L2003	22.8.40-11.10.40
L2075	17.7.40 (DIA 18.8)-22.8.40
L2101	7.9.40 (DIA 12.10)-15.10.40
L2118	29.9.40-EFB 14.9.40
N2455	30.8.40-13.9.40
N2706	31.8.40-29.10.40
P2578	26.4.40-17.10.40
P2754	19.8.40-20.2.41
P2768	30.5.40-s/d 18.8.40 (Morden)
P2801	17.5.40-s/d 15.8.40
P2871	22.5.40-26.9.40?
P2878	19.8.40-FBO2 26.8.40 (crashed Hambledon)
P2963	31.5.40-FBO2 16.8.40
P2966	3.5.40-s/d 18.8.40 (Sevenoaks)
P3109	28.6.40-s/d 14.8.40 (off Dover)
P3111	28.6.40-2.2.41
P3151	11.7.40-31.7.40
P3158	11.7.40-EAO 19.8.40
P3160	11.7.40-s/d 14.8.40
P3161	11.7.40-22.8.40
P3231	12.8.40-FTR 15.2.41
P3380	30.5.40 (DIA 14.8)-27.8.40
P3487	30.5.40-EAO 18.8.40 (Kenley)
P3811	15.8.40-FBO2 10.2.41
P3901	16.8.40-22.8.40
P5201	29.8.40-26.11.40
R4111	19.8.40-s/d 26.8.40 (off Herne Bay)
R4116	19.8.40-s/d 28.8.40 (Throwley)
R4119	19.8.40-9.10.40
R4121	19.8.40-s/d 26.8.40 (off Sheerness)
R4186	17.8.40-EAO 18.8.40
R4192	15.8.40-25.2.41
R4194	15.8.40-7.12.40
R4220	15.8.40-FBO2 17.11.40
R4221	15.8.40-EFB 18.8.40 (Orpington)
V6564	23.8.40-FBO2 26.8.40 (crashed Romford)
V7239	19.8.40-EFA 24.9.40 (on Turnberry beach)
V7312	19.8.40-EFA 29.9.40 (Ayr race course)
V7314	19.8.40-17.10.40
V7316	30.8.40-20.2.41
V7339	19.8.40-22.2.41
V7383	25.8.40-FBO2 29.10.40
V7598	24.10.40-FBO2 12.12.40
V7612	13.10.40-22.12.40

No. 1 (RCAF) Sqn

L1731	26.6.40-9.9.40
L1851	26.6.40-23.8.40
L1973	25.8.40-16.9.40
N2344	27.9.40-15.2.41
N2530	11.7.40-s/d 31.8.40 (Gravesend)
N2590	11.7.40-FAO2 25.7.40
N2608	26.6.40-FAO2 23.7.40
P2647	27.9.40-13.2.41
P2971	28.8.40-s/d 31.8.40 (Staplehurst)
P2993	27.9.40-FBO2 7.10.40
P3041	27.9.40-FAO2 24.10.40
P3068	26.6.40-FBO2 1.9.40 (crash landed Northolt)
P3069	26.6.40-FBO2 26.8.40
P3080	26.6.40-s/d 15.9.40 (Tunbridge Wells)
P3081	26.6.40-s/d 9.9.40
P3181	26.6.40-EFB 9.9.40
P3225	17.9.40-7.11.40
P3534	24.6.40-s/d 11.9.40 (Mayfield)
P3647	20.8.40-s/d 27.9.40
P3670	26.6.40-15.2.41
P3672	26.6.40-FBO2 27.9.40
P3674	20.8.40-FTR 27.9.40
P3757	26.6.40-FAO2 18.8.40

P3858	26.6.40–s/d 31.8.40 (Broomfield)	V6669	3.9.40–27.9.40
P3859	26.6.40–s/d 18.9.40 (Dungeness)	V6670	3.9.40–s/d 11.9.40 (Romney)
P3869	27.7.40–EFB 31.8.40	V6671	3.9.40–9.1.41
P3872	28.8.40–FBO2 26.8.40	V6697	16.9.40–15.2.41
P3873	30.6.40–s/d 5.10.40 (Smarden)	V6746	19.9.40–EFAO 26.11.40
P3874	30.6.40–s/d 26.8.40	V6749	19.9.40–FAO2 25.9.40 (force
P3876	30.6.40–s/d 15.9.40		landed nr Cookham)
P3883	11.7.40–FBO2 26.8.40;	V7287	4.8.40–15.2.41
	11.9.40–16.5.41	V7288	4.8.40–7.10.40
P3899	19.9.40–29.9.40	V7314	17.10.40–15.2.41
P3963	11.7.40–s/d 1.9.40 (Shipbourne)		
P5180	1.9.40–5.9.40		

No. 13 Group HQ

L1381	19.8.40–29.4.41

R4107	1.10.40–24.4.41
R4109	1.10.40–EFAO 18.3.41
R4171	4.8.40–s/d 1.9.40 (West Malling)
V6603	27.8.40–15.2.41
V6605	27.8.40–FAO2 15.11.40
V6609	30.8.40–FAO2 17.9.40

Station Flt, Northolt

N2520	15.6.40–19.12.40

The Vickers-Supermarine Spitfire

Britain's defence against air attack could hold no compromise. Only the best was acceptable. Rapid reaction, fast climb, high speed, massive clout. Hawker Fury squadrons coastal based had been unable to respond fast enough to prevent even relatively slow bombers from penetrating inland, so along which lines was improvement to follow?

Prime fighter for the 1930s had been expected to arise from Specification F.7/30 but it led to aircraft little better than their predecessors. R.J. Mitchell's Supermarine contribution was a gull-winged fighter powered by a complicated steam-cooled Rolls Royce Goshawk. Meeting on 18 March 1933, the Air Staff carefully considered the aircraft and it was on this occasion that the first suggestions for much increased fire power for application to a new Hawker fighter were made. All F.7/30 proposals were for fighters reaching 20,000 ft in 8½ min. A Fury-like replacement was needed, but one to become the standard home defence Bristol Bulldog replacement, RAF fighter.

Slow progress with the Supermarine 224 (F.7/30) caused the contractor to be warned that it must reach Martlesham by the end of 1933, or else... It did not meet the deadline due to major structural changes and engine cooling problems. First flown on 20 March 1934 it only attained 228 mph. The Air Ministry, suspicious about activity at Supermarine, was convinced that Mitchell was neglecting the Type 224 while secretly working on something much better. How right they were!

June 1934 found the Air Staff modifying their OR17 ideas, which now called for a 275 mph machine armed with eight machine guns and having a 1 hr 25 min duration. On 27 July 1934 Mitchell presented to the Air Ministry his ideas for something along those lines. Radical it was, highly streamlined, very slender and with retractable undercarriage and enclosed cockpit. Mitchell, who had chosen for it the new Rolls-Royce PV-12 engine (alias the Merlin), forecast a speed of 265 mph, suggested a four-gun armament and a first flight date in 1935. Without eight guns it did not meet OR17. The Air Staff tried to persuade Mitchell to

67

return to Napier, providers of Lion engines for Supermarine seaplanes, and to adopt their 725 hp 24 cylinder Dagger. That was not at all to Mitchell's liking and on 6 December 1934, with the Merlin forecast to produce 1,025 hp at 15,000 ft, both sides agreed to its use. On 22 December Supermarine received an order for an F.37/34 fighter prototype.

On 26 April 1935 the mock-up was officially inspected, the team telling Mitchell of their desire now for an eight-gun 310 mph F.10/35 fighter. Already it looked as if a modified 37/34 might equate that, although it had provision for only four guns. Fitting more in the thin wing would not be easy due to the strength needed, complicated firing circuitry and little room for the weapons. The chosen solution was to increase wing chord during which process Mitchell wedded elliptical wings to his creation. Not only did this enhance its capability, it also greatly improved the appearance and gave to it an unmistakable and beautiful form that undoubtedly won it wide acclaim.

The eight guns were well spaced along the wings. Adding them caused the fuel load to be reduced from 95 to 75 gallons. Concern also arose over likely difficulties in mass-producing the shapely and clearly exotic design,

whose first flight date was set for October 1935. Instead it took to the air on 6 March 1936, by which time the Hawker monoplane fighter had been flying for five months. Fearing those production delays the Air Staff, wanting 900 fighters, opted for Hawker to supply two-thirds and Supermarine the rest, and placed orders on 3 June 1936. On 28 July the name Spitfire was agreed for the Merlin II Supermarine machine.

News of this high speed competitor had a sobering effect upon Hawker who quickly set to work on a Hurricane replacement with a performance much ahead of rivals. Then, in 1937, Mitchell fell seriously ill and died at the age of 42. That was a bitter blow not only to his closest and dearest, but to the company, the RAF and indeed the nation. Development of the Spitfire would be undertaken instead by a team headed by Mr Joe Smith.

In 1938 Vickers took control of Supermarine, injecting much-needed production know-how as well as cash. The first production Spitfire flew on 14 May 1938 and during August No. 19 Squadron at Duxford began to equip with Spitfires. The process was as forecast painfully slow, only 44 having reached the RAF by the end of 1938.

To boost output of what was

Three Spitfires of 19 Squadron in October 1938. K9795 (nearest) later served with Nos. 64, 603 and 222 Squadrons and K9789 with 65 Squadron.

A three-bladed propeller much improved the Spitfire's performance. The aircraft shown here was used for propeller trials at Martlesham Heath.

unquestionably a superb machine a contract was placed on 12 April 1939 with the Nuffield organization, who initially had planned to build Whirlwinds and would now produce 1,000 Spitfires at a vast new factory at Castle Bromwich. They would be Merlin XII engined Mk IIs to a standard agreed on 17 June 1939. By the time the factory was functioning in 1940 control had passed into other hands.

Spitfire development resulted in the 78th *et seq* examples having the three-bladed two-position propeller, and the 178th onwards a Merlin II driving a constant-speed propeller. Such changes answered repeated RAF demands for its fighter to be improved. An early production Spitfire tested at Martlesham showed a top speed of 362 mph at 18,500 ft, 318 mph when cruising at 15,000 ft reached in 6.5 min. Its service ceiling was 31,900 ft. Small items constantly added to the Spitfires meant weight increases reducing their performance. In July 1939 Fighter Command flew speed tests which revealed that 340 mph at 15,000 ft and 344 mph at 18,000 ft were typical top speeds — which was very disturbing. More power was the only solution, and that was some way off.

Of 305 Spitfires delivered to the RAF by September 1939, 27 had been

Spitfire X4330:QJ-G landing; it was used by 616 Squadron and by 457 Squadron (23 June-16 July 1941) before joining 58 OTU. (IWM)

written off. Ten squadrons were flying Spitfires which clearly needed to be conserved to defend the homeland, releasing Hurricanes for Field Force France (in lieu of hoped-for Defiants) and eventually the Middle East. On 16 October 1939 Nos. 602 and 603 Squadrons drew first blood when they engaged nine Ju 88s attacking naval targets in the Firth of Forth, and destroyed two of them.

Spitfire development was already well underway, a process for which the design was ideal. A Griffon-engined version had been suggested but the Merlin team reigned supreme and a Merlin XII tested on *K9788* resulted in the Spitfire Mk II. Wedding a Merlin XX produced the Mk III whose prototype *N3297* first flew in March 1940. Although its weight of 6,650 lb brought concern over airframe strength, its demise was due more to the decision to install Merlin XXs in Hurricanes. Mk I Spitfires in a variety of modification states mainly fought in the Battle.

Luckily it had been left to the more plentiful, robust Hurricanes to battle for France. Overall an average of 957 Spitfires are officially listed as being in hand in summer 1940, a typical example having a top speed of 350 mph at 18,500 ft increased by about 25 mph by limited application of higher engine boost pressure. A Mk II reached Boscombe Down for trials on 27 June and on 17 July No. 152 Squadron received the first example, for squadron handling. Its 100 octane engine, driving a Rotol CS wooden propeller, peaked at 14,500 ft to deliver 1,150 hp, improving the climb rate and conferring a valuable 6,000 ft higher ceiling. No. 611 at Digby was the first to fully equip, during August 1940, and commenced using the Mk II for wing patrols from Duxford on 31 August although it had scored previously during scrambles. By the end of October 1940 182 Mk IIs had been delivered.

Air Staff commitment to cannon fighters posed a severe problem, which was very evident when Supermarine fitted a 20 mm Hispano gun in each thin mainplane of *L1007* during June 1939. The weapons had to rest on their sides leading to spent rounds failing to eject properly and jamming the gun breech. AFDE Northolt and No. 65 Squadron tested the cannon aircraft late in 1939, and on 13 January 1940 when flown from Dyce by Flg Off G. Proudman it participated in combat during which 602 Squadron despatched a He 111. As big a problem where cannon usage was concerned was the inadequate production, for not until 12 April 1940 did the first example leave the BSA Sparkbrook works.

Beaverbrook, realizing the punishing power of a 20 mm shell, pressed for cannon Spitfires, which led to the decision to embody the guns during production of 30 Spitfire 1s. After fitting out at 6 MU Brize Norton they were delivered before type testing at A&AEE. Late on 1 July 1940 Sqn Ldr P.C. Pinkham, commanding 19 Squadron, Fowlmere, informed his personnel that the squadron was to receive cannon-armed Spitfires, three of which were already at Duxford. Ammunition feed and cartridge ejection problems remained to be solved. The squadron discovered that with the two guns 6 seconds' firing time was feasible, the increased muzzle velocity being a great advantage when the guns fired. A tail chase was not the best means of dealing with a raider, it then seemed, and the squadron practised in flights peeling off from just below cloud cover. The enemy also flew close to clouds! Rubber pads were tried on the spent round deflector to damp rebound, but without much success.

Having received cannon Spitfires the squadron introduced them to operations on 9 July, but not until 2 August was a raider engaged, two of the three Spitfires soon having gun problems. On 11 August a two cannon/four machine gun Spitfire arrived, an advantage for sure. The 16th August saw the cannon Spitfires engage in battle off Harwich during which Flt Sgt G.C. Unwin in *R6776* became the first 19 Squadron cannon

Spitfire pilot to destroy a raider. The main skirmish for the cannon Spitfires took place early on 31 August 1940 when Dorniers and Bf 110s attacked Debden and the Duxford area. R6924 downed a Bf 110, but stoppages led to a couple of Spitfires being shot down by enemy return fire, and to another crashing. By this time only 23 cannon Mk 1s remained and 19 Squadron was relieved to exchange them, even for a set of war-weary eight-gun examples. The precise designation for the two-cannon Spitfires, 'Mk 1b (Spitfire 1/P2)', had been promulgated on 15 March 1940.

The Battle of Britain Spitfires — a brief summary

By 15 October 1940, 1,426 Spitfires had been delivered to the RAF, of which 1,142 saw fighter squadron service between 1 July and 15 October 1940. Grand testimony indeed to the skill with which Air Chief Marshal Sir Hugh Dowding had held back his precious Spitfires for the most momentous air battle of all time. Details of Spitfire operations may be found in *The Battle of Britain — 50 Years On* (PSL).

As with the Hurricane, much servicing backing was provided by civilian organisations, the total number of Spitfires handled during each major month of the Battle being as shown in the table below.

Further back-up was provided by Heston Aircraft, and by de Havilland and Rotol who handled propeller work. Principal Maintenance Units involved with Spitfires were Nos. 6, 8, 9, 12, 15, 24, 37, 48, 49 and 58.

Surviving records suggest that around 125 Spitfire fighters with Battle of Britain pedigrees remained in RAF hands in 1944 during which year at least 34 were struck off charge. A few were being used by the Fleet Air Arm as trainers, but most were in storage by 1945 and their precise dates of demise were not all officially recorded. A census dated 21 June 1947 provided merely a convenient nominal date of disposal.

Among a handful of the earliest examples to survive for long were *L1004* (602 Squadron in summer 1940) converted into a PR Mk XIII for low altitude use in 1944, and *L1031* (222 Squadron) struck off charge on 25 January 1945 after an extensive operational career. Both *K9803* and *K9825* survived the war, and *K9991* (64 Squadron) was one of a small number sold to Portugal in September 1943 at a time when a German invasion of that country was reckoned imminent. *K9871* (74 Squadron) briefly used by 5 Squadron, USAAF, in August 1942, was not struck off charge until June 1945 and at Coningsby, presently the home of the Battle of Britain Memorial Flight.

A handful of Battle survivors chosen for overseas service left Glasgow in December 1942 on ships bound for Port Sudan and 73 OTU: *L1000, P9311* (610 Sqn) and *P9557* (64 Sqn) were among Spitfire 1s on the SS *Alzarab*. Less fortunate were others including *N3278* (ex-234 Squadron) aboard the *Peter Maersk* which on 8 January 1943, was sunk en-route.

Other early Spitfires with long lives included *N3051* (611 Squadron), *N3058* (616 Squadron), *N3098* (41 Squadron and active with 288 Squadron in the closing months of the war), *N3280* (234 and 609 Squadrons)

Spitfires serviced by civilian organisations

Organisation	July	August	September
Air Service Training, Hamble	45	85	104
Cunliiffe Owen, Eastleigh	-	-	9
No 1 CRU, Morris Motors, Cowley	23	33	40
General Aircraft Ltd	9	27	24
Scottish Aviation Ltd .	7	12	23
Westland Aircraft Ltd	3	5	5

and *P9368* (92,616 and 222 Squadrons) which saw operational use in 1941 in the hands of 111 and 132 Squadrons. One meritorious Spitfire was *P9367* (54 Squadron, June 1940 to 1 February 1941); it was among the Mk 1s converted into Mk Vs, which extended this aircraft's operational life to June 1942. It was struck off charge on 6 June 1945.

'R' serial aircraft which survived to 1944 were *R6596*, *R6602* (converted to Mk Va), *R6621*, *R6623*, *R6627*, *R6629*, *R6632*, *R6641*, *R6684* (converted to Mk II), *R6687*, *R6694*, *R6704*, *R6710*, *R6719*, *R6763*, *R6771*, *R6809*, *R6837*, *R6888* (converted to Mk Vb), *R6889* and *R6890* (both converted to Mk Va). *R6916*, *R6957*, *R6958*, *R6959*, *R6960*, *R6963*, *R6976*, *R6777*, *R6979*, *R6986* and *R6987* still existed in 1945. Of these both *R6602* and *R6623* both served during July–August 1942 with the American 52nd Fighter Group. Many of the Mk Ibs taken from 19 Squadron early in September 1940 were in 1941 converted into Mk Vbs, like *R6809* which served with Nos 91 and 302 Squadrons during 1941 and in 1943 was still with front line squadrons including Nos 222, 64, 118, 350 (13 April to 23 May 1944) and was used by the Central Gunnery School from 31 October 1944 until struck off charge on 4 September 1945.

Long-serving Spitfires from the 'X' serial range were *X4021*, *X4030*, *X4051*, *X4058*, *X4068*, *X4162*, *X4165*, *X4172*, *X4173*, *X4177*, *X4180*, *X4274*, *X4319*, *X4416*, *X4481*, *X4488*, *X4551*, *X4558*, and *X4587* all of which soldiered on into 1944. Those which lasted into 1945 and beyond were *X4010*, *X4020*, *X4023*, *X4064*, *X4161*, *X4238*, *X4280*, *X4387*, *X4471*, *X4472*, *X4473*, *X4474* (provisionally sold to the Royal Danish Air Force in August 1947 but soon withdrawn), *X4480*, *X4485* and *X4602*. Less fortunate were *X4267* and *X4269*, both among those lost at sea when the *Peter Maersk* was sunk.

No listing of 1940s Spitfires would be complete without mention of P7350, the Mk II of the Battle of Britain Memorial Flight. Initially delivered to 6 MU, Brize Norton, in mid-August 1940, it probably joined 266 Squadron at Wittering on 6 September 1940 and in October was switched to Hornchurch and 603 Squadron. Necessary repairs soon put it out of use until March 1941 when it joined 616 Squadron, Tangmere, staying until July 1941. In late April 1942 the Central Gunnery School at Sutton Bridge received *P7350* using it until February 1943. For a year commencing April 1943 it served with 57 OTU at Boulmer, and was involved in an accident on 22 April 1944. In July it was received by 39 MU Colerne from where, in 1947, it proceeded to John Dale Ltd to whom it had been sold as scrap. Luckily the firm, recognising it as a long-serving Spitfire, returned it to Colerne where it languished until 1967 when it was surveyed for a possible part in the film *Battle of Britain*. Made airworthy at Duxford in 1968, *P7350* participated in the filming before joining Coltishall's Battle of Britain Memorial Flight in October 1968.

Spitfires used by squadrons 1 July– 15 October 1940

No. 19 Sqn (* — cannon armed, retrospectively designated Mk Ib)

K9799	17.10.38–15.7.40
K9807	11.10.30–7.8.40
K9815	23.1.40–13.7.40
K9825	19.12.38–13.7.40
K9826	21.6.40–2.7.40
K9851	3.9.40–10.9.40
K9874	3.9.40–10.9.40
K9944	17.6.40–18.7.40
K9967	3.9.40–10.9.40
L1018	3.9.40–10.9.40
L1029	29.6.39–25.7.40
L1042	19.6.40–26.7.40
N3039	3.9.40–26.9.40
N3040	15.3.40–22.7.40
N3046	10.9.40 (DIA 11.9)–13.9.40
N3118	12.9.40–14.9.40
N3198	19.4.40–6.8.40
N3199	19.4.40–7.8.40, 3.9.40–17.9.40
N3234	5.4.40–20.7.40
N3238	5.4.40–11.8.40, 10.9.40–29.9.40
N3265	10.9.40–FAO2 18.9.40
N3286	3.9.40 (DIA 5.9)–9.9.40
K/P9836	3.9.40–26.9.40

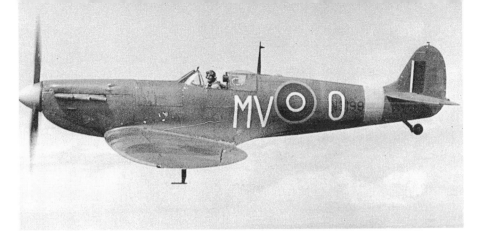

N3199 *served twice with 19 Squadron in 1940, with 57 OTU in 1941–1942 and with 53 OTU from July 1942 until its demise on 6 February 1943.* (Frank F. Smith)

P9391	3.9.40 (DIA 5.9)–26.9.40	*R6833	1.7.40–4.9.40
P9422	3.9.40–s/d 5.9.40 (Birling, Kent)	*R6882	5.7.40–10.9.40
P9431	3.9.40–EFB 15.9.40	*R6888	11.7.40–2.9.40
P9509	18.9.40–26.9.40	*R6889	11.7.40–25.8.40
P9546	3.9.40 (DIA 9.9, 11.9)–14.9.40	*R6890	11.7.40–2.9.40
R6614	31.5.40–FAT 31.5.40	*R6897	11.7.40–11.9.40
*R6623	4.6.40–5.8.40	*R6904	13.7.40–25.8.40, 13.10.40–22.1.41
R6625	31.5.40–11.8.40, 10.9.40–EFB	*R6908	?
	14.9.40 (crashed Orsett)	*R6911	14.7.40–EFB 31.8.40 (FH 43.40)
R6627	31.5.40–FBO2 27.7.40 (crash landed	*R6917	14.7.40–3.9.40
	Duxford)	*R6919	14.7.40–26.8.40
R6687	7.6.40–7.8.40	*R6923	19.7.40–3.9.40
R6688	7.6.40–EFAO 13.7.40 (crashed nr	*R6958	30.7.40–s/d 31.8.40 (FH 32.20)
	Balsham, Cambs)	R6991	12.9.40 (DIA 15.9)–20.9.40
*R6761	27.6.40–26.8.40	X4059	1.9.40–FBO2 4.9.40
*R6770	27.6.40–26.8.40	X4070	10.9.40–FTR 15.9.40
*R6776	27.6.40–4.9.40	X4159	1.9.40–3.9.40
*R6778	1.8.40–4.8.40	X4170	13.9.40 (DIA 18.9)–28.9.40
*R6809	5.7.40–1.9.40	X4173	13.9.40–28.9.40

Some of 19 Squadron's cannon-armed Spitfire Ibs were, like R6923, *modified into Mk Vbs.* (RAF Museum)

P7420, *a Mk II, served with 19 Squadron between 26 September and 15 November 1940.*
(IWM)

X4179	13.9.40-9.8.41	N3108	22.3.40-FAO2 14.9.40
X4231	10.8.40-s/d 31.8.40 (Little Shelford,	N3112	1.3.40-FBO2 29.7.40
	Cambs, FH 23.55)	N3113	1.3.40 (DIA 29.7)-1.8.40
X4237	10.9.40-s/d 27.9.40 (Wye, Kent)	N3118	17.9.40-s/d 24.9.40 (off Dover)
X4267	21.9.40-5.10.40	N3123	18.2.40-13.11.40
X4279	9.9.40-10.9.40	N3126	27.1.40-20.9.40
X4331	13.9.40-28.9.40	N3162	24.12.39 (DIA 5.9)-13.9.40
X4336	13.9.40-26.9.40	N3225	5.10.40 (DIA 5.10)-24.10.40
X4342	9.9.40-10.9.40	N3234	20.7.40-EFB 5.8.40 (crashed on
X4351	13.9.40-EAO2 22.9.40		take off, Manston)
X4352	13.9.40-EFB 27.9.40 (crashed	N3264	3.5.40-FBO2 29.7.40
	Coldred)	N3266	14.6.40-FB02 7.9.40
X4353	13.9.40-5.10.40	N3267	19.9.40-s/d 7.10.40
X4424	18.9.40-26.9.40	N3280	20.10.40-24.10.40
X4425	18.9.40-28.9.40	P9324	13.9.40-s/d 15.9.40
X4473	20.9.40-28.9.40	P9334	1.6.40-FAO2 25.7.40
X4474	20.9.40-5.10.40	P9335	11.10.40-24.10.40
X4475	20.9.40-5.10.40	P9394	13.9.40-FBO2 30.9.40
		P9427	13.9.40-19.9.40
MkII		P9428	13.5.40-EFB 5.9.40 (collided with
P7318	27.9.40-23.1.41		R6635 over Thames Estuary)
P7299	27.9.40-?	P9429	13.5.40-FBO2 28.7.40;
P7372	26.9.40-19.12.40		12.10.40-24.10.40
P7377	19.9.40-14.11.40	P9430	13.5.40-s/d 7.9.40 (nr Rayleigh)
P7379	27.9.40-FTR 27.6.41	P9447	17.9.40-s/d 11.10.40 (Maidstone)
P7380	26.9.40-29.4.41	P9462	3.10.40-14.11.40
P7381	26.9.40-7.11.40	P9500	6.9.40-25.9.40
P7420	26.9.40-EFB 15.11.40	R6597	29.9.40-17.10.40
P7421	26.9.40-11.10.40	R6604	1.8.40-3.10.40 (damaged 24.9.40)
P7422	26.9.40-26.6.41	R6605	1.8.40-EFB 14.9.40 (written off
P7423	26.9.40-EFB 29.10.40		18.9.40)
P7425	26.9.40-FTR 31.7.41	R6611	30.7.40-FAO2 3.9.40
P7427	26.9.40-29.12.40	R6612	30.7.40-FB02 18.9.40
P7428	26.9.40-9.11.40	R6619	10.9.40-FBO2 28.9.40
P7429	26.9.40-24.3.41	R6635	5.6.40-EFB 5.9.40 (collided with
P7430	26.9.40-23.6.41		P:9428)
P7432	26.9.40-FAO2 28.9.40	R6702	19.9.40-20.9.40
P7434	26.9.40-16.4.41	R6755	20.9.40-EFB 27.9.40
P7435	26.9.40-3.11.40	R6756	30.7.40-FTR 8.9.40 (FH 60.10)
		R6757	30.7.40-EFB 11.8.40 (FH 16.25)
No. 41 Sqn		R6885	30.7.40-s/d 5.9.40 (crashed S.
K9890	21.7.40-20.9.40		Benfleet)
N3038	27.9.39-s/d 29.7.40 (Dover)	R6887	30.7.40 (DIA 17.9)-15.3.41
N3059	27.8.40 (DIA 11.9)-21.9.40	X4021	2.8.40-FBO2 5.9.40 (later converted
N3098	21.1.40 (DIA 4.9)-12.9.40		to PR Spitfire)
N3099	21.1.40-FAO2 13.7.40	X4052	19.9.40-EFB 11.10.40 (collided with
N3100	19.3.40-FBO2 28.7.40		X4554)

74

X4178:EB-K *and* EB-N *of 41 Squadron photographed late in the Battle.*

X4060	12.10.40–30.10.40	P9390	25.4.40-EFB 2.7.40 (later *2111M*)
X4068	13.9.40–19.10.40	P9446	1.6.40-FBO2 6.7.40
X4101	13.9.40-FBO2 19.9.40	P9465	27.9.40-EFAO 30.9.40 (repaired)
X4178	25.9.40 (DIA 7.10)-FTR 15.10.40	P9506	1.9.40–12.2.41
	(in Channel)	P9549	4.6.40 (DIA 24.7)-FAO2 25.7.40
X4253	5.10.40–24.10.40	P9558	1.9.40-EFAO 25.10.40
X4317	23.9.40–24.10.40	P9559	1.9.40–3.2.41
X4325	6.9.40-s/d 11.9.40	P9560	1.9.40-EFA 7.9.40
X4338	7.9.40–26.11.40	P9367	12.6.40–1.2.41
X4343	6.9.40 (DIA 11.9)–20.9.40	R6705	10.6.40-EFB 9.7.40
X4344	6.9.40 (DIA 30.9)–7.10.40	R6707	12.6.40-s/d 25.7.40 (in Channel)
X4345	6.9.40 (DIA 30.9)-SOC 10.10.40	R6708	12.6.40-s/d 22.8.40 (off Deal)
X4346	6.9.40–20.9.40	R6709	12.6.40–22.2.41
X4409	16.9.40-EFB 28.9.40 (force landed	R6710	12.6.40–26.7.40
	Stelling Minnis)	R6711	12.6.40-EFB 7.7.40
X4426	19.9.40-s/d 28.9.40 (Lynstead)	R6812	12.7.40-EFB 23.7.40 (crashed
X4445	28.9.40-EFB 2.10.40		Cliftonville)
X4447	2.10.40–24.10.40	R6814	12.7.40–21.8.40
X4545	28.9.40-EFB 2.10.40	R6815	12.7.40 (DIA 12.8)–22.8.40
X4554	28.9.40-EFAO 10.10.40	R6816	12.7.40-EFB 25.7.40 (crashed nr
X4558	29.9.40-FBO2 9.10.40		Kingsdown)
J/X4559	29.9.40-FBO2 1.10.40, Re-Cat EFB	R6832	19.8.40-s/d 28.8.40 (crashed
	8.11.40		Stockbury; FH 16.80)
X4589	7.10.40–24.10.40	R6892	25.8.40–22.2.41
X4492	8.10.40–25.10.40	R6893	9.7.40–30.12.40
X4604	14.10.40–24.10.40	R6895	9.7.40 (DIA 31.8)–17.9.40
		R6898	13.7.40–23.1.41
		R6899	13.7.40-EFAO 3.2.41

No. 54 Sqn

L1042	26.7.40–25.9.40	R6901	13.7.40-FTR 9.9.40
L1093	29.5.40-SOC 16.7.40	R6913	23.7.40–26.8.40
N3097	19.6.40-s/d 15.8.40	R6914	25.7.40-FBO2 12.8.40
N3110	20.8.40-EAO 31.8.40 (bombed just	R6962	28.7.40–2.8.40
	prior to take off, Hornchurch)	R6969	17.8.40 (DIA 25.8)–26.8.40
N3111	13.12.39–10.7.40	R6973	17.8.40–1.2.41
N3160	10.12.39-FBO2 12.8.40 (crash	R6974	17.8.40–12.9.40
	landed nr Dartford)	R6981	9.8.40-EFB 15.8.40
N3173	9.3.40–2.9.40	R6982	25.6.40–2.8.40
N3183	10.12.39-FTR 9.7.40	R6984	25.6.40–2.8.40
N3184	22.1.40-FTR 21.7.40 (off Clacton)	R7015	4.8.40-EFB 15.8.40
N3192	12.6.40-EFB 24.7.40 (force landed	R7017	28.7.40–21.8.40
	on shore nr Sizewell)	R7019	28.7.40-FBO2 15.8.40
P9326	1.9.40–7.4.41	R7021	28.7.40-EFB 30.8.40
P9387	25.4.40-s/d 25.7.40 nr Dover;	X4019	1.8.40–24.8.40
	repaired	X4053	23.8.40-s/d 28.8.40
P9389	19.4.40 (DIA 24.7)-s/d 24.8.40	X4054	23.8.40-s/d 31.8.40
	(Kingsdown)		(Hildenborough)
		X4108	16.8.40–12.9.40

X4163	13.8.40–22.2.41
X4235	25.8.40 (DIA 31.8)–21.11.40
L/X4236	25.8.40–EFB 31.8.40 (bombed taking off, Hornchurch)
X4238	25.8.40–22.2.41
X4242	3.9.40–22.2.41
X4476	29.8.40–28.12.40
X4317	3.9.40–23.9.40
X4318	2.9.40–19.9.40
X4319	4.9.40–22.2.41
X4323	19.9.40–EFB 8.11.40

No. 64 Sqn

K9785	20.4.40–FAO2 13.7.40 (damaged by AA fire, Dover)
K9805	17.4.40–FBO2 13.8.40
K9862	19.8.40–2.1.41
K9895	14.8.40–2.1.41
K9903	3.9.40–EFA 6.9.40 (nr Ternhill)
K9950	29.9.40–EFB 28.11.40 (Tunbridge Wells)
K9958	2.10.40–2.10.40 (damaged by bombing)
W/K9964	14.8.40–FTR 15.8.40 (force landed Calais/Marck)
K9991	17.4.40–FBO2 5.8.40
L1029	25.7.40–s/d 5.8.40 (off Folkestone)
L1030	14.9.40–2.1.41
L1035	19.3.40–s/d 25.7.40 (in Channel)
L1037	29.2.40–FAO2 22.7.40
L1038	29.2.40–FBO2 16.8.40
L1039	29.2.40–s/d 8.8.40 (nr Dover)
L1055	2.7.40–FBO2 25.7.40
L1068	14.8.40–FAO2 16.8.40
L1073	2.5.40–FAO2 19.9.40
N3122	22.8.40–22.1.41
N3230	13.5.40–FBO2 15.8.40
N3231	21.7.40 (DIA 25.7)–31.7.40
N3247	7.10.40–26.11.40
N3273	13.5.40–2.7.40
N3293	17.4.40 (DIA 11.8)–8.11.40
P9369	17.4.40 (DIA 19.7)–EFB 8.8.40 (crashed Capel, Surrey)
P9421	18.5.40–s/d 25.7.40 (off Dover; FH 28.15)
P3432	8.10.40–24.11.40
P9447	2.6.40–23.8.40
P9449	2.6.40–s/d 5.7.40 (nr Rouen)
P9450	2.6.40 (DIA 11.8)–FTR 5.12.40
P9507	2.7.40–20.7.40
P9545	29.9.40–12.10.40
P9554	14.8.40–s/d 16.8.40 (crashed Ockfield)
P9555	16.8.40–22.1.41
P9556	16.8.40–FBO2 21.12.40
P9557	16.8.40–4.10.40
P9563	11.8.40–FBO2 5.9.40
P9564	11.8.40–EFAO 30.9.40
R6623	5.8.40–FBO2 23.8.40
R6639	26.7.40–EFB 9.8.40, subsequently repaired
R6643	26.7.40–EFB 29.7.40, subsequently repaired
R6683	26.7.40–FTR 6.10.40
R6697	8.6.40–FBO2 4.8.40
K/R6700	8.6.40 (DIA 25.7)–22.1.41
R6767	18.7.40–30.7.40
R6813	1.9.40–FBO2 12.8.40
R6895	9.7.40–EFB 31.8.40 (repaired)

R6972	23.8.40–22.1.41
R6975	24.7.40–22.1.41
R6990	26.7.40–FTR 15.8.40
R6991	6.8.40–13.8.40
R6992	6.8.40 (DIA 9.8)–17.8.40
R6995	29.7.40–FBO2 9.8.40
X4018	9.8.40–s/d 12.8.40
X4026	19.8.40–21.8.40
X4031	17.8.40–24.8.40
X4032	17.8.40–FTR 27.9.40 (FH 39.20)
H/X4060	9.8.40 (DIA 12.8)–23.8.40
X4067	11.8.40–1.9.40
X4320	5.9.40–FTR 4.10.40 (FH 45.15)
X4321	5.9.40–FBO2 7.9.40
X4322	5.9.40–EFB 28.9.40
X4547	24.10.40–FBO2 22.11.40

No. 65 Sqn

K9789	12.7.40–28.11.40
K9803	30.8.40–13.9.40
K9903	21.3.39–2.8.40
K9904	19.8.40–29.9.40
K9905	23.3.39–s/d 8.8.40 (nr Dover)
K9907	25.3.39–FTR 8.7.40
K9909	25.3.39–s/d 22.8.40 (at sea)
K9911	28.3.39–EFB 8.8.40 (nr Dover)
K9915	30.5.40–FTR 16.8.40
K9995	27.8.40–EFAO 27.8.40
L1094	6.9.40–FBO2 8.8.40
N3101	2.4.40–17.2.41
N3128	2.4.40–EFB 2.8.40 (crashed on take off, Hornchurch)
N3129	2.4.40–FTR 7.7.40
N3151	3.4.40–FAO2 15.10.40
N3163	8.8.40–9.12.40
N3164	4.1.40–13.9.40
P9436	11.5.40–FBO2 8.8.40
P9454	26.8.40–EFB 1.12.40
P9516	12.7.40–FAO2 3.8.40
P9562	18.8.40–18.11.40
R6602	11.8.40 (DIA 14.8)–29.8.40
R6609	1.6.40–FTR 7.7.40
R6610	4.8.40–9.9.40
R6615	11.6.40–FTR 7.7.40
R6617	1.6.40–EFB 7.8.40 (crashed on take off)
R6618	1.6.40–EAO 16.8.40 (ground strafed, Manston)
R6619	1.6.40–15.7.40
R6620	1.6.40–FBO2 23.8.40
R6712	10.7.40–25.10.40
R6713	10.7.40–FTR 18.8.40 (crashed nr Canterbury)
R6714	10.7.40–EFAO 16.10.40
R6766	13.7.40–EFAO 13.8.40 (crashed Eastry)
R6775	12.7.40–24.7.40, 27.7.40–7.2.41
R6777	12.7.40–EFB 30.7.40
R6799	12.7.40–EFB 2.8.40 (crashed, Hornchurch)
R6803	8.8.40–6.1.41
R6818	26.7.40–EFB 20.8.40
R6837	14.10.40–FAO2 18.10.40
R6883	8.8.40–16.2.41
R6884	12.7.40–FTR 24.8.40
R6886	18.8.40–6.11.40
R6978	31.8.40–FTR 12.12.40
R6982	6.8.40–FTR 12.12.40
R6987	11.8.40–3.12.40

'Trolley-acc' still plugged in, tin-hatted attendant close by, Sqn Ldr R.H.A. Leigh, Commanding, and a 66 Squadron Spitfire are ready for take-off from Gravesend. (via A.S. Thomas)

No. 66 Sqn

K9823	8.6.40-FAO2 3.9.40
K9944	18.7.40-s/d 5.9.40
L1001	28.5.40-FAO2 (crash landed Coltishall)
L1011	7.8.40–17.9.40
L1041	21.6.40-FAO2 12.7.40
L1043	18.6.40–9.9.40
L1083	21.6.40–23.9.40
N3029	28.9.39-FBO2 5.9.40 and damaged further on 15.9.40
N3032	27.9.39-FBO2 4.9.40
N3035	10.10.39-FBO2 29.9.40
N4041	9.11.39-FTR 24.7.40 (in sea)
N3042	9.11.39-EFB 29.7.40 (crashed on Orfordness shore)
X/N3043	24.9.40-s/d 8.10.40 (nr Rochester)
N3044	5.11.39 (DIA 4.9)–10.9.40
N3048	5.11.39-s/d 4.9.40 (crashed nr Mersham)
N3049	30.10.39-EFB 9.9.40
N3060	28.8.40-s/d 5.9.40
N3121	11.1.40-FBO2 4.9.40, EFAO 11.10.40
N3170	18.9.40-FBO2 28.9.40
N3178	15.10.40-FBO2 29.11.40
N3182	2.4.40-FTR 19.8.40 (in sea, off Orfordness)
N3225	4.4.40 (DIA 7.9)–9.9.40
N3285	26.9.40-FBO2 13.10.40
P9362	15.10.40–1.11.40
P9519	18.9.40–4.10.40
R6603	13.9.40-s/d 18.9.40
R6689	7.6.40-EFB 4.9.40
R6715	11.7.40-FTR 30.8.40 (at sea)
R6716	12.9.40–23.9.40
R6754	24.9.40–1.10.40
R6771	8.9.40-FBO2 17.9.40
R6779	10.9.40-s/d 8.10.40
R6800	26.7.40-EFB 17.10.40 (FH 119)
R6925	6.9.40-s/d 18.9.40
R6927	6.9.40-1.11.40
X4010	18.9.40-3.10.40
X4052	21.8.40-FBO2 4.9.40
X4103	7.10.40-6.11.40
X4170	29.9.40-EFB 25.10.40 (FH 45.35)
X4176	6.9.40-31.10.40
X4234	13.10.40-1.11.40
X4254	6.9.40-FBO2 7.9.40
X4255	6.9.40-FBO2 11.10.40
X4266	5.9.40-20.9.40
X4320	5.9.40-FTR 4.10.40 (FH 45.15)
X4321	5.9.40-FBO2 7.9.40
X4322	5.9.40-s/d 28.9.40
X4326	5.9.40 (DIA 7.10)–12.10.40
X4327	5.9.40-EFB 14.9.40
X4339	7.9.40 (DIA 11.9)–23.9.40
X4420	15.9.40-EAO 10.11.40 (FH 47.29)
X4421	16.9.40–21.10.40
X4473	29.9.40 (DIA 5.10)–19.10.40
X4478	23.9.40–2.12.40
X4479	23.9.40 (DIA 13.10)–20.10.40
X4543	2.10.40-EFB 13.10.40 (crash landed Hornchurch)
X4562	9.10.40-s/d 11.10.40 (Elham)
X4593	17.10.40-EFAO 22.11.40 (FH 85.05)
X4598	8.10.40-29.10.40
X4599	8.10.40-6.11.40
X4612	15.10.40-FAT2 15.10.40
X4614	15.10.40-13.11.40
X4615	26.10.40-14.12.40
X4618	27.10.40-2.11.40

Mk II (assigned to 66 Sqn, used by 421 Flt)

P7303	5.10.40-s/d 11.10.40
P7441	5.10.40-s/d 12.10.40

P7444	5.10.40 (DIA 15.10)–30.10.40
P7445	5.10.40–24.10.40
P7446	5.10.40–7.11.40
P7447	5.10.40–7.12.40

No. 72 Sqn

K9828	7.10.40–?
K9840	25.8.40–FBO2 2.9.40
K9847	2.9.40 (DIA 8.10)–12.10.40
K9870	7.10.40–s/d 11.10.40 (Sittingbourne)
K9922	11.4.40–EFAO 27.8.40
K9929	14.4.39–FAO2 3.8.40
K9935	19.4.39–FBO2 5.10.40
K9938	21.4.39–EFB 2.9.40 (in sea, Herne Bay)
K9940	24.4.39–EAO2 6.10.40 (Biggin Hill)
K9942	24.4.39–FAO2 5.6.40
K9958	8.5.39–9.9.40
K9959	8.5.39–FAO2 17.8.40
K9960	5.9.40–EFB 14.9.40 (Orlestone)
K9989	9.9.40–EFAO 5.10.40 (collided after take off)
L1056	24.7.39–FBO2 1.9.40 (crash landed, West Malling)
L1078	17.8.39–EFB 6.8.40 (crashed, Acklington)
L1083	23.9.40–4.12.40
L1092	16.9.40–FBO2 1.9.40
N3068	6.9.40–s/d 27.9.40 (nr Sevenoaks)
N3070	2.9.40–s/d 6.9.40 (nr Maidstone)
N3093	2.9.40–s/d 5.9.40 (nr Tunbridge Wells)
N3094	2.9.40–FBO1 14.9.40
N3221	1.4.40–FBO2 22.8.40
N3228	13.10.40–17.10.40
N3229	2.9.40–FBO2 4.9.40
P9338	6.6.40–FTR 12.10.40 (crashed nr Folkestone)
P9376	2.9.40–12.9.40
P9424	25.8.40–EFB 31.8.40 (repaired)
P9438	12.5.40–EFB 31.8.40 (crashed, New Romney)
P9439	2.9.40–5.9.40
P9444	4.6.40–12.7.40
P9448	4.6.40–FBO2 1.9.40
P9457	3.5.40–s/d 31.8.40 (Staplehurst)
P9458	3.5.40–s/d 2.9.40?
P9460	4.5.40 (DIA 4.9)–17.12.40
R6704	2.9.40–FBO2 18.9.40
R6705	2.9.40–FBO2 18.9.40
R6710	6.9.40–EFB 11.9.40, but repaired
R6721	24.9.40?–EFB 27.10.40
R6777	2.9.40–3.11.40
R6830	13.8.40–EFA 13.8.40
R6881	6.9.40–2.5.41
R6916	22.7.40–19.8.40
R6928	15.8.40–EAO 31.8.40
R6971	610 Sqn aircraft, burnt out at Hartfield 4.9.40 flying with 72 Squadron
R6981	24.7.40–9.8.40
R6984	2.8.40–28.9.40
R7022	6.9.40 (DIA 7.9)–19.9.40
X4013	610 Squadron aircraft, burnt out 5.9.40 when operated by 72 Squadron
X4034	11.8.40–EFB 5.9.40
X4063	9.9.40–EAO 18.8.40

X4068	12.8.40–13.9.40
X4069	12.9.40–17.10.40
X4109	13.8.40–s/d 1.9.40
X4170	28.9.40–29.9.40
X4252	6.9.40–23.1.41
X4254	6.9.40 (DIA 7.9)–12.9.40
X4262	2.9.40–EFB 3.9.40 (Marden, Kent)
X4337	7.9.40 (DIA 18.9)–13.10.40
X4340	9.9.40–EFB 27.9.40 (crashed Stepney)
X4410	17.9.40–EFB 20.9.40
X4413	14.9.40–2.5.41
X4416	13.9.40–24.9.40
X4473	28.9.40–29.9.40
X4478	20.9.40–23.9.40
X4480	20.9.40–22.9.40
X4481	20.9.40–10.10.40
X4483	23.9.40–29.4.41
X4486	24.9.40–20.2.41
X4488	24.9.40–9.10.40
X4544	27.9.40–damaged 5.10 — hit K9989 —, kept until 15.5.41
X4595	9.10.40–2.5.41
X4596	8.10.40–15.5.41
X4600	13.10.40–2.5.41
X4601	13.10.40–31.3.41
X4602	13.10.40–15.5.41
X4643	6.10.40–7.5.41

No. 74 Sqn

K9863	13.2.39 (DIA 10.7)–15.7.40
K9870	20.2.39–FAO2 8.8.40
K9871	21.2.39–FBO2 13.8.40
K9878	1.3.39–4.9.40
K9928	10.5.40–EFAO 3.7.40 (lightning strike, nr Margate)
K9951	2.5.39–12.9.40
K9953	2.5.39–12.9.40
L1001	28.5.40–28.9.40
L1089	12.12.39–4.9.40
N3091	3.1.40–s/d 13.8.40 (FH 158.25)
P9306	6.7.40–16.9.40 (to Science Museum, Chicago 9.44)
P9336	11.7.40–s/d 28.7.40 (nr Dover)
P9379	26.5.40–s/d 31.7.40 (nr Folkestone; FH 88.35)
P9380	12.7.40–FAO2 8.8.40
P9393	3.6.40–EFB 11.8.40 (in sea)
P9398	26.5.40–s/d 31.7.40 (in Folkestone Harbour; FH 72.20)
P9427	21.8.40–13.9.40
P9429	9.10.40–12.10.40
P9465	3.6.40–FBO2 3.7.40
P9492	3.6.40–15.9.40
P9547	4.6.40–FTR 28.7.40 (in Channel)
R6603	10.8.40–13.9.40
R6606	1.9.40–EFB 15.9.40
R6706	12.7.40–FBO2 28.7.40
R6716	10.8.40–12.9.40
R6757	29.7.40–30.7.40
R6759	30.7.40 (DIA 13.8)–25.8.40
R6771	13.7.40–31.7.40
R6772	13.7.40–15.9.40
R6773	13.7.40–17.8.40
R6779	12.7.40–FBO2 2.8.40
R6780	12.7.40–13.9.40
R6839	29.7.40–13.9.40
R6840	29.7.40–15.9.40
R6962	2.8.40–FTR 11.8.40

R6982	2.8.40–6.8.40	K9998	2.7.40–FAO2 22.8.40
R6983	27.7.40 (DIA 31.7)–6.8.40	L1009	18.10.40–?
X4022	2.8.40–FAO2 30.8.40 (collided with X4027)	L1014	14.9.40–1.11.40
		L1077	20.8.40–s/d 9.9.40 (nr Rye)
X4024	14.8.40–4.9.40	L1080	3.6.40–EAO2 19.8.40 (bombing, Bibury)
X4027	14.8.40–14.9.40		
X4060	9.12.10–12.10.40	N3032	19.9.40–12.10.40
X4061	9.8.40–17.8.40	N3040	22.7.40–s/d 18.8.40 (nr Tonbridge)
X4067	4.8.40–12.9.40	N3106	15.10.40–EAO3 10.11.40
X4069	14.8.40–12.9.40	N3125	21.10.40–?
X4101	14.8.40–13.9.40	N3167	30.3.40–FBO2 26.7.40
X4167	16.8.40–1.11.40	N3193	30.3.40–s/d 18.9.40 (nr Gravesend)
X4419	16.9.40–20.10.40	N3248	20.3.40–FTR 20.9.40 (in Channel)
		N3249	20.3.40–FBO2 30.8.40 (crashed nr Bibury)
Mk II			
P7292	11.10.40–22.10.40	N3268	13.8.40–s/d 25.8.40 (St Govan's Head)
P7306	10.9.40–27.11.40		
P7308	10.9.40–15.1.41	N3283	14.9.40 (DIA 18.9)–14.2.41
P7310	10.9.40–15.5.41	N3285	20.3.40–21.8.40
P7312	12.9.40–FTR 1.11.40	N3287	30.3.40–EFA 25.7.40 (crashed nr Chudleigh)
P7316	15.9.40–14.6.41		
P7329	13.9.40–EFAO 8.10.40 (mid-air collision over Coltishall)	P9316	20.7.40–s/d 4.9.40
		P9368	9.3.40–20.8.40
P7352	13.9.40–13.6.41	P9371	6.3.40–EFB 23.9.40 (repaired)
P7355	13.9.40–29.10.40	P9372	27.7.40–s/d 9.9.40 (FH 99.35)
P7356	14.9.40–21.9.40	P9433	23.5.40–FBO2 5.7.40
P7357	26.9.40–13.7.41	P9434	23.5.40–FBO2 8.7.40
P7360	10.9.40–EFB 17.10.40	P9454	4.6.40–FAO2 5.7.40
P7361	10.9.40–18.11.40	P9464	20.8.40–11.9.40 (FH 52.15)
P7362	10.9.40–FTR 23.9.40 (in sea off Southwold)	P9413	7.7.40–FBO2 15.9.40
		P9544	12.9.40 (DIA 27.9)–9.10.40
P7363	10.9.40–7.2.41	P9548	4.6.40–EFAO 27.8.40 (crashed Marlesford, Suffolk)
P7364	13.9.40–FBO2 22.10.40		
P7366	10.9.40–9.3.41	R6596	4.6.40–FBO2 9.9.40
P7367	12.9.40–19.11.40	R6597	4.6.40–29.7.40
P7368	10.9.40–19.11.40	R6613	20.8.40–EFB 11.9.40
P7370	10.9.40–EFB 30.10.40	R6616	31.5.40 (DIA 16.9)–10.10.40 (collided with X4038)
P7373	13.9.40–EFAO 8.10.40 (collided with P7329)		
		R6622	31.5.40–s/d 27.9.40 (Dartford)
P7426	24.9.40–EFB 20.10.40	R6624	31.5.40–s/d 14.9.40 (crashed nr Faversham)
P7431	11.10.40–FTR 22.10.40		
		R6642	26.9.40–FTR 15.10.40
No. 92 Sqn		R6703	7.7.40–s/d 19.8.40
K9793	1.9.40–FTR 11.9.40 (in sea)	R6760	3.8.40 (DIA 27.9)–4.10.40
K9951	12.9.40–1.10.40	R6767	13.9.40–FTR 27.9.40

Spitfire DW-L of No. 610 Squadron, its serial painted over, at Hawkinge in August 1940. Shot down early on 26 August, Peter Else, its pilot, baled out when over the Channel. (Peter Else)

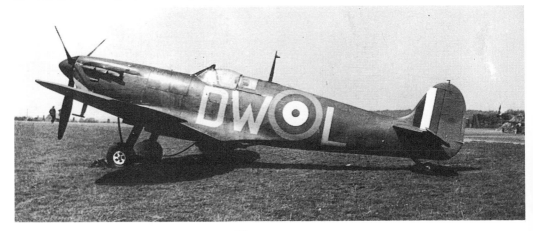

79

R6838	19.9.40–s/d 15.10.40
R6922	15.10.40–FTR 19.10.40
X4037	21.8.40–s/d 24.9.40 (nr North Weald)
X4038	21.8.40–EFAO 10.10.40 (collided with R6616)
X4051	21.8.40–9.10.40
X4069	12.9.40–EFB 30.9.40
X4356	23.9.40 (DIA 24.9)–3.10.40
X4417	17.9.40–EFB 20.9.40 (crashed West Hougham)
X4418	17.9.40–SOC 9.11.40
X4419	20.10.39–13.8.40
X4422	18.9.40–s/d 27.9.40 (Farningham)
X4225	28.9.40–8.3.41
X4224	19.9.40–9.10.40
X4427	19.9.40 (DIA 24.9)–9.10.40
X4480	22.9.40 (DIA 27.9)–22.1.41
X4484	24.9.40–18.5.41
X4485	24.9.40–13.11.40
X4487	24.9.40–FBO2 31.11.40
X4551	28.9.40–FBO2 27.10.40
X4552	28.9.40–FBO3 12.10.40
X4553	28.9.40–SOC 28.10.40
X4555	28.9.40–7.11.40
X4556	29.9.40–27.11.40
X4557	29.9.40–5.11.40
X4591	11.10.40–s/d 12.10.40 (FH 4.45)
X4597	7.10.40–s/d 9.10.40 (Ashford)
X4606	16.10.40–14.11.40
X4607	17.10.40–26.3.41
X4609	17.10.40–24.10.40
X4616	24.10.40–12.3.41

No. 152 Sqn

K9840	23.9.40–24.1.41
K9880	2.1.40–s/d 20.7.40 (off Swanage)
K9882	3.1.40–s/d 26.9.40 (off Isle of Wight)
K9894	2.1.40–FBO2 8.8.40
K9901	16.1.40–s/d 25.7.40 (off Portland)
K9930	23.2.40–10.9.40
K9954	27.12.39–EFB 15.8.40
K9980	15.2.40–EFB 25.7.40
K9982	9.2.40–s/d 26.9.40 (off Isle of Wight)
K9990	(see 611 Sqn)
K9999	15.2.40–s/d 12.8.40 (Isle of Wight)
L1048	3.10.40–5.12.40
L1054	15.2.40–FAO2 7.8.40
L1059	30.9.40–EFB 7.10.40
L1072	27.12.39–FTR 30.9.40 (in sea)
N3039	26.9.40–s/d 7.10.40
N3173	20.9.40–s/d 25.9.40 (nr Frome)
N3176	15.10.40–FAO2 10.11.40
P7286	(Mk II) 17.7.40–6.9.40
P9327	3.5.40–FBO2 25.7.40
P9382	26.9.40–23.3.41
P9391	26.9.40–EFB 11.10.40 (nr Dorchester)
P9432	18.6.40–FBO2 21.9.40
P9440	11.5.40–FBO2 18.7.40
P9442	11.5.40–1.10.40
P9456	25.4.40–FTR 12.8.40 (in sea, St Catherine's Point)
P9463	8.9.40–FBO2 16.8.40, FTR 25.9.40
P9509	26.9.40–23.3.41
P9543	26.9.40–23.3.41
R6607	27.9.40–EFAO 18.10.40
R6608	21.7.40–FBO2 13.8.40; 8.10.40–23.3.41

R6614	26.7.40–FTR 11.8.40 (in Channel)
R6763	22.7.40 (DIA 14.10)–19.10.40
R6764	22.7.40–20.9.40
R6801	26.7.40–12.8.40; 13.10.40–17.1.41
R6810	21.7.40–FTR 25.8.40
R6811	21.7.40–EFB 8.8.40 (crashed Betswall)
R6829	10.8.40–FBO2 28.8.40
R6831	19.8.40–FTR 27.8.40 (in sea)
R6880	13.8.40–EFAO 13.8.40
R6889	27.9.40–12.12.40
R6907	10.8.40–EFB 29.11.40
R6909	19.8.40–FTR 4.9.40 (in sea)
R6910	10.8.40 (DIA 15.8)–9.9.40
R6964	13.8.40–15.11.40
R6968	14.8.40–FBO2 15.8.40, 30.9.40–28.3.41
R6994	15.8.40–FTR 25.8.40
R7016	18.8.40–FTR 23.9.40 (in Channel)
X4012	26.8.40–26.9.40
X4017	9.8.40–15.9.40
X4025	18.8.40–16.12.40
X4164	19.8.40–26.8.40
X4169	13.9.40–FBO2 24.9.40
X4171	15.8.40–23.3.41
X4177	23.9.40 (DIA 25.9)–26.9.40
X4247	28.8.40–7.10.40
X4258	16.9.40–1.10.40
X4381	13.9.40–1.11.40
X4550	27.9.40–EFB 2.10.40

No. 222 Sqn

K9795	14.10.40–FBO2 15.10.40
K9799	31.8.40–10.9.40
K9826	2.7.40–s/d 13.8.40 (Barnham, Kent)
K9962	3.9.40–EFB 4.9.40
K9993	13.9.40–EFB 20.9.40
L1010	24.6.40–EDFB 3.9.40 (crashed Canewdon)
L1089	4.9.40–FBO2 15.10.40
N3119	12.9.40–FBO2 30.10.40
N3164	13.9.40–EFB 8.11.40
N3169	31.8.40–FBO2 7.9.40
N3203	31.8.40–FBO3 20.9.40 (nr Redford, Kent)
N3233	9.3.40 (DIA 31.8)–15.9.40
N3294	9.3.40–EFB 4.7.40 (nr Withernsea)
P9318	3.40–8.40?
F/P9323	16.3.40–s/d 30.8.40 (crashed Sheppey)
P9324	21.3.40–13.9.40
P9325	16.3.40–EFB 30.8.40 (Eastchurch)
P9328	21.5.40–FBO2 1.9.40
P9337	25.3.40–s/d 31.8.40
P9360	16.3.40–EAO 31.8.40 (bombed at Hornchurch)
P9364	11.3.40–FTR 7.9.40?
P9368	2.9.40–FBO2 18.9.40
P9375	17.7.40 (DIA 30.8)–1.9.40
P9378	15.3.40–s/d 30.8.40 (nr Rochford)
P9397	4.6.40–FBO2 15.10.40
P9434	22.9.40–FBO1 30.10.40
P9443	4.6.40–FBO2 25.7.40, s/d 30.8.40 (nr Sittingbourne)
P9447	12.9.40–17.9.40
P4969	21.5.40–s/d 7.10.40
P9492	15.9.40–s/d 30.9.40 (Denham)
P9505	6.7.40–7.9.40
P9542	7.9.40–FBO2 14.9.40

80

Top *Spitfires of 222 Squadron,* ZD-R nearest. (IWM)

Above *Spitfire* P9323:ZD-F *ready and waiting at Kirton-in-Lindsey during July 1940.* (Andy Saunders Collection via A. Thomas/Michael Payne)

R6628	8.6.40–FTR 30.8.40
R6638	8.9.40–FBO2 11.9.40
R6685	6.9.40–18.10.40
R6702	20.9.40–EFB 27.9.40
R6719	10.7.40–5.9.40
R6720	10.7.40–FBO2 30.8.40
R6772	15.9.40–EFB 18.9.40 (Challock)
R6773	15.8.40–EFB 26.10.40
R6809	20.9.40–23.9.40
R6837	1.9.40–FBO2 4.9.40
R6840	15.9.40 (DIA 20.9)–25.9.40
R6881	13.8.40–6.9.40
X4024	4.9.40–FBO2 14.9.40
X4057	1.9.40–EFB 5.9.40
X4058	1.9.40–FBO2 18.9.40
X4067	23.9.40–27.5.41
X4249	3.9.40–EFB 14.9.40
X4265	3.9.40–FBO2 14.9.40
X4275	31.8.40–EFB 14.9.40
X4278	31.8.40–s/d 4.9.40
X4280	31.8.40–11.9.40
X4341	7.9.40–22.12.40
X4540	10.10.40–19.10.40
X4546	29.9.40–30.3.41
X4548	29.9.40–EFB 27.10.40

No. 234 Squadron

K9963	1.9.40–6.9.40
N3057	29.8.40–?
N3061	29.8.40–s/d 6.9.40 (off Weymouth)
N3191	22.3.40–16.1.41
N3231	28.3.40–FBO2 12.7.40
N3239	16.3.40–s/d 24.8.40 (Isle of Wight)
N3241	22.3.40–?
N3242	22.3.40–FBO2 16.8.40
H/N3277	8.4.40–FTR 15.8.40 (force landed nr Cherbourg)
N3278	15.4.40–FBO2 8.8.40
N3279	15.4.40–FBO2 6.9.40
P9319	15.3.40–11.10.40
P9320	15.3.40–FBO2 30.8.40
P9363	15.3.40–EFB 15.8.40 (crashed nr Twyford)
P9365	15.3.40–EFB 31.7.40
P9366	27.3.40–EFB 6.8.40
P9464	20.5.40–8.8.40
P9466	18.5.40–EFB 7.9.40
P9468	20.5.40–FBO2 10.8.40
P9491	20.5.40–FAO2 4.7.40
P9493	20.5.40–EFAO 25.7.40 (crashed nr Porthtowan)

P9494	20.5.40-FBO2 26.8.40
P9508	19.8.40-FAO2 1.11.40
P9519	11.9.40-18.9.40
R6621	5.10.40-FBO2 9.10.40
R6627	8.9.40-11.9.40
R6896	1.8.40-FTR 23.9.40 (FH 66.30)
R6957	17.8.40-12.2.41
R6959	19.8.40-23.3.41
R6967	30.7.40-s/d 16.8.40
R6983	27.9.40-28.3.41
R6985	25.7.40-s/d 15.8.40
R6988	8.8.40-s/d 15.8.40 (nr Swanage)
R7017	9.9.40-27.11.40
R7022	19.8.40-6.9.40
X4009	19.8.40-FBO2 7.9.40
X4010	19.8.40-5.9.40
X4016	11.8.40-s/d 16.8.40 (in sea off Isle of Wight)
X4023	11.8.40-FBO2 26.8.40
X4035	17.8.40-EFB 6.9.40 (FH 10.40)
G/X4036	17.8.40-FBO2 11.10.40
X4182	19.8.40-EFAO 25.9.40 (crashed nr St Mawgan)
X4183	19.8.40-s/d 6.9.40
X4244	9.9.40-28.3.41
X4251	22.8.40-27.3.41
X4354	18.9.40-13.4.41
X4355	10.9.40-6.11.40
X4387	10.9.40-12.40
X4428	18.9.40-FTR 16.1.41
X4608	30.10.40-23.3.41

No. 266 Sqn

K9850	17.8.40-EAO2 18.8.40 (strafed, Hornchurch)
K9864	4.6.40-16.8.40 (re-classified from FBO3)
K9996	17.8.40-7.9.40
L1011	17.8.40-17.9.40
L1043	18.6.40-9.9.40
L1059	4.6.40-FAO2 9.8.40
L1088	4.6.40-EAO2 18.8.40 (strafed, Hornchurch)
N3095	12.1.40-s/d 16.8.40 (nr Canterbury)
N3118	19.1.40-12.9.40, 14.9.40 to 17.9.40
N3127	15.2.40-EAO2 18.8.40 (strafing damage)
N3168	15.2.40-s/d 15.8.40 (Teston, Kent)
N3170	15.2.40 (DIA 18.7)-21.7.40
N3175	19.1.40-s/d 12.8.40 (Bembridge)
N3178	15.2.40-FBO2 13.8.40
N3181	15.2.40 (DIA 15.8)-3.9.40
N3189	11.3.40-s/d 15.8.40 (East of Deal, by He 115)
N3240	11.3.40-s/d 16.8.40 (nr Deal)
N3244	16.2.40-FAO2 18.7.40
N3245	16.2.40-FBO2 15.8.40, 29.8.40 to 20.10.40
P9312	16.5.40-s/d 16.8.40 (Canterbury)
P9333	16.5.40-s/d 12.8.40 (off Portsmouth)
P9424	19.8.40-25.8.40
R6626	20.10.40-11.4.41
R6752	17.10.40-10.1.41
R6762	13.8.40-EAO2 18.8.40 (strafing, Hawkinge)
R6768	21.7.40-s/d 15.8.40
R6920	28.7.40-EAO2 18.8.40 (strafing, Hawkinge)

R6925	19.8.40-6.9.40
R6927	19.8.40-6.9.40
R6991	17.8.40-12.9.40
X4019	17.10.40-16.4.41
X4030	12.8.40-FBO2 16.8.40
X4033	19.8.40-7.9.40
X4061	18.8.40-EAO3 18.8.40 (strafing, Manston)
X4063	13.8.40-EAO3 18.8.40 (strafing)
X4064	11.8.40-4.2.41
X4066	16.8.40-EAO 18.8.40
X4164	17.10.40-11.4.41
X4172	17.8.40-7.9.40
X4173	17.8.40-25.8.40
X4174	17.8.40-7.9.40
X4175	17.8.40-7.9.40
X4176	17.8.40-6.9.40
X4178	17.8.40-25.8.40
X4179	18.8.40-25.8.40
X4252	24.8.40-6.9.40
X4253	24.8.40-11.9.40
X4254	24.8.40-6.9.40
X4255	24.8.40-6.9.40
X4259	17.10.40-FAO2 5.11.40
X4269	27.8.40-12.9.40
X4274	17.10.40-18.4.40
X4347	17.10.40-8.3.41
X4348	17.10.40-18.4.41
X4594	17.10.40-FTR 6.3.41 (FH 183)
X4613	24.10.40-EFB 2.3.41

Mk II

P7285	5.9.40-17.10.40
P7286	6.9.40-17.10.40
P7287	6.4.40-17.10.40
P7288	6.9.40-20.10.40
P7289	6.9.40-20.10.40
P7294	6.9.40-24.10.40
P7295	6.9.40-17.10.40
P7296	6.9.40-10.10.40
P7297	6.9.40-17.10.40
P7307	7.10.40-20.10.40
P7309	5.9.40-17.10.40
P7311	6.9.40-17.10.40
P7313	5.9.40-EFB 11.9.40
P7315	19.9.40-17.10.40
P7324	5.9.40-17.10.40
P7325	6.9.40-17.10.40
P7327	5.9.40-17.10.40
P7328	5.9.40-17.10.40
P7350	6.9.40-17.10.40
P7365	6.9.40-17.10.40

No. 602 Sqn

K9833	10.2.40-5.7.40, 4.8.40-7.9.40
K9839	10.2.40-FBO2 16.8.40
K9881	24.3.40-FBO2 16.8.40
K9890	13.7.40-21.7.40
N/K9892	8.11.39-EFA 1.8.40 (Drem)
K9899	24.3.40-?
K9910	6.3.40-EFB 9.9.40 (crashed Boxgrove)
K9955	8.11.39-FBO3 4.9.40 (became 3276M)
K9969	12.5.39-FBO2 18.8.40
K9995	19.8.40 (DIA 26.8)-27.8.40
L1002	24.9.39-FAT2 10.9.40
L1004	24.9.39-26.8.40
L1005	24.5.40-FBO2 18.8.40
L1027	21.12.39-FBO2 11.9.40

L1040	5.7.40-EFB 31.8.40		X4412	13.9.40 (DIA 15.9)-24.9.40
L1049	23.9.40-?		X4414	13.9.40 (DIA 27.9)-3.10.40
N3068	31.8.40-6.9.40		X4541	2.10.40-FBO2 12.10.40
N3109	24.12.39-22.8.40		X4603	13.10.40-14.12.40

N3119	14.3.40-22.8.40
N3198	6.8.40-EFB 7.8.40

No. 603 Sqn

N3226	7.4.40-s/d 25.8.40 (nr Dorchester)
N3227	7.4.40-s/d 6.9.40 (nr Hailsham)
N3228	7.4.40 (DIA 7.9)-7.10.40
N3242	13.9.40-FBO2 28.11.40
N3282	19.8.40-s/d 11.9.40
P9381	13.7.40-FTR 25.8.40
P9423	13.7.40-s/d 19.8.40 (nr Berstead)
P9446	19.8.40-FBO3 12.10.40
P9461	3.6.40-FBO2 1.8.40
P9463	3.6.40 (DIA 16.8)-22.8.40
P9491	19.8.40-31.8.40
P9510	13.7.40-FBO2 30.9.40
P9515	27.8.40-14.12.40
R6600	19.8.40 (DIA 6.9)-8.9.40
R6601	20.8.40 (DIA 6.9)-14.12.40
R6780	13.9.40-22.11.40
R6834	19.8.40 (DIA 6.9)-8.9.40
R6839	13.9.40-FTR 26.10.40
R6965	31.8.40-14.12.40
X4012	13.10.40-17.11.40
X4030	11.8.40-12.8.40
X4104	12.9.40-14.12.40
X4110	16.8.40-FBO2 18.8.40
X4160	16.8.40-EFB 27.9.40 (crashed, Lullington)
X4161	16.8.40-s/d FBO2 18.8.40
X4162	16.8.40-25.11.40
X4169	15.8.40-30.8.40
X4187	21.8.40-s/d, FBO2 26.8.40
X4188	21.8.40-s/d 26.8.40
X4256	24.8.40-FTR 7.9.40 (FH 15.50)
X4269	27.8.40-FBO2 30.10.40
X4270	27.8.40 (DIA 10.9)-FBO2 2.10.40
X4382	10.9.40-14.12.40
X4389	12.9.40-14.12.40
X4390	12.9.40-14.12.40
X4411	17.9.40 (DIA 26.9)-11.11.40

No. 603 Sqn

K9803	13.9.40 (DIA 18.9)-FBO2 28.9.40
K9807	28.9.40-s/d 7.10.40 (Chilham)
K9833	5.7.40-4.8.40
K9890	20.9.40-7.10.40
K9916	4.2.39-FTR 17.7.40
K9963	6.9.40-EFB 5.10.40
K9995	6.11.39-FBO2 19.7.40
K9996	6.11.39-15.7.40
L1017	1.9.40-6.9.40
L/L1020	15.9.39-EFB 1.9.40
M/L1021	15.9.39-s/d 29.8.40 (nr Lympne)
R/L1024	15.9.40-EAO2 1.9.40
R/L1040	5.7.39-EFB 10.9.40
K/L1046	20.9.39-FTR 28.8.40
L1057	16.9.39-FBO2 7.9.40
D/L1067	19.9.39-s/d 30.8.40 (Snargate)
L1070	16.9.39-EAO2 1.9.40
L1076	1.9.40-s/d 28.9.40
N3026	21.2.40 (DIA 23.7)-29.7.40
B/N3056	20.7.40-s/d 2.9.40
N3099	29.9.40-17.10.40
P/N3105	11.4.40-EFB 28.8.40 (crashed Leigh Green)
N3109	5.10.40-FTR 7.10.40 (FH 195.30)
N3196	3.9.40-FBO2 7.9.40
N3229	11.4.40 (DIA 23.7)-24.7.40
N3244	21.9.40-FTR 27.9.40 (in sea off Folkestone)
S/N3267	11.4.40-FBO2 29.8.40
N3268	11.4.40-17.7.40
H/N3288	31.5.40-EAO2 1.9.40
P9394	30.8.40-13.9.40
P9440	3.9.40-FBO2 15.10.40
N/P9459	6.5.40 (DIA 29.8)-4.9.40
P9467	2.9.40-FTR 7.9.40
P9499	6.9.40-30.10.40
P9553	8.9.40-s/d 2.10.40

Hornchurch at the end of August 1940, with Spitfire X4278:ZD-D *nearest,* X4272: XT-M *of 603 Squadron,* ZD-W *and* ZD-J.

A cross-Channel chase led to Spitfire X4260:XT-D of 603 Squadron being forced to land in France.

Y/R6626	20.7.40–20.10.40
R6717	29.6.40–EFAO 2.8.40 (crashed Inkhorn, Aberdeenshire)
V/R6721	14.7.40–9.9.40
U/R6751	14.7.40–FTR 28.8.40
E/R6752	20.7.40 (DIA 2.9)–10.9.40
GR6753	14.7.40–s/d 29.8.40 (Dymchurch)
R6754	20.7.40–4.9.40
R6755	5.7.40–FBO2 18.7.40
Z/R6808	28.7.40–EAO 1.9.40
W/R6835	14.7.40–FBO2 31.8.40
R6836	20.7.40–24.10.40
X/R6989	8.8.40–5.9.40
R7019	7.9.40–EFB 15.9.40 (Fairlight, Sussex)
R7020	6.10.40–17.10.40
X4019	7.10.40–17.10.40
X4064	20.9.40–17.10.40
Z/X4185	1.9.40–EFB 3.9.40 (off Margate)
X/X4250	30.8.40 (DIA 2.9, DIA 7.9)–27.9.40
X4259	1.9.40–17.10.40
D/X4260	1.9.40–FTR 6.9.40 (FH 9.55)
X4261	1.9.40–FTR 5.9.40 (FH 8.50)
X4263	30.8.40–FBO2 4.9.40
M/X4264	30.8.40–FTR 5.9.40
X4265	14.10.40–EFB 21.10.40
N/X4271	30.8.40–EFB 31.8.40, (Wanstead) (FH 3.50)
X4273	30.8.40–FTR 31.8.40
X4274	30.8.40–17.10.40
M/X4277	30.8.40–EFB 3.9.40, (off Margate) (FH 7.45)
X4323	3.9.40–s/d 18.9.40
X4324	3.9.40–s/d 15.9.40
X4347	8.9.40–17.10.40
X4348	8.9.40–17.10.40
X4349	8.9.40–23.9.40
X4415	14.9.40–1.10.40
X4489	24.9.40–10.10.40
X4490	24.9.40–17.10.40
X4493	8.10.40–17.10.40
X4494	8.10.40–17.10.40
X4613	17.10.40–24.10.40

No. 609 Sqn

K9815	13.7.40–FAO 26.7.40
K9825	13.7.40–26.7.40
K9841	18.7.40–25.8.40 (FB02 12.8.40)
K9997	4.6.40 (DIA 12.8, DIA 15.9)–5.10.40
L1008	8.6.40–FAO2 25.9.40
L1048	28.9.40–3.10.40
L1065	6.9.39–5.11.40
L1069	8.9.39–s/d 11.7.40 (Portland)
L1082	19.8.39 (DIA 24.8)–5.9.40
L1095	6.9.39–FTR 11.7.40 (off Portland)
N3023	8.9.40–s/d 27.7.40 (off Weymouth)
N3024	11.9.40–FTR 14.8.40
N3113	10.8.40 (DIA 7.9)–2.10.40
N3203	25.4.40–EFB 4.7.40
N3221	28.9.40–4.12.40
N3223	28.4.40–EFAO 5.10.40 (crashed Chisenbury)
N3231	25.9.40–s/d 7.10.40
N3238	29.9.40–s/d 7.10.40
N3273	5.10.40–7.1.41
N3280	5.9.40 (DIA 7.9, 25.9)–26.9.40
N3288	18.9.40–FBO2 26.9.40
P9322	8.6.40 (DIA 8.8)–28.8.40
P9369	17.4.40–FBO2 22.7.40
P9467	4.6.40–FBO2 15.7.40
P9503	26.9.40–EFB 27.10.40
R6631	16.8.40–FTR 28.11.40?
R6634	4.6.40–FTR 18.7.40 (in sea off Swanage)
R6636	4.6.40–FBO2 18.7.40 (SOC 26.7.40, force landed Studland Bay)
R6637	4.6.40–FTR 9.7.40
R6690	7.6.40 (DIA 13.8)–EFB 15.9.40
R6691	7.6.40–29.8.40, 17.9.40–FBO2 25.9.40

Top and above *Spitfires of 609 Squadron at Middle Wallop.*

R6692	7.6.40 (DIA 12.8)–28.8.40	X4107	16.8.40–FTR 27.9.40
R6699	7.6.40–FBO2 25.9.40	X4165	16.8.40–9.12.40
R6706	26.9.40–24.2.41	X4173	28.9.40–24.2.41
R6769	21.7.40–12.8.40, 15.8.40 — FAO2	X4234	24.8.40 (DIA 27.9)–13.9.40
	2.9.40	X4331	28.9.40–24.2.41
R6801	14.8.40–28.8.40	X4471	18.9.40–24.2.41
R6915	21.7.40 (DIA on 7.9, 30.9,	X4472	18.9.40–FBO2 7.10.40
	7.10)–14.10.40	X4539	29.9.40–24.2.41
R6922	15.8.40 (DIA 15.9)–17.9.40	X4586	8.10.40–FTR 28.11.40 (FH 37.35)
R6961	13.8.40 (DIA 14.8, 25.8)–24.2.41	X4587	8.10.40–26.3.41
R6977	22.7.40–28.8.40	X4588	8.10.40–9.12.40
R6979	22.7.40 (DIA 26.9)–24.2.41	X4598	29.10.40–2.4.41
R6986	25.7.40 (DIA 25.8)–5.9.40	X4642	27.10.40–24.2.41
R7020	13.8.40–FAT2 13.8.40		
X4104	16.8.40–25.8.40		

No. 610 Sqn

H/K9818	27.2.40-s/d 12.8.40
K9852	15.10.40-31.10.40
K9876	15.10.40-?
R/K9931	7.7.40-25.8.40 (nr Northbourne)
M/K9947	30.8.40-23.9.40
P/K9960	23.7.40-5.9.40
K9970	9.9.40-14.12.40
K9975	14.9.40-23.9.40
M/L1000	2.10.39-FBO2 10.7.40
B/L1009	3.10.39-18.10.40
L1037	30.8.40-s/d 30.9.40 (Fyfield)
H/L1044	3.10.39-s/d 12.8.40 (in sea)
L1045	31.10.40-FBO2 8.8.40
L1075	5.10.39-FTR 9.7.40
V/L1076	5.10.39-7.7.40
L1094	27.10.40-EFB 4.11.40
N/N3124	11.9.40-FAO2 13.10.40
N3170	9.9.40-12.9.40?
S/N3201	28.3.40-EFB 20.7.40 (crashed Wootton)
N3264	13.10.40-EFB 27.10.40
J/N3284	14.5.40-7.9.40
V/P9330	14.9.40-17.8.40, 7.10.40-EFA 7.11.40
P9311	14.9.40-17.12.40
E/P9433	9.9.40-30.10.40
P9439	5.9.40-6.12.40
M/P9451	2.6.40-7.7.40, 28.8.40-EFAO 11.12.40
T/P9452	2.6.40-s/d 18.7.40
K/P9495	2.6.40-EFB 12.8.40
L/P9496	2.6.40-s/d 26.8.40 (crashed Paddlesworth)
Q/P9502	2.6.40-EFAO 12.7.40 (crashed Titsey Park)
D/P9503	11.7.40-6.8.40
P9511	25.8.40-s/d 28.8.40 (Stelling Minnis)
P9512	7.7.40-22.7.40
Q/P9545	11.7.40-19.8.40
O/R6595	7.6.40-EFB 26.8.40
J/R6599	11.9.40-EFAO 12.10.40
S/R6621	24.2.40-FBO2 12.8.40
E/R6629	31.5.40-FBO2 31.8.40
X/R6630	31.5.40-FTR 11.8.40
X/R6641	13.8.40-FBO2 24.8.40
S/R6686	19.8.40-21.8.40 (crashed nr Eastry)
A/R6693	7.6.40-31.7.40 (crashed Hawkinge)
F/R6694	7.6.40-EAO2 18.8.40
P/R6695	7.6.40-s/d 22.8.40 (Hawkinge)
T/R6765	13.7.40-FBO2 8.8.40
Z/R6802	7.8.40-FTR 16.8.40
N/R6806	16.7.40-FBO2 2.9.40
R6807	13.7.40-EFAO 13.7.40 (crashed Titsfield)
Q/R6881	13.8.40-FAO2 12.10.40
D/R6918	28.7.40-FTR 11.8.40
M/R6970	19.8.40-FBO2 26.8.40
R6971	19.8.40-EFB 4.9.40 (on 72 Sqn)
A/R6976	24.7.40-23.11.40
W/R6993	26.7.40-14.12.40
R6996	19.8.40-EFAO 2.9.40 (repaired)
O/X4011	27.8.40-EFAO 5.11.40
X4013	27.8.40-EFB 5.9.40 (on 72 Sqn)
X4014	27.8.40-2.10.40
F/X4028	19.8.40-14.12.40
X4065	12.8.40-23.9.40
X4067	14.9.40-23.9.40

X4070	12.8.40-26.8.40
X4102	13.8.40-s/d 24.8.40 (crashed Fyfield)
X4103	13.8.40-26.8.40
X4105	13.8.40-FBO2 2.9.40
B/X4166	15.8.40-FAO2 12.10.40
X4168	15.8.40-Soc 11.9.40
R/X4239	26.8.40-17.12.40
X4240	7.10.40-14.12.40
S/X4241	30.8.40-FBO2 2.9.40
M/X4245	7.10.40-14.12.40
R/X4239	26.8.40-17.12.40

No. 611 Sqn

K9841	6.6.40-18.7.40
K9918	4.6.40-21.8.40
K9963	4.6.40-1.9.40
K9970	4.6.40-FAO2 28.7.40
K9981	4.6.40-21.8.40
K9989	9.2.40-FAO2 8.6.40
K9990	30.11.39-FTR 18.7.40 (in sea off Isle of Wight; on 152 Sqn)
N3051	1.3.40-21.8.40
N3052	1.3.40-21.8.40
N3059	25.1.40-27.8.40
N3060	25.1.40-28.8.40
N3061	15.2.40-29.8.40
N3062	15.2.40-FAT2 22.7.40 (on shore, Colwyn Bay)
N3065	16.3.40-22.8.40
N3066	16.3.40-29.8.40
N3068	16.3.40-31.8.40
N3070	16.2.40-27.8.40
N3072	18.12.39-23.8.40
R6838	30.7.40-5.8.40
R6921	22.7.40-23.8.40
R6965	30.7.40-31.8.40
R6978	24.7.40-31.8.40
X4015	30.7.40-31.8.40

Mk II	
P7281	27.8.40-24.10.40
P7282	22.8.40-24.10.40
P7283	26.8.40-24.10.40
P7284	26.8.40-24.10.40
P7289	6.9.40-20.10.40
P7290	14.8.40-22.8.40
P7291	14.8.40-30.10.40
P7292	14.8.40-23.8.40
P7298	21.8.40-EFAO 11.9.40 (crashed Shirley)
P7300	21.8.40-24.10.40
P7301	21.8.40-7.11.40
P7302	14.8.40-5.11.40
P7303	14.8.40 (DIA 21.8 and 15.9)-17.9.40
P7304	14.8.40 (DIA 21.8)-17.9.40
P7305	14.8.40 (DIA 21.8, 17.9)-28.9.40
P7314	14.8.40-24.10.40
P7320	21.8.40 (DIA 9.9)-12.9.40
P7321	21.8.40 (DIA 11.9)-17.9.40
P7322	21.8.40-24.10.40
P7323	21.8.40-EFB 11.10.40
P7326	2.10.40-24.10.40
P7354	27.8.40-24.10.40
P7369	19.9.40-EFAO 28.9.40 (crashed Ternhill)
P7371	14.9.40-24.10.40
P7374	14.9.40-24.10.40
P7375	29.9.40-24.10.40

The Battle of Britain Memorial Flight's Spitfire II P7350, now over 50 years old and dressed here as a 41 Squadron aircraft. It saw Battle of Britain service with 266 Squadron.

P7376	14.9.40–24.10.40
P7442	12.10.40–24.10.40
P7443	12.10.40–24.10.40
P7448	11.10.40–25.10.40

No. 616 Sqn

K9803	1.6.40–12.8.40
K9807	7.8.40–FAO2 15.8.40
K9817	17.11.39 (DIA 7.8)–12.8.40
K9819	8.11.39–s/d 25.8.40
K9827	17.11.39–s/d 26.8.40
K9829	15.11.39–FBO2 1.8.40
K9996	7.9.40–4.1.41
L1001	28.9.39–FAO2 5.10.40
L1012	7.11.39–FBO2 30.8.40
L1034	9.2.40–4.1.41
L1036	9.2.40–EFB 16.9.40 (in sea N of Cromer)
N3058	26.8.40–FBO2 24.9.40
N3066	29.8.40–FAO2 18.10.40
N3070	27.8.40–2.9.40
N3271	9.4.40–FAO3 4.8.40
N3275	25.5.40–s/d 26.8.40 (Dungeness)
P9368	26.8.40–2.9.40
P9383	6.6.40–FAO2 26.7.40
R6632	31.5.40–2.9.40
R6633	1.6.40–s/d 26.8.40
R6644	7.10.40–26.2.41
R6696	7.6.40–EFAO 7.8.40
R6698	9.6.40–FAO2 11.8.40
R6701	9.6.40–s/d 26.8.40 (off Dover)

R6702	9.6.40–FAO2 11.8.40
R6704	9.6.40–2.9.40
R6758	18.8.40–s/d 26.8.40 (Adisham)
R6777	26.8.40–2.9.40
R6778	4.8.40–EFB 1.9.40
R6926	17.8.40–EFB 22.8.40 (crashed Elham)
R6963	13.8.40–8.9.40, 12.9.40–26.2.41
R6966	13.8.40–FTR 25.8.40
R6980	27.7.40–26.2.41
R6984	28.9.40–26.2.41
R7018	9.8.40–FBO2 26.8.40
X4020	31.7.40–13.10.40
X4033	7.9.40–26.2.41
X4055	30.8.40–FBO2 15.11.40
X4056	30.8.40–FAO3 8.11.40
X4172	7.9.40–13.11.40
X4174	7.9.40–26.2.41
X4175	7.9.40–26.2.40
X4180	26.8.40–10.9.40
X4181	26.8.40–EFB 2.9.40 (crashed nr Tonbridge)
X4184	26.8.40–EFB 30.8.40
X4248	28.8.40–s/d 30.8.40
X4328	7.9.40–EFB 27.9.40
X4329	7.9.40–26.2.41
X4330	7.9.40 (DIA 14.10)–1.11.40
X4388	13.9.40–26.2.41
X4477	26.9.40–26.3.41
X4614	31.10.40–31.1.41
X4617	26.10.40–26.2.41

The Westland Lysander

Asked to name the four most common operational RAF aircraft during the Battle of Britain, Hurricane, Spitfire, Blenheim would surely hurry to mind — and then, a pause to consider the options. One could do worse than choose the Lysander, 162 of which equipped nine squadrons at the height of the fight. 'What were so many "Lizzies" doing?' you may ask. They were waiting for something to happen.

At dusk and dawn from July to December they daily scoured the coastline in pairs between Land's End and Duncasby Head, searching for invaders. During daylight they trained to provide the Army with such close support as might be needed in the event of enemy landings. It might have involved bombing enemy positions, spotting for gunners and dropping supply containers to the beleaguered. It might have involved strikes upon enemy vehicles including tanks, for some Lysanders had two 20 mm Hispano cannons attached to their wing stubs. Unfortunately only ball ammunition was available — useless against armoured vehicles. They might also have been ordered to spray gas using 'smoke curtain installation' equipment, permitting the dispensing from 500 ft of 15 seconds of poisonous clouds over an area 600 yd long and 60 yd wide.

All that assumed the Lysanders would not face stiff opposition. Flying fairly low, they had during the French campaign shown themselves vulnerable to ground fire, although they evaded fighters by flying slowly. Their biggest handicap was their considerable size, which made them easy targets. Trials had already shown that small Taylorcraft light planes were a far better proposition for artillery ranging. As for ground attack, the Luftwaffe pointed the way with its fighter-bombing Bf 109s, which must have reminded some in authority that British fighters had long had similar capabilities but used only light bombs.

Lysander production was rapid. Indeed, by 15 October 1940 the RAF had received 856 examples. During a major policy review meeting on 17 August, the Air Staff rated as 'embarrassing' the number available of an aeroplane grabbing far too many Bristol engines and 'only really suitable for the North-West Frontier of India'. Yet, with nothing in view to replace it, the Lysander was to soldier on as an army support aeroplane well into 1941.

August 1940 saw it acquire two other roles in which it was to be increasingly involved. First came the delivery of Lysanders to the highly secret No. 419 Flight, North Weald based but using the satellite field at Stapleford Tawney. There was developed, at the height of the Battle, the use of Lysanders to convey and retrieve agents involved in covert activities in France and the Benelux lands. The first such operation using Lysanders was carried out after the Battle.

A second new role concerned the use of Lysanders for spotting survivors of ditched aircraft. Initially, pairs of crews detached from army co-operation squadrons were placed at fighter stations, one of the first such movements being to Roborough, Plymouth.

'Lizzies' were much in evidence in 1940 and surely remain unforgettable in sight and sound for anyone with wartime memories. In my own case I spent many hours watching them at Cambridge where they congregated following the fall of France. Plentiful shrapnel wounds were evident, bodies were mud-splattered and wheel spat plates removed. Many carried an additional rear gun in a cockpit whose covers were usually slid open to avoid the high heat in the greenhouse. Most bore enormous yellow ringed roundels to make sure happy Army gunners recognized them. 'Lizzies' were as much a part of that summer as the fighters. Luckily, they never engaged in the fight for which they trained, although some shots were directed towards them — by friend and foe.

Specification A.39/34 had ended the era of biplane army co-operation machines. Issued in April 1935, it called for a single-engined monoplane with a wide speed range and carrying a two-man crew in an enclosed cockpit. Two forward firing machine guns and rear defence were needed, also dive-bombing capability.

Three manufacturers responded with designs, two being chosen which left Hawker's notions rejected. The Bristol contender, Type 148, was a low wing monoplane of which two prototypes were ordered, one having a Perseus XII engine and the other a Taurus II.

Unmistakable, the 'Lizzie', with its high wing deep fuselage, long 'glasshouse' and hefty spatted undercarriage. P1674:HB-T *belongs to 239 Squadron.*

Westland proceeded carefully, having lately passed through difficult times; they needed a major contract to survive. Army co-operation personnel were questioned about their specific needs and pointed out that a high wing machine was desirable. In that case where could the undercarriage be installed? Initial designs included a stub wing into which the undercarriage could retract, but that was reckoned too weak for field operations. Instead came huge well sprung spats giving the 'Lizzie' crews the chance of trampoline-like landings. With a Browning gun in each spat and stub wings to carry a 500 lb bomb load or light containers, the Westland W.8 went ahead, two prototypes being ordered in June 1935 to be powered by either Mercury or Perseus engines.

K6127, the Mercury IX engined prototype, first flew on 15 June 1936. Its double tapered wing giving it a dragonfly-like appearance was slotted and flapped, as a result of which the take-off and landing space needed was small. Indeed, *K6127* was found to have a stalling speed of 55 mph, which

meant that hovering was almost possible in a fair wind.

Martlesham's trials showed it to have a top speed of 237 mph at 10,000 ft, 221 mph at 5,000 ft. Unstick in a 5 mph wind took a mere 135 yd, ample clearance about 250 yd. Landing run, using brakes, extended about 250 yd. Unquestionably, here was an amazing performer and a gross of Lysanders was ordered, *L4673-4816*.

Rumblings of dissatisfaction began when the aeroplane reached the School of Army Co-operation, Old Sarum, in February 1938, where it was classed as too slow. *K6128*, the second prototype, originally fitted with a Mercury ME 3M(a), was re-engined with a more powerful Perseus XII converting it into the Mk II prototype and sent to India for tropical trials while production of the Mk 1 advanced.

L4673 (890 hp Mercury XII) flew in April 1938, its military load raising its weight to 5,833 lb and cutting its top speed to 229 mph at 10,000 ft, reached after a $5\frac{1}{2}$ min climb. At sea level it could reach only 206 mph, but still stalled at 55 mph. Thus it was little faster than its predecessor, the Hawker Hector biplane, which attained 187 mph at 6,560 ft and reached 10,000 ft in six minutes. To survive in combat, the Lysander would have to rely upon its manoeuvrability. Nevertheless, it had a very useful short field performance, thanks to the excellent shock-absorbing gear, but maintenance was hard going because of the chaotic positioning of equipment behind the power plant. Hopes for general improvement resting with the 905 hp Perseus XII Lysander II were soon dashed when that version was found to be much heavier, with a loaded weight of 6,015 lb. Even so a small speed advance was worthwhile, so instructions were given to fit Perseus engines to *L4739* and subsequent 'L' aircraft. The superior Mercury XV was meanwhile tried in *L4673*, although such engines were needed for Blenheims. As for the sleeve valve Perseus, it was afflicted by technical problems, and most Lysanders had Mercurys.

No. 16 Squadron at Old Sarum became, in May 1938, the first to receive Lysanders. By 3 September 1939 263 had been delivered and 257 were still in use. Their parent No. 22 Group being part of Fighter Command, Lysanders and indeed Hectors had silver and black and then white and black under surfaces, just like front line fighters, and rather than waste them there was a notion that they should fly low level, coastal standing patrols. Seven squadrons were Lysander-equipped pre-war, No. 16 with Mk IIs.

During the 1940 battle for France Lysanders flew about 600 sorties from which 34 failed to return. Once home the squadrons were widely dispersed, mainly close to the coast but also along the main inland defence line stretching roughly from York to the Wash, thence to London and across the south of England. Nos. 2,4,26,225 and 614 Squadrons all had special training to spray gas, each holding 47 × 250 lb 26 gal SCI units, sufficient for 12 Lysanders of each squadron to fly two sorties.

August 1940 saw delivery commence of a refined Lysander, the Mk III. Its engine gave more power, twin guns in the rear cockpit were usual and it had self-sealing fuel tanks. No. 110 Squadron (RCAF) Odiham-based was, on 25 August, given Mk IIIs *R9001–9008*, apparently Mercury VI powered, whereas *R9009*, also delivered that day, had the specified Mercury XVA. The non-operational Canadian squadron, which also carried out development work with the cannon-armed *K6127*, undertook service trials of the III,

Lysander prototype K6127 *fitted with two 20mm cannon and leading the way for similar squadron conversions.*

before Nos. 4 and 16 received examples in October. Cannon, which reduced the aircraft's speed by 12 mph, were being introduced at that time but only at the end of 1940 had enough become available for almost half of the squadron aircraft. They could carry 12 rounds per gun only.

For a variety of reasons establishment of the Lysander squadrons was cut during September 1940 from 18 to 12 each, and 231 Squadron was formed from 416 Flight in Ulster. By 15 October 166 Mk 1s, 358 Mk IIs and 232 Mk IIIs had reached the RAF, 106 (14 per cent) of which had gone overseas and three had been sold to Finland. Only one is known for sure to have been involved in shooting during the Battle period.

Serials of the aircraft delivered to 15 October 1940 are:

MkI: L4673-4738, P1665-1699, R2572, R2575-2600, R2612-2649, R2651-2652.

Mk II: L4739-4816, N1200-1227, N1240-1276, N1289-1320, P1711-1745, P9051-9080, P9095-9140, P9176-9199, R1987-2010, R2025-2047.

Mk III: R9001-9030, R9056-9079, R9100-9135, T1422-1470, T1501-1535, T1548-1590, T1610-1624.

Lysanders which served with operational squadrons 1 July–15 October 1940

No. 2 Sqn, Sawbridgeworth, with detachments at Cambridge from 1.8.40

L4815	10.2.40-13.3.41
L4816	25.2.40-24.10.40
L6847	11.2.40-5.3.41
L6848	11.2.40-18.9.40
N1217	15.6.40-24.10.40
N1242	25.2.40-20.12.40
N1258	24.3.40-EFAO 4.7.40 (force landed, Harold Wood, Essex)
N1259	10.2.40-8.8.40
N1261	10.2.40-7.9.40
N1262	25.2.40-20.12.40
N1318	31.5.40-20.12.40
N1319	31.5.40-24.10.40
P1686	25.2.40-25.8.40
P1727	15.6.40-24.10.40

P1742	31.5.40-24.10.40
P9070	2.7.40-29.10.40
R1989	11.5.40-7.12.40
R1997	31.5.40-24.10.40
R2000	19.7.40-19.12.40
R2001	19.7.40-19.12.40
R2009	19.7.40-24.10.40
R2010	19.7.40-5.12.40

No. 4 Sqn, lodger at Linton-on-Ouse

L4748	11.1.39-20.7.40, 21.8-29.9
L4752	6.6.40-29.9.40
L4755	19.1.39-29.9.40
N1203	14.6.40-EAO 18.8.40
N1204	6.40-24.9.40
N1205	16.6.40-EFB 16.7.40 (crashed into high ground in Berkshire)
N1295	31.8.40-21.9.40
N1300	16.6.40-6.10.40
P1699	27.6.40-21.9.40
P1712	4.7.40-21.9.40
P1734	8.3.40-21.9.40
P9061	8.3.40-25.9.40
P9062	8.3.40-25.9.40
P9101	4.7.40-24.9.40
P9108	19.6.40-23.9.40
P9140	9.7.40-29.9.40
P9184	19.7.40-5.8.40
R1990	16.6.40-8.10.40
R2025	19.7.40-21.9.40
R2026	19.7.40-21.9.40
R2031	19.6.40-EFB 16.7.40 (crashed 4 miles S of Scarborough)
R2032	19.6.40-7.10.40
R2042	28.6.40-8.10.40
R9012	24.9.40-13.5.41
R9013	9.10.40-25.1.41

MkIIIs *R9026, R9028, R9029, R9030, R9056* (EFB 7.10.40, crashed while flying low nr Carlton, Yorks), *R9057, R9075, R9077, R9078, R9079, R9100, R9118* and *R9124* all delivered to the squadron on 20.9.40.

No. 13 Sqn, Speke, to Hooton Park 14.7.40

L4767	6.2.39-10.2.41
L4767	6.2.39-20.7.40
N1220	22.2.40-17.9.40
N1224	5.10.40-13.11.40
P1691	15.6.40-10.7.40
P1713	6.7.40-23.11.40
P1725	6.7.40-25.11.40
P9056	15.6.40-17.9.40
P9059	15.6.40-13.11.40
P9068	22.6.40-25.11.40
P9075	6.6.40-17.9.40
R2007	19.7.40-13.10.40
R2028	16.6.40-17.9.40
R2033	16.6.40-7.10.40
R2034	19.6.40-23.11.40
R2035	19.6.40-11.10.40
R2625	17.6.40-10.8.40
R2626	17.6.40-10.8.40

No. 16 Sqn, Cambridge, to Okehampton 1.8.40, to Weston Zoyland 15.8.40.

L4794	20.3.39–8.7.40, 14.8.40–3.12.40
L4795	20.3.39–16.11.40
L4798	20.3.39–19.9.40
L4802	29.3.39–19.9.40
L4803	30.3.39–15.1.42
L4813	8.2.40–?
N1244	31.5.40–24.10.40
N1265	26.8.40–19.9.40
N1297	30.5.40–25.10.40
P1669	20.1.40–16.11.40
P1673	31.5.40–12.8.40
P1674	31.5.40–19.9.40
P1675	31.5.40–19.9.40
P1678	31.5.40–4.9.40
P1684	19.1.40–3.12.40
P1687	18.1.40–SOC 30.9.40, became 2234M
P9057	6.6.40–24.10.40
P9058	6.6.40–25.10.40
P9077	31.5.40–20.7.40
R9016	13.10.40–19.4.41
R9058	13.10.40–28.5.41
R9059	14.10.40–20.5.41
R9101	14.10.40–EFA 1.11.40
R9102	15.10.40–EFA 28.12.40
R9106	14.10.40–20.5.41
R9107	14.10.40–20.5.41

No. 26 Sqn, West Malling, with 'B' Flt at Cambridge from 3.8.40

L4756	20.5.40–22.7.40
L4776	20.2.39–26.10.40
L4778	23.2.39–26.10.40
L4780	24.2.39–26.10.40
L4788	25.8.40–7.11.40
L4790	25.8.40–7.11.40
L4810	19.7.40–28.10.40
L6848	18.9.40–7.11.40
L6854	3.5.40–EAO 16.8.40 (destroyed by bombing at West Malling)
N1267	25.8.40–EFAO 27.8.40 (crashed at Nettlestead, Kent)
N1268	30.8.40–26.10.40
N1275	13.2.40–22.8.40
N1306	30.5.40–EAO 18.8.40 (destroyed by bombing at West Malling)
P1695	25.8.40–25.8.40
P1697	25.8.40–29.10.40
P1698	25.8.40–29.10.40
P1714	20.5.40–22.8.40
P1726	1.7.40–26.10.40
P9067	27.6.40–26.10.40
P9080	30.5.40–EAO 18.8.40 (destroyed by bombing at West Malling)
P9101	24.9.40–28.10.40
P9107	19.4.40–26.10.40
P9127	18.5.40–3.12.40
P9131	6.6.40–5.11.40
P9132	6.6.40–26.10.40
P9135	6.6.40–26.10.40
R2029	17.6.40–9.12.40
R2030	17.6.40–EFA 24.8.40 (crashed diving low flying nr Haverhill)

No. 110 Sqn, (RCAF), Odiham; used Redhill as advance base from 7.40

K6127	2.8.40, to RAE 9.10.40 (cannon trials aircraft)
L4788	4.4.40–25.8.40
L4789	4.4.40–17.9.40
L4790	4.4.40–25.8.40
N1209	25.2.40–15.10.40
N1265	25.2.40–26.8.40
N1267	25.2.40–25.8.40
N1268	25.2.40–30.8.40
N1301	25.2.40–SOC 17.7.40
P1694	25.2.40–27.8.40
P1695	25.2.40–25.8.40
P1696	25.2.40–27.8.40
P1730	3.4.40–15.10.40
P1731	4.4.40–29.8.40
P1732	6.4.40–27.8.40
P9095	25.1.40–29.8.40
P9104	22.7.40–22.8.40
P9113	25.8.40–10.8.41
P9114	25.8.40–EFA 25.11.40
P9125	25.8.40–5.2.41
P9128	25.8.40–21.1.41
R9001	25.8.40–9.5.41
R9002	25.8.40–31.12.40
R9004	25.8.40–26.1.41
R9005	25.8.40–19.5.41
R9006	25.8.40–19.5.41
R9007	25.8.40–25.1.41; at RAE 17.9.40–9.10.40
R9008	25.8.40–21.8.41
R9119	25.8.40–31.12.41
R9120	25.8.40–29.7.41

No. 225 Sqn, Tilshead

L4753	19.10.39–15.10.40
L4781	10.1.40–7.10.40
L4787	10.1.40–16.7.40
L6856	27.12.39–8.10.40
L6859	2.1.40–28.8.40
L6860	2.1.40–21.7.40
L6865	2.1.40–17.9.40
L6868	27.12.39–17.10.40
N1224	3.5.40–5.10.40
N1250	20.10.39–20.8.40
N1254	20.10.39–12.9.40
N1255	20.10.39–12.9.40
N1256	20.10.39–20.1.41
N1273	10.10.39–10.8.40
N1293	3.5.40–17.9.40
N1294	3.5.40–10.11.40
N1295	3.5.40–31.8.40
N1315	27.12.39–26.8.40
R1999	19.7.40–12.10.40
R2006	19.7.40–17.9.40
R2007	19.7.40–5.10.40
R2008	19.7.40–7.10.40
R9064	29.9.40–8.4.41
R9065	29.9.40–7.6.41
R9076	29.9.40–EFB 29.4.41
R9121	29.9.40–13.5.41
R9122	29.9.40–6.1.41
R9123	29.9.40–31.7.41
R9125	29.9.40–2.6.41
R9127	29.9.40–EFB 9.11.40
R9128	29.9.40–EFAO 21.10.40
R9130	29.9.40–13.5.41

A group of Lysanders of 225 Squadron, N1294:LX-T *nearest alongside* L6865:LX-E. (IWM)

No. 231 Sqn, formed on 1.7.40 from No. 416 Flt, Aldergrove, N. Ireland, within No. 61 Group. To Newtownards 15.7.40

L4748	20.7.40–21.8.40
L4794	8.7.40–14.8.40
L4800	8.7.40–24.11.40
N1213	17.9.40–25.11.40
N1220	17.9.40–16.2.41
N1270	25.5.40–24.11.40
N1276	17.9.40–22.11.40
N1302	25.4.40–22.11.40
P1673	12.8.40–23.11.40
P9056	17.9.40–EFA 20.11.40
P9065	23.4.40–25.9.40
P9075	17.9.40–24.11.40
P9096	23.4.40–24.11.40
P9097	25.4.40–EFAO 1.7.40
	(crashed Castlewellan, Ulster)
P9098	25.4.40–24.11.40
P9184	5.8.40–24.11.40
R2002	19.7.40–28.12.40
R2028	17.9.40–23.11.40
	(pre-1.7.40 examples taken over by 231 Sqn from 416 Flt)

No. 239 Sqn, formed Hatfield 18.9.40, detachments at Cambridge and Gatwick

L4786	19.9.40–28.4.41
L4789	19.9.40–22.4.41
L4798	19.9.40–6.5.41
L4802	19.9.40–6.5.41
L6865	19.9.40–12.12.40
N1254	19.9.40–FAO2 2.10.40
N1255	19.9.40–?

N1265	19.9.40–6.5.41
N1293	17.9.40–31.12.40
P1674	19.9.40–27.4.41
P1675	19.9.40–26.11.40
R2006	allotted 17.9.40–27.4.41

No. 241 Sqn, formed Inverness 25.9.40

N1204	24.9.40–30.11.40
N1295	5.10.40–21.10.40
P1699	21.9.40–11.1.41
P1712	21.9.40–6.2.41
P1734	21.9.40–29.10.40
P9140	29.9.40–16.1.41
R2025	21.9.40–EFA 24.9.40
	(crashed on take-off, Inverness)
R2026	21.9.40–10.11.40

No. 268 Sqn, formed Westley/Bury St Edmunds 30.9.40, detachments at Cambridge in 10.40. No aircraft of its own prior to 24.10.40

No. 613 Sqn, Netherthorpe; to Firbeck 7.9.40

L4740	16.6.40–29.7.40
L4779	2.5.40–26.2.41
L4792	9.4.40–13.11.40
L6855	2.4.40–12.8.40
L6861	3.4.40–16.8.40 (crashed nr Wainfleet during patrol)
L6872	2.4.40–9.10.40
N1295	21.9.40–5.10.40
N1300	6.10.40–3.3.41
P1670	25.4.40–21.4.41

P1671	25.4.40–21.4.41
P1690	19.5.40–24.7.40
P1692	25.4.40–EFB 6.9.40 (crashed Netherthorpe returning from patrol)
P1693	25.4.40–23.11.40
P1724	25.4.40–FB02 16.9.40 (forced landing Scothern, Lincs)
P9078	31.5.40–17.6.41
P9079	31.5.40–17.6.41
P9120	19.6.40–25.1.41
P9176	7.7.40–24.2.41
P9177	7.7.40–31.7.40
R1998	19.7.40–27.11.40
R2000	19.7.40–19.12.40
R2001	19.7.40–19.12.40
R2004	19.7.40–20.4.40
R2005	19.7.40–24.2.40

No. 614 Sqn, Grangemouth

L6850	6.9.40–19.10.40
L6853	27.10.39–3.2.41
N1214	15.5.40–5.1.41
N1225	14.11.39–24.8.40
N1226	15.11.39–18.9.40
N1227	14.11.39–5.11.40
N1240	15.11.39–19.10.40
N1241	15.11.39–5.11.40
N1248	?–21.7.40 (SOC)
N1249	?–?

N1251	?–10.8.40 (damaged on collision with P9186)
N1314	27.12.39–27.10.40
P1677	27.5.40–13.1.41
P1731	29.8.40–7.11.40
P9060	19.5.40–16.10.40
P9076	19.5.40–28.11.40
P9099	23.5.40–5.1.41
P9100	24.5.40–16.1.41
P9121	27.6.40–10.2.40
P9186	19.7.40–EFA 10.8.40 (collided with N1251 nr Dysart, Fife)
P9194	27.5.40–17.1.41
R1991	24.8.40–2.11.40
R9021	9.10.40–31.5.40
R9022	9.10.40–28.4.40
R9024	9.10.40–3.6.41
R9025	10.10.40–24.1.41
R9131	9.10.40–3.6.40
R9133	9.10.40–14.5.40
T1455	9.10.40–11.6.40

No. 419 Flt formed 7.40 at North Weald and based at Stapleford Tawney (renamed 1419 Flt and became 138 Sqn).

R2625	10.8.40–138 Sqn
R2626	10.8.40–18.2.42
T1508	25.9.40–11.6.41

The Seekers

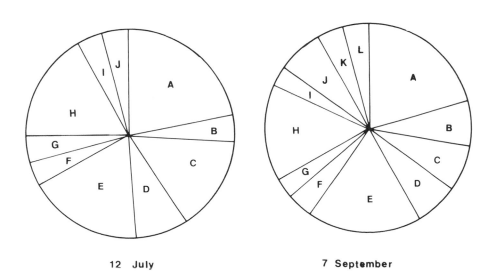

12 July   7 September

Pie charts showing the operational squadron percentage proportions of Coastal Command

LEGEND:

Letter	Identity	12 July	7 September
A	Anson	22	21
B	Beaufort	4	–
B	Blenheim IV(f)	–	7*
C	Blenheim IV(f)	15	7*
D	Blenheim IV GR	8	7
E	Hudson	18	18
F	Lerwick	4	4
G	Stranraer	4	3
H	Sunderland	17	15
I	Swordfish (FAA)	4	–
I	Beaufort 1	–	3
J	PRU	4	–
J	Battle (on loan)	–	7
K	Fleet Air Arm (det.)	–	4
L	PRU	–	4

*each represents two squadrons, two with 24 aircraft each and two with 16 aircraft each.

Coastal Command Anti-Invasion Patrol Areas

From early July 1940 Coastal Command regularly mounted extensive sea area patrols, their purpose the detection of invasion shipping approaching our shores. This map depicts a typical patrol layout for September 1940. Although adjustments to precise patrol lines and areas were frequently made, patrol areas remained similarly positioned.

Coastal Command aerodromes and invasion ports are marked.

LEGEND:
SA1 — night sorties
SA2 and SA3 — sorties made dawn to dusk
SA4 — flown at dawn and dusk
SA5 — flown around midnight
SA12 — short patrols 07:30–08:30 hrs
DUNDEE — Dunkirk to Dieppe — once every 24 hrs
HATCH — Le Havre to Cherbourg — once every 24 hrs
HOOKOS — Hook to Ostend, night patrol dusk-dawn, continuous in moonlight
MOON — moonlight patrols flown when shipping considered likely to be visible

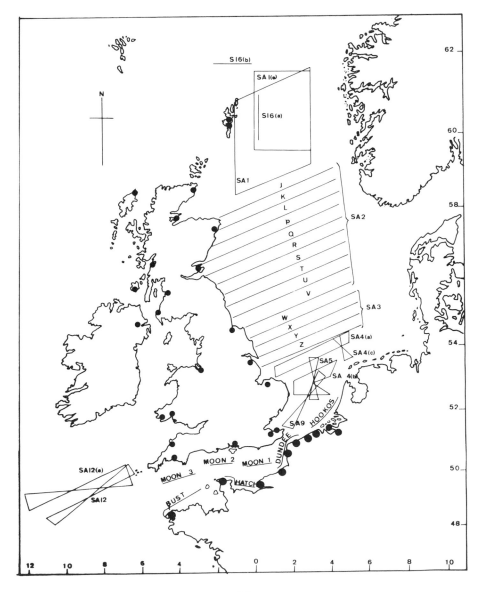

96

Least known, least appreciated, least publicly recorded, yet at all times operating with considerable risk, 'Coastal' was the Cinderella of the RAF. Undermanned and the smallest operational Command, it was called upon to perform in a vast arena stretching along the enemy coast from Brittany to the Arctic, firing the opening rounds of the Battle of the Atlantic while carrying out vital tasks during the Battle of Britain. Bombing, fighting, watching and perhaps most important of all obtaining detailed information concerning the German invasion build-up — Coastal Command crews managed all that. Landplanes, biplanes, floatplanes and flying-boats, fighters, bombers, spy planes, British and foreign, ubiquitous Coastal Command operated them all.

While Blenheims and Hudsons scoured the deeps for German shipping, and struck at fringe targets and scanned the seas for invasion signs, Anson squadrons shepherded coastal convoys and engaged Messerschmitts when the need arose. Sunderlands reconnoitred distant scenes and patrolled over ocean shipping, depth charges ready for troublesome U-boats. Beaufort torpedo bombers came into their own late in the Battle, while the Botha proved ever more inadequate. From much bombed Eastchurch Fairey Battles seconded from Bomber Command waged war on German E-boats whose task was to harry Channel shipping.

All too often small formations of Blenheims from Detling or Thorney Island reconnoitred to the enemy shore risking a pounce by 'Emils'. Not surprisingly their overall losses were the highest of any squadrons during the Battle, while far above in relative immunity and through cloud gaps photo-reconnaissance Spitfires recorded the assembly of the German invasion fleet.

Every operational sortie by Coastal Command was carried out within a very hostile environment, often in atrocious weather and by day and night. As the Battle of Britain evolved into the opening rounds of the Battle of the Atlantic, Coastal Command could face that with skill and bravery dearly bought.

Beaufort L4516:OA-W *of 22 Squadron, and a goodly supply of torpedoes, at North Coates.* (IWM)

The Avro Anson

'Faithful Annie' they called her — and aircraft don't win such affection without good cause. For over 30 years, and wherever the RAF was to be found, sooner or later 'Annie' would appear. By mid-October 1940 the RAF had received 1,795 Ansons. A handful played a vital part in Britain's air defence, hundreds were used to train gunners and navigators, and by the end of the Battle of Britain a total of 396 had served in Coastal Command for whom the Anson had been devised.

Just like its successor, the Lockheed Hudson, the Anson was a simple derivative of a small airliner. Designed to accommodate six passengers, that twin-engined machine known as the Avro 652 originated in 1933 and two were ordered by Imperial Airways. Avro was more famous for its 504 and Tutor trainers, and other airliners, but the onset of the rearmament drive caused the company to consider more offensive needs, one of which was for a coastal reconnaissance bomber. May 1934 found the company invited to tender a landplane design, at a time when agreement had been reached whereby the Royal Navy would patrol the deeps and the RAF would protect coastal waters.

Avro quickly adapted their Type 652, replacing its oval passenger cabin windows with large square types and later fitting a broad, clear strip almost half the fuselage length. This 'greenhouse effect' provided a truly splendid view, among the best available from any combat aircraft. The pilot's canopy also gave an excellent field of view, ideal when he used the Browning Mk II machine gun, aimed through a ring and bead sight, fitted in the port side of the nose. Main defence was provided by a 117 lb Armstrong-Whitworth AW 38 'bird cage' single Vickers GO gun dorsal turret. Engine power came from two Armstrong-Siddeley Cheetah VI radials. Avro's adaptation

Equipment layout of the Avro Anson general reconnaissance bomber

A-Pilot's gunsight; B-D/F screened loop aerial; C-Gun turret, AW11 or AW38; D-Vickers GO gun; E-Draught-proof bulkheads; F-Ammunition drums; G-two 100 lb HE bombs; H-Standard compass Type 0.5 or 0.5A; Type 0.4 for navigator and Type P.7 for pilot; I-Radio installation; J-Four Mk.1 20 lb HE bombs or two Mk.1 practice bombs, or smoke floats or 4 in. Mk.1 reconnaissance flares; K-Radio receiver, Type 3002; L-Position of retracted wheels; M-Browning gun, Mk II; N-Cushion for bomb aimer; O-Bomb sight, Mk.VIIIB; P-Bomb aimer's window; Q-Bomb aimer's nose tip window.

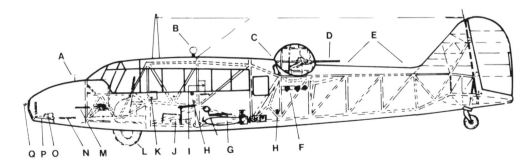

Prototype Anson K4771. *Note the initial side window arrangement.* (IWM)

of the airliner appearing reliable, a prototype (*K4771*) was ordered in September 1934 and first flown from Woodford on 24 March 1935.

Such speed and ease of prototype construction is in marked contrast to that of so many aircraft, and development followed similarly. On 23 April 1935 *K4771* reached Martlesham Heath for assessment, and the Establishment, while viewing it favourably, emphatically stated that it needed far more tailplane area. As a result the tailplane span was later increased by one-fifth. Another hurdle it faced was a de Havilland competitor, a coastal patrol version of the DH 89 Rapide airliner. The two aircraft were matched against each other in late May 1935 at the Coastal Command Development Unit, Gosport, after *K4771*'s arrival there on the 13th. Preference being for the Avro aircraft, an order was placed for 174 production examples equating Specification 18/35 written in August 1935. By then Martlesham had further assessed the Type 652A and asked for unsatisfactory rudder control to be improved before it was returned for further trials. Avro enlarged the tailplane, extended the rudder — which previously would not shift when the aircraft attained over 185 mph — and installed Cheetah IX engines. Larger flaps were fitted to improve the landing performance, and a modification was agreed regarding the

top contour of the fuselage. Between September and 20 April 1936 further trials were conducted at Martlesham and by their conclusion the Anson was in service, such was its speed of development.

K6152, the first production aircraft, flew on 31 December 1935 and served as a development machine. Straightforward was the Anson's construction, fabric and some light alloy covering being fastened to the tubular, welded steel fuselage frame, braced by 3-ply formers and spruce stringers. Within the plywood covered mainplanes two main spars extended from tip to tip. The rudder and tailplane were also of wooden construction whereas the fin was an extension of the metal frame fuselage. Wooden Fairey Reed fixed pitch propellers were driven by the seven-cylinder Armstrong-Siddeley 350 hp Cheetah IX engines. Although *K6152* carried a crew of three, that was subsequently increased to four after further Martlesham trials. The observer (or second pilot) sat on the starboard side of the cockpit, while the nose accommodated a prone bomb aimer's position. Three circular windows in the extreme nose, later a flat panel, gave him a good field of view. Ansons *K6152-6163* held four petrol tanks each carrying 30 gal; subsequent aircraft had 35 gal tanks and provision for a fuselage 40 gal auxiliary tank. On 6 June 1936 *K6153* and *K6154* were delivered to 48 Squadron at Manston so that in less than two years one of the RAF's most popular acquisitions entered service.

Its shape was highly distinctive too, for it was the first expansion period monoplane to enter service, and was the first production RAF aircraft to have a retractable undercarriage whose wheels half protruded to lessen the damage in the event of a wheels-up landing. For thousands the undercarriage came to be the Anson's most memorable feature — dare one say most endearing? To raise the undercarriage meant resorting to an awful lot of winding by hand of a crank lever under the first pilot's seat, the precise number of turns depending upon which particular 'Annie' was in hand! Not until the late-war Mk XI was hydraulic retraction featured.

With the AW 38 turret in place, two guns, full fuel load and a 200 lb bomb load — for that was all the Anson could carry — the all-up weight was 8,500 lb. Empty of disposable load it weighed in at 6,510 lb, about as much as a Spitfire. During a typical $5\frac{1}{2}$ hour escort sortie the aircraft cruised at around 103 knots. A 100 lb HE bomb, or 4 × 25 lb practice bombs, or four smoke floats or 4-in reconnaissance flares could be carried in the root of each 'Mainplane Type 1' fitted to reconnaissance Ansons. The light weapons were accommodated between the spars, with the 100-pounders lying aft of the main spar. Their chamber had spring-loaded doors, forced open by the weight of the falling bomb. Electro-magnetic carriers on the fuselage underside between the spars of some Ansons permitted the carrying of two more 100 lb AS or 250 lb HE bombs. The prototype had attained 188 mph at 7,000 ft, cruised at 158 mph, initially climbed at 720 fpm, had a range of 790 miles and a service ceiling of 19,000 ft. For operational purposes it was the cruise performance that really mattered. In Spring 1937 Ratier two-bladed variable pitch propellers were fitted to *K4771* for comparison with the Fairey Reed type, the former giving a slight all-round improvement in performance. The Ratier type increased the ceiling to 22,000 ft reached in 41.3 min, the Fairey Reed version reaching only 20,000 ft in 40.2 min. In any case the Anson was so ideal for coastal patrol that a second order, for 143 (*K8703–8845*), was placed. From *K8720* enlarged trailing edge flaps were fitted.

That Avro had produced a very useful aeroplane was highlighted by its adaptable and capacious interior. Pilot training aircraft were fairly readily available in the late 1930s whereas the training of navigators,

Anson K8762 illustrated when serving pre-war as 'G' of the School of General Reconnaissance. (R. Gascoigne)

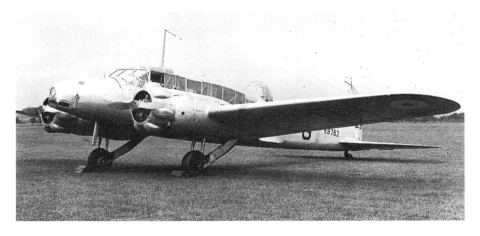

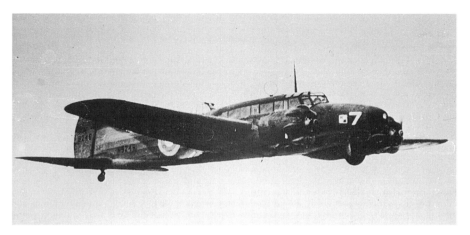

Anson N5246 '7' of No 6 CANS, bearing the marking of free Poland, was one of a large number earmarked for an operational role in the event of an invasion.

observers and air gunners was not so easily catered for — until the arrival of the Anson. The Avro 652 cabin, originally seating six, could accommodate three or four aircrew under training and only 62 Ansons of the second order were delivered for GR use. The remainder, and all 106 with 'L' serial numbers, were produced as navigator/observer trainers despite the bomber camouflage displayed by some. *K8830–8837* had dual control, showing the aircraft's further trainer potential. When subsequent orders were placed, they were mainly for trainer versions along with small batches to replace Ansons sold to other Air Forces who recognized their value. Many RAF bomber squadrons received Ansons to give crews experience of more modern aircraft before they were rapidly converted to much higher performance aircraft. RAFVR crews were trained upon them at Regular squadron camps, and Ansons were also used for operational training in Bomber Command.

Service use and operations

The first squadron to have Ansons was No. 48, equipped at Manston between March and June 1936 and much inflated when it became the School of Air Navigation before being re-established as a GR squadron. Subsequent Anson GR squadrons were:

Squadron	Base	First received	Notes
No. 206	Manston	K6176 — 6 June 1936	Flap-equipped replacements from 7.37
No. 220	Bircham Newton	K6198 — 2 September 1936	Reformed 17.8.36. Complete in 12.36
No. 269	Bircham Newton	K6240 — 19 December 1936	Reformed 7.12.36.
No. 224	Manston	K6284 — 23 February 1937	Reformed at Boscombe Down 1.2.37: to Manston 15.2.37. First sqn to use wing flap examples.
No. 217	Boscombe Down	K6310 — 23 March 1937	Reformed 15.3.37. To Tangmere 15.2.37
No. 233	Tangmere	K8776, '77, '78, '79 — May 1937	Reformed 18.5.37.

Anson squadrons moved between Coastal Command's Groups as expansion took place. Those in south and south-west England were eventually placed in No. 15 Group then, when No. 16 Group formed at Lee-on-Solent on 1 December 1936 with HQ at Wykeham Hall, that took control of Abbotsinch (to where 269 Squadron moved at the end of the month) and 206/220 Squadrons, Bircham Newton. There was further movement of Anson squadrons as more stations became available, and further transfers when No. 18 Group opened controlling stations in Scotland.

The Munich crisis of September 1938 saw squadrons deployed to War Stations: 269 from Abbotsinch to Thornaby, 48 from Eastchurch to Thorney Island and into Reserve status in 16 Group, 224 from Thornaby to Leuchars, 233 from Leuchars to Montrose, and 217 from Tangmere to Warmwell. All had returned to pre-war stations by 10 October 1938, then on 1 November 224 and 233 Squadrons moved to Leuchars joining 18 Group which took over administration of 269 Squadron and Abbotsinch. Between October 1938 and January 1939 10 Ansons were ferried to 4 FTS in Egypt by Anson crews operating from Thorney Island.

Many pre-war exercises involved close co-operation with the Royal Navy. Special air escorts were sometimes also provided, as on 21 March 1939 for the French President M. Lebrun by seven Ansons from Bircham Newton and 10 of 48 Squadron. On 6 May 1939 nine Ansons of 217 Squadron were among the escort when RMS *Australia* sailed for Canada and the USA carrying the King and Queen.

A particularly memorable pre-war Anson involvement came about when on 20 April 1939 a large number of German warships from Kiel sailed through the English Channel and into Spanish waters. This provided a splendid opportunity to view and photograph German capital ships, a task given to 48 Squadron commanded by Wg Cdr J.R. Findlay, MC. *K8704* and *K8771* found three ships, *K8833* acquainted itself with the cruisers *Leipzig* and *Emden*, and *K8706* with *K8707* took a close look at the *Graf Spee*, *Von Scheer* and the *Deutschland*. From the latter a seaplane was hastily catapulted, then flew alongside *K8707* and flashed a terse, apt message: 'Sheer off!'

Additional expansion of the Anson force began in March 1939, with the switch to Coastal Command of three Auxiliary Air Force squadrons. No. 500 (County of Kent) received *N5051* and '*52* at Detling on 19 March, then on 22 March No. 502 (Ulster) received *N5049* and '*50* and No. 608 (North Riding) Squadron took on charge *N5053* and '*54*. All three squadrons reached their established numbers in June, then No. 612 (County of Aberdeen) Squadron began converting on 26 June with the arrival of *N5219*. Coastal Command's strength had much increased.

Among the Ansons a new shape had by then arrived, the Lockheed Hudson introduced to Leuchars and 224 Squadron in May 1939. Its greater range and speed and superior weapons capacity permitted longer duration and more productive bomber/escort sorties, but eight reliable Anson GR squadrons out of Coastal Command's total of 19 squadrons bore the brunt of the early wartime reconnaissance duties.

Ansons commenced operational unarmed North Sea patrols on 24 August 1939, but German warship movements were too distant for them to locate any. No. 16 Group instituted a skeleton watch in its operations room on 25 August, the same day as No. 500 Squadron mobilized at Detling. On 29 August a detached Flight of 48 Squadron arrived there to reinforce the Auxiliaries.

At 13:00 on 3 September a flight of Ansons of 206 Squadron hastily left Bircham Newton to attack a U-boat thought to be 30 miles off Norfolk. None was found, but two days later Anson crews felt sure of success —

they had in error attacked two British submarines.

Luckily such incidents were few, but another on 3 December 1939 proved the inadequacy of the Ansons' prime weapon, the 100 lb bomb. An Anson crew had come upon HMS *Snapper*, attacked it in error and scored a direct hit with one of the bombs which little damaged the submarine. The incident set in motion development of depth charges for dropping from aircraft.

As for the eight remaining Anson squadrons (for by July 1940, although five had converted to Hudsons, two Dutch Navy Anson squadrons—Nos. 320 and 321 — had formed on 1 June 1940 at Carew Cheriton), their tasks remained basically the same throughout 1940. From a string of almost equidistant stations along the coastline the squadrons maintained cover over inshore convoys around the entire length of Britain's shores, each mounting on average six sorties every day. From September 1940 they received help, as much earlier in the war, from Whitleys seconded from Bomber Command and partly equipping 502 Squadron at Aldergrove. That had come about due to the need to cover convoys off

Northern Ireland, and the Botha's failure. The sinking of the *Empress of Britain* by a Fw Condor proved how vulnerable to air attack ships were when some distance from shore and beyond the ability of Ansons and Blenheims to give much protection. Although strikes on enemy ships were tasks given to Blenheim and Hudson crews, 217 Squadron's Ansons made night bombing attacks on Brest and attempted shipping strikes.

An unexpected combat bonus was the Anson's ability to survive fights with German fighters, its slow speed ironically giving the Anson an advantage. That was very evident when in June 1940 three Ansons survived an onslaught off Kent by nine Bf 109s and claimed to destroy two of the enemy and damage one. The Luftwaffe took its revenge on 13 August when at 16:10 Detling was heavily bombed and eight Ansons were mauled. The diversity of Anson operations may be seen from the accompanying survey.

Many Ansons by late summer 1940 were being prepared for shipment to Canada and South Africa for use within the Empire Air Training Scheme. Some were those relinquished when Hudsons replaced them. They

Very active in 1940 were the Ansons of 500 Squadron, one of which is seen here. Note the large Armstrong Whitworth turret and the ample side glazing.

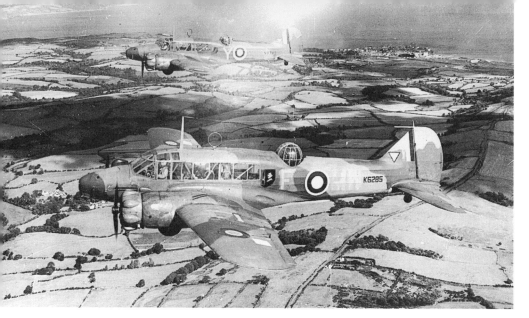

Two Ansons being flown by Netherlands Navy crews, K6285:MW-F *nearest retaining the markings of 217 Squadron by whom it was operated between June 1939 and July 1940.* (IWM)

were taken via 12 MU, Avro Woodford, and often via Burtonwood for preparation and packing, then placed aboard ships mainly in Liverpool but also other west coast ports for their journeys. A total of 65 Ansons with Battle of Britain service in Coastal Command were involved.

Summary of prominent operational events

NB: Throughout the period, Ansons flew — in addition to special operations — many prescribed standard patrols, e.g. Patrols ALD 1 and ALD 2 from Aldergrove, SA 6 from Detling, W4 and W6 from Dyce, etc.

July

1 A/608 Sqn: 07:20 spotted half-submerged He 59 off West Hartlepool — had been shot down by Spitfires. Crew of 4 rescued by RN

2 Z/48 Sqn: 16:30 reported Convoy CV 177 London–Gibraltar being attacked by bombers; near misses

4 612 Sqn: 10:48 WL-F: N5272 (Plt Off Longley) bombed oil streak; red marker flag erected two hours later
W/612 Sqn: 13:10 on W6 patrol 28 miles NW of Cape Wrath attacked suspected U-boat
P/48 Sqn escorting Channel Convoy 178 westbound 12:55 reported 15 enemy aircraft

attacking; 2 MVs abandoned. Two more attacks reported, at 14:43 and 15:00, and by 16:53 three ships were on fire

9 612 Sqn searched for Finnish ship *Lahti*, also for U-boat and survivors of Blenheim YH:L
612 Sqn: 12:10 WL-T:N5370 investigated Dutch ship which left convoy OA180 — thought to have been sunk by sabotage

10/ 500 Sqn: 02:13 MK:F returning from
11 reconnaissance Dunkirk–Dieppe crashed at Sternham; four killed

12 500 Sqn (Plt Off Pain): 08:40 MK:L escorting convoy FS 19 attacked by nine He III and claimed one; three of crew rescued
500 Sqn (Sgt Smith): 12:20 escorting convoy FN 21; 6 He lll and 3 Bf 109 attacked convoy

18 500 Sqn (Sgt Barr): 11:03 MK:G shot down one of four Bf 110s attacking convoy FS 24
612 Sqn WL-A:N5268 (Plt Off Isted) engaged and drove off Do 17 attacking ships

20 612 Sqn searched, with motor boat, for survivors of raider shot down by 603 Sqn 50 miles off Peterhead

21 612 Sqn WL-0:N5366 reported submerged U-boat 15 miles NE Bass Rock

22 612 Sqn WL-0:N5366 (Plt Off Winter-Taylor), escorting convoy HX 56A including HMS *Furious*, attacked suspected U-boat at 10:10, aiding 2 destroyers. Two more sorties joined in, RN signalled 'I think it's a wreck now'.

23 612 Sqn WL-0:N5366 attacked suspected U-boat

24 612 Sqn searched for survivors of He lll shot down off Scotland

31 500 Sqn MK:Z fired upon by AA ships SE of Harwich during convoy escort. Observer Flt Sgt Ward received leg injuries

August

1 612 Sqn *R3413*: special search for U-boat, lengthy oil patch found mid-morning

6 H/217 Sqn: 13:45 attacked a U-boat 82 miles W of Bishop's Rock
W/502 Sqn: 21:30 on convoy escort reported MV *Boma* torpedoed 47 miles NW of Malin Head

9 500 Sqn *MK:B* missing from a *Hookos* patrol

11? 500 Sqn *MK:L* escorting convoy FN 49 during enemy attack engaged by our fighters. *MK:H*, *W* and *R* later escorted convoy
217 Sqn *MW:V* missing from routine SA 12 patrol

12 48 Sqn: 04:45 search for U-boat, no trace. 10:45 searched again off Gunnas Island, no trace

13 500 Sqn dispersal area bombed at Detling 16:10

25 48 Sqn (*K8703*, Sgt Sawyer) late afternoon attacked a U-boat, no success
J/502 Sqn aimed 2 × 100 lb bombs at a U-boat at 55° 04'N/06° 36' W

26 48 Sqn (*R3308*, Flt Lt Rolt): 18:02 surfaced U-boat seen 4 miles ahead, dropped two 100 lb AS Mk III bombs, neither detonated
500 Sqn *MK:Y* crashed taking off, on an area sweep from Detling

30 500 Sqn area bombed at Detling 17:30

31 500 Sqn area dive-bombed and strafed at Detling

September

1 16:36: 500 Sqn area bombed and machine-gunned at Detling
D/502 Sqn attacked a U-boat at 54° 14'N/05° 06'W at 13:55

2 13:13 500 Sqn area bombed at Detling

3 612 Sqn attacked a U-boat

15 48 Sqn *R3369* (Flg Off Brass) convoy patrol 05:45–10:35. At 08:30 found 8,000 ton MV burning at stern after being bombed but not sinking — four armed trawlers standing by
500 Sqn: 17:00 *MK:J* escorting FN 84 attacked by enemy aircraft, gunner injured

20 217 Sqn: 11:05–14:30 six Ansons and three Blenheim fighters from St Eval attempted without success a shipping strike at 48° 33'N/05° 03'W (west of Brest)
217 Sqn: 13:20 *MW-J* attacked a ship in St Peter Port, Guernsey

23 217 Sqn: 01:15–04:15 Ansons (*MW-B:R9599*, *J:K6282*, *G:K8712*, *Q,P:R9628*, *N,S:L9154*, *W,U:L7994*, *X,N4892*) bombed Brest harbour, dropped 16 × 120 lb GP, 14 × 100 lb AS and 6 × 20 lb. PR photographs showed oil floating in harbour

26 217 Sqn: 00:30–03:25 three Ansons bombed Brest dropping 6 × 120 lb GP and 21 × 25 lb incendiaries

26/27 217 Sqn: 21:25–00:25 three Ansons in shipping strike off Brehat Island
217 Sqn: 22:25–23:00 three Ansons in shipping strike/search Ushant-Brehat Is

27 217 Sqn: 00:05–02:55 six Ansons (*MW:B*, *G*, *J*, *N*, *W*, *S*) bombed Brest. Dropped 24 × 120 lb GP, *J* crashed on return.

October

1 612 Sqn *N9741* (Plt Off Watt) drove Bf 110 away from convoy
Two Ansons (Netherlands Navy) burnt out at Carew Cheriton — four seriously injured

2 217 Sqn (*MW:P, N, O, U, T, W*) strike barges 05:30–08:30 Isle de Bas-Ushant-Brest area; *T* dropped 4 × 120 lb GP nr Ile Molene, *R* dropped 4 × 120 GP on Plougeinau. Barges also bombed at 48°36'N/04°34'W
217 Sqn: one Anson evening search for German destroyers, Bishop's Rock area

4 V/500 Sqn on convoy escort 09:55 12 miles East of Southwold engaged a Ju 88 at sea level, claimed hits

13 612 Sqn *WL-G:N5273* searched for U-boat, dropped two bombs on moving oil slick

16 217 Sqn *MW:V* attacked a U-boat with 2 × 100 lb AS west of Bishop's Rock as it submerged and at 09:52 engaged a He 115 near the scene, registering some hits

Ansons used by Coastal Command squadrons 1 July–15 October 1940

(C) after dates = later sent to Canada; (SA) = sent to South Africa

No.22 Sqn (for continuation flying)

N5068	14.8.40–18.3.41 (C)
N5207	14.8.40–15.11.40 (C)

No. 42 Sqn (for continuation flying)

N5053	15.8.40–8.4.41
N5198	15.8.40–EFAO 10.9.40 (ditched)
N5314	4.8.40–SOC 2.3.41
N5359	15.8.40–22.6.41
N9535	4.8.40–3.10.40

No. 48 Sqn

K6175	?–24.7.40
K6231	29.6.38–20.2.41
K6242	13.6.38–FB02 2.12.40
K6279	30.6.38–22.11.40 (SA)
K6284	4.8.39–23.12.40 (SA)
K6292	12.9.39–23.11.40 (sunk en route to Canada, 16.3.41)
K8703	21.6.38–FAT 7.1.41 (Stornoway)
K8706	17.9.38–11.3.41 (C)
K8750	?–25.11.40 (sunk en route to Canada on SS *Horda*, 16.3.41)
K8771	10.6.38–EFA 23.6.41 (crashed Sealand)
K8774	24.5.38–7.10.40 (C)
K8775	8.8.38–FAT 11.7.41 (C)
K8823	8.10.39–22.8.40
N5109	14.10.40–26.11.40
N9895	10.2.40–28.2.42
N9896	14.6.40–25.11.40
N9908	3.2.40–29.8.41
N9930	29.1.40–29.7.41
R3305	18.5.40–3.11.40

R3308	29.5.40–3.4.41
R3318	11.4.40–16.4.41
R3323	4.6.40–5.1.42
R3331	6.6.40–11.9.40
R3369	3.6.40–21.5.41
R9581	9.8.40–15.12.40 (SA)
R9598	2.8.40–11.3.41 (C)
R9629	27.6.40–24.5.41

No. 98 Sqn (for continuation flying)

R3372	17.5.40–12.7.40 (C)
R3375	17.5.40–15.7.41

No. 206 Sqn

K6176	9.11.38–23.9.40
K6178	14.11.38–1.1.41 (SA)
K6288	3.6.39–2.6.41
K8814	15.6.39–4.7.40 (C)

No. 217 Sqn

K6282	?–?
K6285	7.6.39–21.7.40
K8712	?–?
K8752	30.5.38–26.9.40 (C)
K8753	7.12.38–4.7.40 (C)
K8769	14.12.38–EFB 12.10.40 (crashed Trevose Head)
K8782	1.6.37–19.10.40 (C)
H/K8783	7.5.38–EAO 3.10.40 (St Eval)
G/K8785	13.6.38–13.12.40 (FB02 27.10.40)
K8787	17.1.38–10.10.40 (SA)
K8813	7.6.39–FTR 11.8.40 (ditched)
K8829	3.2.38–21.7.40
K8830	12.9.39–8.8.40 (C)
L7994	?–?
L9154	?–?
N4892	15.3.40–13.10.40 (C)
N9888	7.2.40–25.10.40 (C)
N9889	7.2.40–FTR 16.11.40 (ditched)
N9890	7.2.40–EFB 26.9.40 (crashed Rhosille Beach, Caernarvon)
N9894	7.2.40–23.11.40 (C)
R9599	11.8.40–25.10.40 (C)
R9628	27.6.40–15.1.41
R9701	29.9.40–EFB 21.11.40 (ditched)

No.269 Sqn

N9675	14.1.40–28.8.40

No.321 (Dutch) Sqn

K6175	24.7.40–EAO 1.10.40 (burnt out, Carew Cheriton)
K6285	21.7.40–EFA 9.8.40
K8823	22.8.40–EAO 1.10.40 (as K6175)
K8829	21.7.40–EFA 31.7.40
N5202	7.9.40–6.3.41 (C)
N5357	14.8.40–10.11.40 (C)
N9535	4.10.40–6.3.41
Y/N9742	14.8.40–FTR 29.11.40 (ditched)
R3346	16.5.40–1.2.41
R9826	7.10.40–4.1.41 (C)
R9827	7.10.40–20.3.41

No. 500 Sqn

N5051	19.3.39–13.3.41 (C)
N5220	17.6.39–FTR 11.7.40

N5355	9.9.39–22.4.41
N5356	12.9.39–FTR 9.8.40
N9538	?–EAO 2.9.40 (destroyed by bombing, Detling)
N9674	31.5.40–16.5.41
N9686	19.8.40–14.8.41
N9732	6.5.40–EFA 26.6.41
N9898	1.6.40–SOC 6.8.40
N9907	19.4.40–6.4.41 (C)
R3312	23.5.40–30.3.41
R3349	31.5.40–27.8.40
R3350	3.6.40–29.4.41 (C)
R3368	3.6.40–16.5.41
R3387	27.8.40–30.4.41 (SA)
R3396	6.6.40–8.4.41 (SA, sunk en route)
R3434	12.6.40–4.5.41 (C)
R3435	8.6.40–EFAO 19.11.40 (crashed nr Diss)
R3442	13.7.40–7.12.40 (C)
R3466	21.8.40–26.3.41 (SA)
R3468	19.8.40–16.5.41 (SA)
R9632	18.7.40–20.4.41
R9633	18.7.40–2.9.40 (C)
R9650	21.8.40–21.12.40
R9664	11.8.40–16.8.40 (C)
R9698	28.8.40, to Avro (trials) 27.9.40
R9699	4.9.40–31.5.41

No. 502 Sqn

N5049	22.3.39–15.11.40
N5104	25.4.39–26.10.40
N5105	25.4.39–9.11.40
N5106	25.4.39–15.11.40
N5107	25.4.39–28.10.40
N5108	25.4.39–14.4.41 (C)
N5109	25.4.39–14.10.40
N5213	16.6.39–11.8.40
N5214	19.6.39–13.9.40
N5216	16.6.39–26.10.40
N5217	19.6.39–26.10.40
N5228	18.6.39–EFAO 10.7.40 (crashed Detling)
N5229	25.6.39–SOC 26.8.40
N5232	25.6.39–23.4.41 (SA)
N5235	23.6.39–5.9.40
N5236	23.6.39–27.7.40 (C)
N5237	23.6.39–28.10.40
N5374	13.9.39–23.7.40 (SA)
N9765	28.8.40–19.9.40 (C)
N9899	1.6.40–13.9.40 (C)
N9900	22.4.40–13.9.40 (C)
R9630	12.7.40–18.9.40 (C)
R9631	14.7.40–13.9.40 (C)

No. 608 Sqn

N5053	22.3.39–15.8.40
N5054	22.3.39–14.11.40
N5064	30.3.39–14.11.40
N5068	14.4.39–14.8.40
N5195	31.5.39–4.9.40 (C)
N5197	31.5.39–18.6.41
N5198	31.5.39–15.8.40
N5201	31.5.39–21.3.41 (C)
N5202	12.6.39–7.9.40
N5203	13.6.39–13.9.40
N5207	13.6.39–14.8.40
N5357	7.9.39–14.8.40
N5358	7.9.39–4.9.40 (C)
N5359	7.9.39–15.8.40

N5361	7.9.39–21.3.41 (C)
N9742	7.5.40–14.8.40
N9918	26.4.40–31.12.40 (SA)
R3316	18.4.40–25.9.40
R3404	14.5.40–17.4.41 (C)
R9568	26.7.40–3.5.41 (C)
R9577	21.6.40–3.5.41 (C)

No. 612 Sqn

N5268	11.7.39–13.11.40 (C)
N5271	12.7.39–4.10.39 (C, sunk en route on SS *Beaverbrae*)
N5272	12.7.39–31.7.41
N5273	19.7.39–22.12.40 (C)
N5363	11.9.39–10.1.41
N5366	8.9.39–3.2.41
N5367	8.9.39–12.1.41
N5368	8.9.39–3.2.41
N5369	9.9.39–10.1.41
N5370	11.9.39–23.10.40 (C)
N5371	9.9.39–11.1.41
N5372	8.9.39–2.9.41
N5373	8.9.39–12.1.41
N9722	9.5.40–25.1.41
N9741	16.5.40–25.1.41
N9875	1.4.40–3.2.41
N9917	1.4.40–11.1.41
R3333	7.5.40–FTR 6.9.40 (ditched, The Minches)
R3409	11.4.40–15.3.41
R3413	27.5.40–2.10.40 (C)
R9808	20.9.40–10.1.41

Of the 158 Ansons which served with Coastal Command in summer 1940, 52 found their ways to the EATS in Canada, 13 to South Africa. In Britain 15 were still active in 1944, 11 in 1945. Longest survivor appears to have been *N5366* whose career was thus:

Initially to 9 MU 2.9.39 then to 612 Sqn, 1(C)OTU 3.2.41–7.8.41, to 1 AOS 20.10.41, 5 AOS 18.11.41, 1 AFTU 9.2.42, 1(O)AFU 26.8.42–18.12.42 and again after overhaul, 28.6.43–7.11.45, and after storage sold to the Norwegian Government 7.8.47.

N5109, still very active in 1946, was initially delivered to 502 Sqn on 26.4.39, then went to 48 Sqn 14.10.40, 5 AOS 22.11.40, 2 AGS 2.3.43–28.9.43, 14(P)AFU 4.2.44–1.9.44, 83 Grp Support Unit of 2TAF 14.4.45, 83 Grp Comm Sqn 24.5.45, RAF Sylt 6.9.45–25.7.46 and SOC 1.10.46. Of the 'K' serialled aircraft only *K6176* survived to 1944 after being used by 12 OTU 25.11.42, 11(P)AFU 30.3.43–7.7.43, Stn Flt Wick 17.2.44, Comm Flt Leuchars 13.5.44 and Ringway 26.5.44, where it was very soon SOC as obsolescent.

Coastal Command's Whitleys

On 3 September 1940 four Whitley Vs arrived at Aldergrove. These, and four more received next day, were the first to join Coastal Command. They were not the first to operate under Coastal Command control.

The Command's main problem had long been a deficiency in aircraft numbers and the limited duration of most aircraft. To operate deeper water patrols Whitley IIIs of 58 Squadron Bomber Command moved, a few days after hostilities started, to Boscombe Down. From there they assisted Coastal Command by flying anti-submarine patrols over approaches to the English Channel. When St Eval in Cornwall became available patrols and convoy escorts started from there, typical cover being given, on 2 November, to Convoy OB28G comprising 13 merchant ships sailing from Liverpool to join OA28G off Milford Haven. Between 5 and 14 February 1940 No. 58 Squadron returned to Linton-on-Ouse and Bomber Command.

No. 58 Squadron had been no stranger to Coastal Command for, with 51 Squadron, it was Boscombe Down based in 1937 when the station was controlled by the Command. Both squadrons were however administered by Bomber Command. Late November 1939 No. 51 Squadron again found itself liaising with the mariners when one of its Whitley IVs and three Mk IIIs hurriedly took up station at Kinloss, there to attack the *Deutschland* which was expected to creep home along the Norwegian coast. The vessel did not oblige and 51

Squadron's detachment returned home on 6 December 1939.

Further Whitley involvement with maritime affairs was spasmodic until August 1940 when the failure of the Botha in Coastal Command caused no mean alarm. On 17 August the MERPC Committee discussed that serious situation and reviewed re-equipment plans, deciding that 608 Squadron would persevere longer with the Botha and '502' stop conversion training. Statistics before them showed Whitley production rates good, with the aircraft steadily entering squadron service, for it did not draw upon Bristol Pegasus engines which were then in short supply. Whitley operations, although less intense than by other bombers, were blessed by low loss rates, which produced a surplus of aircraft over needs. Suggestions that Whitleys replace Blenheims were not followed through; Hampdens and Wellingtons having higher performances were preferred. The Whitley possessed a good range, and it could be adapted to carry depth charges. Therefore a decision was taken a few days later to divert some Whitley Vs to Coastal Command.

An interim Whitley movement was ordered and on 1 September 1940 an air party of eight Whitley Vs of No. 102 Squadron under Sqn Ldr C.A. Morris, and accompanied by two Bombays and two Harrows with three Harrows following with the ground staff, journeyed to Prestwick. Next day the remainder of the squadron arrived, three Whitleys being detached to Aldergrove for a dual role, operational and training. On 6 September 102 Squadron began escorting convoys off Ireland, the detachment coming under the control of Anson-equipped 502 Squadron, already inflated with detached Flights of Hudsons. Among the 102 Squadron personnel was Plt Off Leonard Cheshire who on 18 September for instance flew DY-Q between 11:20 and 22:00 and escorted convoy HX71.

On 7 August three Blackburn Bothas intended for 502 Squadron had arrived at Aldergrove from 33 MU Lyneham. They never came on squadron strength. Instead, on 23 August, some of '502's' maintenance personnel moved to Abingdon to be instructed in Whitley operating. Then came the first deliveries of Whitleys assigned to the squadron, which by 15 October had received 20 out of the 21 Whitley Vs allocated to it. Operations had commenced on 6 October 1940, patrols lasting about eight hours.

Whitley Vs used by 502 Squadron Coastal Command September–October 1940

N1392 4.9.40–10.4.41
P5010 7.10.40–EFA 5.3.41 (crashed on Loch Foyle shore)
P5045 3.9.40–FTR 21.10.40 (ditched in Galway Bay)
P5050 28.9.40–FTR 4.2.42
P5051 26.9.40–?
P5052 26.9.40–24.11.41
P5054 3.9.40–FTR 18.11.40 (ditched off Co. Antrim)
P5059 14.9.40–FTR 23.10.40 (from ocean patrol)
P5061 26.9.40–12.4.43
P5062 4.9.40–27.11.40
P5063 4.9.40–7.3.41
P5064 4.9.40–EFA 5.11.40 (nr Kinloss)
P5065 4.9.40–30.5.41
P5078 28.9.40–19.2.42
P5081 25.9.40–10.4.41
P5090 3.9.40–EFB 24.11.40 (crashed nr Balquhidder, nr Perth)
P5093 3.9.40–10.4.41
P5096 1.10.40–4.2.41
P5107 6.9.40–17.12.41
T4141 15.10.40–26.10.40

Torpedo bombers: the Botha and the Beaufort

Throughout the war the torpedo remained the most effective weapon with which to sink ships, but aerial delivery was difficult and hazardous. Release was necessary from precise low altitude to prevent the torpedo smashing itself upon water contact. An error in the angle of water entry would prevent the torpedo from running as intended, and during the release phase the weapon's propellers needed to start turning correctly and its guidance system function as intended. Achieving accurate aim and a drop at correct range from the target were often necessary in weather conditions giving cover to the attacker. A torpedo attack was far from simple.

To overcome these problems torpedo-carrying aircraft needed to approach the target on a low, slow and level track which made them highly vulnerable to anti-aircraft fire which in 1940 increasingly came from flak ships providing protective cordons. Losses during anti-shipping operations were high and, since many enemy ships sailed close to shore,

fighters could arrive very quickly. It mattered not whether one or a pack of torpedo bombers operated, the risks were high.

When the war started Coastal Command had only two torpedo bomber squadrons, Nos. 22 and 42, equipped with Vickers Vildebeest biplanes whose design dated from the mid-1920s. The Mk IV (Perseus sleeve valve radial), with a top speed of about 155 mph at 5,000 ft, equipped No. 42 Squadron at Thorney Island, and No. 22 at Bircham Newton had a mixture of Mk IIIs and IVs. Although several times alerted for such action, no Vildebeest ever carried out a torpedo strike from Britain. Instead, they flew inshore coastal escorts and anti-submarine sorties. In December 1940 it fell to 22 Squadron operating from Detling and its antique biplanes (*K4187, K4591, K4592, K4595, K4612* and *K6396*) to escort HM King George VI as he sailed to France. No. 22 Squadron's *K4591* was the last of its Vildebeests to operate and 42 Squadron operated them until March 1940. By then much effort had been

When the war began Coastal Command was still operating two squadrons of Vickers Vildebeest torpedo bombers. K6414, a Mk IV, was used by 42 Squadron.

expended to provide a modern monoplane torpedo bomber for the RAF.

Mid-summer 1935 found the Air Staff contemplating an Avro Anson replacement even before that 'interim' type was in service. Deliberations revolved around an operational requirement (OR) for two differing types. Eventually they specified M.15/35, a three-seat torpedo bomber reconnaissance (TBR) aircraft, and G.24/35, a coastal convoy/merchant ship escort general reconnaissance bomber (GR) aircraft.

As it was easier to develop the GR aircraft was, on 5 September 1935, the first of the two specifications to be issued to attract tenders. A week later the TBR scheme was similarly revealed. The former called for a bomber to fly lone sorties and possess very good observation and navigation facilities, attributes the Anson finely exhibited. The TBR aircraft would be the first British design to carry a 1,900 lb torpedo internally, and as an alternative needed to be able to accommodate a 2,000 lb bomb, 2 × 500 lb or 4 × 250 lb GP bombs. Like the former, it must cruise at not less than 220 mph at 1,000 ft.

Before defining its needs the Air Staff gave advance notice of its requirements to A.V. Roe, Blackburn, Boulton & Paul, Handley Page, Vickers-Armstrongs and Westland. By the end of 1935 several contractors had produced designs, those to G.24/35 being examined in mid-December and the M.15/35 schemes in January and February 1936. Blackburn submitted a G.24/35 design resembling a landplane version of a flying-boat, and among the others was a Bristol Aquila-engined Blenheim variant which ultimately led to the Blenheim IV Anson replacement and a typically radical Westland layout.

Blackburn also tendered to M.15/35, along with Boulton & Paul who had plans for a Goshawk or Pegasus X powered design. Bristol offered a Bristol Perseus version of their G.24/35 idea. Handley Page and Vickers-Armstrongs submitted layouts based upon their latest bomber designs, both unwittingly prophesying far later torpedo-bomber versions of the Hampden and Wellington bombers. In 1936 these were rated too large and unwieldy for torpedo bombing although such a task was promoted in 1940 for the hefty Avro Manchester. Of the contenders Blackburn's B-26 high-wing dual-purpose design found most favour.

Upon hearing of the OR the Bristol team had considered combining the GR and TBR tasks in one design and, through autumn 1935, pressed this idea upon Air Ministry. By December 1935 the Air Staff were favouring such a union, particularly on grounds of cost and simplified production. With combining the needs in one design making sense, the Director of Technical Development on 10 January 1936 formally recommended that, since only four RAF torpedo bomber squadrons were envisaged, a pure TBR aircraft should be dropped in favour of a combined TB/GR machine and that Avro should develop an improved Anson. Before that idea was acted upon the Chief of the Air Staff stepped in and on 23 January 1936 announced his decision — that it would be far better to invite fresh plans for a four-man layout for the combined role, and order two prototypes of each of the three best designs. Whatever the outcome Bristol would supply all the power plants.

On 29 January a start was made in revising the TBR M.15/35 projects, favour remaining with Blackburn's B-26. Bristol Type 150 with Perseus VIs was in second place. During February 1936 discussion revolved around combining the GR/TBR roles and in March 1936 the Air Staff decided upon that course. Blackburn and Bristol, which had combined the roles in its Type 152, were in April invited to a design conference, though not entirely as competitors, for already the Air Staff had intimated that Blackburn would supply Coastal Command needs and Bristol produce an aircraft for tropical service.

Bristol's design now had a crew of four. To improve his view the navigator's station, now in the nose, caused the pilot's cockpit to be raised above the torpedo cell, combing aft being faired into the dorsal turret. Both were told to prepare mock-ups by June 1936 equating a new TB/GR specification, 10/36.

Officials visited Blackburn on 7 May to discuss further the revised version of the high-wing B-26 machine whose twin Bristol Aquila engines were reckoned by the firm to be able to provide the required performance at 5,000 ft for the GR and at 10,000 ft for the TB versions. The RAF disputed this, expressing preference for fitting the more modern Bristol Perseus X while appreciating that these heavier power plants would increase the aircraft's size and weight. Despite the B-26's promise there was some resistance to Blackburn building a major type for the RAF because most of the firm's expertise lay in producing naval aircraft. Nevertheless the go-ahead for the B-26 Botha was given at the end of June.

By June the Bristol 152 mock-up was only two-thirds complete, placing it behind the Blackburn. When on 22 August 1936 production orders were placed off the drawing board for the aircraft under rearmament Scheme F, they called for 78 Perseus VI-powered Bristol Beauforts. Pressure was applied upon Bristol to shift Blenheim production from Filton to make way for the newcomer.

On 7 September 1936 the finalized 10/36 production specification was issued to the two companies. It was based upon a cruising speed of 220 mph at 15,000 ft for the torpedo bomber, and 200 mph at 5,000 ft when a reconnaissance load was carried. With 1,000 lb load the range must be 1,000 miles, with 2,000 lb 500 miles. The pilot's fixed forward-firing gun must fire clear of the propeller disc, and for rear defence two Vickers K guns or Brownings were needed. Bristol's examination of their project led to the conclusion that the Perseus VI engine would give a top speed of 277 mph. On 2 November 1936 they raised with Air Ministry the possibility of fitting instead their new Taurus sleeve valve engine, claiming that it would boost the speed to 294 mph with additional special cooling systems to cope with tropical operation. The torpedo was now to be only half internally carried.

Blackburn received authorization on 17 November 1936 to purchase materials for 242 examples of their design, by now named Botha. Production of both aircraft was scheduled to commence by 31 March 1939 and consideration given to Short Bros. helping with Botha production. That soon was reckoned likely to cause delay and the work was instead sub-contracted to 'Blackburn Denny' at Dumbarton by the Clyde.

Bristol's submission relating to an engine change undoubtedly prompted the Chief of the Air Staff to suggest on 27 November that both variants should attain their top speeds at 15,000 ft. Higher performance would permit faster transit time, allow more rapid and effective search over a larger area at the greater height and give the option of high-level and dive-bombing. Carrying full load, the aircraft must now be able to maintain 10,000 ft on only one engine, a safety factor when operating over the sea.

The requirements had changed so much that in mid-January 1937 Blackburn asked for clarification. Although the modified B-26 mock-up was still only two-thirds complete, it portrayed an aircraft easily and quickly convertible from GR to TBR role, the prototype of which seemed likely to fly before the end of 1937. Fully supercharged Perseus X engines were forecast to give it a top speed of 286 mph. Constant changes in internal layout and equipment being asked for in both designs were, however, bringing repeated delays — not to mention increased weight. Then early in 1937 the Air Staff again radically changed the OR, giving both aircraft bombing as their primary role. It was surely hardly surprising that Maj Buchanan, DTD, visiting both contractors in April 1937, returned to London commenting that progress on the Beaufort was 'very slow', and that Bristol were 'making optimistic promises'. Their aircraft was based upon the Blenheim except that it featured alloy intrusions instead of steel spar flanges which, to the chagrin of the company, the Air Ministry insisted would need testing. The aircraft's weight had been reduced by refined structure and use of light alloys. Blackburn were only just starting detail drawings. The biggest delays, however, concerned the engines.

The latest specification called for fully supercharged engines and a maximum cruising speed to be attained at 15,000 and not 5,000 ft. By 2 July 1937 Bristol were stressing that in their opinion the Perseus Type 152 was incapable of much additional power and development and L.G. Frise, the Beaufort's chief designer, was finally given permission to switch to installing their medium supercharged Taurus III engine in early aircraft. Blackburn unfortunately elected to stay with the Perseus. As there was to be no prototype as such the first aircraft would be used for development. Fully supercharged Taurus IIs would be a later fitment, Bristol stated. The idea was approved by the CAS on 12 July.

On 25 August 1937 both companies received copies of the ultimate, fully revised specification requiring a cruising speed loaded of not less than 220 mph at 15,000 ft when carrying torpedo or bombs. A few weeks later a need for four small bomb containers or SCI for smoke or gas-laying was added. While all aircraft would serve as bombers, GR squadrons would not operate torpedo bombers.

The final Beaufort mock-up conference was held on 2 September 1937. The mock-up had a four-gun turret and DTD ordered that it be replaced by a single Vickers Gun type because of the shortage of Browning guns. When the Air Ministry later wanted a four-gun turret it was impossible to install. The remote reading compass too had to be removed, partly because it would not be ready in time and also because it suffered interference. The biggest problem, though, was the delay particularly caused by the engine change and its novel cooling system, which combined to place it six months behind the Botha. That, coupled with fears that the Beaufort would need a long take-off run, and with only 78 on order, released calls for cancellation. That was too simplistic: Beauforts were scheduled for No. 100 Squadron operating from Singapore or Australia from where, already, there was talk of setting up a second Beaufort production line. Bothas would equip No. 42 and then No. 22 Squadrons of Coastal Command.

Major changes had certainly wrecked progress. At the end of 1937

The Beaufort's rival, the Blackburn Botha, which briefly equipped 608 Squadron. L6264 is depicted here.

Blackburn forecast a Botha first flight in September or October 1938 — about nine months late. An official review of Botha progress in January 1938 revealed production drawings about half complete, with tooling and jigging underway at Brough and Dumbarton. The first two machines would be hand made, the next three jig-built, then the remainder fully tooled. At Brough, where production was scheduled to commence in July 1938, 242 Bothas would be built and according to the makers possibly 20 might be complete before 1939. Air Ministry rated that very optimistic. In November 1936 Bristol had estimated that their first Perseus Beaufort would be ready in June 1938. Now the first example was scheduled to fly in October 1938 and with 350 on order by autumn 1938 production was set to begin in January 1939 and rise to 17 a month by January 1940. To help Bristol in the interim period a stop-gap order for 62 Blenheims to precede the Beauforts was placed on 24 January 1939.

January 1938 saw further delay hit the Botha programme. Viewing the mock-up the DTD pointed out that for the intended prone bomb aimer an optically flat nose panel was essential, whereas the existing nose transparency was fully curved. The pilot's canopy needed clear view openings, screen wipers too, in keeping with latest policy. Blackburn replied that these would cause four months' delay; Air Ministry reckoned the firm could do better than that.

Trouble next hit Blackburn in April 1938 when the company was told that the Botha needed a power-operated two-gun dorsal turret instead of a gun ring, as well as 1,000 rounds of ammunition — double the original load. Choice fell upon an unusual shaped Frazer Nash turret whose pointed top was thought likely to least disturb air flow towards the fin while not increasing drag too much. Weight was another matter, and the aircraft's safe diving speed needed drastic curtailment. Most of the prescribed Botha changes were not of

Blackburn's making — likewise the delays. The company did well to get the prototype *L6104* into the air on 28 December 1938.

The first Beaufort *L4441* was treated as a prototype. It was agreed to fit optically flat nose panels in the Beaufort after the first nine aircraft had been completed because it was already late and further delayed when ground runs revealed excessive engine overheating. It only clocked up 30 minutes' flying in its first three flights due to that problem, and was damaged in a ground collision on 3 March 1939. Necessary modifications were incorporated before further aircraft appeared. Its first flight took place on 15 October 1938. Further aircraft were delayed by a policy causing retardation of production. Excessively high cylinder head temperatures were still being recorded, and as a result *L4441* did not go to Martlesham for official assessment until 17 April 1939. Bristol received it back on 10 May and again set about modifying the engine cooling system. Despite the criticism A & AEE reckoned that the design showed promise, and had recorded a maximum level FS speed of 263 mph TAS at 15,000 ft. Barely did Bristol have time to consider the Martlesham words before Air Ministry asked that the rear armament be increased to two guns! Turbulence aft of the turret also required aerodynamic changes to be made to the rear fuselage contour. On 20 June 1939 the Taurus II was accepted as being the standard moderately supercharged engine for the type, giving better performance at the normal operating height, 6,000–8,000 ft. Because of the mounting problems the CAS approved a plan for the first six Beauforts to be delivered to Home squadrons for intensive flight trials, although the plan reiterated by Air Ministry on 9 June 1939 was for all Beauforts to serve in the tropics and semi-tropics, which emphasized the need for good engine cooling.

It was August 1939 before problems on that score seemed finally cleared,

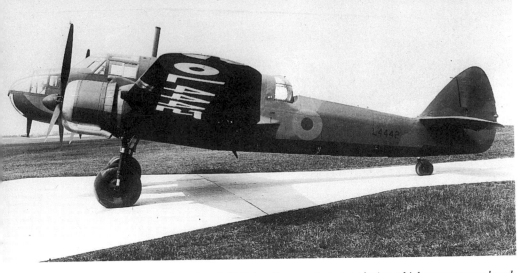

An early production Beaufort, L4442 *has the rounded nose glazing which was soon replaced, along with the initial production exhaust system.* (Bristol)

after introduction of modified inter-cylinder baffles and improved oil coolers. The second aircraft had Taurus IIIs and by 3 July had only done 40 minutes' flying. Engine changes were on 14 August 1939, noted in the issue of new mark numbers for the aircraft. The Mk 1 would now have Taurus IIIs, the main version being the Taurus II Beaufort II.

Overseas use of the Beaufort was obviously out of the question and the Air Staff decided to postpone its Far East debut until at least March 1940.

Arrangements were however made in August 1939 for the third Beaufort to be despatched to Karachi for tropical trials of the engine cooling system and 30–40 hours of flying. *L4443* finally left for India in December 1939. In the meantime Beauforts would undergo intensive flying with Coastal Command. The RAF received its first example, *L4447*, on 28 September 1939, *L4449* soon after.

Although it first flew later than the Beaufort, the Botha beat it in the Martlesham stakes by arriving there in March 1939. Bearing in mind the

Beaufort L4449 *features the more angular nose and revised exhaust layout.*

Botha's tortuous progress, it is surely little wonder that the A&AEE found some serious problems with the preferred machine. A preliminary report issued on 14 June 1939, a week after the second Botha, *L6105*, flew, critized poor longitudinal stability, and even before it flew *L6105* had increased tailplane area. Large horn balanced elevators replaced the smaller, inset type. Rudder control on *L6104* was far too heavy, the aircraft periodically exhibiting sharp yaw which necessitated different gearing and a wider chord rudder trimmer.

Annoying features as these were, they were insignificant when compared with the discovery that the aircraft could not maintain height on one engine when loaded to above 16,000 lb. Although its Perseus X gave 880 hp at 15,500 ft, the power output fell dramatically when 16,000 ft was reached. *L6104* was also rated extremely draughty and when Blackburn made alterations the top speed increased by 18 mph! But the main problem surrounded the power plants — as with the Beaufort but for very different reasons.

Blackburn would need to install more powerful Bristol Perseus Xa engines which gave between 910 and 950 hp at 5,000 ft, the recommended operating height of the original GR aircraft. An official decision was fast taken. The favourite, the Botha, was deemed unsuitable for the TBR role. That task would be undertaken exclusively by the Beaufort upon which development would now be concentrated. When in autumn 1939 Bothas *L6107*, *L6347* and *L6348* underwent torpedo dropping trials at TDU Gosport, it was merely to assess their suitability should the Beaufort eventually fare even worse than the Botha, which luckily was not the case although its 1940 career was far from successful. The Botha had been ruined by repeated alterations; the Beaufort — at the start of the war — looked to be about 12 months away from torpedo operations.

By the end of November 1939 the position was thus: *L4441* AMDP aircraft, *L4442* delivered on 30 November 1939 (Taurus IIIA trials), *L4443* being prepared for Indian trials, *L4444* handling trials at CFS, *L4446* and '47 with 22 Squadron, *L4448* shipped on 21 October 1939 to Australia, *L4449* and '50 with 22 Squadron, twenty-nine examples (some with Taurus III engines) accumulated in flight sheds receiving AID inspections, 50th aircraft *L4490* (Taurus II also in all subsequent 'L' aircraft) in erecting jig, 63rd example in final erection with the jig and production rate now five per week.

Since the Beaufort was now the number one torpedo bomber the decision was taken on 5 December 1939 to acquire sufficient for two years of operations, with 100 being ordered almost immediately. Although production was gathering speed, eight reaching the RAF in November and 17 in December 1939, a report of 9 January 1940 prepared by HQ Coastal Command referred in particular to poor serviceability and defective cylinder baffles. Neither were eased by shortages of equipment to maintain the type. Then came another report, from Boscombe Down, on 6 March. It commented on the very bad single engine characteristics of the Beaufort. To maintain height was only just possible at 120 mph. Coastal Command commented on 12 March that it was thus impossible to clear the aircraft for operations. Another decision was also taken on 6 March — as soon as Blenheim IVs had all been fitted with nose under-gun cupolas, Beauforts too would be fitted with them. Cabin heating was also to be improved.

On 20 April 1940 it was agreed that the Beaufort II (to be Australian built) would have American Pratt & Whitney SC3-G Twin Wasp engines. By 10 July engine modifications were thought to have been well effected after a satisfactory 100-hour type test run was completed. The next week suitably modified engines were brought onto the production line, along with the modification kits for retrospective fitting to squadron aircraft which were to return to Filton as soon as more modern Beauforts could be issued to release the older ones.

On 26 May 1940 the A&AEE issued its report on performance trials conducted with *L4456* (Taurus II) whose tare weight was 11,739 lb and take-off weight for tests 17,705 lb. When carrying a Mk XII torpedo a top speed of 271.5 mph TAS was recorded at 6,000 ft and a maximum cruising speed of 258.5 mph TAS at 7,700 ft. Estimated service ceiling was 19,700 ft and 10,000 ft was reached in 6.2 min. Internal bomb load of 2,000 lb could be supplemented with a 250 lb bomb beneath each mainplane. Later Beauforts with Taurus IV engines could be overloaded to 21,000 lb.

Further increased defensive armament was considered in August 1940. On the 14th a late production Taurus IIa aircraft examined at Filton had a Vickers Gas gun poked from an open window on each beam. It was unsatisfactory because of the draught caused, so Bristol set about fitting a gun poking through the windows.

By 31 October 1940 there was a plentiful supply of Beauforts to draw from, with early examples having been, or in the course of being, re-engined with Taurus IIas at Filton. Delivery by 31 October embraced all the 'L' and 'N' series aircraft and from the 'W' serial batch of which the initial two (*W6468* and *W6469*) reached 37 MU on 17 October. Additional to *L4448* (taken to Australia), 349 Beauforts had been produced. Many of the early 'N' machines, delivery of which commenced on 14 June with *N1000–N1002*, were immediately stored awaiting re-engining before issue to squadrons. Most of the 1940 operations were flown using a handful of the hundreds of Beauforts built. Last to reach the RAF in the period was *W6476*, flown to 18 MU on 31 October. As for the Taurus engine problems, they were never completely solved — except by switching to the Pratt & Whitney Twin Wasp. There was another suggested solution when

on 3 May 1941 a recommendation was made that the Merlin XX replace the Taurus IIa. A month later favour switched to the Merlin 30, for the Beaufort III to enter production in December 1941. A lot had changed by then, and Merlin 30s were earmarked for the Royal Navy's Fairey Barracuda torpedo bomber.

Operations

Following the decision to employ the Beaufort at Home in Coastal Command, No. 22 Squadron at Thorney Island, chosen to conduct its intensive flying programme, received *L4447* on 15 November 1939. By the end of the month it held four Beauforts, very different aeroplanes from the ancient Vildebeests and each carrying up to six 100 lb AS bombs, it was seeking U-boats in the Channel. That activity ceased on 20 December 1939 when *K4591* flew the last such patrol.

Beaufort progress was slow, although a dozen had reached the RAF by the end of December. *L4447* crashed taking off on 8 January 1940 and when *L4446* force landed in the sea off Fort Blockhouse, Gosport, on 16 January the crew was lucky to survive. Weapon trials began on 20 January, using 250 lb bombs on the day that a second take-off crash occurred. By mid-February, with 11 Beauforts on charge, Vildebeests began leaving, the last vacating the squadron on 26 February. Torpedo dropping training from Gosport commenced on 13 February and on the 26th five crews between them achieved eight successful drops. March 1940 found night flying, navigation and gunnery training well underway particularly from Carew Cheriton and St Eval.

It was at this point that Boscombe Down informed Bristol that the Beaufort did not meet the RAF's need because of its very bad single engine flight characteristics. Until the contractor could improve the situation that aircraft could not be released for operations. Bristol worked fast to cure the problems while training continued. On 27 March the first of a series of live torpedo drops was attempted using HMS *Grive* as target ship. Arrival of *L4453* on 5 April brought the first Beaufort squadron to full strength.

On 8 April 1940, and somewhat hastily declared operational in view of serious international developments, 22 Squadron moved with 14 Beauforts to North Coates. Next day, Germany invaded Scandinavia.

Simultaneous with 22 Squadron's move, No. 42 Squadron at Bircham Newton received *L4483*, *L9810* and *L9813*, its first Beauforts. The latter two came from a second order for 137 examples all to be fitted with Taurus II engines, the first two of which (*L9790* and *L9791*) had been delivered on 2 March.

The Beaufort situation was, nevertheless, far from satisfactory. Engines were giving much trouble and there was a general shortage of essential equipment. Crew training had barely begun at the Coastal Command Pool, Silloth, which became No. 1 (Coastal) OTU on 9 March.

No. 42 Squadron, the second with Beauforts, flew its last Vildebeest sorties on 6 April, and on the 8th began conversion using 13 Beauforts. On 9 April the squadron ceased to be operational at Bircham Newton and on the 16th its main party moved to Thorney Island. Two months were to pass before it was operationally fit.

The first operations orders involving Beauforts were given by 16 Group on 12 April. Nine were ordered to Bircham Newton where they were loaded with mines. A tenth aircraft crashed there while landing on the 12th. For three days they stood by. On 15 April the executive order was given, and nine Beauforts took off, at ten-minute intervals beginning at 18:37, to mine the mouth of the River Elbe. At 02:10 the last back landed — Plt Off Fordham and crew (Sgt Greenwood,

LAC Picot and AC Wells) were missing in *L4465*. The remaining eight aircraft mined on the 17th and this time *L4517* crashed on landing, injuring its crew. Bad weather preventing further operations from Bircham Newton, the detachment returned to North Coates.

To play a more direct part in the Norwegian battles the Beauforts needed to be nearer the scene. On 29 April 12 were ordered to Lossiemouth and on 1 May under Wg Cdr Mellor were awaiting orders to bomb Stavanger. The weather was too bad and next day the detachment returned to North Coates, where six aircraft loaded with torpedoes and three with bombs stood by. At night six Beauforts set out on a mining operation only to be recalled due to the weather conditions and the positioning in their target area of a new balloon barrage. Throughout 3 May six crew of the squadron were at standby again at Bircham Newton, weapon loads frequently changing. Afternoon on the 4th found a four-aircraft torpedo strike force ready at Bircham along with a mining (or 'cucumber') force. Five aircraft forming the latter eventually left at 19:30 from North Coates on *Cucumber No. 18*, all returning safely. At Bircham Newton on 5 May the strike force stood by, this time carrying 2,000 lb AP bombs, but poor weather prevented operations that day.

The afternoon of 7 May saw the first anti-shipping strike being flown when at 14:30 six Beauforts each carrying a 2,000 lb AP bomb took off from Bircham Newton to attack a Nuremberg Class cruiser reported between Nordeney and Juist. One Beaufort had to turn back with engine problems while the rest (one of which aimed the first 2,000 lb AP bomb ever dropped) became embroiled with enemy defences. Beaufort *L4464:G* (Fig Off Woolatt) was shot down and Wg Cdr Mellor's aircraft was badly shot about. The next Beaufort loss was in a crash on the beach by North Coates on 8 May when Flg Off

Berryman was killed in *L4466*. Opening of the *Blitzkrieg* on France and the Low Countries placed additional extra pressure on the Beaufort force which once more concentrated on mining until 12 May when six set off from Bircham Newton, escorted by three Blenheims, to attack, with 2,000 lb bombs, ships loading tanks from a jetty at Stavoren. Some 20 miles from the Dutch coast the force was recalled and a likely heavy loss avoided. Instead, Waalhaven was later bombed by six aircraft using 500 pounders and three laid mines. Six bombed a Rotterdam oil depot on 20/21st. Another daylight operation was flown on the afternoon of 29 May, five crews attacking torpedo boats and several other ships at Ijmuiden. Two Beauforts sustained flak damage but there were no casualties. By the end of May 1940 No. 22 Squadron had despatched 50 sorties for the loss of four aircraft. Another six had been lost in accidents. Those were causing considerable concern, with troublesome engines looking likely causes. In particular there were many faults relating to cylinder valves, such problems coming to a head at the worst possible time for on 1/2 June 1940 22 Squadron was ordered to one-hour standby and at 08:30 on the 2nd seven aircraft hurried off in search of a reported approaching invasion fleet which luckily did not materialize.

Nevertheless, and with Beaufort production increasing fast, a policy switch came. Beauforts would now replace Ansons in the general reconnaissance role. No. 217 Squadron at St. Eval received its first three examples on 24 May — *L9804*, *L9805*, *L9807* — and two days later *L9866*, *L9867* and *L9868* joined 48 Squadron at Thorney Island. Both became fully equipped during June 1940 when Beauforts were also introduced into the training programme at No. 1 Torpedo Training Unit, Abbotsinch.

On 5 June No. 42 Squadron with 18 Beauforts commenced operations from Thorney by despatching *L4486*, *L4488*, *L4490* and *L4502* to search for E-boats in the Channel. Next day escort was provided for HMS *Nelson*, then the squadron was ordered urgently to place a detachment at Wick, with Sumburgh in the Shetlands as its advance base, to sink the battlecruiser *Scharnhorst* which was creeping south along the Norwegian coast. From Scotland the first strike was mounted on 13 June, target for four aircraft (*L4486*, *L4488*, *L4489*, *L4490*) being Vaernes airfield in Norway where German fighters were ready to protect the battlecruiser. Resistance was fierce and *L4489* crashed in the sea short of Sumburgh, its ailerons all but shot away. Then on 16 June *L4486*, *L4488* and *L4490* set out with Blenheims and Hudsons on the far more hazardous mission, the sinking of the heavily protected *Scharnhorst*. Bad weather forced their early return, but the presence of the large warship could not so easily be overlooked. On 19 June No. 42 Squadron moved entirely to Wick, from where on 21 June Sq Ldr Smith in *L4503* led a nine-Beaufort force from 42 Squadron to dive-bomb with 500 pounders the ship which had a six-destroyer and MTB escort. It was also close enough to the Norwegian coast for enemy fighters to engage the Beauforts. *L4486*, *L4501* and *L9810* were shot down, leaving *L4487*, *L4491*, *L4503*, *L4507*, *L9812* and *L9890* to land back at Sumburgh, some much battle-scarred.

No. 22 Squadron had also been active off Norway, seven crews setting off on 15 June to attack Bergen, with *OA:J* instead attacking a tanker in Sogne Fjord. On 17 June three crews set off to attack the *Scharnhorst* but abandoned the raid due to bad weather. Two days later the squadron's last operation before grounding involved a search for a U-boat.

With so many Beauforts in service engine problems correspondingly multiplied. So serious was the situation that on 26 June 1940 the Assistant Chief of the Air Staff ordered a restriction on Beaufort flying until aircraft with engines modified or replaced at Filton became available. A crisis situation had arisen for there was now no suitable aircraft immediately available to replace the Anson. Neither the Blenheim nor Hudson was ideal. What of the much maligned Botha?

Fitting the more powerful, heavier Perseus Xa had done little to improve it. Indeed the increased all-up weight made an engine failure at heavy load more dangerous and the aircraft appreciably slower. Those aspects, and not the oft-quoted unreliability of the engines, were its most undesirable features. At the start of the war an instruction was issued to the effect that no Botha was to be flown at a weight exceeding 16,000 lb — and the loaded weight of the Perseus Xa version was almost 17,000 lb. Botha production had nevertheless proceeded apace, the whole programme being reviewed on 17 April 1940. Only Perseus Xa Bothas could ever be suitable for squadron use — and Blackburn stated that retrospective fits were feasible. The ACAS(T) demanded that fuel-jettisoning facilities must be fitted in case of emergency engine failure. By May 1940 sufficient Perseus Xa engines were becoming available for installation on the production lines but it was July 1940 before examples of such aircraft reached the RAF.

On 3 June 1940 four Bothas (*L6107*, *L6123*, *L6124* and *L6126*) had been delivered to No. 1 (C) OTU Silloth where crews would need to train. With the Beaufort also in dire trouble, three Bothas (*L6164*, *L6165* and *L6166*) were on 28 June posted in to No. 608 (North Riding) Squadron, Thornaby, where *L6170–L6174*, *L6188* and *L6388* had arrived by 5 July — while the Beauforts were nearly all grounded. Although by 24 July 250 Beauforts and 150 Bothas had been built the former were in trouble and the latter had never operated. Flying characteristics of the Botha had been much criticized, but the Beaufort too had its idiosyncracies, including a tendency to roll and yaw excessively

— highly undesirable characteristics in a torpedo bomber.

With the Beauforts lying idle, and the Battle of Britain beginning to increase in intensity, the Bothas were committed to action. On 10 August Bothas of 608 Squadron began escorting coastal convoys off Yorkshire — and not without fresh criticism. For any other than the pilot the view from the aircraft was very poor, which made it quite unsuitable for the task allotted. A detailed report on this was demanded from the Director General Research and Development and from HQ Coastal Command. The Anson was by general agreement a far more suitable aircraft for convoy escort for it flew slower and afforded a superb view for its crew. The Botha flew its 309th and last operational escort sortie on 6 November 1940 by which time 608 Squadron had re-equipped with Ansons. Its only future would be as a trainer, and even in that task Bothas provided many problems. For Coastal Command it must be back to the Beaufort.

The Command faced a serious loss of strike capability as the invasion force gathered, and now accepted that, although the Taurus troubles were far from cured, 22 Squadron must resume operations. This it did on 31 August when Flt Lt Bauman attempted to bomb Amsterdam's seaplane station. On 2 September three aircraft attacked Flushing docks, and next evening three more struck at barges in the South Beveland Canal. Thereafter operations were primarily directed at the German invasion forces. Trouble came on 10 September when a heavy fuel loss brought the demise of Sgt Gunn and crew in *R:N1146*.

On 11 September 22 Squadron launched its first torpedo strike operation. Five Beauforts took off at 16:10 for Detling, hoping there to rendezvous with Blenheim fighters. No escort appearing, they proceeded to the position given for a convoy but drawing a blank pressed on until ships were found east of Ostend. Led by Flt

Torpedo release from a Beaufort.

Lt Bauman they went in to the attack. One torpedo exploded on a sandbank, three had electrical release failures but one scored a direct hit and sank a large grey vessel reckoned to be of 6,000 tons. During the attack the Beauforts faced stiff opposition from flak ships, but all returned.

A three-aircraft torpedo roving commission set off from Bircham Newton in the evening of 15 September and this time *OA:K–L4508* (Flt Lt Francis) claimed a torpedo hit on a ship in Ijmuiden. Next it was Cherbourg harbour that attracted No. 22. At 13:30 on 17 September six crews set off for Thorney Island and from there later carried out a torpedo attack on a destroyer and flakships, facing heavy enemy fire and blinding searchlights. One crew could not get into attack position, one had to release outside the mole, two attacked without scoring hits and *L4508* was shot down.

The following evening 22 Squadron was briefed for its biggest possible prize yet, the 30,000 ton liner *Europa* in Wilhelmshaven. Five crews set off at 19:05. 'J' aborted but this time all the other torpedoes ran — but not towards the liner which was only seen by Flt Lt Bauman (*OA:G*) who went down to 100 ft and released his torpedo, without scoring a hit, in the face of further intense searchlight glare. Others attacked smaller merchant ships. On the 20th five operated, this time releasing two torpedoes at a tanker and a merchant vessel, again without success. Another torpedo was released during a night roving commission on the 24th and this time the weapon suddenly angled off during its run. At the end of the month the squadron resumed mining duties, by which time two other Beaufort squadrons were operating.

Engine problems were far from solved as 42 Squadron was made only too aware when engine failure resulted in three crashes at Wick — *L4506* on 9 September, *L9882* when taking off on the 16th, and *L9812* on the 19th. Engine problems also put *L9942* into Sinclair Bay on the 30th and *L4484* with starboard engine problems was burnt out in a crash near Chidham on 8 October. In for modification at Filton the squadron lost *L4507* during the bombing of the Bristol works on 27 September. It was against a background of serious troubles that the squadron was operating.

No. 42 Squadron sent a detachment to Thorney Island while the main element stayed at Wick. Operations were resumed on 28 September by the detachment at Thorney Island which started Channel patrols. Two crews unsuccessfully sought shipping near Ostend on 4 October and were then engaged by four Bf 109s which shot down *L4488* and seriously damaged *L4505* which made a forced landing at base. On the 10th *G:N1150* and *R:L4491* carried out a torpedo attack on ships off Boulogne then both were pounced upon by fighters. The Wick detachment meanwhile operated off Norway.

Although it had received Beauforts in May 1940, 48 Squadron never flew them operationally. The Thorney Island based squadron was too busy operating until early June when four crews became Beaufort proficient. Three of those moved to St Eval in mid-June and nine more crews were able to convert for at St Eval 15 more Beauforts awaited the squadron. Life for all was hard since there was no hangar accommodation for aircraft needing constant attention. Persistently the aircraft's tailwheels would not come down, and each machine needed to have self-sealing tanks fitted. But it was the Taurus engines that gave the greatest cause for concern by frequently cutting out. Repeated testing bringing no real cure, 48 Squadron was ordered to resume operations with Ansons and pass many of its Beauforts to No. 217 Squadron, also St Eval based, and which had experienced the Beaufort's problems over a similar time scale. On 25 September two of its Beauforts carried out a dawn bombing raid on Brest, each dropping four 250 lb GPs in the face of searchlights and AA fire. Unlike '48', No. 217 had been chosen to persevere with the Beaufort in order that squadrons of torpedo bombers could be stationed around the south and east coasts of Britain — 217 at St Eval, 22 at North Coates and 42 at Wick. Detachments and movements common to all Coastal Command squadrons permitted reinforcement and tactical deployment particularly to Bircham Newton and Thorney Island as required.

For the three Beaufort squadrons October 1940 was a busy month with

L9878:MW-R, *a Beaufort of 217 Squadron.*

much training taking place. On the 17th two of 22 Squadron attacked a tanker, escorted by three flak ships, off the Dutch coast, both torpedoes missing. Flt Lt Gibb's aircraft *OA:K* was mauled by flak which injured the navigator and gunner and caused a forced landing at Sutton Bridge. More successful was a roving commission on 23 October when *OA:A* and *OA:G* in low cloud and drizzle came across a convoy north of Ijmuiden, turned into wind and each fired a torpedo. That from *A* hit the stern of a 4,000 ton MV and *G* a 2,000 ton MV whose decks were quickly awash. The third torpedo strike by 22 Squadron came on 27 October when four aircraft on an early morning rovers were able to attack, only to see their torpedoes failing to run correctly. Later that day two more operated off the Dutch coast, both attacking a 4,000 tonner without success. *G* (Flt Lt Bauman yet again) was then engaged by a He 115 and a 30 minute fight ensued at the end of which the Heinkel left with its starboard engine smoking badly. Three more similar operations were flown by 22 Squadron before the end of the month without any ships being confirmed as sunk.

Summary of Beaufort operations — carried out by 22 Squadron unless otherwise stated

Suffix letter to dates: B = bombing operation, M = mining operation, T = torpedo operation
No operations between July and late August 1940
31 August/1 September 1/2B *G: L9790* (Flt Lt Bauman) dropped 6 HE on Schellingwoude

September

2B Op. No. 51, 19:40–23:45: 'G', 'Q', 'C' bombed Flushing; 'G' (flown by Wg Cdr Braithwaite) crashed on landing
3B 19:45–22:15: three to South Beveland Canal, barges bombed
5B 19:30–22:30: 'G', 'Q' to Boulogne harbour
6B 19:30–23:15: 'A' to Ostend harbour, 4 × 250 GP from 7,000 ft; with six Swordfishes
7B 19:15–22:30: 'Q' 'G', 'K' to Boulogne harbour

10B 01:30–01:30: 'G', 'K', 'L', 'Q', 'R' to Boulogne and Calais; 'R' (Sgt Green and crew) missing
10M 19:15–'G', 'K', 'Q' mined 'Eglantine' area
11T 16:10–18:45: 'G', 'K', 'L', 'Q', 'V's intended escort and convoy target not located, made torpedo strike at 17:52 on shipping in Ostend Roads, one ship claimed hit
14T 18:00–21:00: 'B', 'K', 'I' operated from Bircham Newton to Flushing Roads, no attacks
15T 18:30–22:30: 'K', 'P' in Rover off Ijmuiden; 'K' (Flt Lt Francis) made first successful night drop, against 3,000 ton MV
17T 21:15–23:36: 'A', 'I', 'G', 'K', 'Q', 'X' to Cherbourg harbour; four released, 'Q', damaged (crash landed), *K:L4508* missing
18T 19:45–23:00: 'G', 'I', 'J', 'K', 'M' ordered to torpedo the 30,000 ton liner *Europa* in Wilhelmshaven. Bauman located the ship but could not attack due to searchlight glare. 'K', 'M', 'G' released at smaller ships at sea without success.
19T 18:00–22:30: 'G', 'I', 'J', 'M', 'X' in Rover off Den Helder; no attack
20T 19:30–23:20: 'A', 'G', 'I', 'M', 'X' in Rover off Den Helder; no attack
23T 00:01–04:00: 'A', 'G', 'I', 'J', 'K', 'M' in Rover off Den Helder; no attack
24T 03:20–06:25: 'A', 'G', 'I', 'J', 'M', 'U', 'X' in Rover Cuxhaven–Hook; no attack
25T 02:20–06:26: Six in Rover Den Helder–Cap Gris-Nez; one drop missed.
26T 05:00–06:15: 'A' and 'C', of 217 Sqn, dropped 250 lb GP Brest dockyard
27M 01:30–06:18: 'I', 'J', 'M', 'U', 'V' mining 'Eglantine' (off Cuxhaven); only one mine dropped — bad weather
28M 01:33–06:30: 'G', 'I', 'J', 'M', 'K', 'U' mining, four for River Elbe (Yams), 'K' and 'U' in Jade ('Eglantine' area) and Weser — no drops
19:40–00:18: five of 42 Sqn to Lorient: 'R' and 'G' mined river mouth, 'P' abandoned with engine trouble, 'V'—*N1149* — *missing*
29M 18:35–23:00: 'G', 'I', 'J', 'M' to Jade and Weser estuaries
30M 03:00–09:30: two of 42 Sqn. to Lorient
18.00–23:00: mined Jade and Weser estuaries, 'X' and 'M' mined off Heligoland, 'J' dropped mine 21 miles west of Neuwerk, 'G' caught fire (soon extinguished), 'I' abandoned

October

1M 03:00–07:75: 'G' and 'R' of 42 Sqn mined Lorient harbour mouth at 05:08
2 18:00–22:15: 'J', 'M', 'X', 'U' mined Ems Estuary ('Chrysanthemum')
4T 12:35–15:45: *L4505* T/42 Sqn strike off Ostend–Ijmuiden, seriously damaged off Nieuport by 4 Bf 109s. Hydraulics shot away, torpedo jettisoned in Thorney Creek, crash landed Thorney Island 15:45. Other aircraft, *L4488*, FTR

6T	(afternoon operation): *L4502* and *N1150* of 42 Sqn, shipping Cherbourg-Le Havre, no attack
7T	15:45-18:10: 'J', 'U', 'E' to Den Helder Roads; abandoned — no cloud cover 18:00-20:00: *L4484*, *L4491*, *N1150* of Sqn in Rover Cherbourg-Le Havre, no attack
8T	15:32-18:25: 'K', 'W', in Rover Ijmuiden-Ems, no attack 18:30-21:35: 2/3 of 42 Sqn in Rover Le Havre-Dieppe; 'P' early return, 'E' (*L4484*) crashed at Chidham on return
10T	17:00-18:30: *G:N1150* and *R:L4491* of 42 Sqn to Boulogne; 'G' claimed hit on stern of a motor vessel, 'R' released too but without result and was engaged and badly damaged by Bf 109s, crash landed base
17T	11:30-15:30: 'K', 'G' in Rover Ijmuiden-Cuxhaven; 'G' attacked mine-laying tender
23T	13:45-17:45: 'A' and 'G' to attack convoy north of Schiermonnikoog, claimed two hits
25T	00:25-06:05: 'A', 'G', 'I', 'M', 'W' to attack *Europa* in Bremerhaven at 03:35, no success
26T	13:06-17:16: three ('B', 'C', 'N') of 42 Sqn from Wick in Rover along Norwegian coast, Utyoer Light to Brummelo. *L9813* and *N1159*, which had attacked merchant ships in Aspo Fjord, were both shot down by Bf 109s
27T	04:44-08:00: 'A', 'X' in Rover Sylt-Texel 05:27-08:20: 'I', 'E', in Rover Borkum-Texel; 'E', running in to attack a 6,000 ton MV off Den Helder seriously damaged by fire from flakships, 'I' — no attack Two crews of 42 Sqn searched for trace of colleagues lost the previous day 10:30-14:22: 'A', 'G' in Rover Borkum-Hook. 'A' engaged a He 115 for 30 minutes. Both dropped torpedoes at 2/3,000 tonners 9 miles off Ameland and missed. 'G' holed by AA fire
28T	15:25-18:40: 'I', 'U', 'V', 'X' in Rover Wangeroog-Borkum. 'X' near miss on 2,000 ton tanker 16:55 hrs 6 miles W. of Terschelling, 'I' and 'U' each attacked a tanker 21 miles W. of Borkum at 17:05
29T	04:45-08:45: 'G', 'X' in Rover off N. Germany. 'G', released 13 miles off Borkum and missed 05:39-08:45: 'H', 'D' in Rover off N. Germany. 'D' crashed in the sea moments after take-off.

Total operational sorties
1.7.40-31.10.40 = 148

Blackburn Botha used by 608 Squadron

L6170	5.7.40-27.9.40
L6171	5.7.40-31.12.40
L6173	5.7.40-7.11.40
L6174	5.7.40-15.11.40
L6188	5.7.40-1.10.40

L6189	4.8.40-13.11.40
L6190	4.8.40-12.11.40
L6191	3.8.40-28.11.40
L6192	27.8.40-15.11.40
L6193	27.8.40-?
L6194	26.8.40-1.12.40
L6208	8.8.40-13.11.40
L6209	8.8.40-4.9.40

Beauforts used by squadrons 1 July– 15 October 1940

No. 22 Sqn

L4449	11.39-17.8.40*
L4457	24.2.40-18.9.40
L4458	?-17.8.40*
L4459	12.1.40-24.8.40*
L4460	12.1.40-2.8.40*
L4461	19.1.40-21.8.40*
L4462	10.1.40-17.8.40*
L4463	10.1.40-17.8.40*
L4467	27.3.40-17.8.40*
L4472	22.4.40-EFA 1.7.40 (ditched)
L4474	24.2.40-16.12.40*
L4477	24.2.40-16.12.40
L4485	25.5.40-20.9.40
K/L4508	27.5.40-FTR 17.9.40 (in sea off Cherbourg)
L4511	13.8.40-EFAO 5.11.40 (landing St Eval)
L4515	3.4.40-16.12.40
L4516	4.4.40-EFB 18.12.40
L9790	25.5.40-EFA 29.6.41 (crashed on take-off, Thorney Island)
L9791	25.5.40-battle-damaged 18.9.40
L9792	22.5.40-EFAO 29.11.40
L9796	24.8.40-21.9.40
L9800	13.8.40-EFB 29.10.40 (crashed in sea just after take-off)
L9826	13.8.40-10.9.40
L9827	12.8.40-11.9.40; written off after bombing of Filton 25.9.40
L9829	11.10.40-8.1.41
L9830	2.10.40-29.12.40
L9852	2.6.40-EFAO 23.9.40 (crashed, Docking)
L9854	13.8.40-9.1.42
L9855	?-?
L9856	13.8.40-18.9.40 (written off after bombing of Filton 25.9.40)
L9865	13.8.40-19.9.40
L9871	4.6.40-11.9.40, 20.9.40 — force landed Whimple, Devon, 5.11.40
L9879	5.6.40-EFB 2.9.40 (crashed, North Coates)
L9880	22.8.40-14.9.40 (written off after bombing at Filton 25.9.40)
L9889	5.6.40-FTR 26.11.40 (shot down by AA off Den Helder)
L9891	9.6.40-6.1.41
L9892	15.6.40-battle-damaged 3.11.40, became *2387M* (FH 50)
L9946	15.6.40-1.8.40 — EFB 23.11.40 (abandoned, engine failure nr Southwold)

123

N1117	10.9.40–EFAO 27.9.40 (crashed, landing at Docking)
N1118	10.9.40–FTR 27.12.40 (ditched)
R/N1146	6.9.40–FTR 10.9.40 (from Boulogne)
N1147	22.9.40–FTR 6.4.41 (FH 37.15)
N1151	8.9.40–FTR 22.1.41
N1152	9.9.40–9.1.42
N1158	9.9.40–EFA 18.6.41

*passed to 217 Sqn, interim equipment

No. 42 Sqn

L4482	9.5.40–28.8.40
E/L4484	9.5.40–8.10.40 (crashed nr Chidham; FH 95.25)
L4487	8.4.40–14.3.42
L4488	28.7.40–FTR 4.10.40
L4490	3.5.40–3.11.40
R/L4491	3.5.40–battle-damaged 10.10.40, crashed Thorney Island
L4500	8.4.40–29.1.41
L4502	9.5.40–12.8.40, 8.9.40–4.2.41
L4503	9.5.40–3.11.40
T/L4505	3.5.40–4.10.40 (crash landed Thorney Island)
L4506	22.4.40–1.8.40, 21.8.40–9.9.40 (crashed approaching Wick)
L4507	22.4.40–5.9.40 (written off after bombing at Filton 25.9.40)
L4514	5.4.40–EFB 20.3.42 (crashed)
L9812	17.4.40–7.10.40
L9813	8.4.40–30.8.40, 14.9.40–FTR 26.10.40 (shot down in Aspo Fjord, Norway; FH 92.50)
L9838	13.8.40–14.9.40
L9882	26.6.40–EFAO 16.9.40 (crashed on take-off, Wick)
L9890	7.6.40–21.8.40, 20.9.40–EFB 21.12.40 (ditched off Wick)
L9942	27.6.40–31.8.40, 14.9.40–EFB 30.9.40 (in sea off Wick)
L9945	15.6.40–14.9.40
L9965	26.6.40–31.7.40, 8.9.40–29.9.41
L9966	26.6.40–31.7.40
N1145	29.5.40–8.12.40
N1148	23.9.40–EFA 13.9.41 (crashed into hangar, Leuchars)
V/N1149	6.9.40–FTR 28.9.40
N1150	18.9.40–battle damaged 20.11.40
N1159	15.9.40–FTR 26.10.40 (shot down in Aspo Fjord, Norway)
N1160	15.9.40–19.9.40 (overshot Wick, damaged)
N1162	19.9.40–FTR 31.12.40
N1163	19.9.40–FTR 14.10.41

No. 48 Sqn

L4482	28.8.40–19.10.40*
L9820	29.5.40–19.10.40*
L9821	29.5.40–19.10.40*
L9822	3.6.40–19.10.40*
L9823	3.6.40–19.10.40*
L9835	18.6.40–19.10.40*
L9837	19.6.40–19.10.40*
L9838	16.6.40–13.8.40
L9851	16.6.40–19.10.40*
L9853	16.6.40–19.10.40*
L9859	30.5.40–19.10.40*

L9860	30.5.40–19.10.40*
L9861	30.5.40–19.10.40*
L9862	31.5.40–19.10.40*
L9866	26.5.40–19.10.40*
L9867	26.5.40–19.10.40*
L9868	26.5.40–19.10.40*
L9881	19.6.40–19.10.40*
L9883	16.6.40–19.10.40*

*transferred to 217 Sqn

No. 217 Sqn

L4449	17.8.40–4.11.40*
L4459	24.8.40–26.12.40*
L4460	2.8.40–26.12.40*
L4461	21.8.40–28.11.40*
L4462	17.8.40–17.11.40*
L4463	17.8.40–FTR 1.1.41*
L4467	17.8.40–26.12.40*
L4474	17.8.40–FTR 20.12.40*
L4511	27.6.40–13.8.40**
L9796	5.6.40–24.8.40**
L9799	5.6.40–21.8.40**
D/L9800	5.6.40–13.8.40**
L9804	24.5.40–22.5.41
L9805	24.5.40–18.9.41
L9807	24.5.40–FTR 15.12.41 (FH 71.55)
L9826	31.5.40–13.8.40**
L9827	31.5.40–12.8.40**
L9828	31.5.40–10.9.40
L9854	5.6.40–13.8.40**
L9856	5.6.40–13.8.40**
L9865	9.6.40–13.8.40**
N1154	18.9.40–FTR 7.12.40

* received from 22 Sqn
** transferred to 22 Sqn

Summary

By 15 October 1940 345 Beauforts had reached the RAF, of which 123 had seen squadron service. Of those, five survived the war. Of the Beauforts delivered to Coastal Command by mid-October, 30 survived into 1944 and 11 into 1945. Surviving longest were *L9897*, *N1020*, *N1105* and *N1151*, all of which lasted until 1946. Attrition rate to varying causes had been high in 1940, 74 of the total delivered by 31 October 1940 being struck off charge by 31 December 1940.

The Blenheim long-range fighter

Coastal Command acquired the Blenheim more by chance than intent. Prior to hostilities the Air Staff repeatedly considered the value of long-range escort fighters which they eventually rejected in favour of heavily armed bombers. Early air battles proved the vulnerability of such aircraft whose heavy turrets impaired their performance. One explored alternative was to convert some 'heavies' into even more strongly defensively armed aircraft, their task being to give enemy fighters an unpleasant welcome. Lack of manoeuvrability and tactical problems brought an end to such ideas and, after heavy losses in December 1939, Bomber Command looked to darkness mainly to cloak its activities — except for Blenheims.

Thus the RAF went to war without long-endurance fighters. Within a few weeks a serious problem faced Fighter Command, for the Luftwaffe was waging an increasingly effective campaign against shipping sailing between the Shetlands and the Thames Estuary. Short-range day fighters could never provide an effective answer. That could only be given by long-endurance aircraft. It was now that pre-war plans for four 'trade protection' squadrons were enacted and in late 1939 they formed, equipped initially with Blenheim l(f) fighters.

Air Chief Marshal Hugh Dowding rightly considered it costly and wasteful to use Hurricanes and Spitfires for shipping protection duties, so plans were laid to employ the Blenheims virtually as sentinels which would summon the nearest help should likely attack forces be detected.

Barely had the scheme come into play when in February 1940 the four squadrons were switched to Coastal Command which nominated them

'fighter reconnaissance' squadrons. No. 254, which had learned on 7 January that it would be getting Blenheim IVs, was on 28 January moved from Stradishall (where it had lodged on the bomber station) to Bircham Newton and Coastal Command, absorbing Blenheim Flight, alias 'D' Flight of 233 Squadron, which became 'B' Flight, 254 Squadron. No. 235 left Manston for North Coates a month later where on 29 February they were joined by No. 236 from Martlesham. On 26 February No. 248 left Hendon for North Coates. During March and April three squadrons re-equipped with Blenheim IV long-range aircraft converted into fighters by having a gun pack fitted into the bomb bay. These were to be flown by a three-man crew — pilot, air observer and wireless operator/air gunner. No. 236 Squadron retained MK 1(f)s, having a secondary day fighter role.

No. 254 Squadron first patrolled, using *L8717* (Flg Off Baird) and *L6639* (Sgt Rose) on 29 January 1940. Their task was to protect the large East Coast fishing fleet, but they also flew as far as Scotland to discourage enemy bombers, first unsuccessfully engaging a He 111 on 22 February when return fire fractured the spar of Blenheim *L8766* and five times entered *L8841*. Next day *L8784* returned with two bullet holes — produced by gunners on shipping it was escorting.

April 1940 saw a rearrangement of the squadrons. No. 248 moved to Thorney Island on the 8th, there to arm fully with Mk IV(f)s, No. 236 moved to Speke on the 22nd and No. 235 to Bircham Newton on the 25th. From the latter station No. 254 was soon placing detachments at Detling and Thorney Island. The fighting in Norway was beyond the range of the squadrons to interfere from their

A Blenheim IV(f) with four gun ports visible in the belly tray.

present bases, so on the 8th 254 Squadron sent detachments to Lossiemouth, from where on 9 April operations began with a reconnaissance to Bergen. On the 10th two German aircraft and a Ju 88 had been claimed as destroyed by three Blenheims which attacked the airfield and seaplane station at Stavanger. Next day they went again and on the 11th strafed a destroyer in Hjelte Fjord. Such activity continued until 23 April when No. 254 Squadron moved to RNAS Hatston, Orkney, and two days later their Blenheims were escorting British warships off Romsdal Fjord when Plt Off Illingworth (*R3628*) bagged a He 111. The squadron was to see frequent action over Norway to the end of 1941.

Meanwhile it was No. 235 Squadron which on 2 May opened operations off the Dutch coast, then on the 5th *L9261:M* (Flt Lt G.A.P. Mainwaring) and *P4844:K* (Plt Off Wales) carried out a coastal reconnaissance to Wilhelmshaven where three Bf 109s challenged them, putting *L9261*'s port engine out of action. Mainwaring managed to escape only by pulling 9lb boost. On the 7th three Blenheims covered Beauforts and Swordfishes

attempting to mine off Nordeney, then when the *Blitzkrieg* broke forth the Blenheims gave close protection to various ships and their operations. May 12 found *L9245* and *L9404* beating off 17 bombers attempting to sink mine layers off Flushing, and next day the squadron began helping to cover the civilian evacuation of the Hague. The squadron was much committed to such coastal activity, Flt Lt Pennington-Legh destroying two Bf 110s off Ostend on the 18th.

No. 248 Squadron left Thorney Island for Montrose and Dyce on 22 May, re-entering Fighter Command within 13 Group to play its part in the coastal defence of Scotland. Then on the 25th, the day that 236 Squadron rejoined Fighter Command at Filton, elements of '235' moved to Detling from where they provided daylight cover during the evacuation from Dunkirk, leaving others to engage enemy activity off Belgium. Such activity was costly and on the 29th during a patrol off France all three participants including Mainwaring were shot down. By this time some of the Blenheims had twin Vickers K guns in their turrets.

As the evacuation from France moved to more westerly ports No. 235

responded with patrols over Dieppe and on 10 June, operating from Thorney Island, covered the withdrawal from Cherbourg, returning to consolidate at Bircham Newton on 24 June. Two days later No. 248 at Dyce rejoined Coastal Command, initially maintaining its role of coastal defence. Operations over and off the Low Countries meanwhile became No. 235 Squadron's main employment. Seeking the crew of a missing bomber on 27 June, six Blenheims were set upon over the Ijsselmeer by a swarm of Bf 109s and four (*P6958*, *N3543*, *P6957* and *L9447*) were shot down, leaving only Sgt Clarke (*N3541*) and Flg Off Peacock (*N3542*) to return. During June the squadron flew 576 operational hours.

Throughout July No. 235 Squadron was active off the East Coast flying convoy cover, escorting warships, making reconnaissance flights to the Belgian and Dutch coasts and extending its sphere of operations by using Thorney Island and occasionally Detling as advance bases. Flights up to six hours long were carried out, and some support was given to Hudsons making bombing raids. Plt Off Wales with Sgts Needham and Jordan (who had been earlier shot down) managed to acquire a French aircraft and attempted an escape which ended in disaster when they were again shot down and killed near Oegstregst, Holland. In July the squadron managed 747 hours of operational flying, in which it now had further support for on 4 July No. 236 Squadron was transported — with the aid of a Bombay, Flamingo and Rapide — back into Coastal Command at Thorney Island. More of the Blenheims now had an additional turret gun, and a few already had a nose swivel gun for the observer's use. Reflector sights were being installed for pilots.

Meanwhile No. 254 Squadron had been very active off Norway. On 6 July two crews were backing a Skua raid on Bergen by escorting HMS *Southampton* and HMS *Coventry* 50 miles off Stavanger when four Bf 110s attacked. They put holes in the fuel tanks of Blenheim *L8842* of Sgt Tubbs, who was forced to ditch by the destroyer, and they were also soon mourning the death of Sgt MacVeigh. Plt Off Pattison's Blenheim *N3604* was shot down and dived vertically into the sea. Two of the crew were rescued but Pattison was missing.

Busy as the activity off Norway was throughout July and August, the main action had of course switched to the south where Nos. 235 and 236 Squadrons were to be found in the thick of the fighting. From Bircham Newton No. 235 began at the start of August making reconnaissance flights off Denmark and on the 3rd three Blenheims forced a He 115 to alight at sea. On the 7th a group of small ships were strafed in the first such operation by the Blenheims (*N3531*, *N3523*, *P9261*). With Flt Lt Fletcher in command, 'B' Flight moved from Bircham Newton to Thorney Island on 8 August. On their first escort patrol given to a reconnaissance aircraft operating between Le Havre and Trouville mid-afternoon, the three Blenheims flown by Flt Lt Fletcher (*L9446*), Sgt McKnokje (*T1805-M*) and Sgt Marsland (*N3526-K*) were attacked by 15 Bf 110s. During the running fight the Blenheim gunners claimed one attacker. Next day escort was given to minelayers and a reconnaissance flight to the Guernsey area. A further flight developed on 11 August when off the French coast two Bf 109s tackled *L9252-U*, *N3542-X* and *N3553-Q*, and a Messerschmitt was claimed. Fear of attacks on Thorney Island on both 12 and 13 August caused Blenheims to be scrambled to protect the station but no raids developed. Instead, it was left to a trio of Blenheims Bircham Newton-based to engage enemy bombers two days later.

Flg Off Loughlin (*L9404*), Plt Off Jackson-Smith (*T1803*) and Sgt Hall (*T1804*) left Bircham at 13:30 to make a sweep along the Danish coast. When about 150 miles out to sea they saw to their amazement a formation of about

As Blenheim IV(f) LA-R *of 235 Squadron pulls away its belly gun tray us visible, also light bombs beneath the rear fuselage and the twin guns in the turret.* (Bruce Robertson)

40 He 111s which were making for Norway after a disastrous attempt to bomb Tyneside. Smith and his gunner set about one which they claimed to shoot down while the other two severely damaged a Heinkel which was forced down to sea level. The Blenheim crews then resumed their operation during which they attacked a small ship with machine-gun fire and 40 lb bombs which they carried on racks externally fitted below the rear fuselage.

On the 15th fighter defence of Thorney Island also occupied 235 Squadron which on the 16th was busy from both its bases protecting minelayers. On the 17th both 235 (*L9446* Flt Lt Fletcher, *Z5732*, *T1805*, *N3540* and one other) and 236 Squadrons each provided six Blenheims for an evening raid by Eastchurch's Battles on E-boats reported in Boulogne.

'A' Flight of 235 Squadron was scrambled yet again, on the 18th, to defend Thorney Island. This time the enemy was intending to batter the station and the Blenheims fought to defend it with Flg Off Peacock (*L9446*), Plt Off Wordsworth (*N3533*) and Sgt Nelson (*T1869*) each claiming a Ju 88. More station defence scrambles followed although the main activity was shipping cover and reconnaissance. It was on 24 August that 235 suffered its most unfortunate loss when Hurricanes of No. 1 (Canadian) Squadron mistook a flight of defensive Blenheims for Ju 88s and, despite frantic attempts to prove their identity, the Hurricanes fired upon the Blenheims. Woodger (*T1804*) was shot down into the sea off Wittering, Sgt Wright's body, riddled with machine-gun fire, being recovered from the sea. Neish (*Z5736*) had his Blenheim's undercarriage shot about and had to crash land. Flood (*N3531*), who had on the 21st shot down a Henschel Hs 126 off Le Havre, was lucky to have escaped. By the end of a month in which another five defence patrols had been mounted, 235 Squadron had flown 923 hours. Six of their Blenheims had twin turret guns and six had free nose guns.

Since 4 July No. 236 Squadron had also been using Thorney Island, but almost immediately began maintaining a detachment at St Eval for operations off the south-west coast, the Scillies and north-west France — a large area indeed. Unlike 235 this squadron was still flying Blenheim 1(f)s with two-man crews.

First action came on 11 July when Plt Off F. Riley (*L6797*), Plt Off B. MacDonough (*L6816*) and Plt Off C.B.C. Peachment (*L6766*), escorting two destroyers to a crashed enemy seaplane off Start Point, were ordered to engage a Ju 88 which, damaged, had a lucky escape because it was faster than the Blenheims. A further engagement came on 17 July when Flg Off MacArthur took off at 13:45 to sweep along the coast between Selsey Bill and Dungeness. At 14:10 they spotted three Ju 87s, attacked them and concentrated upon one dive-bomber which was driven off low towards France. At 14:10 Flt Lt R.W. Denison set out alone after two other aircraft had to abort, and made for Le Havre to escort a reconnaissance aircraft. The latter turned about when three Ju 88s appeared and these Dension and crew tackled. With a beam attack they scored hits on one. Next day the squadron mounted another such escort to the same area and this time two of the three Blenheims engaged were not seen again after they entered rain and low cloud around heavy AA fire at Cap de la Hague. By this time half the squadron had been equipped with Blenheim IVs, eight being received on 13 July.

A special task assigned to the squadron was the escort of civilian Empire Class flying-boats between Poole and the Scillies. But it was general reconnaissance operations, particularly to Le Havre, that most occupied 236 Squadron. Cotes Preedy was leading a trio of Blenheims in bright sunshine at 13,000 ft in the Cherbourg area on 20 July when six enemy fighters arrived, three attacking in line astern. The Blenheims dived up sun, two Bf 109s pouring their fire into Sgt Lockton's wing. Moments later his aircraft, *L1300-A*, dived steeply into the sea leaving the other two to make for home. Next day Preedy operated again, Sqn Ldr Drew leading, with Sgt Sharp as No. 3. Reaching Le Havre, they dived from 10,000 to 500 ft and into rain. Upon seeing a Bf 109

heading for France they gave chase, but the Blenheims were far too slow and the formation returned to 10,000 ft. Enemy awareness was proven when another Bf 109 tackled them from out of a stall turn. Sharp's gunner, Sgt Chapple, fired into the fighter when it was at the top of its turn, and the pilot then dived away into cloud.

Periodically during the Battle Coastal Command mounted operations combining its bombers and fighters, sometimes involving the naval aircraft under its operational command. On 1 August, after a photo-reconnaissance aircraft reported a large concentration of enemy aircraft at Querqueville, 13 crews of 59 Squadron were ordered to bomb the aerodrome which six crews of 236 Squadron were ordered to strafe. Another four were to stand off as high as possible to bounce any interfering fighters. With conditions fine for the enterprise, 59 and 236 Squadrons set off around 15:00. The bombers made their run, then Sqn Ldr Drew (*K-N3601*) the squadron's commanding officer, Plt Off MacDonough (*N-R2774*) and Sgt Smith (*M-N3603*) streaked across below 100 ft, strafing the aerodrome and nearby gun emplacements. Too much had been demanded of them for both Drew and MacDonough fell to ground fire and *M-3603* came home badly damaged.

Next day brought news of change for 236 Squadron when orders were given for 'B' Flight to move to St Eval and for the rest to follow later. The journey to Cornwall was not without incident for as three crews took up escort of *G-AFCZ* they entered fog off Barnstaple, and then Gladiators of 247 Squadron (Plymouth-based) forced away Plt Off Lumsden's Blenheim, *N3602*, mistaking it for a Ju 88. Meanwhile 'A' Flight continued the usual reconnaissances from Thorney Island. On 4 August, as three Blenheims in tight vic returned from Le Havre, pairs of Bf 109s attacked them from either side. One of these they claimed to shoot down by controlled turret fire which discouraged the enemy. Convoy escorts were being regularly flown by 236 and on 7 August five Blenheims were ordered to cover a convoy after it had come under attack off Swanage. By the time the Blenheims arrived two ships could be seen burning and making for Poole while the remainder, spread out, were heading for Portsmouth. The Blenheims patrolled without seeing enemy aircraft. On 8 August 236 completed the move to St Eval.

Throughout August 248 Squadron operated along the Norwegian coast and flew anti-invasion search patrols off Scotland. Such activity entailed extremely long sorties and the ever-present risk of running out of fuel, which event overtook Plt Off Haviland on 7 August when, after an $8\frac{1}{4}$-hr flight, he was forced to ditch off the Farne Islands, the crew being picked up by a trawler off St Abbs Head and the aircraft being salvaged. Trondheim, Statlandet, Aalesund, all were visited and many SA1 patrols were flown. When ships were found they were strafed and attempts made to hit them with small bombs. Such ventures were far from easy for most ships were well armed and German fighters were usually ready to help defend them.

September brought intense action for both Nos. 235 and 236 Squadrons. Still Bircham Newton based, No. 235 also made use of Thorney Island, as on the 1st when destroyers on anti-invasion patrols were escorted both in the North Sea and the Channel while the now frequent patrols off Denmark continued. There were also some special escorts to bombers as on the 11th when after reconnaissance of the Dutch coast the whole squadron combined to escort bombing raids, 'A' Flight shepherding FAA Albacores raiding Calais and a Flight of 236 Squadron operating from Detling guarding Blenheims of 53 Squadron which were attacking a nearby convoy. Meanwhile 'B' Flight 235 Squadron was protecting Blenheims of 59 Squadron bombing Boulogne. All three operations ran

into German fighters, two of which were claimed as destroyed after they had shot down Plt Off Wicking-Smith. Flt Lt Flood was shot down during the Boulogne raid before one fighter was brought down by Fletcher. Although 53 and 236 Squadrons became embroiled with 36 German fighters they escaped. Next day eight of 235 Squadron escorted Albacores to Le Havre and this time two Blenheims were shot down.

Patrols to protect Thorney Island were still being frequently mounted, three such taking place during each day phase of enemy operations on 15 September. As enemy tactics changed 235 Squadron switched more to sweeps on the Danish coast and protecting east coast convoys from Bircham Newton, although detachments were maintained at Thorney Island for many more weeks.

September 1940 found No. 236 very active from St Eval where it was attacked several times by Ju 88s. Its flying-boat escort duty continued, with some concern arising when early on the 6th the C-Boat *Clare*, homing from the USA, failed to make the rendezvous off the Shannon. Four hours later another three Blenheims began a search in vain for the seaplane. A third patrol left at 11:35 and eventually located it flying over Pembroke en route for Poole Harbour.

By the third week of September No. 236 Squadron had split again, and by the end of the month almost all of 'A' Flight had moved to Aldergrove, there to protect shipping off Northern Ireland from marauding Fw Condors. By that time the squadron had settled down to escort and patrol duties.

The four Blenheim fighter squadrons during the Battle of Britain and indeed beyond displayed enormous courage often in the face of awesome enemy forces. Their targets were often those of opportunity found as often in frightening sunshine as in even more alarming appalling conditions at sea. They fought high, they fought low — bravely, brilliantly.

A formation of Blenheim IV(f) long-range fighters of 254 Squadron including N3537:QY-H *and* V5735:QY-D.

Blenheim 1(f) used by 236 Squadron, Coastal Command

(Sqn moved to Thorney Island 4.7.40. Replacement with Mk IV(f) began on 13.7.40)

K7139	236 Sqn
L1119	236 Sqn
L1125	236 Sqn 7.3.40–25.7.40
L1151	
L1257	L/236 Sqn 7.6.40–9.8.40
L1284	4.6.40–1.9.40
L1300	A/236 Sqn 16.2.39–FTR 20.7.40 (shot down off Cherbourg)
L1305	236 Sqn 4.12.39–9.8.40
L1334	236 Sqn 4.6.40–17.9.40
L1337	236 Sqn 19.4.40–6.8.40
L6676	236 Sqn 2.6.40–10.8.40
L6789	236 Sqn 19.5.40–16.8.40
L6797	236 Sqn 2.6.40–10.8.40
L6801	H/236 Sqn 4.6.40–10.8.40
L6804	F/236 Sqn 4.6.40–14.8.40
L6815	236 Sqn 3.5.40–10.8.40
L6816	236 Sqn 3.5.40–4.9.40
L6840	A/236 Sqn 7.6.40–14.8.40
L8684	D/236 Sqn 4.6.40–8.8.40

Blenheim IV(f) used by Coastal Command Squadrons 1 July– 15 October 1940

No. 235 Sqn

L9252	1.6.40–29.7.40
M,B/L	5.5.40–EFB 3.9.41
L9262	11.5.40–EFAO 30.8.40 (crashed Bircham Newton)
L9393	1.6.40–EFA 29.7.40 (crashed Grimston, Norfolk)

L9396	11.5.40–FTR 11.9.40
L9415	21.7.40–20.11.40
L9446	4.40–20.11.40
J/N3523	7.5.40–21.8.41
N3525	5.6.40–20.11.40
N3526	29.6.40–20.11.40
F/N3531	27.5.40–7.12.41
N3540	23.5.40–EFAO 17.8.40 (overshot Thorney Island)
N3541	23.5.40–FTR 18.7.40
N3542	23.5.40–27.7.40
P4830	10.4.40–EFA 17.9.40 (crashed nr Salisbury)
P4833	15.2.40–9.10.40
P4835	14.3.40–7.12.41
P4845	15.2.40–20.11.40
T1803	2.8.40–EFA 22.2.41
T1804	2.8.40–s/d 24.8.40 by Hurricanes
T1805	2.8.40–EAO 18.8.40
T1807	15.9.40–FTR 23.8.41
T1869	2.8.40–7.11.41
T1946	5.8.40–10.12.40
T1955	5.10.40–FTR 12.6.41
T1999	13.10.40–EFB 23.11.40
Z5724	26.8.40–9.9.40
Z5725	26.8.40–s/d 11.9.40 (off Calais)
Z5730	5.8.40–9.9.40
Z5731	5.8.40–5.12.41
Z5732	5.8.40–23.11.40
Z5741	13.9.40–EFA 14.10.40 (crashed off Thorney Island)
Z5742	5.9.40–FTR 5.5.41

No. 236 Sqn

R/N3600	19.7.40–27.4.41
K/N3601	19.7.40–s/d 1.8.40 (strafing Querqueville)
L/N3602	19.7.40–19.12.40
M/N3603	19.7.40–28.11.41
N/R2774	19.7.40–s/d 1.8.40 (strafing Querqueville)
O/R2775	19.7.40–10.5.41
R2776	19.7.40–EAO 21.8.40 (bombed, St Eval)
R2777	19.7.40–EFAO 30.7.40 (crashed on take-off, Carew Cheriton)

Q/R2799	28.7.40–21.2.41	L8786	15.2.40–EFAO 31.8.40 (crashed Dyce)
R2788	3.8.40–20.10.41		
R2789	28.7.40–21.2.41	L8837	15.2.40–21.7.40
R3878	1.8.40–FTR 21.12.40 (recce. of Brest)	P/L8840	15.2.40–FTR 15.4.41
		C/L8841	15.2.40–2.9.42
R/R3886	28.7.40–30.12.40	L8842	15.2.40–EFB 6.7.40 (ditched)
P/T1806	24.8.40–EFB 25.3.41	N/L9176	27.6.40–20.11.41
F/T1809	24.8.40–24.1.42	L9299	6.6.40–SOC 1.8.40
E/T1810	28.7.40–30.8.41	K,V/L9313	27.6.40–EFA 24.12.41 (ditched)
T1811	28.7.40–FTR 10.9.41	D/L9406	13.4.40–FTR 22.3.41
G/T1812	28.7.40–15.3.41	L9407	13.4.40–EFA 25.8.40 (undershot Dyce)
J/T1942	4.8.40–EFB 24.2.41		
Z/T1943	28.7.40–5.9.41	A/L9408	16.4.40–28.7.41
T1944	4.8.40–EAO 21.8.40 (bombed, St Eval)	N3524	1.6.40–FTR 5.6.41
		D/N3528	13.4.40–FTR 11.2.41
T1945	28.7.40–14.7.41	N3529	13.4.40–EFAO 3.9.40?
T1947	28.7.40–20.8.41	N3530	2.6.40–FTR 9.10.40
T1954	6.9.40–11.12.40	N3608	9.7.40–EFAO 3.9.40
Z5729	3.8.40–7.4.41	H/N3609	9.7.40–FTR 9.4.41
Z5733	3.8.40–FTR 10.3.41	F/N3610	14.7.40–1.1.41
Z5734	3.8.40–22.7.41	N3611	26.7.40–3.7.42
Z5735	3.8.40–20.8.41	R/N3612	27.6.40–24.4.42
Z5736	3.8.40–29.4.41	L/R3623	21.4.40–17.4.41
Z5737	3.8.40–26.5.41	P/R3629	21.4.40–EAO 25.10.40 (bombed, Montrose)
Z5738	3.8.40–26.5.41		
Z5739	24.8.40–26.4.41	O/R3827	19.6.40–EFB 4.3.41
Z5740	24.8.40–29.4.41	R3887	17.6.40–EFA 22.7.40 (crashed Sumburgh)
Z5743	16.8.40–5.1.42		
Z5755	26.9.40–EFB 21.3.41	Q/R3888	27.6.40–27.12.41
		H/T1952	6.9.40–14.10.40 (crashed, Aberdeen beach)

No. 248 Sqn

		G/T1953	6.9.40–EFB 28.2.41
L9302	22.4.40–4.7.40	Z5726	28.8.40–6.12.40
Q/L9392	22.4.40–FTR 3.11.40		
O/L9394	25.5.40–9.8.41		
L9448	22.4.40–?		
L9449	22.4.40–FTR 27.8.40 (from Norway)		
H/L9450	22.4.40–FTR 4.3.41		
V/L9451	22.4.40–FTR 13.9.40 (Statlandet area)		
K/L9452	22.4.40–30.7.40		
X/L9453	21.5.40–FTR 20.10.40		
L9454	21.5.40–9.8.41		
L9455	17.5.40–EFAO 13.12.40		
S/L9456	22.4.40–FTR 7.8.40 (ditched off Farne Is, from Norway)		
S/L9457	22.4.40–FTR 19.8.40 (from Norway)		
N3536	29.6.40–3.2.41		
N6194	18.2.40–5.4.41		
Y/N6233	9.3.40–EFB 10.1.41		
N6239	22.2.40–10.3.41		
P4825	21.2.40–31.1.41		
P4831	22.2.40–21.12.40		
P4847	15.2.40–30.12.40		
P6952	25.5.40–FTR 20.10.40		
B/R3625	21.4.40–EFAO 13.12.40 (ditched)		
R3626	21.4.40–FTR 1.10.40 (from Norway)		
T1808	17.9.40–12.11.40		
T1997	7.10.40–EFA 16.12.40		
T2078	1.9.40–6.7.41		
Z5723	22.8.40–24.7.41		

No. 254 Sqn

L8783	15.2.40–22.6.42
L8785	15.2.40–3.9.40

Of the 125 Blenheim IV(f)s used by Coastal Command squadrons, 20 were destroyed as a result of operations, six crashing during operational flying. In all, Coastal Command squadrons during the Battle operated 206 Blenheims, 35 of which (17 per cent) failed to return, 11 (53 per cent) were written off due to battle damage, 11 were written off due to accidents during operational flying, eight variously crashed and nine were destroyed by bombing — a total of 74 write-offs, or 36 per cent.

Blenheims for reconnaissance and bombing

Ordered as a long-range reconnaissance and photographic aircraft for the Army, it was in that role that the Blenheim IV entered squadron service on 19 January 1939 when *LS4835* was received by Odiham-based No. 53 Squadron which was fully equipped by March. Then on 16 March the other 50 Wing squadron, Andover's No. 59, began receiving Mk IVs and trained pre-war with Aldershot Southern Command. Both were within 22 (AC) Group and administered by Fighter Command. Coastal Command's first Blenheim IV was *L4846*, tried by 217 Squadron between March and August 1939.

Both squadrons entered the BEF's Air Component in September 1939 and moved to France. No. 53's operations began early on 29 September, Sqn Ldr Clements (*L4842*) and Plt Off Read (*L4841*) flying night sorties over north-west Germany. A limited number of such sorties were flown by No. 53 but No. 59 did not operate before May 1940 when both squadrons busily monitored the German *Blitzkrieg* before No. 53 Squadron withdrew to Andover on 20 May, replaced its losses and two days later began daily operations using Hawkinge as its advance base. No. 59 Squadron commenced return to Andover on 24 May and was complete at Odiham by 10 June 1940 from where some PR sorties were flown over France. On 1 June No. 53 Squadron re-established itself at Eastchurch, and continued operations before moving to Gatwick on 13 June, from where it last operated on the 18th.

After France fell the future employment of the squadrons needed to be faced, their main *raison d'être* having been swept away. Both returned to 22 Group control on 23 June, and then came the decision to utilize their reconnaissance expertise in Coastal Command. No. 53 was ordered to Detling (16 Group) and No. 59 to Thorney Island (15 Group), each Group inheriting a highly skilled and tough squadron.

Coastal Command was delighted with its acquisition and within minutes of handover on 5 July had both squadrons operating, No. 53 flying SA9, 'Dundee' and 'Hookos' patrols at the eastern end of the English Channel and also observing shipping in ports between Boulogne and Flushing. No. 59 watched the western end by mounting SA 11s, 'Hatch' and 'Moon' patrols, and observed activity between Dieppe and Lorient. Invariably, each patrol was carried out by one very vulnerable aircraft — with inevitable results. The obvious course of events was confirmed from the start when on 5 July Flt Lt G.T. Palmer's 59 Squadron Blenheim was chased then engaged by three Bf 109s off Dungeness. Next day the 59 Squadron Blenheim of Plt Off A.J. Roe was attacked by two Bf 109s for ten minutes during which encounter the barrel of the turret Vickers gun was shot away!

Very soon both squadrons mounted specially called for reconnaissances. No. 53 began 'Traffic' sorties — observation of road and rail movement around Calais, Dunkirk and St Omer, and during one early patrol Plt Off Mallon discovered Boulogne to be the lair of He 59 floatplanes. Coastal Command was not, however, content to use its Blenheims just for reconnaissance and on 6 July began employing them as strike bombers when five (Operation No. 36) were sent to attack barges in the Ijmuiden–Amsterdam canal. With that began a hazardous, costly series of day and night raids directed against shipping and fringe targets. Next day

'53' went to Ostend and on the 9th tried to bomb E-boats off their Boulogne lair. Thereafter the squadron repeatedly bombed targets including Amsterdam, Flushing, Ghent and Rotterdam. By the end of July No. 53 had despatched 264 operational sorties and flown 641 operational hours, thus exceeding the prescribed total for a GR landplane squadron of 256 sorties.

To the west No. 59 had been equally busy, and mounted two 'spy flights' to Brest on 8 July. Night operations even in summer could end disastrously, as was dramatically illustrated on 9 July when Plt Off Rex, returning from Le Havre and failing to locate Thorney Island, eventually crashed at Peterstone, near Cardiff. His aircraft was burnt out and two of the crew were killed. Less fortunate was Plt Off A.D. Hopkins and crew, for all were killed in a crash at Tenbury. It was usual on anti-invasion patrols to carry bombs, and on the 12th a 59 Squadron crew showed a typical use for them by unloading on an airfield near Boulogne. Coastal airfields, particularly around Cherbourg, at Le Touquet, Caen and around Brest, were often attacked when no surface vessels were observed. With more targets in 16 Group area, No. 59 Squadron often operated there, making its first bombing strike with eight aircraft on oil tanks at Ghent on 14 July and repeating it on the 17th. Although on the 22nd '59' bombed barges in Amsterdam and next night more at Flushing, daylight reconnaissance flights were the norm. Sometimes Blenheim fighters escorted the spying aircraft, as on 20 July when all was far from well. Bf 109s tackled the escort, destroying one over Le Havre and leaving Plt Off C.M.M. Grece to fight his own way home.

On 1 August 59 Squadron mounted a 13-aircraft midday medium level formation attack on Cherbourg. All the participants bombed the target area, but W/C Weldon-Smith was shot down. In addition to search and strike operations the squadrons also escorted Channel convoys, No. 59

seeking survivors of ships sunk on 8 August after a Channel convoy was attacked at dawn by E-boats and later dive-bombed. Next day '59' responded with a dusk raid on Guernsey's fighter airfield. The Channel was universally hostile and when on the 14th three 59 Squadron crews searched for warships off Boulogne they were chased away by Hurricanes. Like their fighter Blenheim companions at Thorney Island No. 59 also flew aerodrome defence patrols — in their bomber Blenheims — when attack seemed likely.

No. 53 Squadron concentrated throughout August on SA 9, 'Hookos' and 'Dundee' patrols, interspersing them with special strikes on Flushing's oil stores and Den Helder docks. When Detling was dive-bombed in late afternoon on 13 August the squadron suffered heavily, particularly when machine-gunning Bf 109s set fire to five bombed-up Blenheims and seriously damaged another pair. Sqn Ldr D.C. Oliver and four more squadron men were killed and five seriously wounded. Nevertheless, patrols continued and strikes were resumed on 21 August when five Blenheims carried out Operation 50 against Abbeville. Next day St Omer airfield was bombed, and when clouds gave cover individual Blenheims bombed airfields. At the end of August Detling was subjected to two more sharp raids, in the second of which Bf 109s strafed the airfield. and on 1 September it was again dive-bombed. Incendiaries and HEs rained down after dark damaging the MT Section. Although the destruction of Detling barely crippled Britain's defences, the enemy appreciated its front line value in the event of invasion, and must have known that its aircraft carried out night and day watch upon German preparations. Detling, on that basis, was a worthwhile target and on both 2 and 4 September the Luftwaffe carpet-bombed the station, hitting dispersal areas but luckily without causing squadron casualties. Next afternoon

Bf 109s dive-bombed remaining buildings.

As the Germans massed barges for the invasion the two squadrons observed and bombed them. With invasion reckoned imminent No. 53 Squadron raided Boulogne's concentrations on the evening of 7 September as the Luftwaffe attacked London, and during the following afternoon struck at shipping off Calais losing two aircraft and crews. On the 9th the squadron again called upon Boulogne and next day tried to sink three merchant ships off Calais.

HQ Coastal Command on 11 September ordered its largest anti-shipping strike so far after No. 53 Squadron shadowed a large convoy sailing west from Ostend. At 16:45, with the array of ships four miles west of Calais, five Blenheims of 53 Squadron, six of No. 59, five Beauforts of No. 22 and six Albacores with an escort of a dozen Blenheim IV(f)s of 235 and 236 Squadrons struck with limited success. Two days later three crews of 53 Squadron attacked another convoy, this time off Boulogne whose barges were bombed at night by 59 Squadron. On 15 September five 53 Squadron Blenheims marked the great day by smiting shipping in the entrance to Boulogne before joining with '59' in a night strike on Le Havre. On the 17th a large scale night attack on Cherbourg was carried out by a combined force of Nos. 53, 59, 22 and 826 Squadrons. Next night No. 59 returned while '53' hit at barges in Den Helder, repeating that raid on the 20th when operating from Bircham Newton to avoid the huge London night barrage.

Shipping off Cap Gris Nez was again attacked in daylight on the 21st, by six of 53 Squadron, and early on the 23rd and again on the 24th raids were mounted on Flushing and Zeebrugge to distract enemy attention from Royal Navy minelayers operating off the two harbours. Meanwhile, the immediate threat of invasion lifted, 59 Squadron on the 22nd and 23rd commenced bombing attacks on Lorient in a new phase of operations. Throughout the more spectacular operations the SAs, 'Dundees', 'Hookos' and 'Hatch' patrols continued, making life for Nos. 53 and 59 Squadrons hectic and hazardous. Between 1 July and 30 September the two squadrons worked through 81 Blenheims, of which 19 failed to return from operations, giving the horrendously high loss rate of 23 per cent. Another 13 Blenheims were written off or crashed due to battle damage and two more crashed during operational flying, making the overall loss on operations no less than 39 per cent of entire strength. By any reckoning that is horrific. The courage displayed by all who flew with '53' and '59', and the many who died, is immeasurable.

Blenheim IV — Coastal Command General Reconnaissance Bomber Aircraft

L4849 53 Sqn 6.3.39, to 5 MU 17.8.40
L8789 53 Sqn 19.6.40-FTR 27.10.40 (Channel shipping strike)
L8791 Y/59 Sqn 23.5.40-16.2.41
L8792 59 Sqn 23.5.40-FTR 1.8.40 (from Cherbourg)
L8793 M/59 Sqn 23.5.40-EFB 25.9.40 (crashed approaching Thorney Island)
L8794 53 Sqn 19.6.40-EFAO 4.8.40 (crashed nr Churt)
L9043 53 Sqn 28.8.40-EFAO 28.12.40 (crashed taking off, Thorney Island)
L9238 53 Sqn 15.5.40, to 13 CTU 15.11.40
L9273 59 Sqn 18.6.40-21.7.40
L9463 L/59 Sqn 11.4.40-EFB 30.11.40
L9471 53 Sqn 28.5.40-SOC 31.3.42
L9473 K/59 Sqn 25.7.40-FTR 25.7.40 from sea rescue
L9474 53 Sqn 28.5.40-EFB 13.7.40 (crashed Bulpham, Essex)
L9475 53 Sqn 28.5.40-FTR 4.8.40 from Emden
N3537 59 Sqn 18.6.40-EFB 1.12.40 (crashed Thorney Island)
N3551 53 Sqn 26.5.40-FTR 14.7.40 from Ghent
N3586 59 Sqn 28.7.40, to 143 Sqn 6.7.42
N3587 59 Sqn 28.7.40-FTR 2.8.40
N3590 59 Sqn 19.6.40-FTR 8.8.40 (recce Cherbourg)
N3615 59 Sqn 18.8.40-FTR 28.4.41
N3630 53 Sqn 14.8.40-FTR 26.11.40
N6169 59 Sqn 25.5.40-FTR 21.8.41
N6195 8 MU, to 53 Sqn 12.9.40-?

P4850 53 Sqn 12.9.40–FTR 11.3.41
R2771 53 Sqn 21.7.40–EFB 5.10.40 (crashed Manston)
R2773 53 Sqn 6.8.40–FTR 4.1.41
R2783 59 Sqn 4.8.40–FTR 23.11.40 from Lorient
R2785 59 Sqn 4.8.40, to 105 Sqn 28.8.41
R2794 F/59 Sqn 11.8.40–EFAO 28.8.40 (crashed Littlehampton)
R2795 59 Sqn 11.8.40–FTR 19.8.40 from Caen
R3631 59 Sqn 17.6.40–FTR 21.8.41
R3635 59 Sqn 28.5.40–FTR 20.9.40
R3637 59 Sqn 28.5.40–EFB 7.7.40 (crashed nr Ludlow)
R3639 Z/59 Sqn 28.5.40–EFB 23.7.40 (crashed Thorney Island)
R3640 53 Sqn 28.5.40–27.8.40
R3668 D/59 Sqn 8.6.40–15.12.41
R3677 53 Sqn 5.6.40–EAO 13.8.40 (bombed at Detling)
R3678 53 Sqn 5.6.40–1.1.41
R3694 59 Sqn 23.5.40–FTR 17.7.40 from Cherbourg
R3697 53 Sqn 10.5.40–EFB 21.10.40 (crashed nr Eastchurch)
R3779 53 Sqn 5.6.40–FTR 8.9.40 from strike off Calais
R3819 53 Sqn 14.6.40–EAO 13.8.40 (bombed at Detling)
R3833 59 Sqn 21.8.40–4.5.41
R3835 59 Sqn 17.7.40–EAO 16.8.40 (bombed at Manston)
R3836 X/53 Sqn 17.7.40–FTR 25.7.40 from SA 9
R3837 59 Sqn 21.8.40–9.10.40
R3844 59 Sqn 20.6.40, to 105 Sqn 3.8.41
R3849 53 Sqn 14.6.40–EAO 13.8.40 (bombed at Detling)
R3880 S/59 Sqn 20.6.40–FTR 31.8.40
R3881 59 Sqn 20.6.40–EFB 11.7.40 (crashed)
R3889 S/59 Sqn 3.7.40–FTR 26.11.40
R3890 59 Sqn 3.7.40–FTR 16.7.41
R3909 53 Sqn 14.6.40–17.9.40
T1801 59 Sqn 19.6.40–FTR 26.7.40 from Cherbourg
T1802 53 Sqn 27.7.40–26.4.41
T1815 59 Sqn 24.7.40–EAO 16.8.40 (bombed at Thorney Island)
T1816 53 Sqn 3.8.40–FTR 11.8.40 from Dundee II
T1874 59 Sqn 15.8.40, to RAE 17.12.40
T1880 P/59 Sqn 19.7.40–EFB 1.9.40 (crashed Thorney Island, from Lorient)
T1937 53 Sqn 7.40–EFB 13.8.40 (crashed Hawkhurst)
T1938 53 Sqn 7.40–EAO 13.8.40 (bombed at Detling)
T1940 53 Sqn 15.8.40–FTR 31.8.40 from Vlaardingen
T1991 59 Sqn ?–?
T1992 53 Sqn 7.8.40–FTR 5.2.41
T2035 F/53 Sqn ?–EFB 24.8.40 (crashed Dover)
T2036 53 Sqn ?–FTR 8.10.40 from Gravelines
T2040 59 Sqn 22.8.40–7.3.41
T2042 53 Sqn 18.8.40–FTR 8.9.40 from convoy attack
T2043 53 Sqn 25.8.40–12.6.41
T2044 53 Sqn 18.8.40–FTR 30.9.40 from Rotterdam
T2045 53 Sqn 27.8.40–FTR 18.9.40 from Berck
T2046 53 Sqn 18.8.40–EFB 28.8.40
T2137 59 Sqn 27.9.40–FTR 2.11.40 from Cap Griz Nez
T2217 59 Sqn 31.8.40–FTR 9.1.41
T2218 53 Sqn 2.9.40–EFB 5.12.40
T2219 53 Sqn 3.9.40–1.11.40
T2220 59 Sqn 2.9.40–1.1.41
T2221 53 Sqn 31.8.30–EFAO 27.9.40 (crashed on take-off, Detling)
T2222 53 Sqn 2.9.40–30.7.41
T2275 59 Sqn 5.9.40–12.5.41
T2319 59 Sqn 28.9.40–FTR 17.10.40 (attacking destroyers off Brest)

Coastal Command Blenheim B/GR and fighter aircraft strike operations

July

3 Blenheim IVs from Bircham Newton in shipping sweep Maas Estuary, dive-bombed ships 7 miles N Hook. One overturned after direct hit, others reported sinking, one aircraft damaged.

6 21:20–23:30: 5 Blenheims 53 Sqn barges near Ijmuiden.

7/ 21:45–22:50: 6 Blenheims 53 Sqn Op. No.
8 37 — shipping Ostend area. Blenheims F and J/59 Sqn near Brest attacked MV *Condorcet* — bombs UX.

9 21:45–22:45: Blenheims 53 Sqn E-boats Boulogne harbour

11 05:30–07:30: 3 Blenheims 59 Sqn sought E-boats 15 miles SW Selsey Bill. None seen. 'E' and 'P' engaged and damaged a Do 17
22:30–23:40: 3 Blenheims ('N', 'P', 'F') 53 Sqn attacked shipping in Boulogne

12 21:00–23:45: 6 53 Sqn Isle of Leidam
J/59 Sqn located 2 × 2,500 ton MVs in Cherbourg, tried to bomb, intercepted by 12 Bf 109s. 'J' damaged, A/G wounded

14/ 21:30–00:50: 5/6 53 Sqn and 6 of 59 to
15 storage depot Ghent–Selzaete Canal

17 14:45: 59 Sqn armed recce Le Havre–Cherbourg where 'Z' bombed the Gare Maritime, 'L' attacked Le Havre docks. Blenheims on a 'Hatch' patrol shot down a Ju 87

17/ 21:20–00:20: 6 of 53 Sqn, 4 59 Sqn petrol
18 tanks at Ghent

18/ 22:15–00:25: 59 Sqn Hatch patrol, strike
19 Caen

19/ 21:30–00:15: 6 Hudsons (206 Sqn) and 3
20 Blenheims from Bircham Newton strike barges and ships at Emden

20 Blenheims of 53, 59 Sqns patrolled Channel. D/59 Sqn attacked by 6 Bf 109s 6 miles NE Cherbourg at 18:30, U/59 Sqn attacked Cherbourg port using 2 × 250 lb GP, 12 × 40 lb GP — typical load

20/ 21:20–23:25: 4/6 59 Sqn and 2/3 Hudsons
21 206 Sqn oil tanks Ghent

21 Blenheim A/59 Sqn reported large MV burning 24 miles 335 off Portland
21/ 22:15–22:20: 1/6 53 Sqn Ghent, all
22 damaged by AA
22/ 23:30–03:23: 6 59 Sqn barges Amsterdam
23
23/ 20:50–00:01: 6 53 Sqn barges Amsterdam
24 01:00–01:10: 4/6 59 Sqn oil tanks Flushing
25 Blenheims K/59 Sqn in sea 15 miles S Portland midday during sea search
25/ 01:00–01:56: 2/6 53 Sqn in poor weather
26 attacked barges nr Haarlem
03:15–04:35: 1/6 ? 59 Sqn oil tanks Cherbourg
27/ 03:15–04:35: 3/6 59 Sqn oil targets
28 Cherbourg
29/ 19:55–00.05: 8 53 Sqn Op. No. 59 —
30 shipping Emden. 4 59 Sqn oil tanks Cherbourg

August

1 13 59 Sqn day raid Cherbourg; Wg Cdr Weldsmith FTR in 'A'
3 6 53 Sqn Emden
9 17:45–20:19: 6/9 59 Sqn dusk strike Guernsey airfield
19:35–21:10: 3 59 Sqn Flushing
20:55–22:49: 6 53 Sqn Op. 52 — Flushing
11/ 22:00–23:20: 8 59 Sqn night strike on
12 Cherbourg oil store; 6 53 Sqn Op: 53 — Amsterdam??
12/ 21:15–00:48: 3/6 53 Sqn Op. 54 — Den
13 Helder
13 16:00: bombing of 53 Squadron area at Detling
15/ 21:35–00:05: 3 53 Sqn and 3/7 59 Sqn
16 repeat Op. 54, Den Helder
16 Main hangar Thorney Island damaged by bombing
17 19:00–22:50: 6 235 Sqn and 6 236 Sqn fighters escort Battles to Boulogne
17/ 22:00–23:45: 8 59 Sqn to Rotterdam
18
?? 22:45–02:33: 8 59 Sqn to Flushing oil tanks
18? 14:45–15:00: 8 from Thorney Island on armed recce Le Havre-Cherbourg. Blenheims on 'Hatch' patrol shot down a Ju 87
Z/59 Sqn dropped 2 × 250 lb HE on Cherbourg Gare Maritime
19/ 22:00–23:46: 2/7 59 Sqn night strike
20 Caen/Carpiquet airfield
22:30–23.40: 6 53 Sqn to St Omer
21/ 22:28–01:15: 3/6 53 Sqn on Op. 59 to
22 Abbeville aerodrome
20:20–22:06: 4/6 Sqn Caen/Carpiquet
22/ 22:42–01:20: 6 53 Sqn on Op. 60 to St Omer
23 airfield — bombed 00:08–00:25 as enemy aircraft landed, 17 HE's burst on airfield
23 02:00–05:00: 4/6 59 Sqn strike Dinard airfield 03:10–03:50
24 E,F,A1/235 Sqn circling Thorney Island 16:15 giving station protection attacked by Hurricanes of 1 (RCAF) Sqn. One Blenheim in sea off Wittering, one made wheels-up, flapless landing
20:15–21:50: 7/7 59 Sqn oil tanks Cherbourg

24/ 23:17–01:22 1/6 53 Sqn Op. 61 Flushing
25 airfield
03:10–05:57: 7/7 59 Sqn Dinard airfield — hits on 2 hangars, fuel store
25 20:25–22:40: 6/7 Sqn oil tanks Cherbourg
S/59 Sqn 'Moon' patrol II — engaged two Hs 126 33 miles SW Selsey Bill 17:05. In battle Blenheim propeller hit the sea; landed safely.
26 X/59 Sqn on SA 11 patrol 20 miles SW Portland — found seaplane tender carrying a He 59; another airborne. Blenheim soon driven off by two Bf 109s
26 20:49–21:08: 6 59 Sqn high level attack on Cherbourg fuel tanks
27 20:04: F/59 Sqn attacked 5 E-boats 20 miles off Cherbourg — no success
27/ 19:05–19:25: 6 59 Sqn fuel installations
28 Cherbourg
28/ 01:45–04:50: 2 53 Sqn strike seaplane base
29 Schellingwoude
20:00–22:10: 6 59 Sqn Caen/Carpiquet
31 19:40–22:25: 6 53 Sqn Op. 50 Vlaardingen
31/ 04:05–05:40: 5/6 59 Sqn Cherbourg
1 Sept

September

1 20:00–23:35: 3/6 59 Sqn Lorient harbour — 'P' crashed in flames 23:40 Thorney Island, crew safe
2 20:10–21:35: 5 53 Sqn ships Ostend
20:55–22:15: 4/8 59 Sqn strike Ostend — one attacked Terneuzen in error. Dropped 18 × 250 lb GP, 39 × 30 lb GP, 52 × 25 lb inc.
3 5 53 Sqn Ostend
4 20:00–21:30: 5 53 Sqn Op. 52, stores at Flushing
21:00–23:30: 8 59 Sqn strike oil tanks Cherbourg
5/ 10 59 Sqn barges Boulogne
6
6 21:15–22:10: 4 53 Sqn ships in Boulogne
21:25–22:10: 10 59 Sqn barges in Boulogne
7 20:00: 5 53 Sqn shipping Boulogne
8 11:42–?: 10 Blenheims (5 each of 53 and 59 Sqn) attempted shipping strike attack on MV convoy off Calais reported by S/53 Sqn; 2 attacked, 2 of 53 Sqn shot down by Bf 109s
9/ 2/4 53 Sqn barges Boulogne
10
10 3 53 Sqn and 5 of 59 Sqn shipping off Calais
11 16:00–18:45: 5 of 53 Sqn and 6 of 59 Sqn with 22 and 826 Squadrons — convoy off Calais, escorted by 12 Blenheim IV(f) 235/236 Sqns
12 15:45–17:10: 4 59 Sqn and 3 Blenheim IV(f) attacked 15 MVs off Cap de la Hague
13 3 53 Sqn shipping approaching Boulogne
18:55–22:40: 5 Blenheims 59 Sqn at 20-min intervals, shipping Boulogne
15 16:00–17:45: 5 53 Sqn strike shipping Sangatte
21:00–22:35: 5 53 Sqn shipping Le Havre
21:20–23:08: 8 59 Sqn shipping Le Havre
16 Strikes cancelled — bad weather

137

17 21:45-23:50: 4/6 53 Sqn, 8 59 Sqn, 22 Sqn and 826 Sqn — Cherbourg
18 14:30-15:30: M/53 Sqn bombed Le Touquet from 10,000 ft
    21:15-22:35: 6 59 Sqn shipping Cherbourg 6 53 Sqn Den Helder
20 04:00-?: 1/5 53 Sqn Willemswoord harbour from Bircham Newton
    16:00-17:50: single aircraft of 59 Sqn, strike airfields at Le Treport, St Aubyn, Bos Robert, Abbeville
    21:30-22:50: 6 59 Sqn shipping Cherbourg
21 13:40-15:30: 5/6 53 Sqn strike MVs off Cap Gris Nez
    15:00-16:40-16:40: 3 59 Sqn intending to attack 3 airfields bombed barges Dieppe area
22 07:08-!!14: S 59 Sqn bombed Lorient
23 04:00-08:45: 4 59 Sqn bombed Lorient
    At 23:00 and 00:15 4/6 53 Sqn to Flushing then Zeebrugge — cover op. 15:30: 3 53 Sqn strike large MV and E-boats 15 miles SE Dungeness
23/ 23:00-00:15: 7 53 Sqn attack Flushing and
24 Zeebrugge, second cover op.
24 18:45-21:00: 3 53 Sqn shipping rover off Holland, abandoned
25 18:30-22:00: 6 59 Sqn shipping Brest
26 01:00-02:20: 4 59 Sqn shipping Cherbourg, 6 53 Sqn Den Helder
27 18:15-20:50 3 53 Sqn torpedo workshops Den Helder
28 19:40-23:45: 3 59 Sqn flare force for Beauforts operating at Lorient

29 17:35-21:40: 6 59 Sqn strike Lorient
    18:25-20:17: 6 53 Sqn Rotterdam
30 04:15-08:35: 2/4 59 Sqn Lorient

N.B. Reference to 2/4 etc = 2 aircraft attacked out of 4 despatched

Fokkers from Amsterdam

After brief action in the Netherlands war of May 1940, surviving Dutch naval aircraft were despatched to Boulogne. Arriving by 09:00 on 14 May, they soon set forth for Cherbourg and reached Brest in the evening. They operated along the French coast for eight days, then flew to Calshot on 22 May, the arrivals comprising: eight Fokker T-8W — R1, R3, R6-R11 inclusive (later impressed as AV958 to AV965); five Fokker C.8W — G1, G2, G3, G5, G6; one Fokker C.11W — W14; 12 Fokker C.XIVW — F3, F5, F6, F13, F15-F18, F22, F23 — a total of 26 aircraft.

The obsolete C.8Ws flew to Felixstowe on 30 May and were scrapped. The C.11 and the C.XIVWs at Calshot were later packed then shipped to Soerabaya, Dutch East Indies, where they served as trainers.

Only the T-8W floatplanes operated with the RAF, after flying to Pembroke Dock where on 1 June No. 320 Dutch Naval Air Squadron formed to use them for routine coastal anti-submarine patrols and convoy escorts. On 13 July the crew of P spotted at 12:12 14° and 40 miles from Holyhead what they were sure was a periscope and bombed with 2 × 250 lb AS 2-sec delay bombs and without success what they claimed was a U-boat. On 26 July R10:R crashed into the sea, witnesses in the convoy under escort later stating that the machine suddenly dived into the water. Bodies of the two-man crew were recovered

Fokker T-8W floatplane R-1 *of the Royal Netherlands Navy.*

and taken to Pembroke Dock. *K* was attacked four times on 13 August by a Ju 88 at 51° 35N/06:30 and landed at base bearing six scars. Another loss involved *R9:D* which also crashed in the sea when returning from a patrol over the Irish Sea on 26 September. Of the six floatplanes remaining two were cannibalized to keep the others active. By the end of September all had been taken out of operational service after flying 120 sorties within the RAF.

In a brief alteration of policy one T-8W flew to Felixstowe for use in one of the first special agent pick-up operations. At midnight on 15 October it set out for Tjeuke Lake in the Netherlands upon which it was to alight then bring back four agents. Visibility was good as the floatplane made its way to Vlieland, but by the time the lake was reached thick mist covered that area. No pre-arranged signals being seen, the aircraft returned to Felixstowe, landing at 04:30. Another attempt was made on 16 October and as the Fokker circled Tjueke Lake the letter 'K', the coded signal, was flashed. As soon as the seaplane had splashed down a small boat headed for it and when 30 yd off it opened fire, to which the Fokker's gunner replied. Searchlights swept the surface of the lake, but the T.8W escaped to land at Felixstowe at 05:00.

As it splashed onto the river a trigger-happy Home Guard patrol opened fire, seaplanes no longer being usual in the area. The crew beached their aircraft which had sustained 40 hits and had empty tanks. It later transpired that the agents had been betrayed and arrested on the 15th, and an ambush was arranged for the 16th.

The floatplanes were not the only operational Fokker types to come to Britain, for a Fokker C.X reconnaissance biplane flew in from Bergen via Rotterdam, and a Fokker G.1 escaped to crash in a field just south of Lowestoft.

The final demise of the T-8Ws remains uncertain. I last saw three resting, dismantled, on RAF 60-foot 'Queen Mary' low loaders in the 54 MU Salvage Section opposite the then Cambridge Borough Cemetery, and managed to penetrate the defences for a close look. All three were an unusual light grey with a light green shade of Sky on their under surfaces. None carried identity letters or numbers, and all had the orange and black 'Free Dutch' triangle below the cockpit. After a month or so nearly all of them left, presumably to participate in a funeral pyre. All that remained in Cambridge — where it proudly still resides — was a small piece of wood wearing two unusual colours!

On Pembroke Dock's slipway is one of the T-8Ws of 320 Squadron. Behind rests a Swordfish floatplane and to the left a Sunderland and a Lerwick. (IWM, via J.J. Halley)

Fokker T-8W

AV958 (ex R-1) Pembroke Dock 2.6.40
AV959 (ex R-3) Pembroke Dock 2.6.40
AV960 (ex R-6) Pembroke Dock 2.6.40, to
                Flexistowe 28.11.40–SOC
                6.41
AV961 (ex R-7) Pembroke Dock 2.6.40, to
                Felixstowe 28.11.40–SOC
                6.41
AV962 (ex R-8) Pembroke Dock 2.6.40

AV963 (ex R-9)   Pembroke Dock 2.6.40
AV964 (ex R-10) Pembroke Dock 2.6.40
AV965 (ex R-11) Pembroke Dock 2.6.40, to
                 Felixstowe 28.11.40–SOC
                 6.41

Fokker C.XIV W

F-3   Pembroke Dock
                 15.7.40–SOC 1.3.41

The Lockheed Hudson

Demands placed upon the British aircraft industry in the mid-1930s were enormous. Long starved of orders, it was suddenly told to produce prodigious numbers of sophisticated aircraft. Across the Atlantic the American industry, with a larger market, had been investigating new ideas. They included in particular all-metal structures, variable pitch propellers and retractable undercarriages. Such features were being applied to civil aircraft, the USA being well away from Europe's alarming events.

British design teams visiting America viewed technical development there with much interest and, once home, incorporated some of the ideas in combat aircraft they were designing, among them the Battle and the Wellington. What remained a problem was the ability to produce sufficient modern aircraft in the given time-span and, knowing of the advanced nature of some American

Equipment layout of the Lockheed Hudson general reconnaissance bomber

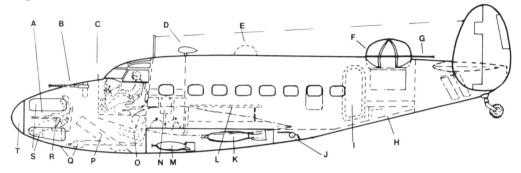

A-navigator's station; B-2 × .303 in Browning guns (1,000 rounds); C-pilot's gun sight; D-Faired screened D/F loop aerial; E-Astro dome; F-Boulton-Paul 2-gun turret (360 rotation); G-2 × .303 in. Browning guns; H-Gunner's compartment and floor leading to central area of roomy fuselage; I-main crew entry door; J-Trailing aerial; K-250 lb HE bombs; L-Rest bunk; M-100 lb HE bombs; N-Wireless operator's position; O-Reconnaissance flares stowage; P-Flare chute; Q-Bomb sight and floor window; R-Navigator's chart table; S-side windows, subdivided on production aircraft; T-Clear nose transparency.

The Anson and the Hudson make for interesting comparison. Whereas the British machine had a metal structure fabric covered, the American aircraft was 'all-metal' and had a stressed skin. Like the Anson it was a military adaptation of an airliner but more capacious, more heavily armed and had a longer normal range. Nevertheless the all-round view from the Anson was superb, ideal for coastal patrol. Additionally it was very suitable for use as a trainer and robust light transport, which qualities enabled it to far outlive the Lockheed 14 in military service. 'Annie' contributed greatly to the British war effort.

---

designs and the means of their rapid production, the Air Council decided to set in motion an exploration into the possibility of Britain supplementing its own production with aircraft from America.

There were two areas in which shortage was very evident. One was that of the advanced single-engined trainer for fighter pilots, the other a medium-ranged reconnaissance bomber to supplement Coastal Command's Ansons. So, in April 1938, a purchasing commission set forth to explore the possibility of US aircraft fulfilling these tasks.

Boeing was busy with large bombers, Douglas with transports and for the future a high speed support bomber. Glen Martin had similar aircraft underway. At North American the commission found a very suitable trainer which was later

purchased as the Harvard, and it was at Lockheed, then a small struggling firm, that the other need was answered.

Although the company was producing small all-metal airliners, it had designed a military variant of its Model 14 which interested the British. By removing seats and furnishing, fitting a bomb bay in its belly and giving it a gun turret and nose guns, this operational training version carrying 644 gal was reckoned able to cruise for about 10 hours. Conversion being straightforward and the performance suitable, the British government in June 1938 ordered 200, named the machine the Hudson and reckoned it suitable for use as an operational reconnaissance bomber.

When news of the purchases was announced the furore was enormous. Why was the British industry and its workers being ignored, H.M. Opposition cried, to which the apt answer would have been, 'because you neglected them!' Newspapers also carried condemnation of the deal in which the aircraft would be shipped to Britain.

October 1938 saw a production specification agreed, the first example flew on 10 December and final adjustments were settled on 1 January 1939 for the four-man Lockheed Model B14L. Two nine-cylinder single row Wright Cyclone GR-1820-G102A radials providing 1,100 hp for take-off and 900 hp (2,300 revs) for cruise-driving constant speed propellers would power the bomber, which was able to carry 4 × 250 lb British bombs or four universal incendiary containers, or 10 × 100 lb bombs and alternatively 10 flares. Two .303 in Colt Browning guns would be mounted on top of the nose and two in a rear turret. Gross weight of the Hudson would be 17,500 lb, almost identical to a loaded Lockheed 14 civil transport, and it would have nose transparencies to cater for the bomb aimer. Agreed fuel load in integral wing tanks — a very novel feature of 1938 — was 607.7 US gal (3,646 lb) and 44 US gal of oil (330 lb). Larger than the Anson, the Model B14 had a wing span of 65 ft 6 in and overall length tail of up to 42 ft 3 in. A maximum speed of 246 mph was forecast with cruising speeds of 200 mph at sea level, 208 mph at 5,000 ft and 220 mph at 12,000 ft. When carrying an operational load the all-metal aircraft would still be able to maintain flight on one engine at 9,000 ft. Take-off at sea level from a hard surface would need a 920 ft run.

The first examples were shipped from Long Beach to Liverpool in February 1939, N7205, N7206, and N7207 reaching Martlesham Heath early in April 1939. Rapid assessment of their capabilities showed them well up to specification, which brought all-round relief. N7208 was received by Boulton Paul on 2 May and its turret was soon resting like an enormous egg atop the rear fuselage. Ample fuselage windows and nose transparencies were favourable features, and the very evident Fowler flaps a great help when landing.

N7209 went to CFS for handling trials and on 27 April 1939 No. 224 Squadron received its first Hudson, N7205. Rapid introduction indeed and on 2 June 1939 '224' received its 12th example. Squadron trials were conducted while other Hudsons were having turrets fitted and in August 1939 No. 233 Squadron equipped. The first month of the war saw Hudsons delivered to 220 Squadron.

Although the value of the upper turret was many times shown, it reduced the aircraft's speed by 15 mph. N7206 with a standard turret had a top speed of 252 mph at 10,000 ft, at which altitude its best cruising speed was around 155 mph.

From the opening of hostilities Hudsons drew upon their excellent duration when patrolling far from home, and particularly off the Norwegian coast in search of German warships heading for the Atlantic. On the second day of war a Hudson engaged a Do 18. One of their most well known early successes was K/220 Squadron's discovery on 24 February 1940 of the prison ship Altmark hiding in Josing Fjord.

The Hudson's early days were not entirely trouble free. In September 1939 the US Neutrality Act came into force prohibiting US citizens from selling arms to the belligerent nations. Rescuing the Hudson deal came the 'cash and carry' Act of 4 November 1939 which led to Hudsons being towed across the border into Canada and then shipped to England.

One annoying problem was a considerable compass deviation which was particularly evident when the aircraft was swung in flying position. There was also concern over the high amount of magnesium alloy used in construction, promoting scares about the aircraft's vulnerability to fire particularly should the integral fuel tanks rupture. Coastal Command and the Air Staff however viewed the Hudson as a very useful acquisition —

Lockheed Hudson 1 N7205 *with turret mock-up for test purposes.* (Lockheed)

and one with a bright future. In October 1939 consideration was given to producing a Mk II fighter version carrying twin 20 mm cannon as well as a turret and two side guns. Tankage for 208 gal could be carried in the bomb bay, the changes raising the all-up weight to a likely 19,817 lb and still providing nine hours' endurance cruising at 175 knots. That suggested an operational radius of 719 nautical miles, including 30 minutes' combat coupled with a top speed of 250 mph at 8,000 ft. Against German maritime aircraft that would have been useful, although the Hudson would not have been fast enough to perform as a general fighter.

December 1939 saw plans for a long-range fighter variant, the Mk III, to be used to protect shipping in the north and north-west approaches until sufficient Beaufighters became available. The Hudson though was valuable in its GR state and, when Coastal Command learnt that it was to have Beaufighters, Hudson fighter schemes faded.

No. 206 Squadron began receiving Hudsons in February 1940 and No. 269 in April 1940. During the evacuation from Dunkirk No. 206 Squadron patrolled over returning ships before joining the other squadrons in patrolling given areas, particularly watching for signs of enemy movement and invasion, and plans involving Norway. As the listing of prominent operations shows, Hudsons also carried out strikes upon

Hudson 1 P5120:VX-C *of 206 Squadron, Bircham Newton.* (IWM)

maritime targets.

During September 1940 genuine Hudson Mk IIs began arriving. Nine reached Britain that month, eight more in October. These with stronger airframe weighed around 19,650 lb loaded, and all featured a ventral 'tunnel' turret which, when lowered, reduced the speed by 10 knots and made the aircraft tail-heavy. Tests also showed that with the turret extended it was difficult to recover the aircraft from a dive. Further modifications led to the Mk IIa (alias Hudson IV — Pratt & Whitney R-1830-SC3G engines) and the Mk IIb (alias Mk V). None of those arrived in 1940, and the faster, longer-ranged Mk III (1,200 hp G-205A engine) also belongs to 1941.

Summary

By 3 September 1939 84 Hudsons had reached Britain. On 1 April 1940 the three operational squadrons held 93 examples, comparative figures for 1 September being five and 101. A total of 189 saw squadron service during the Battle of Britain period and by 15 October 363 Hudsons had reached Britain.

Hudsons used by RAF squadrons 1 July– 15 October 1940

No. 206 Sqn, Bircham Newton

N7275	9.6.40–20.9.40
N7273	9.6.40–EFA 30.9.40
N7293	22.9.40–24.7.41
N7300	16.2.40–EFA 9.11.40
N7302	24.5.40–31.8 40
N7318	31.5.40–23.9.40
N7327	11.6.40–31.7.40
N7343	16.2.40–5.4.41
N7351	16.2.40–EFA 3.9.40
N7362	21.2.40–FTR 14.10.40
N7367	15.2.40–EFAO 1.9.40
N7368	16.2.40–FTR 11.7.40
N7379	22.9.40–13.6.41
N7393	13.6.40–22.9.40
N7395	13.6.40–SOC 12.8.40
N7396	16.5.40–20.9.40
N7401	16.2.40–EFAO 14.8.40
P5133	31.5.40–EFAO 5.8.40
P5137	31.5.40–5.10.40

P5140	4.6.40–7.9.40
P5141	4.6.40–1.1.41
P5143	31.5.40–19.4.41
P5148	10.5.40–29.4.41
P5153	14.5.40–EFAO 6.8.40
P5162	1.6.40–FTR 2.7.40
R4059	19.9.40–13.3.41
T9272	5.6.40–EFAO 6.8.40
T9274	9.8.40–22.9.40
T9276	15.8.40–EFAO 17.9.40
T9281	3.7.40–1.1.41
T9282	8.7.40–FTR 3.8.40
T9283	8.7.40–3.9.41
T9287	16.8.40–20.11.40
T9288	1.8.40–20.12.40
T9289	15.8.40–FTR 11.2.41
T9298	10.6.40–17.4.41
T9300	1.8.40–1.1.41
T9302	6.8.40–1.1.41
T9303	25.7.40–FTR 15.10.40
T9304	17.8.40–EFB 21.4.41
T9310	2.8.40–1.1.41
T9311	4.9.40–29.4.41
T9324	19.9.40–EFB 17.5.41
T9331	21.8.40–FTR 4.2.41
T9332	1.9.40–29.4.41
T9336	2.9.40–FTR 31.12.41
T9338	8.9.40–13.6.41
T9350	9.9.40–FTR 11.2.41
T9357	8.9.40–10.6.41

Mk II

T9368	5.10.40–6.1.41
T9383	13.10.40–30.4.41
T9384	15.10.40–5.5.41

No. 220 Sqn, Thornaby

N7231	24.9.39–EFB 14.7.40
N7233	23.9.39–EFAO 15.9.40
N7267	15.3.40–5.4.42
N7275	20.9.40–30.12.40
N7281	28.8.39–16.3.41
N7291	25.12.39–EFB 7.11.40
N7292	1.9.39–6.8.41
N7293	1.9.39–22.9.40
N7295	5.9.39–EFB 7.11.40
N7297	10.4.40–8.10.40
N7304	27.12.39–24.7.40
N7310	7.5.40–3.4.41
N7311	25.4.40–22.8.41
N7314	19.11.39–SOC 19.3.41
N7316	7.11.39–SOC 30.8.40
N7341	10.4.40–28.1.42
N7379	14.5.40–22.9.40
P5116	24.5.40–11.11.40
P5124	13.4.40–EFB 7.11.40
P5135	24.5.40–EFB 4.12.40
P5146	3.5.40–FTR 2.4.41
P5150	26.4.40–2.11.40
P5151	4.5.40–FTR 16.1.41
P5158	11.5.40–30.7.41
R4059	13.4.40–19.9.40
T9274	22.9.40–1.1.41
T9301	22.7.40–11.7.41
T9317	24.7.40–1.7.41
T9323	?–EFB 6.10.40
T9330	28.8.40–31.7.41
T9354	?–12.6.41
T9355	24.9.40–28.6.41

Lockheed Hudson 1 T9277:QX-W *of 224 Squadron.* (IWM)

Mk II

T9369	19.9.40–19.7.41
T9371	18.9.40–22.1.41
T9273	25.9.40–EFB 27.12.40

No. 224 Sqn, Leuchars

N7222	2.6.39–FTR 21.12.40
N7264	9.8.39–8.8.40
N7265	10.8.39–FTR 9.12.40
N7266	9.8.39–29.11.40
N7272	31.10.39–EFB 20.11.40
N7282	14.10.39–FTR 7.8.40
N7268	10.8.39–FTR 8.9.40
N7298	2.5.40–FTR 11.1.41
N7305	30.12.39–FTR 21.7.40
N7307	2.3.40–5.12.41
N7308	1.5.40–28.5.41
N7315	12.12.39–SOC 19.3.41
N7342	24.3.40–20.6.41
N7358	25.5.40–SOC 28.1.41
P5122	17.5.40–31.8.41
P5136	23.8.40–18.5.41
P5159	23.5.40–1.1.41
P5161	9.6.40–30.5.41
T9273	5.6.40–24.8.40
T9277	2.7.40–FTR 9.12.40
T9278	2.7.40–1.11.41
T9315	11.10.40–6.3.41
T9326	22.8.40–EFAO 30.9.40
T9328	19.8.40–EFB 16.10.40
T9338	21.9.40–EFB 15.11.40
T9344	22.8.40–28.2.41
T9345	22.8.40–EFAO 23.4.41
T9351	24.9.40–16.5.41

Mk II

T9376	3.10.40–16.5.41

No. 233 Sqn, Leuchars; detachments at Aldergrove 8.40

N7224	15.8.39–EFB 31.7.40
N7225	14.8.39–8.8.40
N7226	14.8.39–20.6.41
N7240	15.8.39–FTR 25.10.40
N7242	15.8.39–FTR 21.7.40
N7243	16.8.39–29.1.41
N7251	17.10.39–27.6.41
N7326	26.4.40–4.6.41

N7340	3.3.40–12.6.41
N7252	27.12.39–5.6.41
N7253	26.7.39–8.8.40
N7254	26.7.39–1.1.41
N7257	31.7.39–29.1.41
N7259	4.8.39–30.5.41
N7269	29.12.39–22.12.41
N7280	27.10.39–8.8.40
N7372	17.5.40–13.2.41
N7374	17.5.40–FTR 3.11.40
N7377	17.5.40–EFB 9.7.40
P5117	12.6.40–EFB 5.10.40
P5123	28.8.40–22.1.41 (force landed in Eire)
P5156	2.5.40–1.1.41
T9284	26.7.40–8.4.41
T9313	1.10.40–2.6.41
T9327	22.8.40–27.6.41
T9341	25.8.40–8.7.41
T9361	26.8.40–15.10.40
T9343	19.8.40–FTR 14.10.40
T9365	26.9.40–EFB 4.12.40

Mk II

T9377	29.9.40–FTR 31.10.40
T9378	28.9.40–30.5.41

No. 269 Sqn, Wick

N7274	4.7.40–6.1.41
N7276	3.7.40–13.2.41
N7328	6.7.40–20.10.40
N7331	30.3.40–19.6.41
N7369	4.7.40–22.2.41
N7376	3.7.40–18.2.41
N7392	3.7.40–23.2.41
P5119	19.5.40–6.1.41
P5121	19.5.40–15.3.41
P5125	19.5.40–27.8.40
P5126	23.5.40–6.1.41
P5128	13.4.40–28.2.41
E/P5129	18.4.40–FTR 28.9.40
P5132	26.7.40–FTR 24.10.40
P5152	19.5.40–EFB 23.7.40
P5153	2.5.40–EFAO 6.8.40
P5161	23.5.40–18.2.41
T9270	5.6.40–10.2.41
T9271	5.6.40–29.7.41
T9275	29.6.40–17.8.41
T9291	26.7.40–18.2.41

One of the most secret 1940 machines was this Lockheed 14 alias Hudson, G-AGAR, flown by Sidney Cotton during clandestine 'spy flights' particularly in the Middle East. (via Bruce Robertson)

T9292	15.6.40–8.8.40
T9293	15.6.40–6.4.41
T9293	15.6.40–6.4.41
T9294	15.6.40–6.1.41
T9299	6.7.40–EFAO 23.8.40
T9308	24.8.40–20.6.41
T9312	29.9.40–3.7.41
T9314	1.10.40–30.7.41
T9333	1.9.40–24.4.41
T9334	1.9.40–EFB 8.3.41
T9335	3.9.40–3.7.41
T9336	15.10.40–31.12.40
T9337	1.10.40–18.4.41
T9347	5.9.40–31.12.41
T9349	1.9.40–11.7.41
T9360	21.9.40–EFB 15.5.41

Mk II

T9374	22.9.40–3.7.41

No. 320 Sqn, Leuchars

N7209	15.10.40–8.12.40
N7288	8.10.40–27.9.41
N7302	11.10.40–EFA (missing) 27.10.42

Hudson operations

During the Battle Hudsons flew in the main armed reconnaissances, operating in particular off Norway, Denmark and the Netherlands. Some of the more notable operational incidents are listed here.

July

1/2 02:17 — Hudson bombed De Kooy airfield

2 15:30 Hudson Z/220 Sqn attacked two stationary MVs 25 miles off Lodbierg. 20:45 Hudson E/224 Sqn attacked 50 miles W Lister LV in strong enemy force

3 04:20 M/206 Sqn dive-bombed factory north of Ijmuiden, engaged by Bf 109. A/206 Sqn attacked buildings on Texel

4 N/206 and V/206 Sqn missing from ASR search for Hampden 17:50 D/224 Sqn attacked MV 20 miles off Bergen A/233 Sqn attacked 4 small ships 182° Alsboen Light

7 05:20 V/220 Sqn attacked 3 small minesweepers 12 miles NNW Terschelling. Z and M/233 Sqn attacked ships off Obrestad. W/233 Sqn on SA2 attacked group of 3 DRs and 6 MVs 40 miles off Karmo, Bf 110 engaged. Z/48 Sqn escorting Convoy 177 London–Gibraltar 16:30 reported convoy being bombed

8 O/233 Sqn on SA2 attacked force of 4 DRs and a MV 111 miles 262° Lister Light. M/233 Sqn attacked 2 minesweepers 7 miles off Lisdesnes. D/220 Sqn attacked 3 Danish fishing vessels 32 miles off Lotbrerg. F/206 Sqn attacked MV *Willemsoord* with 4 × 250 lb bombs

10 T/224 Sqn engaged Do 18 068 Kinnaird's Head 82 miles, radio operator wounded

9? 23:15–04:00 5/6 Hudsons 269 Sqn Wick strike on Faltoens nr Bergen, attacked bridges and an ammunition dump

10?? Hudson K/206 Sqn escorting south-bound east coast convoy which came under air attack. Engaged raiders. Anson D/500 Sqn escorting south-bound east coast convoy No. 17 drove off enemy aircraft.

12/13 22:15–02.45 6 Hudsons and 3 Blenheims strike Emden docks

13	05:35 F/220 Sqn attacked two minesweepers 30 miles NW Terscelling
14	18:50 B/220 Sqn found He 115 inverted on the sea 050° Flamborough 113 miles
17	F/233 found 13 ships and 6 U-boats 260° Lodbierg 94 miles and attacked using 10 × 100 lb AS bombs
19	18:00–22:30 5 Hudsons from Leuchars shipping strike 80 miles NW Horns Reef
19/ 20	21:30–00:15 6 Hudsons and 3 Blenheims from Bircham Newton strike barges and ships at Emden
20	Hudson O/233 Sqn on SA2 patrol bombed W/T station Utsire 4 × 250 GP, 3 × 25 inc.
20/ 21	21:20–23:25 4/6 Blenheims 59 Sqn and 2/3 Hudsons 206 Sqn strike oil targets Ghent. K/206 Sqn also unsuccessfully engaged He 115 off Lowestoft. Other 206 Sqn aircraft attacked Rotterdam
21	07:18 Hudson Y/233 Sqn reported enemy force R/U seen including 10,000 ton tanker, Do 18, 34 miles from Lister Light. Attacked 15,000 ton MV 06:16. X/224 and Z/233 Sqn FTR from strike on R/U. Hudson J/224 Sqn attacked 4,500 ton MV 4 miles from Lister
21/ 22	00:35 Hudsons R, U, M/233 Sqn strike Emden basin. 12 × 250 GP, 12 × 25 lb inc
24	04:05 M/269 Sqn engaged Do 18 019° Fair Island 81 miles. V/269 Sqn later reported Do 18 in trouble. 21:13 A/269 Sqn attacked U-boat 068° Mukkle Flugga 81 miles. 18:00 N/224 Sqn shadowed 8 DRs and 6 MVs 235° Lister 88 miles, and another 224 Sqn aircraft saw a Do 18 there, two more later, attacked and bombed one
28/ 29	00:30–03:30 E and K/206 Sqn strike oil tanks Amsterdam; 'Q' aborted 8 × 250 GP, 3 × 25 inc.
29	04:48 O/269 Sqn saw U-boat 285° Harmo 72 miles
29/ 30	6 Hudsons 206 Sqn strike oil tanks Amsterdam, 'Q' and 'U' damaged
31/1 Aug	Hudson E/220 Sqn attacked U-boat 160 miles E St Abbs Head

August

1	09:00 E/233 Sqn saw a U-boat 218° Malin Head
1	12.04 E/220 Sqn attacked 3 MVs 25 miles off Terschelling
6	23:50 0/206 Sqn crashed from SA4A patrol
7	02:10 X/206 Sqn crashed from SA5 patrol
	F/224 Sqn missing from recce Norwegian coast
9	S/206 Sqn crashed from SA4 patrol
10	16:34 P/220 Sqn 055° Cromer 48 miles saw large floatplane thought to be a Ha 140, engagement 16:30
15	06:00 E/206 Sqn engaged He 115 290° Terschelling 50 miles in 40 min battle
18	07:55 E/220 Sqn dive-bombed 4 small ships 241° Horns Reef 42 miles
19	N/206 Sqn on convoy escort vigorously

	engaged He 111 067° Lowestoft 23 miles
21	15:10 A,O.B.X/220 Sqn 241° Horn's Reef 180 miles dive-bombed two escort ships. Fierce battle with Bf 109s. 'X' badly hit, belly landed. All escaped into cloud
22	F/233 Sqn attacked a U-boat 55° 56′N/09° 27′W
25	X/233 Sqn attacked a U-boat at 57° 57′ N/11° 30′ W

September

4	17:30 U/224 Sqn engaged a He 115 105 miles off Flamborough. D/220 Sqn on an SA3 engaged He 115
5	11:12 T/233 Aldergrove attacked suspected U-boat 56° 23′ N/11° 10′ W
6	19:44 B/206 Sqn engaged He 115 090° Cromer 40 miles at 250 ft; W/206 later attacked it and enemy forced onto the sea, engines stopped, asking for help; bombed
8	12:51 L/233 Sqn Aldergrove attacked U-boat 56° 00′ N/10° 15′ W 19:10 V/233 Sqn Aldergrove attacked U-boat 56° 08′ N/10° 34′ W and claimed 4 near misses
11	08:45 M/220 Sqn on an SA2 attacked a U-boat 310° Horn's Reef 71 miles
12	V/206 Sqn on SA5 attacked MV 203° Maas Light 5 miles
14	15:27 Hudson engaged 2 He 115s 350° Terschelling 80 miles
21	11:15–15:15 4 Hudson and 6 Blenheim Bircham Newton strike 2 destroyers and a U-boat 60 miles SW Horns Reef — targets not found 6 Hudsons 206 Sqn attacked 2 MVs 53 miles SW Horn's Reef, dropped 12 × 250 GP and 12 × 250 AS Hudson B:P5137 reported 3 cruisers in Lorient
25	16:45 H/233 Sqn attacked off Lister Light by Bf 110s
26	08:12 L/220 Sqn engaged two He 115s 072° Flamborough 72 miles — explosive bullet entered cockpit. X/220 Sqn gave help and at 09:15 P/220 Sqn engaged them
28	08:43 F/220 Sqn found dinghy off Spurn Point 80 miles; watched till help arrived 17:40 — two men rescued
29	08:22 O/224 Sqn Aldergrove attacked surfaced U-boat 56° 08′ N/09° 40′- W
30	04:45 V/224 Sqn crashed taking off to escort Convoy 74 inbound from Halifax; 5 killed

October

1	Throughout daylight Blenheims from Bircham Newton gave cover to naval units operating off Texel. Ansons and 812 Sqn Swordfish swept sea area between Hunstanton and Gt Yarmouth while 3 Beauforts sought any U-boats off the east coast. Hudsons sought enemy shipping being Karmo and Lister.
3	19:14 Hudson on SA4B 064° Gt Yarmouth 52 miles — 2 He 115 engaged

<table>
<tr><td>10</td><td>16:04 M/220 Sqn attacked two small ships 219° Heligoland 91 miles</td><td>13</td><td>06:30 S/206 Sqn attacked 4 MVs 315° Terschelling 49 miles</td></tr>
<tr><td>11</td><td>P/48 Sqn Port Ellen saw a Fw 200 56° 22′ N/07° 41′ E drop 12 or 15 HEs on a convoy; no hits. 'P' engaged, no hits. F/269 Sqn attacked 1,500 ton MV 004° Elsborn Light 64 miles with 7 × 100 lb AS</td><td></td><td>16:40 Hudson attacked U-boat 317° Barra Head 50 miles</td></tr>
<tr><td></td><td></td><td>16</td><td>B/206 Sqn missing from SA5. F/224 Squadron crashed on return</td></tr>
</table>

The Saunders-Roe Lerwick

That the Lerwick ever entered RAF service is remarkable, for much that it possessed — apart from its crews — was stamped 'failure'. Water handling, aerodynamics, power plants, performance — all were condemned. Only a desperate need to replace 1931-conceived 100 mph biplanes caused its continuation, and led to nearly a month of service during the Battle.

Needing a London/Stranraer replacement the Air Staff outlined such a small general purpose flying-boat within specification R/12.35. Minor adjustments to the needs followed, resulting in R.1/36 issued March 1936 outlining a highly seaworthy, robust six-man flying-boat of 25,000 lb all-up weight able to ride out rough seas when moored in 'sheltered waters'. 'Reasonable accommodation' for the crew was not

to impede performance! That included a top speed of at least 230 mph at 5,000 ft and a range of between 1,500 and 2,000 miles, allowing it to be able to reinforce Mediterranean stations. Three gun turrets would defend it, 2,000 lb of bombs must be carried and take-off be achieved in 1,000 yd. The Air Staff plan was for six home-based general purpose flying-boat squadrons — pairs of Londons, Stranraers and Sunderlands — each established at 6 IE + 2 IR and each with a War Reserve of two aircraft. Overseas would be based four medium/large boat squadrons each established at 4 IE + 2 IR, No. 202 with Scapas and Nos. 203, 205 and 230 with Singapores until Sunderlands were available.

R.1/36 was intended to show considerable advance over the London, Stranraer and Sunderland,

Three Lerwicks at the Cowes factory of Saunders-Roe, L7248 displaying a modified fin and tailplane finlets and a fairing in place of a tail turret. (Saro)

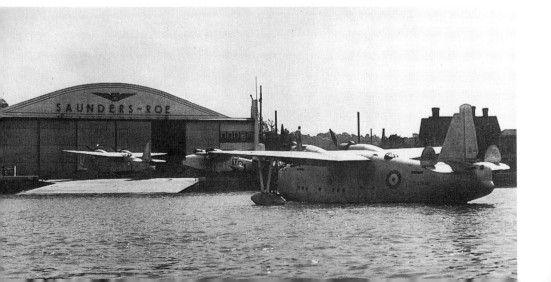

drawing upon the Rolls-Royce Vulture for power. Air Staff forecasts were for an ultimate design able to reach 239 mph, weigh 28,000 lb and cruise at 200 mph for 1,500 miles.

Short Brothers produced a Vulture-engined project whose power plants rested on struts above the 66 ft mainplane. Saro exhibited plans for a 75 ft span gull wing boat claiming a speed of 271 mph by fitting two Bristol Hercules HE 1SM radials. Supermarine's 91 ft span contender, the best, was Vulture-powered. Saro soon had a second idea on hand, a Hercules HE 1M engined 61 ft span machine with more conventional wings. Only enough boats to equip and support two squadrons were needed, so that costing played a major part in the tender process. The small Saro 'after thought' won the order.

First flown in November 1938, the prototype *L7248* proved troublesome from the start, bad porpoising in the water calling for many modifications to the hull step. Take-off run was longer than expected and the aircraft slower than required. Aerodynamics too were poor, and led to a variety of tail unit modifications in attempts to improve stability and extra wing incidence, a very dramatic modification. Single-engined flying proving impossible, load limitations were imposed bringing about the removal of items of limited usefulness.

Cancellation of the Lerwick was considered, but the small GP boat was needed and eventually 21 Lerwicks materialized, the first three powered by HE 1Ms, *L7252-7260* by Hercules IIs and the final eight, *L7261-7268*, by Hercules IVs. A top speed of 214 mph was about the norm, cruising speed was 166 mph and range was around 1,500 miles.

No. 209 Squadron, Oban, was first to receive Lerwicks late in 1939. Although patrols off Scotland were frequently made the aircraft exhibited many problems.

During July 1940 the squadron exchanged bases with No. 240, and had moved to Pembroke Dock by the close of a month in which average serviceability was only 25 per cent and 216.10 hours were flown, quite a considerable proportion of them by a Flt Lt Denis Spotswood, a future Chief of the Air Staff. On average two or maybe three escort patrols were flown. On 4 July for instance *L7262*, operating between 03:15 and 08:20, escorted the SS *Eastern Prince*, while *L7256*, flown by Flg Off Pain, watched over three large merchant ships, a cruiser and two sloops. Next day *L7260* and *L7262* escorted the *Luarentia*; on the 8th *L7256* looked after the cruiser HMS *Glasgow* and on the 9th kept company with HMS

Far too much spray for comfort being hurled over a Lerwick's tailplane. (Saro)

Norfolk. Additionally Lerwicks flew standard Oban patrols 0.3 and 0.5 with special sorties including a submarine search on 13 July in the Barra Head–St Kilda area.

On 26 July the last operational sortie of the Battle period was flown, by *L7262* between 16:00 and 17:45 south of St Govan's Head, where a Fokker T-8W had ditched and was found in tow behind the trawler *King Edward*. By then the squadron was almost completely at Pembroke Dock where on 3 August all Lerwicks were 'grounded' to receive modified Hercules II engines. Corrosion resulting from excessive spray splash also needed attention, and because the aircraft's centre of gravity was so far aft wing tip floats were modified. Flight characteristics were also being attended to by trim tab modifications.

On 16 August Sqn Ldr Winn and Flg Off Wyllie flew *L7262* to test the modified float tips, which were a useful item, and the new rudder tabs which were still insufficient to keep the aircraft straight in single-engine flight. Making the modifications was a slow affair and by 27 August *L7262* was still the only one complete with the remainder 'grounded' in September. No operations were flown during September and October 1940.

Lerwicks used by 209 Squadron July–October 1940

L7250 8.9.40–19.11.40
L7251 1.1.40–sank at Stranraer 21.11.40, recovered
L7254 4.5.40–7.7.40
L7257 17.1.40–30.4.41
L7258 20.2.40–22.1.41
L7259 4.40–9.5.41
L7260 31.5.40–16.5.41
L7262 1.7.40–21.10.40
L7263 8.9.40–22.2.41
L7264 8.9.40–16.5.41

L7255:WQ-A *of 209 Squadron displays the service version of the tail unit, but it was still a very unsatisfactory aircraft.*

Short Sunderland — the 'Flying Porcupine'

'Achtung! Fliegende Stachelschwein!' So said the Germans, warned after the Sunderland was discovered to be a far tougher adversary to tackle than many, due to its excellent manoeuvrability and the siting of dorsal guns in the hands of two gunners, along with four guns in the tail turret. 'Porcupine' though was surely a misnomer for such an impressive, majestic, delectable flying boat.

Surprising it is that with our reliance for survival upon sea trade Britain has never shown overwhelming interest in seaplanes (in the generic sense). Yet ironically it was a seaplane that led to the Spitfire, and flying boats in the 1920s and '30s much helped to police the Empire.

That latter aspect, developed by the RAF, attracted the interest of Imperial Airways. In the mid-1930s, after concluding that seaplanes offered a better means of linking Empire routes than landplanes, the company asked Shorts to build for them a suitable flying-boat. That request was expressed as the company was exploring the Air Ministry's new R.2/33 specification for a long-range patrol/general purpose flying-boat. Short's team was already interested in modern American metal monoplanes and in 1934 decided that the biplane flying-boat belonged to the past.

Flying boats had very distinct requirements. Before take-off could be effected the aircraft needed to rise sufficiently out of the water to ride on a central step, which meant first overcoming water's high drag. Considerable power was then required to lift the machine from the water. Inevitably, take-off runs were lengthy and plentiful engine power was needed. Since there would be much splash the mainplanes, power plants, propellers and tail unit were necessarily positioned as far as possible beyond the reach of the spray. The result was a high wing monoplane with a deep hull. Its narrowness (to meet aerodynamic demands) was also effected by the need for a very strong wing/hull junction. Good hull hydrodynamics were vital, the planing bottom needing very skilful design. Four engines were required by the new Short designs to give sufficient take-off power, along with ample fuel tanks permitting duration of at least 10 hours for the R.2/33.

Shorts based the designs upon their small Scion Senior four-motor flying-boat. Doubling its size and power, they devised the basis of both new designs. Although they looked similar the civil aircraft was less complicated. Imperial Airways' Short S.23 Empire or Imperial Boat involved less technical risk, and relied upon more tried construction methods. Good maintenance qualities in rough conditions and special hull protective treatment were important military needs, and by the time the S.25 was being designed more use of metal extrusions was in any case being made. The military boat also featured shallower forefoot and a broadly tapering planing bottom of reduced drag terminating in a very sharp rear. Its fin was smaller and the flight deck was set further back from the nose. High wing loading was compensated for by the Gouge flaps which slid out of the mainplanes increasing lift at take-off by 30 per cent. The S.25 was slightly smaller than the Empire Boat.

The S.25's internal layout was a novel adaptation of the civil transport. Nose entry for the crew of nine led to a bunk-equipped wardroom sited below a flight deck with dual pilots' controls. In the rear of the cabin sat the navigator, radio operator and flight engineer whose controls included engine temperature gauges, cabin heating controls, APU, fuel supply and electrics. The galley was behind the weapons room where bombs were loaded on to racks electrically wound out beneath the mainplanes. A cargo door was situated on the port side of the deep hull which also contained a small workshop.

One prototype of the Short S.25 was ordered as *K4774* and one of a competing Saro design, the A.33. In March 1936 the Air Ministry, considering progress on both very satisfactory, ordered a further 11 of each. S.25 production details were listed under Specification 22/36/Pl. On 3 July 1936 the first S.23 Empire boat *Canopus* flew amid much well-earned admiration for it was indeed a very beautiful aeroplane. Always it has been said that 'Shorts can never build a landplane'; but my goodness they built superb seaplanes!

Interest in the S.25 increased, then at a late stage in prototype construction the Air Ministry requested dramatic changes. As a result of successful trials with 37 mm cannon in the Blackburn Perth this newcomer was also to feature a similar anti-ship cannon in its bow. But its weight was so high that instead of a cannon the Air Ministry ordained that the S.25 must have a one-gun (Vickers or Lewis) nose turret able to slide rearwards to facilitate mooring. Ample space would also be available for a bomb aimer. For rear defence a four-gun FN 13 turret would now replace a single tail gun.

The effect of these modifications upon the centre of gravity was dramatic. So far did it shift aft that a very major change was needed to make the layout acceptable. It was achieved by cropping the rear spar then increasing the leading edge sweepback by $4\frac{1}{2}°$ which produced the curious canting of the engine nacelles, and by shifting aft the main step which was reduced in depth to maintain the drag coefficient. *K4774* being in advanced state, the decision

was made to fly it initially with the new armament layout then, after a few flights, modify the mainplanes.

K4774 (4 × 950 hp Pegasus X) first flew on 16 October 1937 and, despite its centre of gravity problem, handled well. Structural modifications commenced after the fourth flight and also the fitting of more powerful 1,010 hp Pegasus XXII engines. Flight testing was resumed on 7 March 1938, then *K4774* was passed to the Marine Aircraft Experimental Establishment (MAEE) Felixstowe for official testing. Loaded take-off weight, with 1,520 gal of fuel, was listed as 44,321 lb and tare weight 29,635 lb.

MAEE's general report on the Sunderland stressed many fine qualities. Manoeuvrability to 150 knots was good although the rudder then became heavy. It was 'very comfortable to fly for long periods without the autopilot', the cabin was comfortable and noise not excessive below 2,250 engine revs. View forward and sideways was excellent, and the controls were well harmonized.

L2158, the first production aircraft, flew close on its heels on 21 April 1938. Its all-up weight was assessed as 45,189 lb, against 44,600 lb of the prototype. Trials showed a top speed of 182 knots TAS (almost 210 mph) at 10,000 ft, economic cruising speed of 115 knots TAS, service ceiling of 15,800 ft, take-off run of 683 yds/32 sec and a landing speed of 77 knots. *L2159*, which first flew on 4 May, went to MAEE on 9 May and a month later 210 Sqn flew it to Singapore, reporting an average cruising speed of 177 mph.

With *L2160* first flown on 18 May 1938 Shorts soon attempted to prove that the Sunderland was quite able to cope with far higher loadings. Indeed, *L2160* made two successful take-offs from the river Orwell at 48,500 lb and then demonstrated fuel jettisoning of about 350 gal prior to safe landings at 44,600 lb. Staff at MAEE were greatly impressed that the aircraft could perform so well at a higher weight, with far aft centre of gravity, and yet

Sunderland L2159 prior to delivery to Nos. 209 and 230 Squadrons. It was destroyed on 7 May 1941 during an air raid on Greenock. (via Bruce Robertson)

retain excellent waterborne characteristics. The outcome was a long saga which led to astonishing increases in the Sunderland's capability and particularly its range and duration. Using *K4774* with its take-off weight increased to 49,000 lb, a flight of 14 hr 4 min at 2,000 ft at a mean speed of 149 mph was achieved. Carrying a typical service load, the range on 2,050 gal was 2,750 air miles.

During *K4774*'s spell at MAEE many relatively small but worthwhile equipment changes were called for, so much so that a new production standard, Mk.1/P2, was drawn up to cover Mk 1 production. By mid-August 1938 11 Sunderlands had

flown and by the end of September 230 Squadron at Seletar had its full complement of eight. At home No. 210 Squadron had received *L2162* and *L2163*. Saro's A.33 suffered a grievous blow in rough water on 25 October 1938 and was discontinued because the Sunderland was so very good. After 2,725 hours at moorings a Sunderland had shown no weakness, and the hull, mainly aluminium coated light alloy anodically treated prior to riveting, had stood up remarkably well to poundings. Not surprisingly 10 more, *L5798-5807*, had already been ordered, the first flying on 1 September 1938 and the last on 4 January 1939. Three more —

L2163:DA-G, a Sunderland I of 210 Squadron during a summer 1940 patrol. (Shorts)

N6133, N6135, and N6138 — were also on order along with two extra batches, N9020-9030 and N9044-9050, all of which were flying before hostilities commenced. Flight testing of production Sunderlands showed that whilst they were slightly slower than the prototype their take-off and range qualities were superior.

The Royal Australian Air Force now began expressing interest in the Sunderland following Australian experience with the Empire Boat, and in 1939 19 Sunderlands (A18-1 to 19) were ordered for the RAAF. Not having been delivered before the war they were passed to the British (as P9600-9606 and P9620-9624) to arm No. 10 Squadron, RAAF, based in England.

By June 1939 trials had been successfully flown at MAEE with a Sunderland weighing 55,000 lb at take-off taking a minute to get airborne. Rated no mean achievement, enhanced operational potential included a feasible range in reconnaissance stance of 2,008 miles and endurance of 20.3 hrs, carriage of 13,500 lb weapon load for an operational radius of 500 miles, or the safe carrying of 62 passengers for 1,000 miles. All that was a vast advance on the original concept of a flying-boat with 10.5 hrs' duration

and a range of 1,500 nautical miles when carrying a 2,900 lb bomb load. A week before hostilities commenced Sunderland squadrons began operations by patrolling sea areas north of Scotland to watch for German naval ships sailing into the Atlantic. On 3 September 1939 L2165 of 210 Squadron was on patrol when war was declared and next day L2167, L5798, L2168 and N9026 were out on patrol from Pembroke Dock.

By the outbreak of war attention was being focused on taking full advantage of the Sunderland's suitability for operations at much higher all-up weights than was at first thought possible. It was dependent upon one thing — increased engine power. Discussion of the problem began a few days after war started with a review of three contenders — the Bristol Hercules, 100 octane Bristol Taurus or the 100 octane Rolls-Royce Merlin RM2SM, of which the latter soon found most favour. Calculations showed it likely to permit operations at a starting weight of 52,800 lb and give much improvement over the Pegasus XXII version (performance bracketed here following Merlin forecast): top speed of 245 mph at 9,500 ft (211 mph/6,600 ft), cruising speed 225 mph at 11,000 ft (178 mph/6,000 ft) and range 1,780

Sunderland N9030 *floating on the Medway in 1939.* (Shorts)

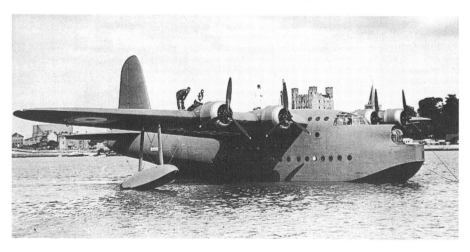

miles on 2,040 gal (1,780 miles/1,520 gal) or 2,900 miles on 2,230 gal (2,900 miles/2,030 gal). Thus the greatest improvement was in speed — useful for transit to patrol zone and for better deployment generally.

Exploration followed two possible trends. One was for a Sunderland Mk II Merlin powered and fitted with a 20 mm cannon turret and wings reverting to the original form. That would take at least a year to design. A simpler alternative was more favoured, a Merlin Sunderland with original wings and with modified forebody to ensure that water was not thrown into prop discs when the aircraft took off at higher weight and was of course deeper in the water. A stiffer hull and wing would confirm safe, heavier loading, and larger wing floats would be needed. With the intention to order 62 more Sunderlands it was decided that only the first 20 should be Mk I/P3, improved by the fitting of the FN 4B tail turret and redesigned bomb gear, the rest the Merlin Mk II, with Saro and Blackburn building Sunderlands too.

The success of the aircraft prompted an order for another 62, but it was reduced in October 1939 to 20 of a refined variant, the Mk 1/P3 still Pegasus XXII-powered. November 1939 then brought a most surprising suggestion, to use Pytram laminated paper in construction of the aircraft, and also the Stirling bomber. It came in response to fears that the huge quantities of metal and wood needed in aircraft construction could be in short supply, but was soon declared 'unsuitable'.

Between November 1939 and January 1940 the MAEE (now at Helensburgh) had increasingly loaded a Sunderland until it was taking off at 58,000 lb, at which weight some damage occurred when water was hurled onto the inner propellers. Landings had also been successful at 52,000 lb. At the latter weight the service ceiling was 12,000 ft, and 9,500 ft at 56,000 lb. By any criteria these were outstanding figures and encouraged development of the aircraft.

Shorts were by now very busy with an even more important aeroplane, the Stirling bomber. Clearly there was mileage even in the Pegasus-engined Sunderland and so the Merlin Sunderland was abandoned to prevent Short's design office becoming overloaded. Instead, against a revised new order of February 1940 for 70 Sunderlands, it was decided that in place of the much altered Merlin version 50 of the latest order would be simpler Mk 1As (later redesignated IIs) powered by Pegasus XVIIIs driving constant speed propellers which were initially proposed for a Mk 1/P4. T9042 however was chosen in March 1940 to be the prototype of a more modified version whose main features were its modified hull forebody planing bottom, revised main step fairing, extra 540 gal wing tankage, extra bomb station for 8 × 250 lb or 4 × 500 lb bombs, quieter flight deck and if feasible retracting wing tip floats. Wing tip extensions were to follow later. Throughout 1940 this aircraft was under development, but it did not fly until 28 June 1941 by which time it had become the Mk III for which repeatedly amended production plans were laid in April for Shorts to build 50, Blackburn 40 and Short & Harland another 25. Shorts at this time were hoping to have the Mk III flying by autumn 1940, with production commencing at Blackburns in November 1941.

The need for heavier bombs and depth charges was apparent from the early weeks of the war. Only a heavy weapon hitting a submarine stood a chance of sinking it. Coastal Command's first success though fell to Sunderland Y of 228 Squadron when on 31 January 1940 it finished off the U-55 which had been damaged by naval depth charges.

April 1940 saw the return to Rochester of L2158 for modification to Mk 1/P3 standard by the trial fitting of a new tail unit embracing an FN 4B turret and stainless steel control chains. Other development aircraft at this time included P9623 which had a smooth finish to its forward hull bottom which improved water performance. *P9624* had a modified faired main step to reduce in-flight drag thereby increasing range and to be featured by the Mk III.

Since early in the war Sunderlands had been operating with two mid-upper open gun positions, some having Poucher twin-gun installations. By July 1940 various modifications had lifted the average weight of a Mk 1 to 48,539 lb. But the additions were all of value and July 1940 saw the start of another — the fitting of an FN 7M dorsal turret tested late 1940 on *T9073*.

The contribution of the Sunderland to the war at sea was out of all proportion to its numbers. Ultimately 75 Mk 1s, 58 Mk IIs, 407 Mk IIIs and 143 Mk Vs were to be built. Sunderlands bore the brunt of airborne convoy escort duty over the Atlantic in 1939–40 and in so doing contributed strongly to the Battle of Britain.

Operations

Long, monotonous patrols were daily carried out by Sunderland crews far, far from home and often in atrocious weather. Unable to climb above bad conditions the crews had to face extremely discomforting flights and there were even occasions when storms turned the aircraft onto their backs! Following the fall of Norway, and then France, ventures requiring great courage were undertaken into fighter defended areas. But by and large their greatest enemy was nature, and the moments of action between July and October 1940 such as are listed here were relatively rare events.

July

1   H/210 Sqn reported U-boat attacked by destroyer (DR) 270° Ushant 220 miles — much oil
P9603: H/10 Sqn (Flt Lt Gibson): 05:57 SS *Zarian* seen torpedoed off Sterns Light. 06:00 *U-26* seen, dived as 4 bombs were dropped. U-boat *U-26* surfaced. 06:13 4

bombs dropped close, crew jumped into sea, 06:17 sank stern first, 41 rescued by HMS *Rochester*

2   11:08 K/204 Sqn reported *Arandora Star* sunk 260° Bora Head 100 miles, many in water, 13 lifeboats and rafts visible. By 16:20 RN had rescued survivors.
Three of 10 Sqn carrying depth charges (DC) operationally for first time

5   *P9623* of 210 Sqn ordered to leave convoy 13:45, attack U-boat. 14:45 found sinking ship, patrolled until rescue arrived

6   *P9601*: F/10 Sqn, seen moving oil patch 06:15 59° 27′ N/08° 18′ W 06:50 4 bombs dropped and Destroyer D83 continued attack without success
E/210 Sqn dropped 2 depth charges and 4 × 250 lb bombs without success on a U-boat at 48° 40′ N/07° 25′ W

7   *P9600* of 10 Sqn patrolling 22:10 Swedish MV *Bissen* — been torpedoed, D83 effected rescue
N9048 of 10 Sqn found sinking Portuguese tanker *Alferrbede* and lifeboat 12:12, gave cover. 16:06 signal — U-boat attacking SS *Manistee* — upturned ship located

8   *L5800:S*/ 201 Sqn DC attack on U-boat 04:26 followed by attack by destroyer D39
N6133: Y/201 missing from patrol
H/10 attacked U-boat

11 *N9050*: D/10 Sqn saw Norwegian MV sinking 06:00, crew in two boats
H/210 Sqn dropped 4 × 250 lb AS bombs on a U-boat 49° 42′N/08° 18′N 06:51

12 *N9049* of 10 Sqn (Sqn Ldr Pearce) up 07:15 for recce of Bordeaux and St Nazaire, in target areas 10:47–12:13 secured photos, slight flak damage, landed 19:00

13 *N9050*: D/10 Sqn (Sqn Ldr Gibson) — attacked twice by Bf 110 15:01 48° 30′–/09° 15′W — scored 25 hits on Sunderland, holed fuel tanks
N9048: A/10 Sqn (Flt Lt Choen) — He 111 approached convoy 15:34, driven off

15 *P9603*: H/10 Sqn (Flt Lt Birch) in search for enemy transports. 14:25 5 He 111 seen attacking ships 48° 50′/06° 52′W, driven off by Sunderland; 5 He 111 engaged then 2 He 111 shadowed the Sunderland.

16 F/10 — DCs on suspected U-boat 51° 00′N/06° 00′W

19 *N9027*: J/210 Sqn patrolling Ireland, 13:30–21:30 crossed oil track 55° 21′/09° 14′W, 5 bombs dropped, no success
N9023 of 204 Sqn suffered battle damage Cat. FB02

28 *P9601* of 10 Sqn (Flt Lt Birch). Ju 88s active in escort area. 09:49 4 lifeboats seen, from *Auckland Star*. 16:15 Sunderland landed alongside, boats empty.

29 *P9602*: G/10 Sqn (Flt Lt Birch), en route Gibraltar 07:06 attacked by Do 18 47° 58′N/06° 52′W, returned to base

30 F/10 Sqn 09:03 50° 32′N/08° 30′W engaged Ju 88s bombing Force PK

31 *P9601*: B/10 Sqn engagement with Ju 88s attacking SS *Moolthan* B/10 Sqn attacked crash-diving U-boat 56° 08′N/09° 37′W

August

2 *N6138*: V/201 Sqn 10-min low-level inconclusive engagement with Do 17 N off Shetland

7 *N9022* of 210 Sqn (Flg Off Lombard) 11:32 flew into unpennanted kite cable flown from MV. Cable cut into leading edge back to main spar, landed safely Oban 14.10

11 *P9624*. H/210 Sqn patrolling, *California* torpedoed, called for help from 20 miles, Sunderland escorted until rescue came

14 *N9027*: J/10 Sqn passed over *Britannic* 13:28, 13:35 56° 26'N/12° 40'W Fw 200 attacked from rear, shells hitting Sunderland's starboard wing and fuel tanks — forced to abandon mission

15 B/204 Sqn 11:25 twice attacked a U-boat, with bombs and depth charges

16 *P9624*: H/210 Sqn 14:15 56° 35'N/12° 05'W 2 DCs direct hits on U-boat — blown out of water, sank sideways. AS bombs dropped ahead of wash. 30 yd oil patch visible by 15:05

26 C/204 Sqn off Tromsoy attacked 8 moored He 115s, claimed to destroy 3 and damage others

27 Sunderland from Sullom Voe sought U-boat SE of Yell, Shetlands 11:38–20:35. B/210 Sqn dropped 2 DCs 56° 24'N/90° 24'W; U-boat altered course

28 Operation off Yell repeated 17:00–23:30 U-boat reported 290° Sumburgh Head 12 miles. Another ordered to search from Oban for U-boat off Borra Head
R:P9606 of 201 Sqn located burning MV *Staresby* unmanned off Cape Wrath. H/210 Sqn dropped DCs and 3 250 lb AS bombs at 56° 40'N/10° 41'W, then destroyer *Mackay* attacked, claimed to sink U-boat

September

2 *P9620* of 10 Sqn crash landed Oban

6 F/204 Sqn 07:10 56° 30'N/08° 10'W attacked U-boat

15 F/204 Sqn 13:20 56° 08'N/08° 09'W attacked U-boat

20/ 21 *L5802*: U/201 Sqn night recce Narvik area, included attempted bombing of Harstaad oil tanks

23 *P9605* of 10 Sqn — search for Do 24 after attack on ship

25 B/10 Sqn 280° Slyne Head — spotted lifeboat from *City of Benares*, attempted to alight but sea too rough. 14:23 made visual contact with *P9624* (E/210 Sqn) 292° Slyne Head 200 miles. Guided it to lifeboat. E/210 Sqn contacted survivors and guided RN to their rescue. Very many anti U-boat sorties currently being mounted
F/210 Sqn 08:22 55° 35'/11° 47'W engaged twin-engined aircraft
P9600: E/10 Sqn 11:15 engaged Do 18° 49' 29"N/08° 58'W without much success
H/10 Sqn 08:11 55° 28'N/11° 40'W engaged Fw 200

28 *P9600*: E/10 Sqn (Sqn Ldr Cohen) 245° Bishops Rock 90 miles 08:35 engaged a Do 17 for 15 min

29 E/210 Sqn 12:15 58° 37'N/16° 54'W attacked U-boat

October

1 *P9600*: E/10 (Sqn Ldr Cohen) on 182° Land's End 55 miles engaged by 3 Bf 110 17:30. 2 Do 17 and 4 Bf 109s also seen

4 F/10 Sqn attacked a U-boat at 49° 04'N/12° 31'W

15 L/204 Sqn 270° St Kilda 52 miles 14:10 escort vessels picking up survivor from sunken MV, joined search

16 D/210 Sqn from Oban attacked a U-boat at 59° 56' N/15° 00'W

17 E/10 Sqn picked up 25 survivors of SS *Stangrant*
P9624: H/210 Sqn, DC attack on U-boat submerging at 59° 11'N, 17° 50'W at 08:17; two subsequent naval attacks, air bubbles seen
P/210 Sqn 342° Rockall 150 miles, attacked a U-boat with DCS
D/10 Sqn west of Bishop's Rock engaged then bombed and claimed to sink a U-boat

19 J/210 Sqn 270° Bloody Foreland 185 miles DC on suspected U-boat

20 B/210 Sqn saw 10:30 lifeboats from torpedoed *Janus* (Swedish) 205- Rockall 90 miles. E/210 Sqn 12:45 dropped supplies and chart to lifeboat of survivors

28 W/210 Sqn at 12:48 reported lifeboats with survivors 86 miles W. of Bloody Foreland, *Empress of Britain* burning aft

29 K/204 Sqn crashed in sea

Short Sunderland 1 — examples in Britain during the Battle of Britain period

L2161	from Middle East to Calshot 7.7.40 (for overhaul), to 230 Sqn ME 19.8.40
L2163	G/210 Sqn 24.6.38–18.12.41
L2166	Middle East, to UK 1.7.40, arrived Calshot 10.8.40, returned ME and 230 Sqn 11.8.40
L2168	Z/201 Sqn, to Calshot 4.7.40 for overhaul
L5798	A/210 Sqn 8.9.38–31.7.41
L5800	S/201 Sqn 4.4.40–1.8.41
L5802	U/201 Sqn 4.4.40–31.5.41
L5805	Y/228 Sqn 24.11.38, to Pembroke Dock 2.7.40, to 201 Sqn 16.7.40–17.3.41
N6133	Y/201 Sqn 6.5.40–FTR 8.7.40
N6138	V/201 Sqn 13.4.40–damaged when driven ashore in gale at Pembroke Dock 2.10.40, used again 10.10.40–19.12.41
N9021	204 Sqn 26.4.40, to 201 Sqn ?, then Pembroke Dock St Flt from 16.7.40, to 201 Sqn 19.10.40–EFB 15.12.40 (crash landing at Invergordon)

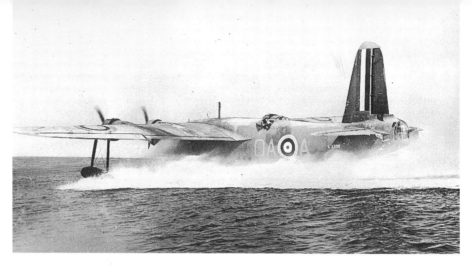

Sunderland L5798:DA-A *splashes down at the end of a 1940 patrol.* (IWM)

N9022	210 Sqn 26.9.39–27.12.40	P9605	10 Sqn RAAF 21.12.39–14.3.42
N9023	Calshot, to 204 Sqn 16.7.40–battle damaged 27.7.40	P9606	R/201 Sqn 4.4.40–11.8.41
N9024	204 Sqn 10.2.40–7.8.41	P9620	K/204 Sqn 21.4.40–EFB 29.10.40 (crashed in the sea)
N9028	A/204 Sqn 26.4.40–FTR from Trondheim reconnaissance 21.7.40	P9621	228 Sqn 7.6.40, to 201 Sqn 30.9.40–4.12.40
N9044	204 Sqn 26.4.40–4.8.41	P9622	228 Sqn 7.6.40, to Pembroke Dock 8.8.40, to W/201 Sqn 30.9.40–EFB 29.10.40 (crashed near Wick)
N9046	F/204 Sqn 26.4.40–EFA (burnt out Sullom Voe 11.12.40)		
N9047	204 Sqn 26.4.40–10.6.41	P9623	210 Sqn 13.4.40–22.1.41
N9048	B/10 Sqn RAAF 30.11.39–EAO (burnt out in air raid 27/28.11.40)	P9624	210 Sqn 19.4.40–8.2.41
		T9042	Mk III prototype at Shorts for R & D
N9049	10 Sqn RAAF 30.11.39–destroyed during air attack on Malta 10.5.41	T9043	Pembroke Dock 19.8.40, to 210 Sqn 26.8.40–FTR 2.9.40
N9050	10 Sqn RAAF 30.11.39–17.3.41		
P9600	10 Sqn RAAF 30.11.39–19.11.41	T9044	Pembroke Dock 1.9.40, to 210 Sqn 9.9.40–sunk in gale, Pembroke Dock, 2.10.40
P9601	10 Sqn RAAF 30.11.39–EAO (burnt out in air raid 27/28. 11.40)		
P9602	10 Sqn RAAF 30.11.39–EFA 2.9.40 (crash landing, Oban)	T9045	Pembroke Dock 20.8.40, to 204 Sqn 30.9.40–EFB 29.10.40 (ditched off Strathy's Point and sank 200 miles NNW Cape Wrath)
P9603	10 Sqn RAAF 30.11.39–EFB (crash landing Pembroke Dock 24/25.6.41)		
P9604	J/10 Sqn RAAF 18.12.39–29.10.41	T9046	Pembroke Dock 8.10.40, to 201 Sqn 6.11.40, to 228 Sqn 16.11.40

The biplane 'boats —
Supermarine Stranraer

So beautiful to view, so stately in passing, the RAF's handful of inter-war biplane flying-boats had become little more than memories by July 1940. The few remaining Singapore IIIs were with the Flying Boat Training Squadron and 240 Squadron had, at the start of June, bade farewell to its Londons. Only the more curvaceous Supermarine Stranraer remained operationally active in Britain, shepherding shipping with 240 Squadron off the west coast of Scotland.

The Stranraer resulted from a requirement for a coastal patrol flying-boat carrying 1,000 lb offensive load during a 1,000 mile sortie and able to operate safely on one engine. Its predecessor, the Scapa, being unable to achieve that, Supermarine redesigned it to meet the R.24/31 demand, continuing the task after the Saro London was selected and then being rewarded with an order. The prototype first flew in the hands of 'Mutt' Summers on 27 July 1934.

Seventeen Stranraers (*K7287–7303*) were ordered in August 1935 to Specification 17/35, the first being delivered in April 1937 and the last, to 209 Squadron, on 3 April 1939.

On 4 June 1940 six Stranraers and a reserve were assigned to No. 240 Squadron whose Londons then headed for Calshot, refurbishment and Gibraltar's 202 Squadron. There was little to choose between the two aircraft, both having all-up weights around 19,000 lb and cruising at 100 mph. The London's advantage was its 1,740 mile range compared with the 1,000 miles of the Stranraer, both being able to extend theirs by carrying external long-range tanks. Even so, Londons remained preferable for guarding Atlantic convoys passing Gibraltar, leaving shorter duration Stranraers patrolling busy waters off Ulster and the west of Scotland.

No. 240 Squadron Pembroke Dock based in July initially operated in Stranraers off Wales. On the 8th for instance *K7292* spent a long time protecting convoy HX53, and on the 14th *K7298* escorted HG37 for over seven hours. Change had by then started, for the squadron on 10 July began moving to Stranraer, Scotland, placing *K7287* and *K7302* at Oban on 17 July to provide cover while 209 Squadron persevered with its ailing Lerwicks.

Moving a flying-boat home was a complicated process and not until 30 July was it completed, *K7291*, *K7299* and *K7301* having arrived late afternoon on the 29th. Throughout July the Stranraers had been very busy. *K7292*, west of Skokholm at 500 ft early on 23 July, saw a He 111 pass close, and another soon after near St Ann's Head. Both were too fast for a Stranraer to tackle. Instead, it was gunners at Pembroke Dock who did the firing — as *K7292* was on its landing approach!

Plt Off Hayter (*K7299*) left at 02:25

The prototype Supermarine Stranraer, K3973. (Supermarine)

to escort the 25 merchant ships and two escort vessels of convoy OB191 steaming at a mere 7 knots. Soon after 13:00 hours, during the long vigil, a torpedo struck the SS *Jersey City* on her port side. Immediate search· for the U-boat was instigated, without success, before two huge explosions tore *Jersey City* apart. She sank at 14.10. *Z* of 240 Squadron relieved Hayter and crew who landed at 16:25, amply demonstrating the duration of their aircraft. *K7291*, *K7292*, *K7298*, *K7299*, *K7301* and *K7302* were all busy at this period.

Wasting no time after arrival, 240 Squadron flew five sorties on 31 July, Plt Off Holmes (*K7302*) seeing a U-boat which escaped and *K7301* searching for survivors from a torpedoed ship. *K7291*, *K7299* and *K7298* each operated patrols which were generally of about eight hours' duration.

All seaplanes need to be of rugged construction, all contact with the water imposing enormous stress upon their structures. They have also to face inclement weather at mooring, something which overtook *K7301* off Stranraer on 21 August. Lashed by a fierce storm, it was torn from its mooring to sink alongside a Singapore III of the FBTS suffering similar fate. Five days later the sad wreckage was hauled ashore for cannibalization.

Three types of operations were being flown, viz. convoy escorts, set area patrols and 'special patrols' seeking U-boats known to be present or for survivors from sunken ships. On 23 August Plt Off Holmes set out in *K7302* to attack a reported U-boat and, as was so often the case, had no sighting. Not so the crew of *K7287* who at 04:55 next morning coming out of cloud spotted a periscope, quickly marked the spot with a flame float then attacked. The submarine had a lucky escape, leaving the Greek freighter *San Gabriel* sinking. Gratitude among her crew must have been great when those aboard *K7287* guided a ship to their rescue. Drama had by no means ended. A large Dutch vessel, the *Volendam*, was then spotted bows down, and this time destroyers sought the attacker.

Locating submarines was difficult, destroying them equally so for the effect of the weapons in use was limited. September found No. 240 among others participating in attempts to improve the effectiveness of bombs used at low levels and assessing the Stranraer's ability to use depth charges.

Whatever the task there was always the possibility of seaplane hull damage whilst afloat. On 6 September *K7303*, holed when taxiing, had to be beached, something normally only

Stranraer BN-L *of 240 Squadron pulls away during weapon trials.* (IWM)

undertaken after each period of 30 hours' flying. *K7300* was another which had hull damage, this time during take-off, which brought alarming moments spent bringing the boat into shallow water.

Battle of Britain Day 1940 passed more quietly, *K7292* flown by Flt Lt Porteous between 19:25 and 04:34 on an 0.3 patrol winning the distinction of being the only British biplane to fly operationally during the momentous day!

For the rest of September and indeed until April 1941 the Stranraers operated in their allotted western area, *K7291*, *K7292*, *K7295*, *K7299* and *K7302* carrying out most of the tasks and escorting some very important convoys and famous ships. Command of the squadron passed from Wg Cdr Bates to Wg Cdr Carter on 27 September and the squadron remained based at Stranraer.

October's activity brought its first highlight on the 6th when *BN:Y* attacked a suspected U-boat at position 55° 29′N/007° 14′W. On 16 October *C/K7291* took off at 06:30 to escort a 38-ship convoy, and at 11:15 15 miles off Rathlin Island came the closest yet to sinking a U-boat. A periscope was sighted, oil too, so two attacks were delivered without success. *K7291* landed at 14:55, *K7292* was by then carrying out a five-hour escort stint over another convoy of 20 merchant ships, two escorts and two destroyers. A lifeboat was spotted, 25 men seen aboard. But the conditions were bad, contact was lost. That was one of the toughest aspects for anyone who served in Coastal Command, for its primary role was the saving of life — increasingly by preventing its extinction at sea.

Stranraers used by 240 Squadron July–October 1940

K7287	4.6.40–14.5.41 (SOC 25.6.41)
K7290	4.6.40–19.6.40 (Calshot for overhaul), 24.9.40–sank in gale, Stranraer, on 21.11.40
K7291	4.6.40–EFA 10.11.40 (sunk in collision with small vessel)
K7292	19.6.40–13.5.41
K7295	4.6.40–10.4.41, later used at 4(C) OTU
L/K7298	4.6.40–13.4.41
K7301	4.6.40–sunk in gale 21.8.40 (Stranraer)
K7302	4.6.40–13.8.40
K7303	the last Stranraer, used by 4 (C) OTU 4.41–10.42, was struck off charge on 31.10.42.

Spying Spitfires

Battle of Britain and 'Spitfire' have come to be synonymous despite the more extensive use of Hurricanes. But the Spitfire's vital role as a spy in the sky was never so well known, and has been all but forgotten. Yet, without a handful of special Spitfires flown by a few very brave souls, the extent of the build-up of the invasion fleet might not have been appreciated, and the need to bomb congregations in Channel ports might have been overlooked. Admiralty daily assessments, while including reports from agents and other sources, drew their most accurate findings from superb photographs obtained by cameras carried aboard PRU Spitfires.

The decision to form a Photographic Development Unit was taken on 22 March 1939 by Air Ministry Directorate of Operations, in particular to photograph naval activity by using high speed aircraft painted to be barely visible. Heston Special Flight formed to enquire into these problems, acquired two Blenheims and set about increasing their speed by polishing and filling cracks in the skinning.

Acting Wg Cdr F.S. Cotton commanding the Flight used a Lockheed 12a before the war to photograph enemy installations in 'cloak and dagger' activities, but Cotton felt that a fast aircraft like the Spitfire would be far better for photo-reconnaissance sorties. A paper prepared by Flt Lt M. Longbottom of the Unit outlined a lightened unarmed aircraft relying upon speed and height for safety. Air Chief Marshal Dowding approved of the idea and, when approached, managed to have two Spitfires sent to RAE Farnborough for cameras to be installed. On 3 October 1939 the Flight became No. 2 Camouflage Unit. Apt, indeed, for the existence of the PR Spitfires was kept secret for many years.

Both Merlin III Spitfires had an F.24 camera fitted in each wing, a $29\frac{1}{2}$ gal fuel tank being fitted behind the pilot's cockpit in a third example. The first two were retrospectively designated Spitfire 'A', the third being a 'B'. On 3 October 1939 the nucleus of the PDU formed at Heston within Fighter Command. Offices and an Airwork hangar were requisitioned, also the Aero Club and Post Hotel which provided officers' accommodation. The Blenheims were replaced by a pair of Spitfires, which joined Cotton's Lockheed 12a and a Hudson. Then in great secrecy, Spitfire N3071, the Lockheed 12a and a Hudson equipping the 'Special Survey Flight' under Flt Lt R.H. Niven left for Lille/Seclin from where, on 18 November, Flt Lt Longbottom made the first operational sortie to the unfortunately cloud-clad Aachen area. A sortie from Bal-le-Duc on the 22nd proved more successful, photographs being taken in hazy, cloudless conditions.

On the third sortie, flown in excellent weather on 21 December 1939, success came. Longbottom returned with photographs taken between Bitburg and Waxweiler, but there was concern over the strong contrail his aircraft produced. Such trails were not widely understood at the time, but it was known that only by flying at non-trailing altitudes could the give-away sign be avoided, which was far from easy. Nevertheless, Longbottom braved that problem on 29 December 1939 to secure photographs of Aachen, Duren and Cologne, and visited that area again before the Flight came home on 11 January 1940. Medical problems of high flying had also been dramatically displayed when, on 2 January at 32,000 ft and east of Weisbaden, Flt Lt Niven dropped his map. Endeavouring to pick it up from the cockpit floor he blacked out, and although he regained consciousness at 25,000 ft he was unable to control the Spitfire before it had spun down to 5,000 ft.

At Heston the third PR Spitfire variant, the 'C', was devised. This was the first to feature a fuselage camera as well as two under the starboard mainplane, balancing 30 gallons of additional fuel in the port mainplane. It also had the additional fuselage tank and extra oxygen.

PDU became fully operational on 1 April 1940, its establishment 2 Blenheims, 2 Spitfires and 3 Hudsons. Actual strength was a Blenheim, 2 Hudsons, a Harvard 1 and four Spitfires with individualistic modifications including exotic paint schemes. Ranging through cream, pale green to blue, the shades finally chosen were a greyish blue for high fliers and a muddy shade of pink for low-level operators. On 1 May Flt Lt le Mesurier in a Spitfire C P9308 reached Heligoland, later reporting that at 33,000 ft he could not shake off contrails. On 29 April Cotton's Lockheed 12a, impressed as long ago as 15 December 1939, came on unit strength.

As soon as the *Blitzkrieg* began PDU Spitfires watched activity around the Dutch coast. Flt Lt Wise headed for Cuxhaven on 15 May only to have his cameras ice up, a common occurrence at the high levels at which the Spitfires operated. He flew around hoping for a clearance until

Photographed in mid-1940, this grey-blue Spitfire displays PRU's LY identity in light grey, along with an uncertain serial.

eventually, short of fuel, force landed in a field near Horsham St Faith. That station was used as starting point for some flights as on 18 May, busiest day yet, when four sorties were flown and *N3116* photographed large areas of the Netherlands.

PDU needed a supporting organization to extract information from the photographs, and 'Air Intelligence 8' was formed within the Intelligence Branch, Air Ministry, Wembley, during May 1940 to undertake interpretation work. During May 20 sorties had been despatched, providing much useful information for the Navy along with photographs of gun emplacements, bomb damage and tactical items which PDU had not been formed to survey. Clearly its potential was great, although the small scale of the prints was not ideal. That prompted low-level and oblique photography — far more risky. The loss of Plt Off Coleman (*P9308*) on a sortie to Hamburg and Bremen emphasized that high levels did not provide immunity either.

PDU still made considerable use of Stradishall as an operations starting point for sorties to cover north German ports. Viewing the enemy progress into France was the small No. 212 Squadron which had formed with Blenheims and Spitfires at Heston on 10 February 1940. It was detached to France, but forced home on 14 June by the German advance. Flt Lt Wise managed to fly home in a 'captured' Fairey Battle, in company with no less than five airmen!

PDU passed from Fighter Command into 16 Group, Coastal Command on 18 June, because of its reconnoitring and maritime duties. A few penetrations into Germany were however made, one on the day of the change when *P9385* overflew Dulmen, Munster, Rheydt and Salzbergen. As the Battle of Britain period approached almost all the flying was to enemy coastal regions.

Operations and the Battle of Britain period

On 1 July PDU divided itself, 'A' Flight forming at Wick and receiving Spitfires *P9310* and *P9530* with which to photograph the Norwegian scene. 'B' Flight formed at St Eval, with *P9313* and *P9336*, to reconnoitre activity along the French coast from Normandy to Bordeaux. The same day from Heston Flt Lt Wise flew *P9382* to photograph Le Havre and Barfleur from 34,000 ft, *N3116* photographed Le Bourget and secured shots of Nantes and Rouen. *P9385* took evening photographs of Le Havre.

From Wick and St Eval first sorties were flown on 3 July. Flg Off Blount (*P9550*) turned his cameras on Stavanger and Flt Lt G.P. Christie (*P9396*) was successful at St Nazaire

N3117 was very successful in its PRU activities. One of the early conversions, it was later modified into a PR V and posted missing on 9.12.41. (Bruce Robertson)

and Nantes. On the 6th Flt Lt Wilson's cameras misted over, clearing sufficiently for him to secure pictures of Hardanger Fjord from 34,000 ft. To achieve that meant a lonely crossing of the sea and enduring intense cold, such long flights relying upon oxygen and the ever-present risk of interception in an unarmed aircraft. It certainly took courage to fly a PRU Spitfire sortie.

On 8 July PDU became the Photographic Reconnaissance Unit (PRU). Next day Flg Off Taylor left Heston at 16:41 in *R6598* for one of the longest sorties so far. He refuelled at Coltishall then photographed Bremen, Delmenhorst, Leeuwarden and Wilhelmshaven before landing at Heston at 21:05. There was now a mixture of operations, *N3117* on 18 July making a low-level rainy dash to Flushing from where it was chased by a Ju 88. When the weather was clear PR pilots had unique views of famous Battle of Britain engagements being enacted below, as on 20 July when Flt Sgt J.D. Taylor (*N3116*), heading for Rotterdam, gazed down upon an attack around 17:30 on a mid-Channel convoy. By the end of that day photographs had been taken of Caen (*P9310*), Brest and Ushant (*P9313*),

the Scheldt (*P9310*) and Lorient (*P9396*). Two sorties a day by individual Spitfires were now quite frequent, even to Norway. Necessary clear weather was a more limiting factor than serviceability.

Heston's element split into two Flights, 'C' and 'D', on 24 July. Next day 'E' Flight formed, to conduct trials using two Wellingtons (*L4342* and *R2700*) and four Spitfires (*N3117*, *P9384*, *P9453* and *R6804*).

An average of five or six sorties were being flown, 25 July proving a successful day. *P9310* covered Antwerp and the Dutch coast, *P9385* the strip from Le Havre to Boulogne and *R6598* the Dutch coast. Cap Gris Nez was twice photographed, in the afternoon, by *P9385* and *R6598*. Three days later eight sorties were completed, by *P9307* (Boulogne), *P9310* (Scheldt), *P9313* (Brest and St Malo), *P9313* (Cherbourg), *P9382* (took off 15:35 for Lindesnes and Kristiansund, landed 18:50), *P9385* (Boulogne and Ostend), *P9385* (Caen to Cap Gris Nez) and *P9550* (Stavanger-Bergen).

Emphasis was increasingly on discovering the extent of the invasion build-up. The Dortmund-Ems Canal, a vital route for such movement, was photographed from *R6598* on 1 August. Then *P9310* managed pictures of Boulogne and Le Havre through cloud gaps on the 2nd, and on the 4th *N3116* recorded the contents of the docks at Rotterdam and Flushing while *P9385* photographed activity between Boulogne and Ostend. Clear weather on the 5th allowed *P9385* to visit Delfzil and Emden while *N3116* was over Rotterdam and the Maas.

As the Battle of Britain gathered momentum, on the 12th *N3116* snooped on canals around Antwerp, and *P9385* looked again at Calais, St Omer and Boulogne. Information gleaned from such sorties and those of 2 Group Blenheims confirmed that invasion forces were gathering. On 12 August Wg Cdr Tuttle flew across the Channel in poor weather to photograph heavy guns near Calais. His was a special event for he was using *K9787*, literally the 'First of the Few' Spitfires, ironically in action on the day the enemy launched his main Battle of Britain bombing campaign.

While heavy fighting ensued on 15 August six successful PR sorties were flown, by *N3116* (Hague-Rotterdam-Scheldt), *P9385* (Den Helder-Amsterdam and later Ghent-Bruges), *P9550* (Wilhelmshaven-Emden), *R6804* (Kiel) and *R6998* (Bremen, Hamburg). Throughout August, photographs in their thousands became available to intelligence gatherers searching for inland shipping and seaborne vessels. Nine sorties on the 26th were among the most successful, *P9310* going twice to the Netherlands and to Belgium, *P9313* covering Ushant and Brest, *P9382* visiting Bergen and Stavanger, *P9384* Kristiansund, *P9385* Dieppe and Calais, *R6804* Terschelling and Den Helder, *R6894* Rotterdam, and another to Brest and Lorient.

The importance to the British of these spy flights was undoubtedly known by the enemy, for a determined attempt was made on 26 August to destroy Heston. Bombs killed three in Hayes, but far worse was to come, although not before PRU had

provided plentiful detail of the invasion build-up. On 2 September *P9385* filmed the coast between Zeebrugge and Calais and next day *R6894* photographed Boulogne and Calais. Between 10:00 and 12:20 on the 4th (when nine sorties were flown) *P9310* photographed Ostend, Zeebrugge and Dunkirk and later visited Le Havre, Dieppe and Boulogne. *P9385* meanwhile filmed the Netherlands North Sea Canal, Rotterdam and Amsterdam before Flg Off Taylor took *K9787* on an evening visit to Boulogne. On the 5th four of the six sorties were to the main concentration areas, photographs resulting in the identification of over 600 barges and other vessels.

Invasion build-up was now rapid. On the 7th nine sorties were flown including two by *R6598* (Scheldt and Ghent; Le Touquet and Fecamp), two by *R6804* (Ostend and Delfzil; Deauville to Cherbourg) and one by *N3117* (Zeebrugge to Le Touquet) covering the set of ports being used by the massing invasion forces. Intelligence assessment based on their photographs showed nearly 900 barges in place in addition to transport ships. That evening, after heavy bombing of London's dockland, 'Alert 1' — invasion expected within the next 24 hours — was ordered. In the absence of an assault Flg Off Taylor (*P9310*) set off at 06:50 on the 8th to search for and photograph the enemy shipping situation at Calais, and seek signs of mass movement. There were none, and seven other flights (by *K9787*, *P9561*, two by *R6804* and by Hudson *N7301* to Den Helder and Ijmuiden) reported no major sailing. Tidal state favoured this and a few more days. When they had passed the Alert state was reduced.

Another 33 sorties were flown before the next 'Alert 1' was ordered, on 15 September when five sorties were flown to the Channel Ports. This time *N3241* and *X4350* had successful sorties, but Flg Off Hyde-Parker was missing from a sortie over Belgian ports. Losses had been remarkably low, the results from operations outstanding, so that those who gave their lives did so not in vain.

Hyde-Parker's loss coincided with a series of serious incidents at Heston which began on 12 September when two AA shells exploded on the Met Office and a hangar. Early on the 17th nine HEs were dropped in a NE–SW stick, the largest falling on tarmac by a hangar. On the 18th two more HEs and lots of incendiaries landed on the eastern part of the landing ground, then came the very destructive blow of 19 September. At 22:48 a parachute mine descended on the main tarmac, immediately detonated and demolished the main hangar and damaged other important buildings. Amazingly, the Spitfires escaped with little harm. *P9313* had windscreen and canopy damage, *P9307*, *P9426*, *X4029* and *R6900* all had splinter damage and were repaired on site. Extensive damage was caused to Cotton's famous Lockheed 12a, the RAF Inspector General's Percival Q.6 *P5636*, DH Hornet Moth *G-AELO*, and *G-AFTL (AX857)*. PRU's daily sorties to bring home the latest news of invasion preparations were not much interrupted, their cameras recording by the end of September nearly 2,000 barges present, a state which continued far into October.

A change on 1 October resulted in 'C' Flight replacing 'A' Flight at Wick. Next day oil bombs damaged the interpretation centre in Wembley. Then came the traumatic event of 8 October. Flg Off Parker was heading out over Kent when two Bf 109s attacked his Spitfire, vulnerable in such a situation. The aircraft burst into flames and Parker baled out, his flying suit on fire. Upon deploying his parachute he suddenly found himself inverted, and his burning clothing was torn away. Badly burned, he managed to survive the horrific ordeal. More Spitfires were now arriving, PRU having proved its worth. There were more near misses by German bombs too before on 29 October three large bombs hit Heston, one producing a giant crater 30 ft deep and 64 ft across and which demolished east end buildings. Impressive as that was, Flg Off S. Millon's sortie on the same day was far more important. Leaving at 16:20 in *P9551* he made the longest PR flight yet, to reach Stettin and Rostock. No longer was the PRU watching the enemy massing his striking power, it was gathering the evidence with which Bomber Command would one day wreak gigantic vengeance.

Small in number, enormously brave, the pilots of PRU had contributed much to Britain's survival. Soon they would play a very great part in her victory.

Great concern was expressed over the risk of exposing PR Spitfire positions by their contrailing, this mid-war example producing a vapour trail at about 30,000 ft. (via Bruce Robertson)

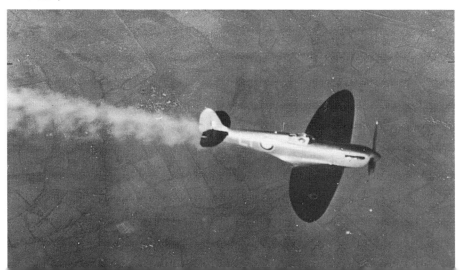

Summary of sorties

	Total flown			Known to have provided useful photographs		
	Heston(a)	**Wick(b)**	**St Eval(c)**	**a**	**b**	**c**
July 1940	78	9	38	57	9	28
August	112	21	30	93	13	25
September	126	13	44	100	8	30
October 1–15	88*	–	–	?	?	?

*Total sorties flown by PRU in the given period

Spitfires used by the PRU 1 July–15 October 1940

NB: Inclusive dates for PRU service include periods when aircraft were being modified/repaired by the Unit/Heston Aircraft Ltd

Serial	Sorties flown					History
	July	**Aug**	**Sept**	**Oct**	**Total**	
K9787	–	4	11	2	17	First production Spitfire. 8 MU Lt Rissington 25.6.40, PRU 11.7.40–FTR 30.6.41
N3111	–		2	2	4	PRU 23.8.4I–FA 21.4.42; ex-54 Sqn 13.12.39–10.7.40
N3116	9	12	–	–	21	2 Cam Unit 39, PRU, damaged 15.8.40, SOC 26.8.40
N3117	3	2	1	–	6	2 Cam Unit 39, PRU, conversion to PRIV, returned PRU, FTR 9.12.41
N3241	–		2	4	6	fighter with 234 Sqn 3,40, converted to PR 'G', PRU 15.9.40–31.8.42, 542 Sqn 10.12.42, 8 OTU 5–6.43; SOC 22.3.45 at 6 MU
P9307	8	1	1	–	10	PDU/PRU 11.2.40–FTR 10.4.41
P9310	10	9	12	6	37	PDU/PRU 11.2.40–8.12.41 8 OTU 27.7.42–missing 2.10.42
P9313	16	10	8	–	34	PRU 21.3.40–FTR 9.11.40
P9315	2	6	21	11	40	PRU 3.7.40–9.11.40; 1 PRU and 3 PRU, SOC 23.2.41
P9382	7	4	5	2	18	PRU 7.5.40–FTR 8.10.40 (Kiel) (FH 113)
P9384	–	11	4	6	21	PRU 19.7.40–missing 29.10.40 flying Heston to Wick
P9385	18	19	2	2	41	PRU 1.4.40–15.11.41; 8 OTU 20.8.42–9.12.44
P9396	14	–	–	–	14	212 Sqn 7.4.40, to PRU, to AST 8.8.40; PRU 14.11.40–FTR 10.4.41
P9453	4	3	2	–	9	PDU 22.4.40–FTR 14.9.40 (FH 22.20)
P9550	13	8	–	4	25	PRU 20.5.40–2.1.41, PRU 29.4.41–140l Flt 1.9.41–FTR 7.11.41
P9561	–	5	11	2	18	PRU 19.8.40–FTR 16.2.41
R6598	14	20	22	–	55	PRU 20.5.40–FTR 22.2.41
R6804	1	17	17	8	43	PRU 25.6.40–missing (EFA) 22.7.41
R6805	–	–	5	–	5	PRU 25.6.40, battle damaged 16.9.40; repaired by SAL 26.9.40; also 2.2.41–FTR 3.5.41
R6844	–	1				
R6879	–	1	1	–	2	PRU 13.8.40–FTR 13.9.40 (FH 14.40)
R6894	–	7	11	5	23	PRU 3.8.40–EFAO, SOC 8.10.40
R6900	–	–	1	6	7	PRU 17.9.40–27.3.41, converted to PR IV, PRU 17.4.41–12.11.41; with 8 OTU 30.7.42–7.10.43; SOC 15.3.45
R6902	–	–	8	6	14	PRU 9.7.40–10.3.41, converted to PR IV, used by 3 and 1 PRUs and 8 OTU, SOC 22.3.45 at 6 MU
R6905	–	–	4	11	15	PRU 9.7.40–30.6.41; later used by 140l Met Flt, 521 Sqn, 8 OTU; SOC 22.3.45 at 6 MU
R6906	–	–	1	–	1	PRU 13.7.40–FTR 17.1.41

Serial	Sorties flown				Total	History
	July	Aug	Sept	Oct		
X4332	–	–	–	2	2	PRU 31.8.40–EAO 29.10.40 (destroyed during raid on Heston; FH 11.10)
X4335	–	–	–	–	–	PRU 31.8.40–10.3.41, 27.3.41–31.5.41; 542 Sqn and 8 OTU later. SOC 6 MU 22.3.45
Unknown	4	5	–	4	13	Serials not recorded in unit diary

Spitfires with PRU during the period, but which did not operate

K9817	20.9.40–9.10.40		*P9551*	18.9.40, to Malta 27.4.41
K9879	11.7.40–EFAO 1.8.40 (crashed NW of Crewkerne, Somerset)		*X4028*	3.8.40–FTR 31.3.41
			X4333	31.8.40–7.10.41
K9959	9.10.40–EFAO 22.1.41 (crashed Long Marston, Herts)		*X4335*	31.8.40–25.5.41
			X4350	15.9.40–FTR 16.10.40 (FH 54.15)
L1055	9.10.40–EFA 5.3.41, SOC 10.3.41		*X4384*	12.9.40–28.3.41
L1081	from 2.10.40		*X4385*	17.9.40–23.11.40
P9309	11.10.40–12.11.40		*X4386*	29.9.40–24.11.40
P9426	1.4.40–10.4.40, 18.6.40–26.6.40, EFA 21.11.40			

Lockheed Hudsons used for photographic and meteorological reconnaissance

	Sorties flown				
	July	Aug	Sept	Oct	
N7301	–	1	1	1	16.1.40–FTR 26.10.40
N7321	–	2	–	–	17.7.40–EFA 22.8.40
N7336	2	3	–	–	On loan from RAE?
P5137	–	–	–	5	5.10.40–26.12.40
P5139	–	2	1	1	10.7.40–5.1.41
P5160	1	1	3	–	15.4.40–4.11.40
T9290	–	–	4	2	25.8.40–11.11.40

Hudsons were used mainly for weather reconnaissance around enemy coastal regions.

The Blind Approach and Development Unit

The Blind Approach Training and Development Unit which re-opened at Boscombe Down on 13 June 1940 and was closely controlled by Air Ministry through Fighter Command, is nevertheless best included within the seekers. Although perhaps not strictly 'operational', crews from this unit confirmed the existence of German *Knickebein* radio beams. For its investigative task (code named *Headache*) the unit acquired three Whitleys and eight Ansons. Among the latter fitted out by 19 June to seek out the beams were *L7967*, *N9938* and *N9945*. Sqn Ldr H.E. Bufton arrived on 20 June from Stradishall to command the unit and made the first *Headache* sortie later that day with another on the following night. On 22 June he flew *N9945* to Wyton from where further operations were flown.

Three Whitleys (*P4943*, *P4944* and *P5019*) reached the unit on 1 July but on 5 July the two eldest examples were replaced by *P5047* and *P5057*. Anson *R3313* also joined them. *N9938* crashed at Wyton on 6 July and *P5019* at Boscombe Down on 12 July. BAT&DU was indeed unfortunate in its equipment for a further four Ansons (*K6241*, *K6258*, *K6318* and *N4953*) arrived in such poor state that on 23 July *R9812*, *R9813*, *R9814* and *R9815* were flown in direct from Avro at Woodford to replace three of them.

One Anson in July briefly operated from Leuchars, searching for beams directed from Norway. By 12 August the Wyton detachment held four Ansons and crews until next day when *L7967* became the second to crash there. Special duty flying hours amounted to 59.15 in July, and 86 by day and 39 at night in August. No. 80 Wing absorbed the specialist staff at HQ Fighter Command and on 30 September the unit was renamed the Wireless Intelligence Development Unit, forerunner of No. 109 Squadron. By then its equipment also included Ansons *R9828*, *R9829*, *R9830*, *R9837* and *R9838*.

The Bombers

Bomber Command went to war split into three parts — the strategic bomber force, an advanced strike force of Battles in France, and No. 2 Group, Blenheim-equipped and home based, held in reserve to support the army.

'Western Plans' prescribed strategic targets — WA6 oil installations, WA7 U-boat bases, WA9 preventing use of the Kiel Canal, WA12 the sinking of warships and WA15 minelaying. To these in 1940 were added railways, waterways, aircraft plants, aluminium works and various factories, spreading targeting over a wide spectrum.

Wellingtons of 3 Group, East Anglian based, initially concentrated upon anti-naval activities, later attacking ports as well as a variety of targets within enemy territory.

Hampdens, the most numerous night bombers and preferred by Command senior officers because of their good load-carrying capacity and smaller crew number, were Lincolnshire based and operated by 5 Group. Their targets were in particular communications, and they were responsible for mining enemy waters and attacking coastal shipping and airfields.

Whitleys of 4 Group, Yorkshire based, could readily be fitted with additional internal tankage and were capable of safely operating at all-up weights far in excess of those originally envisaged. Consequently they were suitable for raids on very distant targets, including Italian.

All bombers could carry 250 lb and 500 lb general purpose (GP) bombs including specialized variants. They also delivered 4 lb hexagonal shaped incendiary bombs packed in small bomb containers (SBC) which distributed loads rather at random. Hampdens were the first to deliver 2,000 lb bombs and carried HEs on external racks beneath each mainplane.

Whereas by the summer of 1940 all of the aforementioned operated at night, Blenheims of 2 Group operated by day and night. Between 9 May and 4 June 1940 Nos. 3, 4 and 5 Groups flew 1,696 sorties losing 39 aircraft; 2 Group Blenheim squadrons managed 856 day sorties losing 56 aircraft and having 10 more written off due to battle damage. Such was the measure of 2 Group's contribution to the fight for France. The slaughter was far from over for on 3 June 2 Group squadrons were ordered to fly day raids to attract and divert German fighters from supporting their army. It was a cruel role which 3 Group was to exercise until late 1943.

On 5 June 1940 the Group was ordered to continue close support to the BEF left in France, then on 6 July came an instruction to attack airfields and barges in occupied territory. Since the outbreak of war the Blenheims had flown PR sorties over Germany and from 23 July these were stepped up by a new Directive ordering damage assessment flights and a widespread watch on the invasion build-up. As if that was not enough there remained Group Ops. Order No. 11 — lone penetrations, using cloud cover, to attack enemy targets and rouse fighter response. Hundreds of such sorties were despatched, few finding vital cover to allow them to proceed. When they did the results could be disastrous, as happened in a bright blue sky over Denmark when a Blenheim squadron was all but wiped out.

On 17 August 1940 a major conference discussed the future equipment of Bomber Command and in particular uses for the lightly armed Blenheims. 'Replace them', 'disband 2 Group' were the most numerous cries. 'More Hampdens' called some, while others pointed to the good record of the Whitley. Wellingtons attracted less favour, but engine and airframe production forced the final outcome. Whatever happened, the RAF with invasion pending needed to honour a pledge to maintain 250 Army support aircraft. Some Blenheim squadrons would eventually re-equip with 'Wimpeys' — but not until late October did the process of making Bomber Command a medium/heavy force begin. Although a few Short Stirlings reached the Command in August and September, heavies were not operational until long after the Battle. Backing all activity were the Operational Training Units controlled by Nos. 6 and 7 Groups of Bomber Command. Three OTUs (Nos. 10, 11 and 16) flew a limited number of night sorties over France during the Battle of Britain.

From the start of July 1940 a proportion of Bomber Command was held at standby to attack a German invasion at sea. During August two Fairey Battle squadrons were loaned to Coastal Command, their prime task to sink E-boats protecting an invasion flotilla. On 7 September, with invasion rated imminent, the whole of Bomber Command was switched to attacking German shipping in Channel ports during night-long onslaughts.

Bomber Command resumed strategic operations by October while 2 Group harrassed German airfields particularly at night, making intruder raids long before Fighter Command's similar campaign opened.

As can be seen from the operations listings, targets throughout the Battle extended over a wide area. Often they could not be located beneath the clouds or in the haze, even when aircraft flew low encountering flak and searchlights. Precisely where many bombs fell is uncertain since few records remain. What is certain is that Bomber Command contributed much to the Battle of Britain, and particularly by attacking invasion vessels in the Channel ports.

Abbreviations used in bomber operations notes

afd *airfield*
gw *gas works*
myd(s) *marshalling yard(s)*
ps *power station*
ry *railway*
sy *shipyard*
10/11, 6/9 etc = 10 out of 11 bombers despatched attacked a target, 6 out of 9, etc

Coded Target Identity

During the first two years of the war many bomber operations records list targets usually within population centres using a special identity system. The most common targets thus identified and attacked in summer 1940 included these:

A — Synthetic/oil refineries

A2	Bremen
A5	Hamburg
A7	Hamburg
A8	Hamburg
A10	Rhenania Ossag, Hamburg
A17	Misburg
A18	Hanover
A25	Emmerich
A27	Monheim
A28	Rhenania Ossag, Düsseldorf/Reisholz
A69	Bottrop

A70	Scholven Buer, Gelsenkirchen
A71	Nordstern, Gelsenkirchen
A72	Köln/Wesseling
A75	Kamen
A76	Bohlen/Gotha
A77	Merseburg/Leuna
A78	Magdeburg
A79	Sterkrade Holten
A97	Zeitz
A104	Politz/Stettin
A108	Dortmund
A160	Magdeburg
A161	Frankfurt
A163	Ludwigshafen

B — Power stations

B8	Hamburg
B56	Berlin West
B57	Berlin, Klingenburg
B58	Berlin, Charlottenburg
B59	Moabit, Berlin

C — Chemical industry

C37	Leverkusen

CC — Channel ports

CC7	Flushing
CC11	Zeebrugge
CC13	Ostend
CC24	Le Havre
CC26	Lorient
CC29	Boulogne
CC37	Calais

D — Docks/Harbours

D1	Hamburg
D2	Blohm & Voss, Hamburg
D3	Kiel
D4	Kiel (Krupp)
D5	Wilhelmshafen
D11	Bremen
D184	Naval base, Emden
D197	Naval base, Wilhelmshafen

E — Engineering works

E8	Krupp, Essen

F — Aircraft factories

F1	Focke-Wulf, Bremen
F18	Gotha
F19	Kassel
F23	Henschel, Berlin
F40	Mockau, Leipzig
F49	Wenzendorf
F69	Junkers, Bernberg
F74	Dornier, Wismar

G — Motor and engine manufacturers

G20	Hirth, Stuttgart
G82	Frankfurt
G161	Siemenstadt

H — Aircraft support unit

H52	Enschewege

Pie chart showing the squadron percentage proportions of Bomber Command

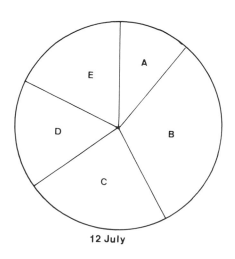

12 July

LEGEND:		No. of	
Letter		squadrons	12 July
A	Battle	4	11
B	Blenheim IV	11	31
C	Wellington 1a/1c	8	23
D	Whitley V	6	17
E	Hampden	6	18

172

K — Aircraft storage depot

K1	Diepholtz
K9	Paderborn
K52	Göttingen
K54	Kolleda (stores for Junkers, Bernberg)

L — Aluminium works

L82	Grevenbroich
L83	Heringen
L84	Köln
L86	Bittefeld
L89	Bittefeld, I.G. Farben

M — Marshalling yards/rail facilities

M25/25A and M58	Aqueducting, etc., Dortmund–Ems canal
M61	Duisburg
M101	Krefeld
M116	Soest
M122	Schwerte
M431	Osnabruck
M434	Hamm
M440	Ruhrort
M448	Essen
M461	Schwerte
M464	Köln/Eifeltor
M465	Köln/Gremberg
M466	Köln/Kalk Nord

M469	Koblenz
M472	Krefeld
M480	Ehrang
M482	Mannheim
M499	Tempelhof/Berlin
M501	Berlin

Z — Aerodromes

Z29	Fokker, Amsterdam
Z36	Rotterdam
Z40	Brussels/Évère
Z57	Schiphol
Z66	Eindhoven
Z83	Brussels/Melsbroek
Z86	Antwerp/Duerne
Z131	St. Inglevert
Z141	Lille/Seclin
Z145	Amiens/Glisy
Z151	Cambrai/Niergues
Z158	Ambes
Z159	St. Nazaire
Z204	Villacoublay

Other specialized targets

F152	Škoda, Pilsen
U172	Fiat, Turin
W1	Pirelli, Milan
X2	Aosta steel works

The Armstrong Whitworth Whitley

Nose down, slab-sided and plank-winged lumbering giant; unforgettable wartime sight, the Whitley. Was it really the aeroplane which, on the first night of the war, ventured far over Germany distributing millions of now highly collectable notelets? Did Whitleys in June 1940 open wartime trans-Alpine excursions to so far distant Italy? Yes, and they achieved far more than ever expected, equipping front line squadrons of Bomber Command until May 1942.

The Whitley originated from the Czech Government's 1934 request to Armstrong-Whitworth Aircraft (AWA) for the firm to devise an aircraft to bomb Berlin. Czech interest soon faded, then the company passed details of the bomber to the Air Staff. They were keenly interested because restrictions on bomber weight were being lifted.

Specification B.3/34 for a night bomber/transport was rapidly drawn up around the design. Approved by DTD on 3 July 1934, it reflected the changed situation regarding bombers. Outlined was an aircraft with maximum speeds of at least 205 mph at 5,000 ft and 225 mph at 15,000 ft, a service ceiling of 25,000 ft, bomb load of 2,500 lb and fuel for a 1,250-mile range at 15,000 ft after a half-hour climb from take-off at maximum engine revs.

AWA having originated the idea, three other contractors (Fairey,

Handley-Page and Vickers) were sent informative copies of the specification and invited to a conference held on 1 August to discuss the bomber. The Air Staff considering the AWA design praiseworthy and worth adopting, there was none of the conventional 'invite to tender' process, although a design was submitted by Vickers. The Chief of the Air Staff, (who was not keen on a second geodetic bomber) also considered the Vickers price too high and on 16 August 1934 approved an order for two prototypes of the AWA design. A contract was signed on 14 September 1934 stipulating delivery of the first in February 1936, the second two months later.

Although a direct descendant of the company's C.26/31 bomber transport and retaining its angular 'easy' to construct form, the new machine, defended by three gun turrets, would differ by having a light alloy monocoque fuselage, which impressed the Air Ministry. Wing construction would also differ, and power would be provided by two Armstrong-Siddeley Tiger radials.

A mock-up conference took place on 20 December 1934, followed by a second on 16 January 1935 to discuss details. Although particular building difficulties arose, the Air Ministry was soon pressurizing the firm to speed construction to build what was now viewed as a very important aeroplane. Lacking a modern heavy bomber for the near future within the May 1935

K4586, *the Whitley prototype*. (AWA)

Expansion Scheme C, the Air Staff pressed the Cabinet to approve an order off the drawing board. Sanction was soon extracted, an order for 80 Whitleys being placed on 23 August 1935 — the day after the first Blenheims were ordered.

On 16 March 1936 the 18,100 lb first prototype K4586 (Tiger IX) undertook its maiden flight from Whitley, Coventry. Flight tests showed it to be markedly unstable laterally, a condition later cured by 4° outer wing dihedral and increased rudder areas. Otherwise very satisfactory test summaries reached London, along with gratifying news that the structure could accept heavier loading than at first envisaged. Expectation was that 52 Whitleys would reach the RAF by mid-1937, but the Ministry's Resident Technical Officer (RTO) estimated in November 1936 that delivery would begin in January 1937. Although a 19,500 lb production Mk I first flew on 23 December 1936, the second did not emerge until 11 February 1937. Delivery commenced in March 1937 with four examples, and the second prototype, now intended to test new stability improvements later on, had only just emerged and did not reach Martlesham until 24 March. By June 1937 only 14 Whitley 1s had been delivered, 24 by October. Even so the company had done well to start delivery a mere three years after project conception. They also had in hand an order for 12 four-engined Ensign airliners for Imperial Airways, a type sharing the Whitley's new alloy

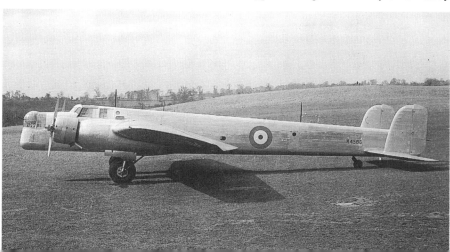

construction system replacing steel tubing in box spars. Like Supermarine, AWA was doing its best in tackling the largest contracts it had ever received — and the Ensign now had to take second place, which also meant its late delivery.

The Whitley 1, built to Specification 21/35, had Tiger IX engines and was designed to carry 4 × 250 or 500 lb bombs in the fuselage, 3 × 120 lb bombs inboard of each engine nacelle and 3 × 250 lb HEs in outboard wing cells. By the time it entered service this was clearly not the bomber the Air Staff wanted for a knock-out blow on Germany. Much more in line with their needs was the 14,000 lb bomb load, four-engined B.12/36 and the medium P.13/36. Go-ahead had also been given to the B.1/35, a redesigned enlargement of the Wellington which became the Warwick. All were surely greatly superior to the interim Whitley. They were, however, many years away from service so to fill the gap repeated Whitley orders were placed, ultimately keeping it in Bomber Command until Spring 1944. Its amazing structural strength allowed weight increases throughout its life, the Mk 1 rising to 21,200 lb and later to 23,500 lb.

The second prototype, *K4587*, which first flew on 11 February 1937, exhibited within a few weeks the additional dihedral from the bolted joint of the mainplanes outboard of the engine nacelles. That much improved the stability of *K4587*, first flown in that state on 13 April 1937, further improvement coming from larger rudders and smaller fins, testing of which began on 10 May 1937.

To further improve the aircraft, whose increased load potential was good, Tiger VIIIs with two-speed blowers were featured by the Mk II, the first of which, *K7217*, flew on 8 December 1937. Now, and under rearmament Scheme F, the Whitley order increased to 240, all of which were planned to be built by March 1939. Air Ministry secretly hoped that half might not by then be delivered so the order could be cancelled, saving money for the P.13/36. But by February 1938, with the latter programme slipping, an additional 140 Whitleys were ordered — and to a new Specification, 20/36, which produced the Mk III.

Review of the entire bomber programme during the planning of 1938's Scheme L found the Air Council anxious not to accept any more Whitleys than those on order, believing better things were coming. AWA was now to be approached to build 64 Wellingtons instead of Whitleys, then switch to P.13/36, but the company's production rate was so slow that a change would have taken many months to achieve. Instead, additional Whitleys were ordered to keep the work force intact.

That encouraged further improvement of the Whitley by re-engining, yet it still compared unfavourably with the Wellington. One hundred Whitleys had been delivered by the 1938 Munich crisis, with the remaining 304 due for delivery by December 1939. In yet another attempt to speed production another 100 were ordered in October 1938 to encourage AWA to enlarge its labour force. A year later, with production still too slow, the Air Ministry decided Whitley production must end whatever the consequences. An SBAC consultative Committee looked into the problem, concluding that Whitley production offered a sounder return than cancellation and change. Another 150 Whitleys were ordered to hold AWA intact.

Surveying aircraft production in mid-May 1940, Beaverbrook decided the Whitley, a major component of Bomber Command, must continue and ordered 300 more Whitleys, another 300 in June 1940 and even an additional 300 in September 1940, to ensure AWA carried on for another year when, hopefully, the company could start building Lancasters. In the event the last Whitley, a very different machine from the Mk 1, was completed in June 1943.

Apart from engines, much improvement had been made to the

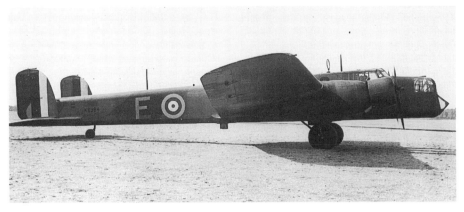

Whitley III K8984 serving with 10 OTU in the summer of 1940. (IWM)

Whitley's armament by fitting Frazer-Nash front and mid-under turrets, first featured by *K7183* and first flown on 14 March 1938. The first 20 Mk III P/1 Tiger VIII aircraft (*K8936–8955*) had twin Vickers guns in the tail turret and no mid turret, and the main Mk III/P2 aircraft (*K8956–9015*) were able to carry 2 × 2,000 lb AP bombs. All Mk Is and IIs were withdrawn before the 1940 action but the Mk III remained in regular use at OTUs until late 1942, the last example retiring in March 1943.

The biggest advance came when Rolls-Royce Merlins replaced Tiger engines. Flight trials of *K7208* (Merlin IIs) fitted at Rolls-Royce began on 4 April 1938. Although tipping the scales at 25,500 lb, its top speed of 239 mph at 16,000 ft made it the fastest Whitley yet. Nevertheless, develop-

ment of Tiger versions continued, *K8936* the first production Mk III flying on 7 September 1938, and from Baginton where a new large AWA factory had opened. Initially weighing 23,983 lb all-up, the Mk III was later cleared to operate at 25,400 lb. *K8936* featured an AWA manually operated tail turret replaced, in *K7183* during 1938, by the four-gun tail turret for Merlin aircraft, which entailed lengthening the fuselage.

In an attempt to provide even more power Whitley *K7243* was re-engined with the experimental Armstrong-Siddeley Deerhound and first flown on 6 January 1939. That programme abruptly ended when the aircraft crashed on 6 March 1940.

Main development in 1939 centred on the Whitley IV (Merlin IV engines), the first of which, *K9016* flown on 18

Whitley V N1503 of 19 OTU Kinloss during the summer of 1940. (IWM)

April, featured the smaller fin and larger rudder already tried. In this version the top speed rose from 190 mph of the 21,000 lb Mk 1 to 239 mph in the latest version. April 1939 brought the first flight of the even better Merlin X-powered 26,000 lb Mk IV. Early Mk IVs had Vickers GO guns in nose and tail and a Browning in the dustbin turret.

Repeated weight increases were reflected in increased operational loadings, A&AEE trials being conducted in June 1939 using a 26,500 lb Mk III. On 22 July 1939 the first of seven production Mk IVas (Merlin X) flew, making the Air Staff disappointed that only the final seven Mk IVs could be thus completed. They decided that 33 earlier aircraft should be modified into IVas as soon as possible, a situation made more difficult due to problems in fitting Rotol propellers.

The Mk IVa lay half-way between the IV and the most prolific Whitley, the Merlin X Mk V of which 1,466 were built. *N1345*, the first example, flew on 4 August 1939 and had a top speed of 225 mph at 16,700 ft. Although normally operated at weights up to 26,000 lb, the Mk V proved itself capable of operating at 30,000 lb during October 1939 tests at Boscombe Down. Doubling the bomber's operational weight, and increasing possible load from 3,080 lb to 8,000 lb, was an outstanding achievement.

Many changes had indeed been made since the design of the Mk I — able to carry 4 × 500 lb HEs in the fuselage cells, 6 × 250 lb HE in the inner wing cells and 6 × 112 lb HE in the outer wing cells — hence those very deep mainplanes. The bombs were originally released through automatic spring-loaded doors in the skinning. Mechanically operated doors were next fitted, but only to the front fuselage cells where 250 lb bombs or incendiaries in SBCs were carried. When the 112 lb bomb became obsolescent the six outer wing cells were dismantled and their doors permanently closed. Much later some Mk Vs had the outer cells modified, then permitting carriage of 60 × 50 lb bombs.

All turrets in the Whitley I and II were of AWA design, featuring freely mounted Lewis guns with Vane-type ring and bead sights. Hand-operated turrets being unsatisfactory at the aircraft's speed — and particularly the nose turret — a change was made in the Mk III whereby the FN 16 power-operated turret with rigid mounted Vickers GO gun and reflector sight was introduced in June 1938. Amidships was sited the retractable FN 17 twin-Browning and reflector sight, power-operated 'dustbin'. Avro produced the AW 38 bulbous tail turret and fitted it with a Vickers GO gun on many Whitleys before the Mk V. Not surprisingly, so many changes produced a number of hybrid Whitleys.

Further turret changes were also

Whitleys popped up their tails and then eventually drifted off — nose down. (AWA)

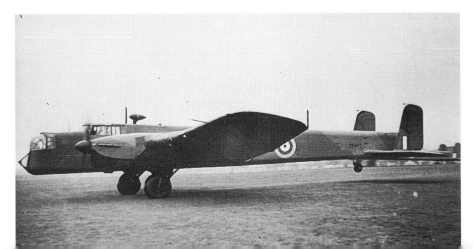

featured by the Mk V form, in which the under turret was deleted and the manual AW 38 rear turret replaced by the four-Browning FN 4. Beam defence featured by other bombers was lacking in Bomber Command Whitleys, although some Coastal Command GR VIIs had beam-mounted GO guns.

Turret change again took place in June 1940. This time the tail turret was removed making way for a paratroop exit. An easier way out was soon chosen and by September 1940 investigation was underway into the possibility of troops parachuting from the one-time mid-under turret position. Hinging doors were fitted, and a tube in the rear fuselage upon which static lines ran on rollers. A 10-in deep shield was fitted ahead of the hole breaking the airflow, and the tailwheel became spatted to discourage a line tangling around it. Even before this activity a Whitley was chosen for glider towing trials, commenced late autumn. Unforeseen at birth, Whitleys were to play a major part in training Britain's airborne forces. The aeroplane that many did not want exceeded most expectations.

Whitley delivery March 1937–December 1940

	Jan	Feb	Mar	April	May	June	July	Aug	Sept	Oct	Nov	Dec	Total
1937	–	–	4	3	3	4	3	3	4	6	4	–	34
1938	10	9	10	7	7	3	–	2	11	6	8	20	93
1939	15	12	5	1	9	15	7	15	17	19	23	19	157
1940	22	18	21	30	40	50	45	39	39	32	27	24	387
Total													671

Delivery on 15 October 1940: *T4263*, '*64*, '*65*

Whitleys Mk I to IV with operational potential which served between July and October 1940

Mk I — none operational in 1940; last example *K7189* struck off charge at 44 MU 11.43

Mk II (with 10 OTU from 18.4.40)
K7221 to 33 MU 13.7.40
K7222 to 37 MU 3.9.40
K7229 to 33 MU 13.7.40
K7234 to 37 MU 23.7.40
K7254 to 33 MU 15.7.40
K7256 to 37 MU 22.7.40
K7257 to 33 MU 20.7.40

Used from July 1940 at the Central Landing School, Ringway, for paratroop training:
K7218, K7220, K7230, K7231

Mk III (10 OTU)
K8936
K8940 18.4.40–19.8.40
K8941 13.8.40–18.3.41
K8942 9.7.40–20.10.40
K8945 25.8.40–12.9.40
K8946 13.8.40–19.6.42
K8949 28.6.40–10.5.41
K8951 25.8.40–12.9.40
K8954 13.8.40–10.3.41
K8956 25.6.40–27.9.40
K8959 15.6.40–14.6.42
K8962 27.4.40–20.11.42
K8972 25.6.40–27.4.42

K8973 3.7.40–14.12.42
K8975 25.6.40–16.11.41
K8976 18.4.40–23.1.41
K8977 18.4.40–6.1.41
K8979 24.6.40–5.4.42
K8981 24.4.40–5.11.41 (crashed Stanton Harcourt)
K8986 12.7.40–11.3.43
K8987 18.4.40–13.11.40
K8991 18.4.40–23.6.41
K8992 18.4.40–18.8.41
K8994 26.6.40–30.4.42
K9003 18.4.40–21.6.42
K9004 27.6.40–18.9.40
K9005 5.7.40–5.8.41
K9010 21.5.40–23.9.40
K9011 18.4.40–16.6.42
K9013 18.4.40–6.9.41
K9014 18.4.40–7.1.42
K9015 18.4.40–6.8.40 (crashed)

Mk IV
Although *K9019*, '*23*, '*25*, '*29*, '*33*, '*36* and '*42* served with No. 10 OTU from May 1940, none flew on operations. They joined surviving Mk IVas at 19 OTU Kinloss during August 1940.

Between 1 July and 15 October 1940, 270 Whitley Vs saw squadron use, of which 28 per cent were in all struck off charge (75 aircraft). Included were 60 written off during operational flying, seven which crashed during training flights, one destroyed in a ground accident and eight by bombing.

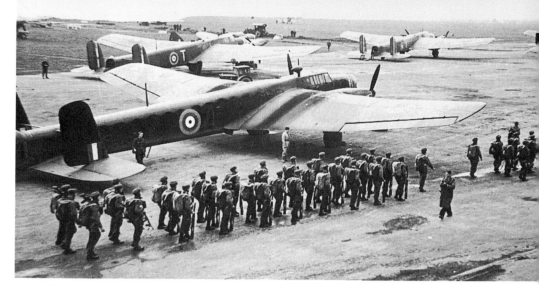

From the autumn of 1940 Whitleys began to play what became a very major part in the establishment and training of Britain's airborne forces. The Mk.V in the foreground shares the task at Ringway with Tiger-engined versions.

Operations

Date	No. sorties completed/ despatched	Targets listed as attacked
July		
30.6/ 1.7	20	Bremen (oil) 10/11, Köln and Hamm MY 6/9
1/2	13	*Scharnhorst* in Kiel 5, Hamm MY 8
2/3	16	Évère and Hingene 6/10, Hamm 4/6
3/4	7	Merville afd 3/4, barges Rotterdam 2/4
4/5	12	Hamburg sy 5/6, Wilhelmshaven 4/6
5/6	12	Merville afd, Wilhemshaven dry dock 5/6
6/7	10	Kiel sy 3/10
7/8	12	Kiel sys, Hamm MY 2/4
8/9	12	Kiel and Évère afds 6/12
11/12	5/8	Köln, Leverkusen chemical wks, Seigburg
12/13	22	Kiel 5/12, Emden 10
13/14	14	Monheim 7/14
14/15	22	Diepholtz (K3) 12, Paderborn (K9) 10
19/20	29	Gelsenkirchen, Hamm MY, Dorsten, Münster, Gelsenkirchen 11/14, Bremen 12/15
20/21	16/21	Wenzendorf and Wismar acft fact, Hamburg, Neuminster
21/22	26	Kassel and Dorsten 16/20, Hamm and Soest MY 5/6
22/23	23	Bremen, Hanover, Hamburg, Diepholz, Delmenhorst 10/11 Paderborn afd, Bielefeld, Handorf, Bernburg 7/12
23/24	24	Kassel, Hamburg (oil), Osnabruck, Oldenburg, Dortmund, Schiphol
24/25	12	*Bismarck* in Hamburg, *Tirpitz* in Wilhelmshaven 2/12
25/26	24	Bottrop, Sterkrade, Bottrop, Kamen, Duisburg, Ruhrort; 18/24
26/27	9	Wilhelmshaven 4/6, Hamm MY 3
28/29	11/15	Wismar acft factory, Travemunde afd
29/30	16	Reisholtz 9/12, Hamm MY 2/4
August		
1/2	13/15	Monheim, Reisholtz, Rattingen
2/3	11/14	Erdol and Salzbergen oil refineries
3/4	6/7	Rhenania Oil at Monheim
4/5	10/11	Sterkrade, Krefeld afd (one aircraft engaged off Dutch coast by Bf 110)
5/6	10/15	Wismar Do works, Kielvic oil depot, Neuminster afd

179

Date	No.	Target
9/10	11/13	Ludwigshafen chem. wks and two afds
10/11	15/20	Frankfurt, Knapsack, Köln/Eifeltor, Hoescht afd, Hengelar
11/12	13/15	Gelsenkirchen, Hattingen PS, Remscheid, Krefeld
12/13	6/15	Harringen aluminium wks, Munset, Witten, Dortmund area
13/14	32/35	Turin and Milan acft facts, Cassano bridges
14/15	21/22	Ambes (oil)
15/16	3/4	Turin aero engine wks 2, Milan (Caproni) 2
16/17	36/48	Bohlen oil targets, Me factory/Augsburg, Karl Zeiss Jena, Waldorf & Helgongen furnace, Sondershausen, Halle area
18/19	4	Turin, Milan
	17/20	Rheinfelder aluminium wks, Walschart chem. wks, Freiburg, Hapshiem afd
19/20	12	Scharnowitz PS Halle
24/25	6	Sesto Sangiovani acft fact, Calindi, Milan, Basto Arsizio
	16	Daimler Benz/Stuttgart, IG Farben/Ludwishaven
25/26	23?	Berlin (Siemens & Halske), Berlin (Siemens & Schukert), Bremen
26/27	9/11	Sesto Sangiovanni and Marelli magneto wks, Turin (Fiat)
27/28	9	Me factory Augsburg, oil store and MY Mannheim, nr Koblenz
	2/6	Fiat, Sesto' and Marelli-Turin
28/29	7/10	Dessau Junkers factory 7, Reisholtz 2, Dortmund 1
29/30	4	Autobahn nr Mannheim, Diest and Dusseldorf afds
30/31	8/12	Berlin 8, Hamburg docks and afd 4
31/1.9	6/9	Köln lignite wks 3/6, Levrkusen 3

September

Date	No.	Target
1/2	6	Fiat Turin 2, Sesto Sangiovani Marelli magneto wks 2, River Po bridge Alessandria
	5	Munich — BMW 1, MY 4
2/3	12	Genoa (Conserta power station), Frankfurt (A161 oil); 2 ditched

Date	No.	Target
3/4		
4/5	12	Berlin 6, Magdeburg 6
5/6	15	Turin and Regensburg 10, Warzburg and Karlsruhe 5
6/7	2/5	Berlin
7/8	7	Attack barges in Boulogne and Ostend at hourly intervals
8/9		Bremen sy
9/10	15/20	Bremen sys 7, Berlin Neukoln gw 3, BMW Berlin 1; Wesermunde, Wisburg, Hamburg 4
10/11	/22	Wilhelmshaven 2, Bremen Fw factory 3, Potsdam 6/7, Bremen oil 3/10
11/12	20	Berlin 5, Borkum 2, Bremen sy 13
13/14	19	Dunkirk 9, Calais 9/10 — barges
14/15	11	Antwerp shipping 10, Flushing 1
15/16	24	Hamburg sy 2/13, Berlin 3/4, Wesermunde, Wilhelmshaven, Cuxhaven, Dunkirk, Wangeroog 7
17/18	15/29	Hamburg docks 5, Ostend 10 — barges
18/19	28	Le Havre 2, Zeebrugge 7, Antwerp 6/8; Hamm, Krefeld, Mannheim, Neubeckham 10/13
	2/3	leaflet drop by 6 Group on Amiens, Rouen, Brest
20/21	18	Mannheim, Ehrang, Soest, Krefeld, Schiphol, Trier, Duisburg, Brussels, Den Helder, Antwerp, Flushing 3
	1	leaflet drop by 6 Group Lille-Amiens-Rouen-Brest
21/22	21/22	Boulogne
22/23	12	Lauta aluminium wks 4/8, Lauta & Dresden rly lines 4
23/24	21	Berlin 9, shipping Boulogne 5, Wismar 2, Gifhald, Hamburg, Cuxhaven, Brunsbuttel, Jever
24/25	20	Berlin (Friedrichsielde transformer station, B120 Finkenherd, Markische electric wks)
25/26	19	Gneisenau, Scharnhorst and Lutzow in Kiel — 6, Antwerp 9
26/27	15	Shipping Le Havre
27/28	11	Shipping Le Havre 1 and Lorient 10

T4131: EY-W *of 78 Squadron, photographed after completing 36 sorties.*

28/29	14	Berlin W. ps, Friedrichselde transformer, Hanover station, Charlottenburg gw, Neukoln gw, Waldeck ps, Amsterdam Fokker factory 3, Wilhelmshaven 3, Spandau, Hamburg, Stendaal, Magdeburg
29/30	?	Misburg, Magdeburg, Antwerp, Schiphol, Hildesheim
30/1.10	8	Berlin 6, shipping in Le Havre 1, Verden 1

October

1/2	16	Sterkrade Holten oil, Rotterdam
2/3	18	Rotterdam, Stettin, Finkenherd ps (B120)
8/9	17	Gelsenkirchen, Hanau, Amsterdam (Fokker factory)
9/10	1	Special reconnaissance, shipping, Le Havre
10/11	21	Leuna (synthetic oil plant), Amsterdam (Fokker) and afds including Merseburg

Whitley Vs used by Squadrons 1 July– 15 October 1940

No. 10 Sqn, Dishforth; to Leeming 8.7.40

N1483	28.3.40–FTR 30.9/1.10.40 (ditched, Irish Sea; returning from Berlin)
N1496	9.3.40–FTR 15/16.8.40 (Kiel)
N1497	6.6.40–FTR 15/16.8.40 (Milan)
P4935	21.8.40–FTR 6/7.9.40 (Berlin)
P4937	16.7.40–23.7.40
P4946	6.6.40–? (FH 389)
P4952	1.5.40–FTR 15.10.40
P4953	1.5.40–15.6.41
P4955	5.5.40–FTR 16/17.8.40 (crashed in Netherlands; Jena)
P4956	5.5.40–10.4.41
P4957	8.5.40–EFB 30.10.40
P4958	5.5.40–25.7.40
P4959	5.5.40–EFAO 27.10.40
P4961	8.5.40–EFB 21.12.40
P4964	8.5.40–4.8.40
P4965	8.5.40–FTR 14.8.40 (ditched off Dymchurch; Milan)
P4966	10.5.40–FTR 15.9.40 (ditched off Yorks; Antwerp)
P4967	10.5.40–EFB 4.9.40 (crashed Northallerton; Berlin)
P4990	18.6.40–FTR 26/27.8.40 (shot down at Valera nr Varere, Italy; Milan)
P4993	11.7.40–EFB 14.10.40
P4994	14.7.40–EFB 22.10.40

P5001	21.6.40-FTR 5.11.40 (ditched)	N1462	14.5.40-EFB 18.6.41
P5018	14.7.40-FTR 1.7.41	G/N1466	1.3.40-FBO2 5/6.9.40
P5048	16.8.40-FTR 11.5.41	J/N1470	1.3.40-EFB 24.9.40 (crashed,
P5055	18.8.40-FTR 28.6.41		Linton-on-Ouse)
P5094	18.8.40-EFB 8/9.9.40 (Ostend)	N1472	3.7.40-FTR 22/23.7.40
T4130	10.9.40-FTR 30.9/1.10.40		(Paderborn)
	(Berlin)	S/N1527	18.5.40-21.12.40
T4143	6.9.40-EFB 15.10.40	P4941	13.7.40-23.7.40
T4148	18.9.40-26.9.40	P/P4943	12.8.40-FTR 7.11.40
T4152	8.9.40-FTR 22.10.40	Q/4951	24.5.40-20.9.40
T4176	17.9.40-20.10.40	L/P4988	19.6.40-15.11.41
		N/P4991	23.6.40-FTR 3.6.41
		T/P5002	24.6.40-FTR 31.8.40 (ditched off

No. 51 Sqn, Dishforth

N1414	17.4.40-EFB 8.9.40 (ditched off		Hornsea)
	Wells, Norfolk)	P5003	21.6.40-26.8.40
N1425	18.8.40-29.8.40	M/P5008	4.8.40-?
N1464	21.8.40-21.7.42	R/P5028	16.8.40-EFB 27.11.40
N1481	16.8.40-FTR 2/3/41	P5058	12.8.40-FTR 21.10.40 (ditched)
N1485	20.9.40-EFB 14.12.40 (in Wash)	D/P5059	14.9.40-EFB 23.10.41
N1488	1.5.40-11.10.41	P5097	20.8.40-19.8.40
N1504	7.8.40-31.7.41	Q/P5098	10.9.40-EFB 23.12.40
P4934	29.5.40-FTR 28.2.41	J/T4134	3.9.40-FTR 10/11.9.40 (Bremen)
P4968	12.5.40-FTR 19/20.8.40	K/T4137	4.9.40-EFB 9.10.40
	(Zcharndoitz)	A/T4146	5.9.40-16.3.41
P4969	15.5.40-14.7.40	T4150	12.9.40-EFB 15.10.41
P4970	12.5.40-22.8.40	J/T4159	26.9.40-FTR 23.12.40
P4972	15.5.40-EFB 30.10.40	T4170	3.10.40-FTR 14.11.40
P4973	21.5.40-FTR 4/5.9.40 (ditched;	T4171	3.10.40-EFB 21.10.40
	Berlin)	X/T4174	20.9.40-FTR 14.11.40
P4974	18.5.40-EFB 12.2.41 (ditched)	T4210	3.10.40-FAO2 7.2.41
P4981	18.5.40-EFB 12.2.41 (ditched)	T4211	5.10.40-EFB/SOC 31.12.40
P4982	18.5.40-EAO 15.8.40 (Driffield)	T4213	10.10.40-EFB 11.2.41 (FH 92.35)
P4983	21.5.40-FTR 11/12.8.40		
	(Gelsenkirchen)		

No. 77, Driffield; to Linton-on-Ouse 28.8.40, to Topcliffe 5.10.40

P4984	23.5.40-EFB 29.11.40	N1353	10.10.39-EAO 15.8.40 (Driffield)
P4985	23.5.40-8.1.41	X/N1355	26.9.39-EFA 22.9.40
P4986	27.5.40-FTR 16/17.8.40 (Bohlen)	N1365	20.10.39-29.10.40
P4987	23.5.40-20.10.40	S/N1367	14.10.39-31.10.40
P4996	16.7.40-20.7.40	N/N1371	5.12.39-13.10.40
P5007	26.6.40-FTR 19/20.7.40	N1390	17.5.40-2.10.40
	(Wilhelmshaven)	A/N1410	20.4.40-13.10.40
P5011	16.7.40-EFA 3.9.40	K/N1413	17.4.40-EAO 15.8.40 (Driffield)
P5013	22.7.40-FA02 12.2.41	N1415	13.9.40-1.11.40
P5020	22.7.40-2.4.41	E/N1425	29.8.40-FTR 19.9.40 (Soest)
P5021	13.8.40-FTR 9/10.9.40 (ditched	D/N1431	9.7.40-EFA 11.9.40 (crashed,
	off Firth of Forth; Berlin)		Linton-on-Ouse)
P5095	19.8.40-1.12.40	N1435	11.6.40-10.8.40
P5105	10.9.40-28.12.40	N1473	3.6.40-FTR 25.8.40
P5106	10.9.40-FTR 10.5.41	A/N1474	7.40-17.6.41 (FH 180)
P5108	9.9.40-FTR 2.3.41	N1501	27.5.40-EAO 15.8.40 (Driffield)
P5112	6.9.40-EFB 7.12.40 (ditched)	N1506	13.6.40-EAO 15.8.40 (Driffield)
T4145	5.9.40-1.1.41	B/N1508	5.5.40-18.9.40
T4175	25.9.40-30.5.41	O/N1524	16.9.40-10.10.41
T4218	9.10.40-EFB 17.11.40	C/P4938	16.8.40-12.8.41
T4224	13.10.40-9.5.41	L/P4942	16.8.40-7.10.40
		P4947	7.6.40-EFAO 3.4.41

No. 58 Sqn, Linton-on-Ouse

P/N1424	20.3.40-FTR 12.7.40?	P4950	17.7.40-FTR 29.11.40
N1426	11.3.40-10.12.40	H/P4969	29.8.40-13.12.41
K/N1427	21.3.40-FTR 3.9.40 (ditched,	V/P4989	17.7.40-14.2.41
	Thames Estuary; Genoa; FH	L,T/4992	15.6.40-FTR 18/19.9.40
	226.65)		(Antwerp)
B/N1428	16.5.40-22.10.40	U/P5004	21.6.40-21.12.40
D/N1433	2.3.40-23.8.40	P5017	16.8.40-4.9.40?
E,T/N1434	15.3.40-FTR 2.10.40 (Frankfurt)	X/P5023	21.8.40-1.1.41
N1436	13.9.40-9.10.40	K/P5042	1.7.40-FTR 10.11.9.40 (Bremen)
N1444	25.5.40-27.10.40	P5044	5.8.40-EFB 14/15.8.40 (collided
A/N1459	25.5.40-FTR 2/3.9.40 (ditched		with Southampton balloon
	off Felixstowe; Genoa)		barrage)
N1461	19.4.40-FTR 1/2.7.40 (Kiel)	P5046	19.8.40-FTR 23 24.9.40 (ditched)

P5056	5.8.40-EAO 15.8.40 (Driffield)
P5091	19.8.40-EFB 8.10.40
T4134	1.9.40-3.9.40
M/T4151	13.9.40-EFB 6.11.40 (ditched)
B/T4158	12.9.40-4.5.41
L/T4160	27.9.40-EFB 24.11.40 (ditched; FH 115.40)
F/T4169	28.9.40-EFB 24.11.40
R/T4172	20.9.40-15.11.40 (ditched)
O/T4200	25.9.40-23.12.41
S/T4205	3.10.40-EFB 4.12.40
T4206	3.10.40-EFB 15.10.40 (FH 16)
T/T4208	30.9.40-FTR 13.11.40
K/T4212	10.10.40-EFB 31.7.41
T4226	14.10.40-EFB 16.12.40 (FH 84.05)

No. 78 Sqn, Linton-on-Ouse; to Dishforth 15.7.40

N1350	21.9.39-28.7.40
N1389	18.1.40-14.10.40
N1393	18.5.40-14.10.40
N1394	27.5.40-28.7.40
N1407	9.6.40-28.7.40
N1409	17.4.40-14.10.40
N1412	6.12.39-19.11.40
N1416	27.2.40-19.10.40
N1437	18.5.39-13.10.40
N1478	18.6.40-FTR 14/15.9.40 (Antwerp; FH 74)
N1485	20.9.40-EFB 14.12.40 (ditched, Wash)
N1486	17.6.40-FBO2 18.11.40
N1487	17.10.40-FTR 21.7.40
N1490	5.8.40-EFB 12.2.41 (crashed New Milnes, Ayrshire)
N1525	17.6.40-FTR 1.3.41
P4937	23.7.40-EFB 4.1.41
P4941	23.7.40-9.8.40
P4964	4.8.40-FTR 1/2.10.40 (Sterkrade)
P4996	20.7.40-FTR 27.2.41
P5056	30.7.40-FTR 28.11.40
W/T4131	18.9.40-19.9.41
T4147	11.9.40-FTR 9.5.41
T4156	9.40-FTR 19.11.40
T4165	3.10.40-15.2.41
T4166	3.10.40-1.3.41
T4167	3.10.40-SOC 20.2.41
T4203	3.10.40-FTR 9.1.41
T4209	5.10.40-FTR 9.7.41

No. 102 Sqn, Driffield; to Leeming 24.8.40. Operating with Coastal Command from Prestwick and Aldergrove 1.9.40-10.10.40, thence based at Linton-on-Ouse

N1375	9.7.40-24.7.41
B/N1377	8.7.40-FTR 26/27.7.40 (crashed Spkiemisse, Netherlands; Mannheim)
Q/N1378	10.1.40-EAO 15.8.40 (Driffield)
G/N1379	16.10.40-3.11.40
N1385	1.1.40-FTR 17.8.40?
M,P/N1386	17.1.40-1.11.40
H/N1391	16.5.40-8.7.40
D/N1415	4.12.39-13.9.40
J/N1419	29.5.40-3.11.40
S/N1420	16.12.39-EAO 15.8.40 (Driffield)
N1433	23.8.40-1.11.40

R/N1471	26.5.40-28.7.41
E/N1475	2.7.40-18.9.40
C/N1489	5.5.40-EFB 29.8.40 (crashed, Siloden Moor)
E/N1502	27.5.40-FTR 12/13.7.40 (ditched off Cromer; Emden)
B/N1523	19.5.40-FTR 6/7.7.40 (Kiel)
O/N1524	19.5.40-16.9.40
F/P4933	8.7.40-EFB 19.10.40
M/P4936	19.6.40-FTR 14.11.40
L/P4945	11.6.40-25.7.40
E/P4995	14.7.40-FTR 7.10.40
N/P5005	23.6.40-2.6.41
G/P5012	22.7.40-FTR 15.12.40
B/P5022	27.7.40-8.10.40
P5046	16.8.40-19.8.40
D/P5073	16.8.40-EFB 24.10.40
O/P5074	16.8.40-EFB 24.11.40
B/P5077	28.9.40-FTR 28.11.40
L/P5082	19.8.40-EFB 27.10.40 (ditched)
P5091	16.8.40-19.8.40
Q/P5097	19.8.40-EFB 15.11.40
S/T4135	16.8.40-21.3.41
H/T4136	16.8.40-EFB 26.10.40

Whitley Vs available for operations at No. 10 OTU Abingdon/Stanton Harcourt

N1349	8.7.40-30.4.42
N1350	28.7.40-30.11.40
N1359	3.7.40-9.11.41
N1394	28.7.40-20.7.42
N1407	28.7.40-SOC 19.5.41
N1411	27.6.40-EFA 21.4.41
N1429	30.6.40-EFA 10.10.41
N1438	16.7.40-21.3.42
N1440	16.7.40-21.7.40
N1479	16.7.40-22.5.41
N1482	20.5.40-EFA 16.11.40
N1494	21.9.40-FAT 17.1.41
N1495	16.7.40-EFA 9.8.40 (undershot Abingdon)
N1526	21.5.40-1.7.40
P4931	30.8.40-FTR 17.9.42
P4932	6.6.40-13.9.44
P4939	16.7.40-EFA 29.4.41
P4940	16.7.40-EFA 5.6.41
P4944	25.8.40-FTR 25.6.42
P4962	8.5.40-EFA 1.5.44 (crash landed Stanton Harcourt)
P4997	25.8.40-FA 3.1.43
P5079	
P5100	25.8.40-12.5.41
P5101	25.8.40-?
T4132	28.9.40-?
T4133	28.9.40-SOC 22.9.44 (obsolete)
T4173	28.9.40-?
T4178	23.9.40-EFA 15.4.41
T4179	23.9.40-28.2.41

No. 419/1419 Special Duties Flt, North Weald (renamed 138 Sqn 25.8.41)

P5029	15.9.40-31.12.41

The Bristol Blenheim

'Britain First': noble gesture as worth pursuing by the British people in the 1990s as it was when Lord Rothermere generously donated an outstanding aeroplane to the nation. From a combination of his desire and forethought, and the skill of the Bristol Aeroplane Company, came one of 1940's most prolific performers, the Bristol Blenheim.

While in summer 1933 the Bristol Aeroplane Co. was busy designing a fighter, Frank Barnwell and Roy Fedden of the company devised a six-passenger transport, the Type 135, powered by two 500 hp sleeve valve Bristol Aquila radial engines first run in September 1934. High and low-wing layouts of this were schemed, the latter chosen as most likely to provide better performance. Bristol was also developing metal structures for military aircraft to make possible incorporation of large doors for easy internal access.

Early in 1934 Lord Rothermere, proprietor of the *Daily Mail*, at a lunchtime meeting with editors and associates, let it be known that he wanted to own 'the fastest commercial aeroplane in Europe', Europe's answer to the new all-metal Douglas sleeper transport and DC-1, which types he knew Beaverbrook had his eyes upon. Attending the function was Robert T. Lewis, Editor of the *Bristol Evening News*, who revealed to Lord Rothermere the existence of the Bristol designs. Rothermere at once asked him to find out more and on 6 March 1934 Frank Barnwell replied, describing a version fitted with more powerful Bristol Mercury engines and likely to attain at least 240 mph at 6,500 ft, making it faster than RAF fighters of 1934.

Rothermere was very impressed, as a result of which an excited Lewis telephoned Roy Fedden on 26 March 1934 telling him that Rothermere wanted one of these aircraft for private use. Rothermere, eager to promote the use of aircraft by businessmen, also wanted to show the Air Ministry how outdated were existing RAF fighters. What Rothermere knew of plans for the Hurricane, Spitfire and Messerschmitt 109, one can but surmise.

On the day after Lewis phoned Bristol, the firm's directors hastily convened a meeting, for they were confronted by a tricky situation. By going along with Rothermere they could offend the Government upon which they depended for survival. By ignoring him they would lose publicity and prestige which the aeroplane, and indeed the Press, could bring to bear. They decided to compromise — meet Rothermere in two days' time and ask him to define his requirements and plans.

Lord Rothermere said that he was prepared to pay £18,500 for a six-seater twin-engined transport crewed by two and having the suggested performance, which much satisfied the company. What, they pondered, would be the Air Ministry's attitude to their plans? A tactful approach resulted in more official enthusiasm than expected, particularly since Government funding was absent from the proposals! Bristol decided to build two prototypes, one Bristol Mercury powered for Rothermere and designated Type 142, the other a slightly enlarged version (Type 143) carrying eight passengers yet having less expensive Aquila engines.

News of the project spread fast, various organizations showing interest in Type 143. One was the Finnish government which appreciated the military potential of such an aircraft — particularly if it had more power. Bristol's plans for a mixed-role version included fighter-bombing within its capabilities, made possible by using a variety of fuselages. A dorsal gun position was feasible, even a forward firing 20 mm cannon. Contractual discussions for nine

The Bristol 142 alias R-12 *and* G-ADCZ *became better known as* K-7557 *and 'Britain First'.*

Finnish Type 143Fs were well underway when Lord Rothermere's prototype Type 142 first flew on 12 April 1935.

Lack of a high performance army support bomber to replace the Hart had been causing official concern. The May 1935 Second Interim Report by the Sub-Committee on Air Parity pointed out that no type in that category was planned within expansion Scheme C. It recommended urgent steps to remove the deficiency — and at this ideal moment the Bristol 142 arrived on the scene.

Early flight trials showed it living up to expectations and in June 1935 it flew to A&AEE Martlesham for airworthiness testing. At once it created a sensation for, fully loaded, it was indeed 50 mph faster than the latest interceptor, the Gloster Gladiator, reckoned as the best British fighter likely to be in service until maybe 1940. The Hawker Fury Monoplane and Supermarine's offering, although not far away, were nevertheless paper aeroplanes.

So impressive was the '142' that within two weeks the Air Ministry was asking Lord Rothermere if they could have it on extended loan to review its bomber potential. An undercarriage failure occurred before performance figures were completed, yet the 142 was obviously a most promising design. On 1 August 1935 the Secretary of State wrote to Lord Rothermere asking if he was prepared to sell the aircraft. Rothermere, highly delighted with all that he had achieved, went one better. He named his aeroplane 'Britain First', gave it to the nation, announced the event in the *Daily Mail* — then paid Bristol in settlement.

The prototype, marked *R-12*, was never to carry its civil registration *G-ADCZ*. Instead it became *K7557* and one of the most important of Britain's new monoplanes. Rothermere soon approached Bristol with a request for an even faster Type 142. His luck was out; so outstanding had the Type 142 become that all production was now earmarked for military purposes. As for the Type 143, which first flew on 20 January 1936, it served only as a test bed for the Aquila engine.

Plans for a two-man Type 142 bomber conversion were drawn up late May 1935, its top speed — if Aquila powered — reckoned to be 262 mph at 15,000 ft. The Air Staff wanted it based on a 1,000 lb load/1,000 mile range formula with all-up weight limited to 9,600 lb. If powered by Bristol Mercuries its speed would rise to 278 mph, but gross weight to 10,400 lb. Bristol's proposals were discussed at Air Ministry on 9 July 1935 when details of a three-seat military conversion were revealed. A wing raised about 16 in to a mid-fuselage position would permit a bomb bay below. A retractable dorsal gun turret could be installed, and an enlarged tailplane would be higher set in a strengthened tail section. Even more impressed, the

Competitor to the Type 142 was the Type 143 (R-14). (Bristol)

Air Ministry (secretly disturbed that neither the Hampden nor Wellington were yet suitable for production) on 22 August 1935 ordered 150 Type 142Ms (*K7033–K7182*) to a standard described in Specification 28/35. Since the aircraft had stemmed from a form of private venture, Bristol was permitted to export some examples.

Easy it is to relate the Blenheim story as a complete private venture. Yet within its conception was to be found the Bristol Bombay transport for which RAE and the Air Ministry had given guidance relating in particular to metal structures, for a company which had hitherto concentrated on small aircraft. Details of seven different metal wing spars had been officially provided. A mock-up of the metal monocoque Type 142M, by now named Blenheim, was ready by January 1936. When Air Ministry officials inspected it they were surprised to find so many radical changes incorporated in what was really a completely new design.

Being confronted with what for April 1936 was an obviously outstanding aeroplane, the Air Ministry within rearmament Scheme F expressed a desire for 1,320 Blenheims, proposing 620 be built by a second contractor within the new

Nearest to a Blenheim prototype was K7033. (Bristol)

Blenheim 'prototype' K7033 *after being camouflaged.* (Bristol)

Shadow Scheme. By April 1938, when Scheme L came into vogue, orders for 1,700 Blenheims had been spread across three firms, Bristol, Avro and Rootes Securities.

K7033, the first example which served as prototype, flew on 25 June 1936 and during its Martlesham trials between November 1936 and February 1937 confirmed the initial favourable impression. That prompted more orders.

Delivery of production aircraft — lacking much equipment — began in March 1937. Even a year later Blenheims were reaching a disturbed Service incomplete, so rapid had the whole process been. A major setback concerned the Bristol-designed dorsal turret produced by Daimler who could not maintain the necessary production rate. So slow was output that no turrets were fitted to Blenheims until nearly 200 had been delivered. Not until October 1938 was the Blenheim 1 declared fully operational within No. 2 (Bomber) Group whose main task was Army support.

By 1938 standards the Blenheim was exceptionally fast and versatile, but its all-up weight had risen to 12,000 lb by the time it entered service, resulting in its 1,000 lb load being able to be carried for only about 670 miles. Its top speed was around 270 mph TAS at 13,000 ft. That began to raise questions, such as how would such an aeroplane fare against monoplane fighters — and could it be improved?

Meanwhile, a replacement for the Avro Anson general reconnaissance bomber was being sought, the requirement outlined in Specification G.24/35 whose tortuous path is discussed on pages 109 to 116. Bristol had already tendered their Type 149, an enlarged, Aquila-powered Blenheim whose top speed was forecast as 254 mph at 5,000 ft and whose wide fuselage accommodated a navigator's station amidships and a radio operator's compartment ahead of its more roomy turret. Although not accepted, the design aroused considerable interest, suggesting the basis for bomber and reconnaissance Blenheim development. The Type 149 had a nose extended 3ft allowing it to accommodate navigation and radio stations. More important was an increased fuel load, partially sited in the outer wings and which raised its possible range to 1,460 miles when carrying a 1,000 lb load. Take-off weight was forecast as about 14,000 lb and demanded a stronger undercarriage.

Blenheim *K7072* was taken from the line for conversion into the Type 149 Blenheim III prototype, modified in accordance with Specification 11/36 into an army reconnaissance bomber, then renamed Bolingbroke. It first flew on 24 September 1937, the pilot

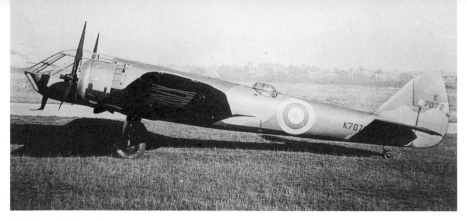

K7072 with lengthened nose converting it into a general reconnaissance bomber, and sometimes designated Blenheim Mk IIIA.

at once complaining that the windscreen was too far ahead of him. Redesign resulted in much altered nose contours to bring the windscreen nearer the pilot while leaving the navigator's station ahead below the pilot's line of sight. Further improvement to the pilot's forward view was achieved by scooping away the port portion of the upper glazing giving the nose a peculiar appearance. This version, approved for production in summer 1938, was again redesignated, this time as the Blenheim Mk IV because of the ease of exchanging parts with the MK 1. No Mk III (the long-range wing version of the Mk 1) ever joined the Service. The Mk IV was introduced first to No. 53 in January 1939 and

was also used by 59 Squadron, both of which were assigned specific Army reconnaissance duties.

By the time the Mk IV entered production, Blenheim I output had rapidly increased from new lines at Avro's Chadderton works and Rootes's Liverpool works. Ubiquity was indicated by its being given in February 1939 four roles: Field Force bomber in 2 Group, general reconnaissance bomber attached to the Army, bomber for Overseas squadrons and auxiliary fighter.

In March 1939 Bomber Command, too, began rearming the 2 Group squadrons with bomber Mk IVs. Most had 100 octane 920 hp 9 lb boost rated Mercury XV engines instead of the $5\frac{1}{2}$ lb boost Mk VIII which provided

Further development of K7072 led to its nose being lowered ahead of the pilot, which led to the Blenheim Mk IV. (Bristol)

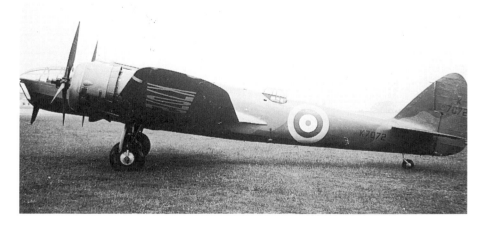

increased take-off and combat power. By the outbreak of war all home-based 2 Group Blenheim bomber squadrons had Mk IVs, around 150 of which were, on 3 September 1939, in front line Home service.

Blenheim IV *N6215* of 139 Squadron, Wyton, flown by Flg Off Andrew McPherson, holds the distinction of opening Bomber Command's campaign soon after the declaration of war by reconnoitring German warships off Brunsbuttel. Next day 15 Blenheims joined Wellingtons in the first RAF bombing raid of the war and for months thereafter 2 Group Blenheims carried out daylight reconnaissance flights, some deep into Germany (see *2 Group*; Faber & Faber). When Norway was invaded squadrons moved to Lossiemouth from where they attacked German forces particularly around Stavanger.

Those operations demanded enormous courage during long, tough flights across the sea in harsh conditions. They were soon followed by shorter range missions, if anything more hazardous, for it fell mainly to 2 Group's Blenheim squadrons to attempt to halt by bombing the German advance into France and the Low Countries. Choke points, airfields, main roads and particularly bridges mostly heavily defended were the main targets, around which were hastily placed anti-aircraft defences used to break apart unescorted Blenheim formations. Bf 109 fighters could then pick off the scattered bombers. Loss rates were exceptionally high, as high as any sustained by the RAF during the entire war. Between 10 May and Bomber Command Blenheim losses during operations in Europe totalled 122 aircraft.

Even at the start of hostilities the Blenheim was known to be at a grave disadvantage when facing German fighters. But it was easy to construct, large numbers were already available, and there was a lack of any alternative type. These factors had resulted in embarrassingly excessive production.

Bristol was winding down Blenheim output when the war began to make way for the Beaufort and, from March 1940, the Beaufighter, at which time Rootes really swung into action. Their initial order for 600 Blenheims was boosted by another for 400 when the war began, 400 later in 1939, and then construction of 220 originally to have been Avro built was switched to Rootes. Another 800 were ordered in January 1940 raising the Rootes target to 2,270. When their production ended in June 1943 the company had built 3,500 of the total production of 5,421. On 15 May 1940 Lord Beaverbrook ordered production to centre on only five existing aircraft types, including the Blenheim. He extended Avro involvement, ordering 820 to be built there, which could only delay Avro's own Manchester bomber. Rootes's order book reached 3,050 by September 1940, by which time the Air Staff was far from satisfied with the Blenheim's capability.

In an attempt to improve its performance, the closing weeks of 1939 had seen attempts to clean up the aircraft, an obvious feature being much smoother paint and a pale green underside (Camotint) applied to Wyton's Blenheims. By January 1940 the decision had been made to fit twin Vickers K-guns in the dorsal turret. In March 42 sets of a periscopically controlled gun in a blister under the nose hatch arrived at Wyton and by April all of the aircraft of XV and 40 Squadrons and many at Wattisham had been fitted, while 21 and 82 Squadron's aircraft was having theirs installed. Main turret production was still inadequate, Bristol having to build 500 to supplement Daimler's output.

None of these modifications could remove the basic fact that already the Blenheim was outdated, a fact proven so harshly during the May 1940 battles. Once France fell the question of the Blenheim's future bomber employment — if any — had to be faced. Some formation attacks on French airfields and a variety of

Handing over of a Rootes-built Blenheim IV, R3740.

operations on fringe targets were flown before it was decided to use the considerable number of Blenheims for cloud cover attacks even into Germany. The Blenheim position was brought to a head on 17 August 1940 when the Medium Expansion Re-equipment Policy Committee met to discuss the use of Blenheims in Bomber Command. The AOC-in-C had recently suggested that 'it would pay us to roll up some if not all the Blenheim squadrons and convert them into heavy bomber squadrons', suggesting those be equipped with Hampdens. His view was that 'although they are doing a certain amount of useful work in the form of cloud flying by day, far better value would be obtained by applying the personnel in a smaller number of heavy bomber squadrons'.

Bomber Command, obsessed by the belief that Germany could be beaten by heavy bombers, never had much time for the exceptionally brave 2 Group Blenheim performers. Just what many had endured was shown on 9 July when 21 and 57 Squadrons, Lossiemouth based and daily keeping watch for signs of a German invasion, were ordered to bomb Stavanger/Sola in daylight. AA guns at the target forced the formations apart, then in came the Messerschmitts. Two of 57's aircraft fell into the sea, but only after 20–30 min fights. *R3608* crash landed and *R3883* came home badly

damaged. Of 21 Squadron's six, four were shot down. Next day it was 107 Squadron's turn to be similarly dealt with when six crews attacked an airfield near Amiens. Only Flt Lt Pleasance and crew, in *T1850* returned. What did much to keep the Blenheim in Bomber Command was the fact that if an invasion came Battle and Blenheim medium bombers would be needed for intensive close army support operations — to which Command replied that Hampdens (the favourite bombers) could perform just as well. But the Air Council had promised the Army that it would maintain a force of 250 medium bombers to give close support — i.e. 15 squadrons. At this time there were more than that number, and some wind-down of the Blenheim squadrons and re-equipment of Battle squadrons was planned at the height of the Battle of Britain with the decision to re-equip Nos. XV, 40, 57, 101 and 218 Squadrons with Wellingtons. That change did not become effective until November 1940.

The question of a Blenheim replacement was never resolved. The closest it ever came was in the form of the Bristol Buckingham which absorbed a prodigous amount of effort yet never saw operational service. Bristol had, in January 1940, proposed a Taurus-engined Mk IV specifically designed as a direct army support bomber with a fighter/ground strafer variant. February 1940 found the Air Staff incorporating their own ideas in Specification B.6/40 for a dedicated army support aircraft able to dive- or level-bomb transport, troops, railheads, dumps, etc. Discussions rumbled on through Spring and Summer 1940 and led to plans for a Blenheim Mk IV powered by Mercury XV engines with cropped impellors and using 100 octane fuel. Air Ministry suggested that Rootes share the design work of what they called the Bisley, and that building could start in September 1940.

Bristol objected, claiming that the design work would become over-complex. July 1940 found the Air Staff having second thoughts about the Bisley whose range would be only 600 miles because it was to carry 600 lb of armour and have an effective operational level limited to a mere 6,000 ft. The War Office let it be clearly known that it wanted this direct support aircraft, so the Air Staff decided to have the project redesigned. Not until September 1941 did the dedicated prototype emerge,

not as the Bisley but the Blenheim V. History was repeating itself. By February 1942 when the Mk V entered service as a night intruder, it had been outdated by the fighter-bomber. But not until June 1943 did Blenheim production cease.

The Blenheim's most important feature was its strong airframe which conferred both a good survival rate despite extensive battle damage and a long life. Also, it was capacious enough to be improved on the basis of operational experience. Fitted with Mercury XV engines a typical Mk IV (all-up weight 14,513 lb) could reach 271 mph at 11,800 ft. *L4835* (Mercury XV) during tests at 15,000 lb had a ceiling of over 24,000 ft after a take-off run of 415 yd. A specially cleaned and prepared Blenheim, *L8748*, reached 285 mph at 9,000 ft. That was about the best that could be hoped for, and apparently it could be sufficient, for on 30 October 1940 Sqn Ldr Little and crew in a 40 Squadron Blenheim were on a training flight near Ely when they came across Ju 88 L1 + GS which they soon shot down at Stuntney.

Blenheim IV R3600 *of 110 Squadron being loaded with 250 lb GP bombs and SBCs at Wattisham in 1940.* (IWM)

Operations summary

Date	No. sorties completed/ despatched	Targets listed as attacked
July		
1	6	PR of N. French coast, cloudy
2	1/1	Barges W. of Gorinchem bombed
3	16	Industrial, rail targets in Germany
	1/12	Barges in R. Lek
	4/6	Brussels/Évère afd
	8/15	Industrial targets (Hamm, Leunen, Osnabruck, Wismar)
4	11/20	Rys — Hamm, Soest; industrial — Hanover, Emmerich; afds — Évère, Schiphol; shipping W. of Den Helder
5	5/12	Afds — Flushing, Rotterdam; industrial — Dijkshausen; convoy 6 miles W. Callantsoog
6	6/8	Afds — Knocke, Ypenburg; barges — Zwolle, E. of Katwyk
7	2/24	Enschewege afd (1 missing), rest abortive
8	12/12	Afds — Ledeghem, Soissons, Roye amy, Douai; barges — Goringhem, Pappendrecht, Lekkerkirk, SW of Zwolle, SW of Amsterdam, in Zuyder Zee
	9	Shipping Aalborg
9	6/23	Afds — Stavanger/Sola, Caen, barges in Holland
10	6/37	Afds — Amiens/Glisy, St Omer
11	5	Afds — Boulogne, Schiphol, Kastrup; Furnes Canal barges
13	5/18	Évère afd; factory Monheim, barges Bruges-Ostend canal
15	4/17	Evreux and Lisieux afds
16	11/15	Afds Trier, St Inglevert; barges W. of Armentières
17	2/13	Barges Zuyder Zee, Bruges Canal, Inkhuisen
17/18	6	First night operation of period, directed against afds at Merville, Morlaix, Caen, Lannion, St Inglevert
18	22/48	18 attacked shipping Boulogne; barges — Zuyder Zee; Airfield St Omer
19	1/15	Dortmund/Borhalle
20	1	Afd Flushing
21/22	9/12	Afds Carpiquet, Querqueville, Lannion 23:02–02:35 hrs
22/23	5/8	Schiphol
23	4/16	Afds — Abbeville, Amiens, St Aubin; barges—Hague
23/24	5/10	Afds — Halberstadt, Schiphol, Wunstorf, Wernigerod
24	1	St Aubin attacked 16.00
25	0/5	All abandoned — or 18 of 114 and 139 Sqns harassing 7 afds in daylight
25/26	8/10	Afds including Lisieux, St Inglevert
26	3/14	Afds — Schiphol, Waalhaven; Dortmund ps
27	3/15	Shipping — Wilhelmshaven, barges near Ijmuiden
28	1/9	Leeuwarden
28/29	1/6	Afds — Brest, Boulogne, Carpiquet, Morlaix
29	6/14	Diepholtz acft depot; oil targets — Hamburg, Gelsenkirchen; Leeuwarden afd; 3 ships
30	14/23	afds — Amiens, St Inglevert, Carpiquet, Cherbourg, Querqueville, Zeebrugge, Leeuwarden; barges — Walcheren, N. Beveland, ry Ostend; oil plants Zeebrugge, Colommes; shipping
31	8/28	Paderborn acft park; barges 15 miles N. Nordeney; oil tanks Burhafe, flak ships near Emden; Vollenhove docks
August		
1	5/12	Leeuwarden, Hamstede afds; flak ship
2	23/35	Afds—Waalhaven, Leeuwarden, Soesterberg, Évère, Hamstede, Schiphol, Flushing, Merville; lock gate Ijmuiden, AA guns Knocke, ry at Haarlem
6	1/	Le Bourget
7	2/29	Querqueville, Hamstede

8	2	Schiphol, Valkenburg
9	2/15	Afds Guernsey, Brest/Poulmiac
10	8/22	Afds Guernsey, Schiphol, Waalhaven, Carpiquet, Dinard, Querqueville, Flushing
11	9/16	Afds — Guernsey, Brest, Dinard, Caen
12	1	De Kooy
12/13	4	Afds — Querqueville, Caen, Dinard
13	10/31	Afds — Waalhaven, Brest/Lanvioc, Querqueville, Brest, Morlaix, Carpiquet, Hingene
	12	12 crews 82 Sqn set off to bomb Aalborg; only one returned
13/14	4/6	Afds and seaplane stations — Brest, St Brieuc, Querqueville, Dinant
14	3/24	Afds — Morlaix, Dinard, St Omer
14/15	6/13	Afds — Ureil, St Inglevert, Soesterberg, Boos, Lisieux; Foret de Guines
15	1/8	De Kooy
15/16	12/18	Afds — Leeuwarden, Chartres, Boos; guns Cap Gris Nez; Foret de Guines
17	2/3	Fecamp, Dieppe
17/18	29/36	Afds — St Inglevert, Lille, Lesquin, Carpiquet, Cormeilles-en-Vixen, Lisieux, Hingene, Borg, Beauvais, De Kooy, Longeville, Schiphol, Maupertuis, Querqueville, Abbeville, Dinard, Angers, Tours, Amiens/Glisy, Orleans/Bricy
19	2/15	AA guns Flushing; Amsterdam
19/20	24/36	
21	13/21	Afds — Jersey, Rennes, De Kooy
22/23		Angers, Chateroux, Lannion, Vannes, Orleans/Saran, Caen/Carpiquet, Cap Griz Nez
23	35	Afds — Belgium, France, Holland; Cap Gris Nez guns
24	4/9	Afds — Hingene, Schiphol, Schellingwoulde; 6,000 ton ship in Zeebrugge
24/25	19	Afds
25	6/18	Afds — De Kooy, Texel, Bergen/Alkmaar, Wunstorf

25/26	7/12	Afds — Boulogne, Fecamp, St Inglevert, Plouscat, Le Treport, Lisieux; searchlights Hardelot
26	2/12	De Kooy; stores depot Rothenburg
26/27	17/18	Afds in France and Belgium including Hoya and De Kooy
27	1	Ship at anchor off Den Helder
28	0/2	No attack
28/29	13/15	Afds in Belgium, France and Netherlands
29	7	Afds — De Kooy, Bergen/Alkmaar; shipping off Den Helder
30	0	Unsuitable weather
30/31	12	8 attacked Emden docks (00:23-02.45); afds De Kooy, Pappenburg, Cap Gris Nez guns
31	18	Paderborn, PR of Dortmund Ems Canal
31.8/ 1.9		16/20 Cap Gris Nez guns (3), docks and shipping Emden (12); afds Ypenburg, Bremerhaven (2)

September

1	2	Afds — Ypenburg, Évère, Schiphol
1/2	10	Petrol depot Nordenhem, ships at Emden
2	2/18	Ypenburg afd
3	0/3	Unsuitable weather
3/4	12/15	Afds — Forets de Guines, St Omer, Abbeville, Calais
4/5	18	Afds — Foret de Guines, St Omer, Dunkirk, Mardyck, Abbeville, Twente; Hamm myds, flakship W. of Alkmaar
5/6	7/12	E-boats Boulogne, guns Cap Gris Nez, searchlights Calais
6/7	18	Cap Gris Nez; afds Amiens–Abbeville area 21:50-05:09; barges and ships in Calais
7/8	12/13	Barges in Dunkirk (9), others Calais and searchlights
8	24/28	Alkmaar afd, destroyers in convoy, Dunkirk and Boulogne basins recces of Dunkirk, Ijmuiden, Ameland, Ostend-Boulogne targets — Rothenburg,

193

		Paderborn, Diepholtz, Witzendorf, Gelsenkirchen, Bremen — mostly not reached
8/9	5/16	Boulogne and Ostend barges 20:52–04:37, also Emden and Brussels myds
9	0	None completed
9/10	21	Ostend barges 20:40–22:47
10/11	22/30	Flushing barges 22:07–00:10 (5), Calais barges (6), Ostend docks (9/10)
11/12	35	Barges etc. Calais, Flushing, Ostend; guns Cap Gris Nez
12	0/8	Channel ports reconnaissances all abandoned—poor weather
13	3/13	Calais, barges near Rotterdam, 6 ships off Zeebrugge
13/14	29/34	Barges Calais (11), Dunkirk (9), Ostend
14	1	Hamstede afd
14/15	11	Cap Gris Nez guns (4), barges Dunkirk (1), Ostend (4)
15	0/6	Unsuitable weather
15/16	48	Barges Boulogne (11/12), Dunkirk (23/24), Flushing (1), Cap Gris Nez (11)
16	5/10	Barges etc. Calais, Dunkirk, Ostend, Zeebrugge, convoy, Hamstede afd
17	3/15	Shipping in Antwerp, off Ostend and the Hook, in Zeebrugge
17/18	40/46	Barges Dunkirk (27), Boulogne (13)
18	1	Abandoned
18/19	46/53	Barges Calais (11/12), Dunkirk (9), Ostend (16/17), Cap Gris Nez (5)
19	1/12	Dunkirk–rest no cloud cover
20	0/3	No cloud cover
20/21	45	Dunkirk (25) and Calais
21	9/12	Shipping — Flushing, off Blankenburg, Calais, and barges being towed away from Channel ports
21/22	26	Dunkirk (21), Ostend (5)
22	15	Flushing, barges in Beveland, 52-ship convoy off Zeebrugge, Waalhaven
22/23	33	Calais (12), Dunkirk (5), Ostend (10), Zeebrugge (6)
23/24	33	Calais (22), Calais/Marck (6), Ostend (13)
24/25	32	Calais, Le Havre, Ostend
25	12	R-boats in the Channel
25/26	27	Boulogne and Calais (with 27 Wellingtons), Antwerp, Brussels; 6 flew security patrol over Calais/Marck
26	1/6	Offensive recces along French-Dutch coasts
26/27	15/16	Boulogne (5), Calais (6), Ostend (5)
27	3/12	6 small ships in convoy heading to Rotterdam
27/28	19	Calais (8), Boulogne (2), Dunkirk (1), Ostend (8)
28	2/7	Dunkirk, Ostend
28/29	34/47	Boulogne (30), Calais and Dunkirk (10), Cap Gris Nez guns (7)
29	0/3	Shipping recces off Dutch coast
29/30	21	Calais (5), Boulogne (5), Flushing (1), Le Touquet (1), Ostend (5), Bittefeld aluminium wks (4)
30.9/ 1.10	34	Boulogne, Calais, Ostend, Dunkirk

October

1/2	21	Myds at Mannheim, Ehrang, Köln/Eifeltor, Gremberg, Koblenz; shipping in Boulogne, Calais, Dunkirk
2/3	8/14	Calais, Gremberg, Köln/Eifeltor, Ypenburg
3	9	Oil targets Homberg, Reisholtz, Emmerich, Sterkrade; ship in Dunkirk
4/5	30	Oil target Reisholtz, shipping in Ostend, Rotterdam
5/6	8	Widely assorted targets
6	11/21	Bombed alternatives — Calais, Boulogne, Den Helder, Harlingen, Stavoren, Einkhuisen, Dordrecht, Ostend, Diepholtz
7	2/12	Shipping in Dutch waterways
7/8	32	Boulogne, Calais, Flushing, Cap Gris Nez
8/9	38	Boulogne, Calais, Flushing, Le Havre
9/10	5/8	Homberg, Warendorf, Texel airfields, barges
11/12	6	Boulogne, rail targets
12/13	36	Fokker at Amsterdam, Dunkirk, Le Havre, Hamm, Köln/Eifeltor

194

13/14	33	Duisburg, Soest, Krefeld, Köln/Kalk Nord, Schwerte
14	3/12	Flak ship, factory nr Jever, Ostend
16	/28	Embankment Dortmund Ems Canal

Blenheim IVs used by Bomber Command Squadrons 1 July– 15 October 1940

(Bracketed numbers indicate the number of operational sorties flown, where known, while aircraft served with the squadron)

XV Squadron, **Wyton (satellite Alconbury)**

L8800	10.12.39-12.11.40
L8848	10.12.39-26.8.40
L8850	10.12.39-16.12.40 (25)
L8855	16.12.39-EFA 6.7.40 (15)
L9413	19.6.40-10.9.40 (18)
L9469	13.6.40-FTR 25/26.7.40 (10) from Wilhelmshaven
N3588	6.6.40-EFA 15.10.40 (5) (crashed at Exeter)
N3267	1.8.40-14.1.41 (12)
N6166	20.9.40-23.9.40
R2766	27.7.40-FTR 14.9.40 (5) from Ostend
R2791	1.9.40-12.11.40
R2796	23.9.40-1.11.40
R3594	16.8.40-10.11.40 (14)
R3603	23.5.40-FTR 18.7.40 (10) (ditched)
R3604	23.5.40-20.11.40 (23)
R3704	19.5.40-13.11.40 (20)
R3764	24.5.40-FTR 30.7.40 (14)
R3766	24.5.40-10.11.40
R3767	24.5.40-20.11.40 (16)
R3768	24.5.40-FTR 12/13.8.40 from St Malo
R3769	24.5.40-EFAO 4.9.40 (31) (crashed nr Kettering)
R3770	24.5.40-FTR 15.8.40 (15) from Forêt de Guines
R3771	24.5.40-EFAO 4.8.40 (crashed nr Whitchurch)
R3777	29.5.40-27.11.40 (24)
R3803	23.7.40-4.8.40
R3894	12.6.40-21.11.40 (16)
R3896	12.6.40-FTR 1.7.40 (3)?
R3905	14.6.40-12.11.40 (17)
T1859	8.7.40-12.9.40
T1924	12.7.40-21.11.40 (21)
T1956	23.7.40-18.8.40
T1957	23.7.40-18.8.40
T1986	23.7.40-17.8.40
T2002	14.8.40-21.11.40
T2127	?-?
T2138	15.9.40-22.11.40
T2226	12.9.40-21.11.40
T2227	12.9.40-7.11.40
T2231	2.9.40-21.11.40 (9)
T2276	5.9.40-13.11.40 (10)

No. 18 Sqn, **West Raynham (using Great Massingham from 9.40)**

L8862	15.3.40-4.7.40
W/L8864	30.5.40-31.5.41 (35)
L8866	4.3.40-FTR 4.7.40 from NW Germany
D/L9040	30.5.40-19.5.41 (29)
L9170	18.7.40-28.2.41
L9188	16.8.40-EFB (crash landed Gt Massingham)
Q/L9192	12.2.40-FTR 2.6.41 (37)
C/L9240	30.5.40-FTR 30.7.41 (37)
L9247	30.5.40-FTR 13.4.41 (22)
L9251	30.5.40-EFB 16.7.40 (3?) (crashed Welwyn Garden City)
L9378	18.7.40-EFB 31.8.40 (crashed nr Weasenham, Norfolk)
L9387	18.7.40-5.12.40
L9390	5.9.40-15.10.41
L9472	13.5.40-FTR 8.8.40 from France
N3552	2.7.40-26.9.40
N3553	3.8.40-23.10.40
N6166	6.9.40-20.9.40, 23.9.40-4.10.40
P6931	28.5.40-? (22+)
P6933	28.5.40-FTR 16.7.40 (3)
P6934	1.6.40-EFB 28.11.40 (overshot Gt Massingham)
R3662	31.5.40-FTR 6.7.40 from French coast
R3663	31.5.40-EFB 2.9.40 (crashed Gt Massingham on return)
R3669	29.5.40-15.10.41
R3734	16.5.40-9.8.41 (19)
X/R3741	26.8.40-FTR 7.5.41 (11)
R3841	17.6.40-4.41
R3842	17.6.40-EFAO 19.7.40 (crashed nr Gt Massingham)
F/R3843	17.6.40-FTR 20.9.41 (17); the aircraft which dropped a metal leg to Douglas Bader at St Omer
T1814	23.6.40-26.11.40 (13)
T1829	8.7.40-FTR 11.4.41 (22)
T1862	7.7.40-14.7.41
T1882	5.7.40-FTR 14/15.8.40
T2004	14.8.40-1.4.41
T2034	14.8.40-21.8.40
T2232	3.9.40-28.4.41
T2254	5.9.40-4.12.40
Z5744	4.9.40-27.12.40

No. 21 Sqn, **Lossiemouth**

F/L8737	16.9.39-EFA 1.11.40 (crashed during night flying training
L8745	13.2.40-1.11.40 (15)
B/L8758	6.11.39-EFAO 3.5.41 (19)
M/L8872	1.4.40-FTR 9.7.40 from Stavanger
L9029	24.2.40-EFAO 12.4.1 (14)
L9422	30.5.40-FTR 28.4.40 from Holland
N3538	9.7.40-12.4.41
O/N3564	9.7.40-EFA 16.9.40
N3574	30.7.40-10.8.40
N3584	30.7.40-3.7.41
K/N3618	14.6.40-EFAO 26.2.41
N3619	14.6.40-FTR 9.7.40 from Stavanger

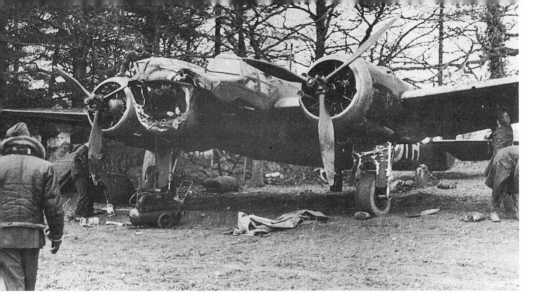

Blenheims were able to absorb enormous punishment and survive, like this 21 Squadron example. (RAF Museum)

N6166	21.5.40–10.8.40
D/P6954	18.1.40-EFA 28.7.41 (22)
N/R3636	9.7.40-EFB 18.3.41 (crashed nr Bodney)
A/R3675	27.5.40–14.8.41
R3687	2.6.40-EFB 16.11.40 (crashed at Longfield, Kent)
R3708	20.8.40–27.8.40
L/R3732	26.5.40-FTR 9.7.40 from Stavanger
R3755	25.5.40-FTR 5.9.40 from sea sweep
U/R3758	28.5.40–5.7.41
R/R3760	13.6.40-EAO 26.10.40 (damaged by bombing, Lossiemouth)
P/R3761	25.5.40–3.7.41
J/R3820	9.6.40-*EFB* 23.7.40 (ditched off Lossiemouth)
O/R3822	13.6.40-FTR 9.7.40 (from Stavanger)
P/R3872	13.6.40–29.7.40
R3875	13.6.40–19.8.41 (17)
Q/R3876	13.6.40-FTR 9.7.40 from Stavanger
G/R3900	14.6.40–31.3.41
L/T1878	13.7.40–16.6.41
Q/T1925	12.7.40–26.8.40
T2233	6.9.40-EAO 26.10.40 (destroyed by bombing, Lossiemouth)

No. 40 Sqn, Wyton (satellite Alconbury)

T/L8757	2.12.39-FTR 2.9.40 from Schlebusch
L8796	14.6.40-EFB 2.9.40 (crashed West Raynham)
L8828	3.12.39-SOC 10.10.40 (FH 118.15)
L8836	3.12.39–9.7.40 from PR of Lisieux
L8876	3.12.39–22.7.41
L9270	27.5.40–12.8.40
H/L9326	30.5.40–30.8.40 (crashed on take-off, Wyton)
L9386	3.9.40–9.11.40
U/L9402	27.5.40–8.11.40 (11)
L9412	19.5.40–10.9.40 (18)

N3570	27.8.40–1.11.40
N3575	27.8.40–20.11.40
N3589	7.9.40-EFAO 13.9.40 (missing)
N3591	14.6.40–10.9.40
N6236	10.5.40–3.11.40 (01)
P4918	6.12.39–6.10.40 (17)
P6901	3.12.39-SOC 10.10.40
R2787	27.7.40–8.11.40
R2793	1.9.40–27.11.40
R3607	13.9.40–24.11.40
X/R3609	24.5.40-FTR 15.8.40 (Chartres)
R3611	24.5.40–8.11.40 (11)
V/R3612	7.6.40–9.9.40 from Ostend
R3682	25.5.40–15.7.40 (4)
R3689	24.5.40 (10)–22.7.40
R3743	8.6.40–28.7.40
R3744	23.5.40-EFA 16.12.40 (crashed on take-off, Horsham St Faiths)
S/R3745	7.6.40–24.7.40
R3763	7.6.40-FTR 25.7.40 from Eelde
G/R3811	3.6.40–25.8.40 (8) from Maupertuis
R3899	28.7.40, to 9.9.40
T1829	29.6.40–8.7.40
T1830	8.7.40–8.11.40
T1848	29.6.40–25.11.40
T1849	29.6.40–8.11.40
T1858	11.7.40–8.11.40
F/T1927	12.7.40-FTR 26.8.40 from Querqueville
T1939	17.8.40–8.11.40
T1989	17.8.40–18.11.40
T2134	12.9.40–6.11.40
T2278	9.9.40–7.11.40
T2279	9.9.40–8.11.40

No. 57 Sqn, Lossiemouth (used Elgin satellite from 8.40)

L9027	9.7.40–3.12.40
L9183	25.4.40-EFB 23.12.40
L9188	5.6.40–9.7.40
L9244	15.3.40–29.11.40
L9268	9.7.40–26.11.40
L9272	9.7.40–26.11.40

L9462	11.4.40–EFAO 23.8.40	U/R3730	19.5.40–FTR 8.9.40
N3583	16.7.40–21.11.40	C/R3756	23.5.40–FTR 14.7.40
N3598	25.6.40–18.1.41	R3759	23.5.40–EFAO 9.7.40 (crashed at
P4856	28.8.40–12.11.40		Hendon)
P6928	9.4.40–FTR 26.8.40	R3765	10.6.40–FTR 11.11.40 (ditched nr
R3591	3.6.40–9.7.40		Outer Dowsing Light)
R3594	3.6.40–9.7.40	R3800	28.6.40–FTR 13.8.40 from Aalborg
R3638	3.6.40–9.7.40	R3802	28.6.40–FTR 13.8.40 from Aalborg
R3666	3.6.40–9.7.40	A/R3808	14.8.40–7.7.41 (18)
R3667	3.6.40–1.9.40	R3812	7.6.40–4.3.41
R3680	3.6.40–EFA 4.7.40 (overshot Dyce)	R3821	9.6.40–FTR 3.8.40
R3682	15.7.40–21.11.40	R3904	28.6.40–FTR 13.8.40 from Aalborg
R3708	27.8.40–5.12.40	R3910	15.6.40–FTR 10.8.40
R3750	5.6.40–FTR 9.7.40 from Stavanger	R3913	15.6.40–FTR 13.8.40 from Aalborg
R3751	5.6.40–15.11.40	R3914	15.6.40–FTR 26.11.40
R3752	5.6.40–21.11.40	P/R3915	15.6.40–FTR 8.9.40
R3825	5.6.40–27.12.40	T1813	13.7.40–EFB 4.12.40 (crashed nr
R3830	5.6.40–26.11.40		Downham Market)
R3832	5.6.50–13.11.40	T1827	8.7.40–FTR 13.8.40 from Aalborg
R3882	17.6.40–EFB 4.9.40 (crashed nr	T1928	29.6.40–18.3.42
	Elgin)	T1889	12.7.40–FTR 13.8.40 from Aalborg
R3883	17.6.40–5.8.40	T1933	15.7.40–FTR 13.8.40 from Aalborg
T1824	11.7.40–14.11.40	T1934	15.7.40–FTR 13.8.40 from Aalborg
T2038	27.8.40–13.11.40	T2031	14.8.40–FTR 27.2.41
		T2032	14.8.40–EFA 8.10.40 (crash landed
			Bodney)

No. 82 Sqn, Watton (satellite Bodney)

L9389	31.7.40–FTR 24.3.41
L9468	10.5.40–FTR 10.7.40
N3569	14.8.40–FTR 10.4.41
N3578	14.8.40–EFAO 4.12.40 (crashed nr
	Southend)
F/N3594	11.6.40–7.10.40
L/P4839	22.8.39–16.6.41 (15)
J/P4843	22.8.39–FTR 7.7.40
H/P6895	18.10.39–FTR 2.7.40 (14)
R2772	24.6.40–FTR 13.8.40 from Aalborg
R2784	14.8.40–30.12.40
T/R3619	18.5.40–FTR 29.7.40 from Bremen
W/R3690	10.6.40–FTR 11.7.40 from N.
	France
R3701	25.5.40–FTR 14.7.40
R3707	19.5.40–12.9.40
D/R3708	19.5.40–12.9.40

T2033	14.8.40–18.3.42
T2118	14.8.40–2.4.41
T2122	10.10.40–18.3.42
T2162	14.8.40–18.3.42
T2165	14.8.40–FTR 26.8.41
T2225	10.10.40–FTR 10.12.40
T2277	9.9.40–1.1.41
T2280	9.9.40–2.12.40

No. 101 Sqn, West Raynham

L4893	14.4.39–20.9.40
L4899	21.4.39–2.1.41
L8870	11.4.40–EFB 26.8.40 (collided with
	balloon cable, Eastleigh, Hants)
L9250	11.7.40–8.8.40

A trio of Blenheim IVs of 101 Squadron up from West Raynham in August 1940.

L9257	4.3.40-9.2.41
L9419	22.4.40-20.8.40?
L9420	22.4.40-20.12.40
L9421	3.5.40-12.7.41
N3545	13.5.40-3.1.41
N2552	26.9.40-FTR 3.4.41
N3574	10.8.40-EFB 20.8.40 (ditched off Lowestoft)
N3616	14.6.40-21.12.40
N6140	24.4.39-FTR 5.7.40 from Bremen
N6141	27.4.39-30.6.41
N6142	26.4.39-22.12.40
N6143	2.5.39-18.6.41
N6174	9.4.40-FTR 25.7.40 (PR of Cherbourg)
N6175	?-EFA 9.7.40?
N6176	9.3.40-EFB 9.7.40 (crashed nr Brampton, Hunts/Cambs)
N6181	29.3.40-13.9.40
Z/N6182	15.3.40-23.1.41
N6238	26.7.39-FTR 24.11.40
P6905	2.4.40-EFB 25.9.40 (crashed S. of Swaffham)
P6908	18.4.40-23.6.41
P6924	30.11.39-FTR 18.7.40 from Cherbourg
P6955	4.3.40-FTR 8.9.40 from Boulogne
R2778	27.7.40-FTR 8.9.40 from Boulogne
R3617	11.4.40-9.2.41
R3801	18.8.40-14.5.41
R3803	4.8.40-10.5.41
R3845	12.6.40-4.1.41
R3846	13.6.40-FTR 19.3.41
Y/T1825	11.7.40-FTR 3.5.41
T1866	7.7.40-19.8.40
T2034	21.8.40-EAO 27.10.40 (destroyed by bombing at Gt Massingham)
T2039	21.8.40-FTR 16.12.40
T2047	27.8.40-21.5.41
T2161	12.9.40-23.9.40
H/T2234	12.9.40-FTR 3.5.41
T2246	9.9.40-EFB 30.10.40

No. 105 Sqn, Honington; to Watton 10.7.40

L8788	4.7.40-17.8.41
L9209	4.7.40-31.12.40
L9338	28.6.40-10.8.40 (damaged)
P4918	6.10.40-27.4.41
R3707	12.9.40-FTR 25.5.41
R3838	15.8.40-3.7.41
T1826	5.7.40-8.11.40
T1884	12.7.40-EFB 27.11.40
T1885	12.7.40-3.5.41
T1886	12.7.40-EFA 26.11.40
T1887	12.7.40-17.8.41
T1890	11.7.40-FTR 15.11.40
T1891	11.7.40-FTR 28.10.40 from Hamburg
T1892	11.7.40-EFB 21.3.41
T1892	11.7.40-FTR 28.11.40
T1894	14.7.40-FTR 9.9.40
T1895	14.7.40-1.3.41
T1896	14.7.40-FTR 2.10.40
T1897	14.7.40-FTR 12.12.40
T1930	13.7.40-28.6.41
T1931	13.7.40-24.4.41

T1936	13.7.40-28.6.41
T2329	5.10.40-FTR 16.11.40

No. 107 Sqn, Wattisham

L4847	15.10.40-?
L4893	20.9.40-13.10.40
L9170	17.1.40-18.7.40
L9306	19.4.40-24.7.40
L9414	24.6.40-FTR 23.7.40
N3568	13.8.40-FTR 1.8.41
N3620	15.6.40-FTR 29.8.40 from De Kooy
N3629	17.8.40-21.9.41
N6183	23.3.40-15.11.40
N6191	21.6.39-EFB 30.9.40 (crashed taking off for Calais from Wattisham)
N6228	20.4.40-11.9.40
N6237	11.8.39-11.9.40
P4856	5.3.40-28.8.40
X/P6894	26.4.40-FTR 10.7.40 from Amiens
B/R3606	29.5.40-FTR 10.7.40 from Amiens
R3615	3.6.40-15.11.40
R3737	19.5.40-EFAO 15.11.40 (crashed nr Stowmarket)
R3740	19.5.40-FTR 18.4.41
T/R3815	3.6.40-FTR 10.7.40 from Amiens
J/R3816	3.6.40-24.6.41
R3824	8.6.40-EFAO 4.9.40 (night collision landing Wattisham)
R3870	10.6.40-30.6.40
R3873	10.6.40-FTR 18.8.41?
R3916	16.6.40-FTR 10.7.40 from Amiens
D/T1831	11.7.40-FTR 8.9.40 from Ostend
T1850	1.7.40-FTR 11.8.40 from Dinard
T1851	1.7.40-FTR 8.9.40 from Ostend
T1852	1.7.40-FTR 19.9.40 from Calais
T1853	1.7.40-29.9.41
T1854	14.7.40-17.7.41
T1860	2.10.40-FTR 19.12.40
T1881	11.7.40-EFA 10.10.40
T1883	11.7.40-FTR 25.9.40 from Calais
T1921	11.7.40-FTR 7.6.41
T1923	13.7.40-24.7.40
T1928	13.7.40-FTR 23.11.40 (ditched)
T1959	23.7.40-17.8.40
T1987	21.7.40-24.7.40
T1988	21.7.40-24.7.40
T2080	9.9.40-FTR 29.11.40
T2139	12.9.40-EAO 3.11.40 (destroyed by bombing, Wattisham)
T2141	26.9.40-26.3.41
T2229	4.9.40-EFB 28.10.40 (crashed nr Bircham Newton)
T2230	12.9.40-16.6.41
Z5794	11.9.40-FTR 11.12.40
Z5795	11.9.40-FTR 24.4.41

No. 110 Sqn, Wattisham

L8751	18.8.39-23.11.40
L8755	1.4.40-25.6.41
L8787	24.6.40-EFA 28.3.41
L9208	28.6.40-11.2.42
L9305	28.7.40-9.12.41
L9310	25.7.40-EFB 8.10.40 (crashed nr Wattisham)
P4858	14.9.39-7.10.40
P4860	15.9.39-23.11.40
R3600	26.5.40-FTR 6.5.41

R3681	26.5.40-2.8.41
R3684	26.5.40-24.4.41
R3736	19.5.40-EFAO 4.9.40
R3738	19.5.40-FTR 25.7.40 from Lunen?
R3741	19.5.40-FTR 18.4.41
R3748	26.5.40-FTR 24.7.40 from Bernberg
R3749	26.5.40-FTR 27.10.40 (destroyed by bombing, Wattisham)
R3772	25.5.40-28.7.41
R3773	25.5.40-EFB 31.8.40 (crashed at Offton, Suffolk, returning from Emden)
R3775	25.5.40-FTR 10.8.40 from St Inglevert
R3807	4.8.40-EAO 27.10.40 (destroyed by bombing, Wattisham)
R3814	11.6.40-25.7.41
R3831	13.6.40-EFA 11.11.40
R3874	11.6.40-25.6.41
R3906	10.10.40-15.12.41
T1797	28.6.40-EFB 10.12.40 (crashed nr Dedham)
T1800	31.7.40-16.5.41
T1923	24.7.40-EAO 20.8.40 (destroyed by bombing at Kenley)
T1958	24.7.40-17.8.40
T1960	24.7.40-17.8.40
T1993	1.9.40-EFB 28.11.40
T2133	13.9.40-EAO 3.11.40 (destroyed by bombing, Wattisham)
T2253	5.9.40-EFAO 29.11.40 (hit trees on approach to Wattisham)

No. 114 Sqn, Horsham St Faith (using Oulton satellite from 8.40)

L4847	26.9.40-15.10.40
L9020	23.9.40-3.8.41
L9204	17.6.40-EFA 23.7.40 (crashed Nantwich)
L9265	17.6.40-FTR 13.8.40
L9267	17.6.40-FTR 24.5.41
L9303	25.8.40-21.11.40
L9375	25.8.40-23.11.40
L9383	25.7.40-11.11.40
L9466	15.4.40-28.3.41
N3532	14.6.40-8.11.40
N3544	14.6.40-19.8.41
N3613	13.6.40-3.5.42
N3617	17.6.40-EFAO 9.12.40
N3626	1.8.40-14.1.41
N3628	2.8.40-21.11.40
R3672	14.6.40-EFA 11.12.40
R3753	11.6.40-FTR 10.11.40
R3804	12.6.40-FTR 5.7.40 from Soest
R3805	12.6.40-11.11.40
R3806	12.6.40-16.10.40
R3809	11.6.40-FTR 25.9.40 from Boulogne
R3813	11.6.40-11.11.40
R3884	14.8.40-1.11.40
R3891	13.6.40-1.1.42
R3892	17.6.40-FTR 19.8.40
R3895	12.6.40-FTR 31.7.40 from Aalborg
R3897	12.6.40-FTR 31.12.40
R3898	12.6.40-FTR 1.8.40 from Hamstede
T1793	21.8.40-25.11.40
T1861	6.7.40-FTR 29.10.40 from Le Havre
T2224	9.9.40-10.7.42
Z5797	11.9.40-23.7.41

No. 139 Sqn, Horsham St Faith

L8756	30.11.39-7.8.41
L9239	13.6.40-FTR 3.8.40
L9303	13.6.40-25.8.40
L9304	13.6.40-FTR 7.8.40 (ditched off Wells, Norfolk)
L9375	4.8.40-25.8.40
L9461	7.5.40-7.8.41
N3631	5.8.40-11.11.40
R3671	13.6.40-FTR 14.10.40
R3673	13.6.40-28.11.40
R3698	12.6.40-3.1.41
R3705	12.6.40-11.11.40
R3757	13.6.40-1.11.40
R3885	14.8.40-FTR 12.5.41
R3901	12.6.40-19.7.40
R3902	12.6.40-11.11.40
R3903	12.6.40-FTR 4.6.41
R3906	14.6.40-10.10.40
R3907	14.6.40-2.5.41
R3908	14.6.40-3.10.40
R3912	13.6.40-11.11.40
T1794	12.6.40-FTR 24.9.40
T1795	12.6.40-FTR 8.6.41
T1796	12.6.40-13.9.40
T1798	17.6.40-13.9.40
T1799	27.7.40-7.3.41
T1832	9.7.40-FTR 16.6.41
T1871	6.8.40-FTR 7.11.40
T1922	12.7.40-22.8.41
T2161	23.9.40-29.10.40
T2281	9.9.40-1.12.40
T2282	9.9.40-18.11.40
T2318	25.9.40-28.11.40
T2320	25.9.40-EFAO 19.11.40
T2328	26.9.40-FTR 31.12.40
T2330	26.9.40-18.11.40

No. 218 Sqn, Mildenhall; to Oakington 18.7.40

L8848	26.8.40-FTR 8.9.40
L9264	5.7.40-18.8.40 (collided with T1929)
L9298	3.8.40-23.11.40
L9306	24.7.40-25.11.40
L9327	9.9.40-23.11.40
L9381	25.7.40-23.11.40
N3561	16.7.40-26.11.40
N3562	16.7.40-15.11.40
N3563	16.7.40-11.9.40
N3573	20.8.40-26.11.40
N3585	16.7.40-21.11.40
N3625	3.8.40-11.11.40
P6960	5.7.40-21.11.40
R3597	28.6.40-EFAO 13.7.40 (crashed nr Bedford)
R3666	12.9.40-10.11.40
T1863	15.7.40-21.11.40
T1864	15.7.40-21.11.40
T1865	15.7.40-15.11.40
T1888	15.7.40-15.11.40
T1929	3.8.40-EFA 18.8.40
T1987	24.7.40-26.11.40
T1988	24.7.40-15.11.40
T1990	3.8.40-FTR 23.8.40
T1996	3.8.40-22.11.40

The Fairey Battle

'If only...'. History is littered with that sentiment, very well applied to the Fairey Battle saga. There wasn't all that much wrong with the aircraft; indeed, it featured rugged advanced construction, a retractable undercarriage — and a famous 'Merlin', in which rested its undoing for the Battle was conceived to take the much more powerful Griffon. Griffon? In 1933, I hear you say? Yes, but not the Griffon engine of Spitfire days, but a predecessor of the same name, a development of the engine which propelled the Schneider winner. When that engine faltered in 1934 Fairey turned to a powerful and too advanced complex engine of their own making. When that too became a non-starter the company was forced to opt for the Merlin which gave about 800 less horse power. Little wonder the aeroplane, far too large for a 1,000 hp engine, was hardly a success.

Few aircraft have suffered at the hands of friend and foe as much as the Battle. Dismissed by a British official history as being 'as well adapted for air fighting as hackneys for winning the Derby', it was more brutally disposed of by the other side. Devised as a replacement for the outstanding 4,700 lb, 184 mph Hawker Hart biplane day bomber, and obsolete before hostilities commenced, the single-engined newcomer was intended to have a top speed of over 200 mph at 10,000 ft and a range of 600 miles when carrying a 1,000 lb bomb load. Night flying equipment and longer range would have pushed its weight beyond the 6,000 lb tare limit.

The P.27/32 Hart light bomber replacement specification was approved by DTD on 12 April 1933, tenders being invited on 29 June from a dozen companies. No advanced Hart-like bomber could result from the existing requirement so range was extended to 720 miles, 195 mph top speed to be attained at 15,000 ft.

Additional tankage should extend the range to 1,200 miles. Eight firms had submitted ideas by November 1933. Fairey, with the Fox high speed bomber to their credit, entered a design for which a top speed of 223 mph at 15,000 ft was forecast. Judged the best, it was followed by Armstrong-Whitworth's featuring a dorsal turret. One example of each aircraft was ordered and almost immediately delay set in.

When the use of that projected Rolls-Royce Griffon was abandoned Fairey seized the chance to press for the use of their spectacular 24-cylinder Prince 'double' engine, each bank of 12 cylinders driving one of the two counter rotating propellers. Somewhat desperate to save the important new bomber, April 1934 saw the Air Staff agree to this unconventional power source even though the engine had not yet passed the standard 100 hour type test. If necessary, they stated, yet another engine would have to be substituted. A switch to the Rolls-Royce Merlin almost inevitably followed, producing a very underpowered aeroplane.

Contracts for both P.27/32 designs were confirmed on 11 June 1934, almost simultaneously with the British government's decision to abandon the 6,000 lb restriction on bomber weight. Officials from Fairey then visited the United States to view latest developments there, following which they redesigned their project, improving its layout and incorporating modern construction methods to achieve higher performance. In further similarity to the Vickers B.9/32, Fairey requested that prototype delivery be postponed until December 1935, much displeasing the Air Staff who, needing the aircraft, agreed very reluctantly. As *K4303*, the Battle prototype did not fly until 10 March 1936.

Brief Martlesham trials in July 1936 revealed the aircraft's inferiority when

A possible alternative to the Battle was the Armstrong Whitworth AW 29.

compared with its B.9/32 twin-engined companion, destined to become the famous Wellington. The single engine imposed both an operational weight limit, and prohibited incorporation of modifications entailing much additional weight which could have resulted in a superior aeroplane. This was how the loaded prototype compared (official figures):

Type	Top speed/ height	Range	Associated bomb load
P.27/32	252 mph/ 15,000 ft	910 miles	1,000 lb
B.9/32	258 mph/ 15,000 ft	1,380 miles	2,000 lb

An inferior aircraft was on offer, to enter service at about the same time as a brighter performer, the superior unexpected Bristol Blenheim. Within Rearmament Scheme C of 1935 the Air Staff wanted 150 Battles before April 1937, instead of which it was not even accepted for Service use until May 1936, when, two months after the prototype flew, 155 examples (*K7558-7712*) were ordered to Specification 23/35.

Already obsolescent, *K7559* on 20 May 1937 became the first Battle delivered to a squadron, No. 63 at Upwood. The Air Staff, desperate to acquire new bombers, had ordered by November 1936 within the later Scheme F a total of 1,368 Battles. Fairey had built a new factory at Heaton Chapel, near Stockport, to produce *K9176-9486, N2020-2066, N2082-2131, N2147-2190* and

The Fairey Battle prototype K4303, a very elegant looking aeroplane but much underpowered. (Fairey)

The Battle was rarely seen with spinners fitted because the rear of its fairing too easily chafed on the engine cowling. The latter was difficult to remove, too.

N2211-2258 — 505 Battles in all. Another 863 were to be built by a daughter firm.

Design work proceeding on more advanced bombers showed that one Avro P.13/36 (later called the Manchester) had an operational capability equivalent to three Battles, but such aircraft were far in the future. Nevertheless the Battle was so disappointing that a decision was taken to cancel those not received by 31 March 1939. Development of later types of bombers was soon lagging so badly that policy reversal resulted in stopgap orders being placed, firstly for another 400 Battles. Austin Motors had set up a production source at Birmingham/Elmdon to build their 863 Battles, *L4935-5797*.

Further concern arose in September 1938 over what the RAF considered painfully slow Battle production rates. To encourage the manufacturer to now complete production by an agreed 31 March 1940, a further 200 examples were ordered on 7 September. Fairey then increased its labour force, introduced night working, and the Air Ministry authorized an order for 50 more Battles. On 1 December 1938 yet another order was placed, for a further 200 to maintain the labour force fully intact until such time as the company could switch to building Avro Manchesters.

When compared with the 1940 Wellington, the Battle I showed its inferiority:

	Top speed/ height	Loaded weight	Range/ bomb load
Battle (Merlin 1)	243 mph/ 16,200 ft	10,900 lb	1,050 miles/ 1,000 lb
Wellington Ic	235 mph/ 15,000 ft	28,500 lb	1,805 miles/ 2,750 lb

The first 136 Battles powered by the Merlin I were designated Mk I. From *K7695* the Merlin II was factory installed, launching an unusual style of mark allocation as this version became the Battle Mk II, the remainder being Merlin III Mk IIIs, likewise those in the range *R3922-R4045*. Austin-built Battles to *L4993* were Mk IIs, the remainder being Mk IIIs. All 'K' and 'N' serialled aircraft had been produced by the outbreak of war, at which time deliveries had reached about *P2310* and *L5320*.

Because of its obsolescence as a bomber new uses for the Battle were devised. A decision not to lengthen its life by development — apart from training variants and target towers — was taken in March 1939. Two hundred examples, *L5598-L5797*, were subsequently ordered to be completed on the line as target towers, the first being delivered on 7 March 1940. A further 66 (*V1201-1250* and *V1265-1280*) were also built as target towers. Another 200 (*P6616-6645, P6663-6692, P6718-6737, P6750-*

6769, *R7356-7385*, *R7399-7448* and *R7461-R7480*) were produced as twin cockpit Battle (Trainer) aircraft. In Service many a Battle had a change of engine mark, and therefore aircraft mark numbers often changed too.

Eventually 2,196 Battles were built, 1,164 by Fairey's Stockport works and the rest by Austin Motors. Production breakdown between the sources was as follows:

Stockport		**Austin**	
May-December 1937	81	September-December 1938	28
January-December 1938	352	January-31 August 1939	351
January-31 August 1939	341	September-December 1939	173
September-December 1939	172	January-December 1939	480
January-November 1940	218		
Totals	1,164		1,032

Operations

No other type of British bomber suffered so harshly at the hands of the enemy in such a short time as the Fairey Battle. Between 10 May and 20 June 1940 115 were officially listed as being destroyed during operational flying, and others were written off due to crashes and enemy air attacks.

On 1 July 1940 ASUs held 151 Battles, 100 of them ready for issue. By 15 July that total had risen to 440. Although there was no shortage of replacements to re-equip the smashed squadrons, the value of reissuing Battles was reviewed. The outcome was that several squadrons found themselves switched to 2 Group — and soon converting to Blenheims.

All Battle squadrons were theoretically armed with 16 aircraft, including Sydenham-based Nos. 88 and 226 Squadrons which in June 1940 joined 61 Group (soon renamed RAF Northern Ireland) and patrolled the seas and beaches of Ulster. Of 98 Squadron, a late arrival in France, very little remained, many of its personnel being lost when the SS *Lancastria*, carrying over 5,000 troops, was bombed and sunk off St. Nazaire on 17 June. A new 98 Squadron based at Gatwick in July introduced the Battle to Coastal Command, with the specialized task

of attacking E-boats in the Channel. On 31 July it was transferred to Kaldadarnes, Iceland, as a striking force to repel any invaders, its place in Coastal Command being taken by 12 Squadron. A 98 Squadron Battle, *L5343* is displayed at the RAF Museum.

Remaining squadrons Nos. 12, 103, 142 and 150 joined a new 1 Group reconstituted at Benson on 22 June and which moved its HQ to Hucknall before the month ended. Resurrected at Stradishall, 150 Squadron joined 103 Squadron at Newton on 23 July. No. 12 Squadron had reformed at Finningley on 16 June 1940 and moved to Binbrook on 3 July to work with 142 Squadron. By 12 July the four squadrons with 47 serviceable aircraft were declared operationally fit, the Newton pair resuming operations on 21 July when they tried to bomb Target Z3, Rotterdam's oil tanks.

At about 16:00 hrs on 27 July a flare loaded aboard *L5528* of 150 Squadron for the night's operations fell to the ground and ignited. About seven minutes later the first of the four 250 lb HEs on the aircraft exploded and was soon followed by two more. Seven men near the aircraft were killed and four badly injured.

Newton's two squadrons were taken off operations at the start of August for anti-invasion training. On 15 August they searched the North Sea for survivors of the Luftwaffe raid on Yorkshire, but not until 7 September did they resume bombing by joining the campaign against shipping in the Channel ports.

Their period of operational inactivity was in contrast to that of Binbrook's squadrons. On 7 August both were placed at the disposal of Coastal Command. No. 12 Squadron moved to 16 Group's station at Thorney Island, but before operating moved on 12 August to Eastchurch, joining 16 Battles of 142 Squadron which arrived the same day. An action-packed three weeks ensued. At 07:00 hrs next day Eastchurch was heavily bombed by Do 17s, the operations block being hit and 12 RAF personnel killed and 40 injured. Airmen's quarters and hangars were damaged but although there were 18 craters on the flying ground no dispersals or Battles were hit. Nevertheless only 25 could be made serviceable. In an afternoon raid two days later neither squadron suffered, but Wg Cdr V. Blackden, No. 12's Commanding Officer, had flown to Martlesham Heath where a bomb destroyed his Battle, *L5093*. Because of Eastchurch's cratered landing ground, 142 squadron temporarily moved to Detling from where, on the evening of 17 August, Battles of both squadrons escorted by Blenheim fighters attempted a daylight raid on Boulogne. Twelve crews had been briefed but only four of 142 Squadron and five of No. 12 attacked. Plt Off Hayten had to crash land *P2331*, its port wing very badly damaged by AA fire.

On 19 August Detling was bombed and *P2331* was further damaged. Another of 12 Squadron's aircraft, *L5491*, was badly riddled by shrapnel during an afternoon attack upon Eastchurch on 20 August. Both squadrons continued using Detling as an advance base from where to interfere with E-boats operating out of Boulogne against Channel convoys.

Despite the ease with which Bf 109s disposed of Battles during the battle for France, several daylight raids were attempted. On 23 August Battle *L5569* of 142 Squadron flown by Plt Off Stevenson was one of six detailed to bomb E-boats and floatplanes at Boulogne. The aircraft was hit by flak and the crew, driven from their objective, aimed their bomb load at a factory south-east of the town. As they turned for home two Bf 109 fighters swept in to dispose of the bomber whose gunner, Sgt Duckers, fired 600 rounds at them while they chased it to the Kent coast. With wireless operator Sgt Hemmings and the gunner injured by enemy fire Stevenson crash landed at Whitchurch, Asford. Two others, *L5503* (Midshipman Taylor) and *L5582* (Sgt Pierce), fell to fighters which damaged Sgt Green's *L5584*.

Only 11 Battles were left serviceable in Coastal Command by 26 August and two days later Eastchurch was again bombed. This time two Battles of 142 Squadron were destroyed. A further attack on 31 August left both squadrons unscathed and with 22 aircraft between them ready for operations. German raiders were more successful on 2 September when at 12:30 the Eastchurch bomb dump close to 142 Squadron's dispersal area was hit by incendiaries. After a few minutes there was a tremendous explosion which damaged beyond repair five of the squadron's Battles. Later that day the enemy called yet again but without causing much damage. Only 16 Battles were available for the flight next day. Still not satisfied, the Luftwaffe dealt with Eastchurch yet again, carrying out a dive-bombing and strafing attack on 5 September and causing considerable damage. Delayed action HEs by SHQ forced the establishment of temporary headquarters near Eastchurch village. Clearly placed in an untenable position, both squadrons were next day ordered to return to Binbrook and to Bomber Command on 7 September. No. 12 Squadron flew away five aircraft and left six behind unserviceable. Both Binbrook squadrons resumed operations, against the Channel ports, on 17 September.

By then No. 1 Group had been expanded by the addition of two Polish bomber squadrons. Polish personnel had been gathering on 27 March 1940 at Hucknall in order to join a new unit, a Battle-equipped Polish OTU soon retitled No. 18 OTU. The first two weeks of this eight-week course were devoted to learning basic English then followed a fortnight's training for pilots in 'A' Flight and wireless operator/air gunners in 'B' Flight. Crew teams learned how to operate the Battle before proceeding for training in bombing and gunnery at Penrhos where the first group comprising six Battles of 'D' Flight was detached on 26 May. These Poles first came under attack on 29 July when a surprise raid developed on Penrhos. The officer in command, Flg Off B.P.H. Page, was killed by splinters. Two Battles were damaged by machine-gun fire, *K9474* quite seriously. By the time the OTU was a flourishing concern the Battle's operational part in the war was ending, and on 25 November 1940 No. 18 OTU received its first Wellington. Nevertheless this and 12 OTU had

trained sufficient crews to enable two Polish Battle bomber squadrons, Nos. 300 and 301, to commence operations from Swinderby on 14 September. Next day 1 Group's nominal strength stood at 96 Battles of which 79 were serviceable. That latter figure steadily rose — to 85 on 28 September — but fell to around 55 over the following two weeks as raids on the Channel invasion ports took a roll. Two further Polish-manned Battle squadrons were formed, No. 304 at Bramcote on 22 August and No. 305 a week later. Neither flew Battles operationally. Ample supplies remained to the end of the Battle of Britain period, 211 Battles being available for use from ASUs on 31 October 1940.

The usual bomb load delivered per Battle during July 1940 was 2 × 250 lb GP HE and 8 × 40 lb fragmentation bombs dropped during level attacks made at about 10,000 ft. By September Battle loads had increased to 4 × 250 lb GP HEs, sometimes supplemented by 16 × 40 lb bombs, and eventually 6 × 250 lb GPs was a frequent load.

The last operational bombing sorties by Bomber Command Battles were flown on 15/16 October 1940. Between 21 July and the final operation Bomber Command Battles

Battles of 300 (Polish) Squadron in September 1940.

had flown 237 sorties in addition to those undertaken during detachment to Coastal Command. Underpowered, poorly armed, outdated even before hostilities began, the Battle still had a considerable part to play as a trainer.

Summary

On 1 July 1940 743 Battle bombers were in RAF use, 770 on 31 October 1940 and mostly in training schools. Bomber squadrons held 114 on 1 July and 141 on 31 October 1940. A further 123 Battle target towers were in active service on 1 July and possibly 93 Battle(T), the latter total rising to 157 by the end of October. A very large number of Battles, bombers and trainers, were being prepared for or were on route to either Australia, Canada or South Africa for use in the Empire Air Training Scheme. Many had seen operational service in 1940, some as used in raids on the Channel ports being overhauled in MUs then despatched overseas.

Of the first production batch of Battles only 29 were active by July 1940, 22 on 31 October 1940, and only two — with 142 Squadron — during that period. Comparative figures for the second 'K' batch are 122 and 87 respectively. The largest contingent was from the 'L' series, Austin-built, of which 362 were active on 1 July and 309 on 31 October 1940.

When in July 1944 all Battles remaining in the UK were declared obsolete, there were two flyable. Of those that carried out bombing sorties in August–October 1940 only a few remained airworthy overseas to end the war. The last Battle to have active life in Britain was probably L5776 of the Gunnery Research Unit. Still airworthy at Wittering in the summer of 1944, it was struck off charge on 12 December 1944 following a flying accident a few days previously.

Operations flown by home-based Battles July–October 1940

Date	No. sorties completed/ despatched	Targets listed as attacked
July (under 1 Group Bomber Command)		
21/22	3/6	Rotterdam(Z3) — 2/3 of 103 Sqn attacked alternatives
22/23	6	Schiphol (Z57) — 2/3 of Sqn attacked and 3 of 150 Sqn operated
28/29	5	Active afds — Brussels/Évère attacked
29/30	3	Waalhaven afd (150 Sqn) — all abortive
August (under 16 Group Coastal Command)		
13	3	Boulogne (142 Sqn)
17	10	Boulogne 19:40–23:59; (12 Sqn) L5391, L5495, P2331, L5359, L5404; (142 Sqn) L5569, L5566, L5503, L5501, L5560 daylight raid, Blenheim escorted
18	9/12	Boulogne shipping 20:20–22:20 (12, 142 Sqns)
19	1	E-boats in Boulogne 23:00–00:45, from Detling
19	10	Boulogne 23:00–00:20 (12, 142 Sqns)
21	1	Boulogne (142 Sqn L5584 — evening sortie from Detling)
23	6	Boulogne barges and E-boats 18:30–19:45 from Detling (142 Sqn)
24	5	Boulogne barges and seaplanes 02:15–03:30 from Detling — only 2 of 142 Sqn attacked
25	1	Boulogne E-boats 04:40–06:00 (L5451:C/12 Sqn)
26	2/3	Le Crotoy afd 01:05–03:45 from Eastchurch (142 Sqn)
26/27	4	Boulogne 23:45–03:15
27	4	Calais E-boats 02:45–05:00 (3 of 12 Sqn, 1 of 142 Sqn)
29	1	Mardyck afd 12:30–13:05 — abandoned (12 Sqn L5398)
September		
3	1	Calais 00:01–01:45 from Eastchurch (142 Sqn)
Operations under 1 Group Bomber Command (resumed):		
7/8	11/12	Calais (103, 150 Sqns)
9	6	Calais 19:00–23:30 (103, 150 Sqns)
10/11	6	Boulogne (103, 150 sqns)

11/12	5/6	Boulogne (103 Sqn, 150 Sqns)		23/24	11/12	Boulogne (12, 142 150 Sqns)
14	12	Boulogne 19:50–23:40 (103 Sqn *L5336*, *L5431*, *P2306*; 150 Sqn *L5057*, *L5058*, *P2312*; 300 Sqn *L5317*, *L5427*, *L5353*; 301 Sqn *L5551*, *L5556*, *L5448*)		24/25		Boulogne 02:40–06:10 (103, 150, 300, 301 Sqns)
				25	12	Boulogne 03:00–07:00 (103, 142, 150, 301 Sqns)
15/16	12	Boulogne 19:50–01:00 (103, 150 and 300 Sqns)		25/26	14	Ostend 02:45–06:05 (103, 150, 300 Sqns)
17/18	20	Boulogne (12 Sqn *L5415*, *L5398*, *L5451*; 103 Sqn *P2307*, *N2157*, *L5536*; 142 Sqn *L5080*, *L5464*, *N2103*; 150 Sqn *L5593*, *L5057*, *L5548*; 301 Sqn *L5536*, *L5445*, *L5392*, *L5549*, *L5048*, *L5551*)		26	4	Dunkirk 01:50–07:00 (2 of 103 Sqn and 2 of 150 Sqn)
				26	1	E-boats in Channel 03:00–03:45; 142 Sqn *L5507* failed to locate, crashed on landing
				October		
18/19	12	Boulogne — 11 attacked dropping 14 ×250 lb + 16 × 40 lb HEs (103, 300 Sqns)		9	8	Calais 18:23–22:30 (301 Sqn)
				10	8	Calais 18:23–22:08 (300 Sqn)
19	12	Boulogne (103, 150 and 301 Sqns)		11	5	Ostend (12, 103, 142 Sqns)
20	3	Cap Gris Nez 03:00–06:40 (12 Sqn)		12	6	Ostend and Calais (301 Sqn — 3 to each)
20/21	12	Boulogne (103, 150, 301 Sqns)		13	6	Calais 18:15–21:30 (12, 142 Sqns)
21	2/3	142 Sqn *L5560* (Boulogne), *L5311* (guns Cap Gris Nez), *L5228* (aborted)		13	6	Boulogne 17:40–22:30 (300 Sqn)
21/22	6	Calais (103, 150 Sqns)		15/16	4	Shipping Calais 20:20–23:45 — abortive (12 Sqn *L5399*, *L5076*, *L5240*, *L5259*; 142 Sqn *L5259*, *L5240*)
22	3	Boulogne (150 Sqn)		16		CC29 19:44–00:15 (301 Sqn *L5448*, *L5445*, *L5549*, *P6567*, *L5556*, *P6569*)

Total Battle day and night sorties under Bomber Command 237
missing   3 (and 4 under 16 Group)
written off due to battle damage 5
Tonnages of bombs dropped: July 1940   4
August   ?
September 6
October   25

Fairey Battles used by Squadrons 1 July– 16 October 1940

(C) after serial = later to Canada, (A) after serial = later to Australia, (SA) after serial = later to South Africa, (SA*) = lost at sea en route to South Africa, aboard the SS *Huntingdon* (sunk 24.2.41)

No. 12 Sqn: Binbrook 3.7.40, Thorney Island 7.8.40, Eastchurch 12.8.40, Binbrook 7.9.40

L5011	4.10.40–10.10.40
L5076(C)	20.8.40–22.12.40
L5093	destroyed by bombing 15.8.40
L5127	17.7.40–25.8.40 (written off in ground accident, Eastleigh)
L5220(C)	27.8.40–16.12.40
L5359(C)	27.6.40–28.11.40
L5391	21.8.40–10.9.40
L5398(C)	26.6.40–12.12.40
L5399(C)	26.6.40–21.8.40
L5400(C)	26.6.40–21.8.40
O/L5415(SA)	19.5.40–28.11.40
P/L5420(C)	23.5.40–5.11.40
Z,C/L5451(C)	21.5.40–16.12.40
L5458(C)	16.6.40–17.12.40
L5491	27.6.40–damaged 20.8.40, SOC 6.9.40
L5493	2.8.40–SOC 31.8.40
L9495	12.6.40–1.1.41
L5521(C)	17.7.40–25.9.40
L5532(C)	6.10.40–5.1.41
L5568	16.6.40–1.8.40 (shot down by British night ftr nr Skegness)
L5629	17.7.40–27.7.40
L5630(A)	24.8.40–7.11.40
N2166(A)	22.8.40–17.12.40
P2311	21.8.40–FAO2 25.8.40, SOC 13.9.40
P2331	16.6.40–17.9.40 (seriously damaged by bombing, Detling)
P5236(C)	29.8.40–16.12.40

P5237(C)	16.6.40–22.12.40
P6571	26.7.40–EFAO (Wainfleet)
V/P6597	16.6.40–FTR 19.8.40
P6597	16.6.40–FTR 19.8.40

No. 88 Sqn, Sydenham, N.I., from 23.6.40

K9322(A)	6.10.38–18.9.40
L5285(SA)	2.3.40–16.11.40
L5330	23.5.40–?
L5361	15.6.40–EAO 4.5.41, SOC after bombing raid
L5389(C)	25.5.40–17.7.40
L5393(C)	9.6.40–5.9.41
L5478	8.6.40–17.7.40
L5544	?–27.6.41
L5558	17.7.40–30.10.40
L5559	21.7.40–31.12.41
L5561	6.6.40–EAO 4.5.41, SOC after bombing raid
L5565	17.7.40–5.9.41
L5571	21.7.40–31.12.41
L5572	21.7.40–EAO 4.5.41, SOC after bombing raid
L5574	17.7.40–22.4.41
L5590	17.7.40–5.9.41
L5594(A)	?–6.9.41
L5596(A)	17.7.40–31.12.41
N2236(A)	26.5.40–17.7.40
N2237(C)	26.5.40–21.7.40
P2156(C)	9.6.40–29.7.40
P2159	23.5.40–EFB 20.3.41 (crashed nr Lardglass, N.I.)
P2320(C)	21.6.40–21.7.40

No. 98 Sqn, Gatwick; to Kaldadarnes, Iceland, 31.7.40

K9213(C)	8.6.38–13.7.40
K9215(C)	13.6.38–14.7.40
K9219(A)	28.6.38–13.7.40
K9229(C)	28.6.38–13.7.40
K9350(C)	12.4.40–26.7.40
K9365(C)	21.6.40–21.7.40
K9386(C)	19.11.38–13.7.40
K9414(C)	9.10.39–13.7.40
K9422(A)	8.10.39–17.7.40
L5063(C)	13.7.40–20.8.41
L5073(C)	?–?
L5099	.7.40–23.6.41
L5331(C)	14.7.40–?
L5332(C)	14.7.40–?
L5343	13.7.40–EFA 13.9.40 (missing from Iceland)
L5357(A)	21.8.40–30.11.40
L5394(C)	2.6.40–13.7.40
L5412(C)	14.7.40–?
L5442(C)	13.7.40–?
L5505(C)	14.7.40–?
L5547	14.7.40–?
L5550(C)	14.7.40–26.8.40
L5552(C)	14.7.40–?
L5553(C)	14.7.40–?
L5554(C)	14.7.40–?
L5628(A)	17.4.40–?
L5629	18.5.40–16.7.40
L5630	17.5.40–16.7.40
N2167(C)	14.7.40–?
P2330	14.7.40–FTR 26.5.41

P6570	14.7.40–EFAO 14.9.40 (crashed Kaldadarnes)

No. 103 Sqn, Honington; to Newton 3.7.40

K7671(C)	2.9.40–2.10.40
K9247(A)	3.10.40–7.10.40
K9460(C)	5.8.40–2.10.40
N/K9471(SA)	5.8.40–2.10.40
H/L5038(A)	5.8.40–12.10.40
C/L5010	17.7.40–FTR 9.9.40
L5011	27.9.40–4.10.40
L5125(SA)	6.40–7.40
L5237	30.9.40–4.10.40
L5244(A)	?–18.8.40
F,J,P/L5336(C)	16.6.40–4.10.40
L5358(A)	23.8.40–21.10.40
L5363(C)	5.9.40–10.11.40
L5381(C)	23.5.40–?
P,Q/L5395(SA)	26.6.40–10.10.40
E/L5431(SA*)	6.7.40–11.10.40
L,G/L5432	6.7.40–20.10.40
L5433	6.7.40–EFA 3.8.40 (crashed on approach, Cottesmore)
L5444(A)	16.6.40–2.7.40
L5469(C)	26.6.40–29.11.40
L5479(C)	16.6.40–20.7.40
F,P/L5525(SA)	16.6.40–12.10.40
L5532	10.9.40–6.10.40
L5629(A)	27.7.40–4.1.41
R/N2157(SA*)	26.6.40–11.10.40
T/N2163(A)	26.6.40–10.10.40
N2255(A)	16.6.40–2.7.40
P2304(C)	26.6.40–10.9.40
E/P2305(A)	16.6.40–10.10.40
D/P2306(C)	9.40–10.10.40
K/P2307(SA)	9.40–12.10.40
G/P2308(C)	9.40–15.10.40
P2311	25.6.40–21.8.40

No. 142 Sqn, Waddington; to Binbrook 3.7.40

K7647(A)	25.8.40–3.10.40
K7652(C)	30.8.40–26.9.40
K9406(C)	19.9.40–2.10.40
K9444(A)	19.9.40–3.10.40
L5042(C)	3.10.40–10.10.40
L5068(C)	4.9.40–17.12.40
L5077(SA)	4.9.40–2.12.40
L5080(C)	19.7.40–11.10.40
L5113	?–EFA (crashed Middleton Stoney, Bicester)
L5259(C)	31.8.40–10.40
L5367(C)	25.8.40–29.9.40
L5368	26.8.40–1.11.40
L5391	10.9.40–EFA 23.10.40 force landed 6 miles N. of Binbrook)
L5428	31.8.40–EFA 13.10.40 (crashed nr Torksey, Lincs)
L5453(C)	15.6.40–16.9.40
L5456	15.6.40–18.9.40
L5464(SA)	21.5.40–16.12.40
L5501(C)	26.6.40–9.9.40
L5502	26.6.40–FTR 28.7.40
L5503	26.6.40–FTR 23.8.40
L5504(C)	26.6.40–19.12.40
L5507	26.6.40–EFB 26.8.40 (crash landed Eastchurch)
L5533(A)	15.6.40–26.9.40

L5560(C)	8.8.40-3.11.40
L5566	30.7.40-22.9.40
F/L5569(C)	8.8.40-12.9.40
L5582	29.5.40-FTR 23.8.40
L5584	?-FTR 28.7.40
L5586(C)	21.5.40-25.9.40
L5589(C)	30.7.40-1.1.41
N2025	25.8.40-6.9.40, SOC 12.9.40
N2103(C)	4.9.40-1.1.41
N2189(C)	19.9.40-25.9.40
L2248(C)	17.7.40-2.9.40
P2177(SA)	15.6.40-27.10.40
P2302(C)	25.8.40-26.9.40
P2310	25.8.40-SOC 4.9.40
P2321(SA)	22.5.40-22.12.40
P2325(C)	15.6.40-1.9.40
P2327	3.10.40-EFA 22.10.40 (crashed Binbrook)
P2329(C)	29.8.40-1.1.41
P6568	26.7.40-28.8.40
P6572	26.7.40-14.8.40
P6600	21.5.40-22.9.40
P6602(A)	30.9.40-2.12.40
P6603	25.8.40-16.9.40

No. 150 Sqn, Stradishall; to Newton 3.7.40

K7647(A)	3.10.40-7.10.40
K9323(A)	21.5.40-24.8.40
K9444(A)	3.10.40-7.10.40
L5042(C)	26.6.40-3.10.40
L5067(SA*)	?-11.10.40
L5058(SA)	?-11.10.40
L5103(SA)	29.7.40-11.10.40
L5106(C)	?-?
L5237	?-30.9.40
L5421(C)	12.8.40-5.11.40
L5434(A)	19.7.40-14.10.40
L5447	11.7.40-11.10.40
L5510(C)	21.5.40-11.10.40
L5524	16.4.40-FTR 13.7.40
B/L5528	11.7.40-27.7.40 (burnt out in ground incident)
L5543(SA)	19.5.40-19.7.40
A/L5545(SA)	28.4.40-10.10.40
L5548(SA)	19.7.40-11.10.40
L5563(SA*)	16.5.40-19.7.40
L5579(C)	21.5.40-13.10.40
L5592(C)	15.6.40-17.10.40
L5593(C)	15.6.40-17.10.40
L5630(A)	16.7.40-24.8.40
N2169(SA)	26.7.40-11.10.40
P2312(C)	25.6.40-14.10.40
P2327(C)	?-3.10.40
P5236(C)	26.4.40-29.8.40
P6568(C)	26.7.40-28.8.40
P6602(A)	21.5.40-30.9.40

No. 226 Sqn, Sydenham

K9210(C)	17.7.40-2.8.40
K9211(C)	17.7.40-13.8.40
K9351(C)	23.5.40-26.7.40
L5035	23.5.40-14.8.41
L5037	25.6.40-?
L5326	9.6.40-19.8.41
L5337(C)	9.6.40-6.8.41
L5401(C)	9.6.40-6.8.41
L5419	20.5.40-10.7.41
L5428	3.8.40-31.8.40

L5452	1.6.40-EAO 4.5.41 (destroyed by bombing of Sydenham)
L5460(SA*)	20.5.40-31.7.41
L5468	17.7.40-28.1.42
L5498	23.5.40-14.8.41
L5564	?-10.4.41
L5576(SA*)	
L5595(A)	?-14.8.41
P5233(C)	26.5.40-6.8.41
P5234(A)	17.5.40-6.8.41
P6601	17.5.40-EFB 22.10.40 (crashed nr Cushendall, Co. Antrim)

No. 300 Sqn, formed Bramcote 1.7.40, to Swinderby 22.8.40

L5317(C)	26.8.40-10.11.40
L5318(C)	26.8.40-13.11.40
L5353(C)	29.6.40-10.11.40
R/L5356	29.6.40-EFA 29.10.40 (crashed at Sutton-on-Trent, Notts)
L5425(A)	28.6.40-30.11.40
W/L5426(C)	28.6.40-10.11.40
K/L5427(C)	?-22.10.40
L5429	28.6.40-12.9.40
F/L5490(C)	29.6.40-10.11.40
M/L5492(C)	1.9.40-13.11.40
Y/L5499	29.6.40-EFB 13.10.40 (stalled at low altitude back from Boulogne, crashed Oxton, Notts)
L5529(A)	3.7.40-?
A/L5530(C)	3.7.40-10.11.40
L5532	29.6.40-10.9.40
L5537	29.6.40-7.11.40
S/L5567(C)	30.8.40-13.11.40
N2127(C)	29.6.40-10.11.40
Q/N2147	29.6.40-10.11.40
N2241(C)	29.6.40-16.11.40
P2309(C)	29.6.40-10.11.40
R7402	31.7.40-16.12.40

No. 301 Sqn, formed Bramcote 26.7.40, to Swinderby 8.40

L9247	26.9.40-4.10.40
F/L5048(C)	29.8.40-12.10.40
L5074	24.7.40-28.8.40
L5237	4.10.40-23.11.40
L/L5316(C)	4.8.40-11.11.40
N/L5351	3.8.40-EFB 25.9.40 (crashed nr Brandon, Suffolk)
M/L5392(C)	3.8.40-?
R/L5445(C)	3.8.40-20.11.40
K/L5448	3.8.40-16.11.40
P/L5449	3.8.40-16.11.40
S/Q/L5535(C)	3.8.40-20.11.40
S/L5536(C)	3.8.40-15.11.40
J,P/L5549(SA)	24.7.40-20.11.40
B/L5551(A)	24.7.40-20.11.40
H/L5555(C)	23.7.40-11.11.40
G/L5556(C)	23.7.40-20.11.40
L5557(C)	30.8.40-11.11.40
A/L5575(C)	7.8.40-20.11.40
L5597	23.7.40-EFA 8.8.40 (crashed near Bramcote)
F/N2189(C)	25.9.40-11.11.40
E/P6567(C)	24.7.40-20.11.40

D/P6569(C)	24.7.40–11.11.40
R7401	31.7.40–20.11.40

No. 304 Sqn, formed Bramcote
22.8.40; non-operational

K9332	26.8.40–23.12.40
L5043(C)	26.8.40–15.11.40
L5044(C)	26.8.40–10.11.40
L5062	8.40–5.11.40
L5070(A)	26.8.40–10.11.40
L5173(A)	2.9.40–10.11.40
L5368	26.8.40–1.11.40
L5429(C)	12.9.40–10.11.40
L5435(A)	26.8.40–10.11.40
L5441	26.8.40–5.11.40
L5488(A)	26.8.40–10.11.40
L5518(C)	26.8.40–10.11.40
L5522	26.8.40–10.11.40
N2106(C)	26.8.40–5.11.40
N2233(A)	26.8.40–10.11.40
P2300(A)	26.8.40–10.11.40

No. 305 Sqn, formed Bramcote
29.8.40; non-operational

K7632	?–14.11.40
L9147?	?–14.11.40
K9399	14.9.40–14.11.40
K9417(A)	14.9.40–14.11.40
L4693(C)	15.9.40–14.11.40
L5009(C)	14.9.40–14.11.40
L5041(C)	15.9.40–14.11.40
L5050(A)	15.9.40–14.11.40
L5052	15.9.40–1.11.40
L5056(SA*)	15.9.40–14.11.40
L5059(SA)	15.9.40–14.11.40
L5064(C)	15.9.40–14.11.40
L5160(SA)	15.9.40–14.11.40
L5197(C)	2.9.40–14.11.40
L5315(C)	14.9.40–14.11.40
L5352(C)	3.9.40–14.11.40
L5476(C)	15.9.40–14.11.40
L5563(SA*)	14.9.40–14.11.40

Between 1.7.40 and 15.10.40 277 Battles saw squadron service and 9 FTR from operations. 124 subsequently served in Canada, 37 in Australia and 21 were despatched to South Africa.

The Handley Page HP 52 Hampden

It is certainly surprising that an Operational Requirement of July 1931 for a multi-engined Boulton & Paul Sidestrand medium bomber replacement could have resulted in two aeroplanes as different as the Hampden and Wellington. Turreted, ideal for lengthy development, suitable for long coastal patrols and limited transport duties, the Wellington served long and well, whereas the Hampden incorporated unusual ideas which ultimately limited its development potential. That is not to say it performed ineffectively, for it undertook a major part in the bomber offensive until 1942. The Hampden's very existence was a near-run thing, for Bristol also prepared an equally well thought of design. Handley Page, though, had long been in the big bomber business. Indeed, several of its biplane Heyford bombers served as

bombing and gunnery trainers in 1940.

A draft specification outlining the new medium day bomber was written in June 1932, approved on 17 September 1932 and issued to attract tenders. Handley Page's entry in the B.9/32 competition tendered in February 1933 was forecast to have a top speed of 211 mph at 12,700 ft, a range of 1,200 miles and a tare weight of 6,425 lb. On 29 May 1933 the Handley Page scheme was chosen from seven tendered designs as a back-up to the favoured Vickers design, with £15,000 and eighteen months sanctioned for its development.

B.9/32 outlined a twin-engined landplane bomber whose tare weight was limited to 6,300 lb. Little known is a stipulation that the wing — not to exceed 70 ft in span — was to be able to fold naval style for hangar storage.

Structural features contributing to the aircraft's strength in flight were to be of metal, but could be fabric covered. A single gun for the wireless operator was to have an unrestricted field of fire aft of the mainplane over the rear hemisphere. A Lewis gun in the front gunner's station was to be backed by two gunners' positions to the rear of the mainplane, and each would be fitted with a Lewis gun. Bomb load would total 1,500 lb.

Handley Page's interpretation was an unorthodox layout whose deep forward fuselage, a mere 3 ft wide, preceded a slender boom carrying twin fins and rudders prohibiting fitting a tail turret. All devised to reduce skin surface area, and thus drag, similar ideas led to the German Dornier 17 and Messerschmitt Bf 110. Thought advantageous initially, the compact layout and cramped crew area limited technical development. Construction features were unorthodox too, in particular a D-type spar attributed to Messerschmitt influence upon the firm's designer, Dr Lachmann. As for its 65 ft span broad chord and highly tapered mainplanes devoid of any dihedral, they were designed for the specified folding while being similar to those of the G.4/31 HP 47 reconnaissance aircraft. Folding

geodetic construction wings for the Vickers design were reckoned too complicated to proceed with, and abandoned in August 1933 allowing both projects to go ahead with fixed wings.

A prototype of the HP 52 was ordered on 24 February 1934, four months after the decision to proceed had been taken. Two Bristol Mercury VI engines were chosen as power plants. Both firms having great difficulty in keeping tare weights within the stipulated limit, permission to raise them but by a mere 200 lb was given on 1 March 1934. On 7 June 1934 the Geneva Convention weight restriction on British bombers was abolished, unfortunately after Handley Page had agreed to deliver their aircraft, already subject to varying delays, in August 1935. Accordingly, Handley Page had now to redesign their bomber and increased its wing span. Planned tare weight dramatically rose to 14,000 lb, embracing increased structure weight and higher stressing levels. Additional power was of course demanded and in August 1934 the design was modified to take two Bristol Perseus engines. Development of those being very slow, a switch to Pegasus power plants was made. Early production aircraft

The prototype Hampden K4240 *bore limited resemblance to the production version.* (HP)

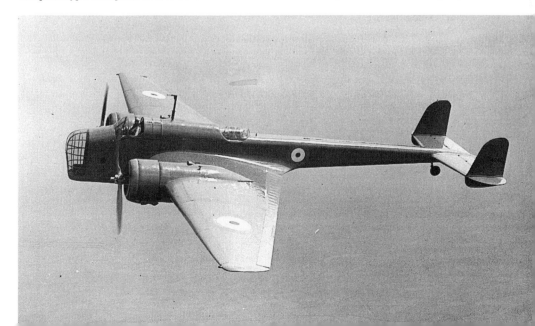

Variously nicknamed 'the pan handle' and 'flying suitcase', the prototype seen here at a Hendon display looked a strange machine.

would have Pegasus XX, later ones the more powerful Mk XVIIIs. Handley Page then stated that although the aircraft's top speed would increase to 238 mph it would inevitably take longer to develop.

A further basic alteration to requirements was introduced on 30 April 1935. The aircraft must now be suitable for day and night bombing. Handley Page requested an extension and were given until December 1935 for prototype delivery to Martlesham. The Air Ministry realized that was optimistic and it was 21 June 1936 when the prototype first flew, from Radlett. After brief testing at Martlesham a production order under Scheme F, for 180 of the aircraft (now named Hampden), was placed on 15 August 1936.

Only a few more flights followed before the end of the year because serious damage was caused when on 29 August 1936 the prototype's starboard undercarriage collapsed on landing causing the aircraft to overturn and fracture a mainplane. Sufficient flying had been undertaken for the issue of a more accurate claim of its capability showing this comparison with the RAF's requirement:

B.9/32	
Top speed	190 mph at 22,000 ft
Bomb load/range	1,500 lb/720 miles
All-up weight	11,300 lb

HP 52	
Top speed	254 mph at 13,800 ft
Bomb load/range	4,000 lb/1,200 miles
All-up weight	22,500 lb

Numerous modifications were incorporated during repair of the prototype including full night flying gear and provision for two guns in both the dorsal and ventral cupolas.

Production drawings were begun on 2 September 1936 to the standard described in specification 30/36, work on production aircraft commencing on 31 December 1936. A completely new nose and addition of dihedral to the mainplanes delayed delivery — agreed to start in August 1937 — until September 1938. Prior to that *L4033* underwent trials at Martlesham in July 1938. By the end of September 1938 seven Hampdens were in RAF hands and 500 were on order. Ten days after the prototype's second arrival at Martlesham on 11 November 1936 for more tests a contract was signed for Short & Harland of Belfast to build 100 Hampdens.

Production Hampdens revealed an all-up weight some 2,300 lb above the prototype's, resulting from increased load and range. Most noticeable was the entirely new glazed nose replacing the original Hubbard type with its simple turret. Plans long existed for a novel turret with gun movement in both horizontal and vertical planes, but they never came to fruition.

Above and below *Production Hampden* L4032. *Although it had no power-operated gun turrets it could carry a 2,000 lb bomb, a mine, yet was too small for much development.* (HP)

Production aircraft featured a redesigned fuel system for increased tankage allowing a range of 1,500 miles, and bomb gear installation permitting loads of up to 6 × 250 lb, 4 × 500 lb or 2 × 2,000 lb HE bombs. A gun mounting replaced the ventral revolving turret. Modified engines increased speed at higher levels, a revised undercarriage was installed and the internal layout much improved.

Tested at Martlesham between March and June 1938, the prototype K4280 had received critical appraisal. Elevator control needed to be more effective during take-off and rudder control improved, for low speed flight and longitudinal stability were none too good. These features were answered by modifications incorporated in Hampden 1/P2 production aircraft, the first of which, *L4032*, reached the A&AEE for brief testing during July 1938. The behaviour of *K4280*'s carburettors when the slots were open had been described as more annoying than dangerous, and its navigation facilities were rated 'poor' with physical communications between the crew difficult. Both were improved in later examples.

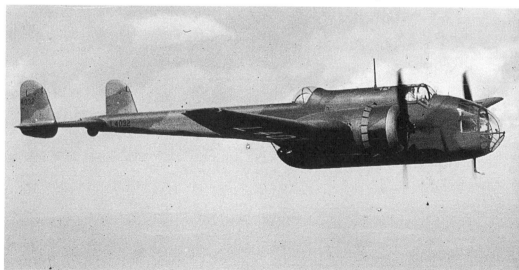

Hampden production posed major problems, for Handley Page was also committed to building its P.13/36 bomber (which became the Halifax), reckoned far more important than the Hampden. Forecast was that by December 1939 320 Hampdens could be delivered from Cricklewood and the Armstrong Siddeley works if the latter was assisted by Ranton & Smith, and a further 100 or so if the British Aircraft and General Aircraft works at Hanworth built Hampdens. Neither plans were implemented, nor another for production in Belgium.

Production planning called for the first Hampden to be delivered by 19 August 1938, 25 by 29 November and 180 by 26 June 1939. Eventually, between September 1938 and the end of that year 38 Hampdens had joined the RAF, and 200 more were ordered on 2 September and a further 120 on 7 November 1938. Delivery rates were then set at 100 by 22 March 1939 and 180 by the following June. A new production source was chosen, English Electric of Preston, with whom a stopgap order was placed for 150 Hampden 1/P3 on 5 April 1939. Further Hampdens designated Mk 1/P4 would be built in Canada from where airframes only would be shipped to Britain.

A Hampden on approach to Cottesmore.

Supply of sufficient engines for all the new aircraft types raised much concern and Handley Page considered alternatives to Bristol and Rolls-Royce designs. Napier, who had provided the famous Lion, were interesting themselves in liquid-cooled sleeve valve designs and had their E.108 Dagger in hand. At the time, January 1937, standards for Short-built Hampdens were under review and by mid-March an idea of fitting them with Dagger engines found favour. Such a combination had first been proposed on 10 June 1936, for a variant designed Hereford 1/D.P.1. With only one HP 52 prototype available the new version was for the distant future. Just how well the engine would fit was problematical too, and Handley Page considered that having two engine types must delay production generally. New jigs and tools would certainly need to be made at Belfast. Napier stated that the Dagger would be ready in summer 1938, but by late 1937 only three hand-made engines were in existence — insufficient even for type trials. Using one of the HP 53 Hampdens to be supplied to Sweden as a Dagger test bed was suggested, although that version was not compatible with the British Hampden.

Short & Harland reckoned they could commence Hereford design

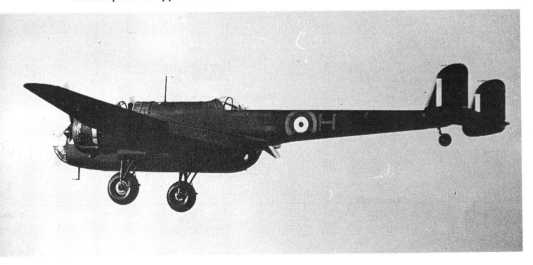

work in September 1937 and Pegasus Hampden production in summer 1938 before switching to the Hereford at the end of that year. That was impossible due to the shortage of Dagger engines. In any case considerable redesign was needed to produce revised mainplanes, suitable nacelles for Daggers and modified undercarriage, although there had to be as much interchangeability with the Hampden as possible. Short & Harland already had an order for 80 Bristol Bombay transports because Bristol had no capacity to build them, in addition to 100 examples of the Short B.12/36 Stirling bomber. Nevertheless it was decided to proceed with the E.108 Hereford, an order for 222 being agreed with an order to proceed with the first 50 being issued in June 1938 and planning being for 120 to be in service by March 1940.

By the end of 1938 36 Hampdens were in RAF hands, and by the outbreak of war 173 were in service equipping ten squadrons. The first, No. 49 Squadron, began to receive Hampdens in September 1938.

In its general wartime form the Hampden (wing span 69 ft 4 in, length 53 ft 4 in) had a fuel capacity inboard, outboard and forward fuel tanks of 656 gal. A fixed Vickers K nose gun with forward and downward field of fire, and one or two Vickers K guns in dorsal and ventral positions amidships were fitted. Additional to previously mentioned loads it could carry a 500 lb bomb under each mainplane and a mine internally.

Operations

Hampden operations commenced on 3 September 1939, when like other bombers they participated in early operations directed against naval ships. In April 1940 they were the first British bombers to lay mines, sown in shipping lanes off Norway. They carried out their first bombing operations against the Continental mainland on 11/12 May and throughout the Battle of Britain period were very active as the following survey illustrates. It was following a night attack on Ostend on 15 September that Sgt John Hannah was awarded the Victoria Cross after he extinguished a fire aboard *P1355*, 'W' of 83 Squadron. Flt Lt R. Learoyd (in *P4403* of 49 Squadron) received the VC for his part in the 12/13 August Dortmund-Ems Canal raid.

Unmistakable outline, Hampden PL-L *of 144 Squadron.*

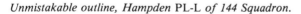

Date	No. sorties completed/despatched	Targets listed as attacked
July		
30.6/1.7	26/28 + 6	Osnabruck (4 aircraft — myds), Hamburg (10/12—A7 oil), Dortmund area (4/12) — alternative Salzburgen
1/2	16/30 + 6	*Scharnhorst* in Kiel dry dock — 8 bombed, Homberg, Osnabruck, 5/6 mining
2/3	7/14 + 6	Hamburg — oil — 7 bombed, and 4/6 mining 'Quince'
3/4	24 + 6	Soest, Munster, Grimberg, 6 mined 'Quince'
4/5	10/19 + 6	*Scharnhorst* in Kiel, Dortmund aqueducts, 5/6 mined 'Forget me not'
5/6	13/15 + 12	Kiel, Dortmund-Ems Canal, 12 mined 'Eglantine'
6/7	10/11	Mining 'Quince'
7/8	18 + 12	Bremen sy, Soest, Duisburg, Rohrorthafen, 11/12 mined 'Hollyhocks'
8/9	12	Mining 'Hollyhocks'
9/10	15/16 + 10/12	Wilhelmshaven — 11 attacked *Tirpitz*, NW Germany, Rotterdam, Waalhaven, 9/12 mined 'Yams'
11/12	9/17	Wanne Eickel (A80) 7, Dortmund Ems-Canal (M24) 3
13/14	17/29 + 12	Dortmund-Ems Canal (M24) 3, Hamburg (D2) 15, Hamburg (C4) 11, Munster, Enden, afds Deijkshausen (F8) 14, 12 mining
14/15	7/12 + 9	Wenzendorf (F49) and Kassel (F19) airframe factories, 5 mined 'Daffodils' and 4 'Krauts'
15/16	15/21 + 12	Paderborn (K2) 12, Hanover (A18) 9, 12 mined 'Daffodil'
17/18	3	Mining
18/19	32/37	Essen, Paderborn, Bielefeld, Krefeld, Duisburg
19/20	14 + 5	Paderborn 5/6, *von Scheer* in Wilhelmshaven (D197) 8, 4/5 mined 'Pumpkins' and 'Undergrowth'
20/21	20/23 + 12	*Tirpitz* in Wilhelmshaven (D197), Enschwege afd (H52), mining 'Daffodils'
21/22	8/20 + 8	Wismar acft fact, 8 mined 'Nasturtium'
22/23	18 + 4	Enschede, Gelsenkirchen, Hamm, 4 mined 'Nasturtium'
23/24	12/14	Wezendorf; Schiphol 6 — no attack, 1 bombed searchlights Ijmuiden
24/25	2/13 + 6	Wezendorf — all aborted. 6 of B/6 dropped leaflets Le Havre, Rouen, Lille, Dunkirk, Caen, Rennes, Brest
25/26	40	Wanne Eickel, Castrup Rauxel, Dortmund-Ens Canal
26/27	21	St Nazaire, Nantes; Hamm (3)
27/28	7 + 8	Hamburg (oil), 12 mined 'Crown' and 'Endive', 8 B/6 dropped leaflets Brest-Beauvais
28/29	18/23 + 12	Hamburg (oil), Bremen (oil), 12 mined 'Daffodil' and 'Quince'
29/30	15/22 + 12	Frankfurt, Dortmund-Ems Canal, 12 mined 'Daffodil' and 'Sweetpea'
31/1.8	12/17 + 12	Misburg (A17), Osnabruck (M431) 12 mined 'Forget me not' and 'Radish'
August		
2/3	2/14	Hanover, Emmerich, Gelsenkirchen
3/4	20 + 12	*Gneisenau* in Kiel, Dortmund-Ems, 12 mined 'Forgetmenot'
6/7	12	Night reconnaissance 'Tomato' and 'Undergrowth' areas
7/8	13/17 + 12	*Gneisenau* in Kiel, 12 mined 'Quince'
8/9	14/18	Homberg, Reisholtz, Schwerte all recalled
10/11	17	Homberg (oil)
11/12	14/18 + 12 + 15	Dortmund and forest area to E., 12 mined off Kiel, 5 of B/7 dropped leaflets on Caen, Rennes, Brest
12/13	9 + 12	Dortmund-Ems Canal 12 mining
13/14	24/27	Bernberg, Dessau, Hanover, airfields
14/15	23/28	Pauillac, Köln/Eifel tour, Hamm, Osnabruck and Soest myds, Dortmund-Ems Canal
15/16	8/21 + 6	Gelsenkirchen, Essen, Reisholtz; 6 dropped leaflets
17/18	20 + 5	Krupp/Essen, 5 mined Elbe Estuary
19/20	12/14 + 5	Ambs (oil) — one crashed Lyme Regis, 5 mined off Aalborg
21/22	25/38	Ship lifts Hohenwalthe 2/6, Magdeburg, Hanover, Osnabruck

Date	No.	Target
22/23	15/24 + 12	Frankfurt acft fact, Duisburg, Goldenburg, 12 mined Great Belt
23/24	40	All mining
24/25	25	All mining; 11 operated off St Nazaire and 12 off La Pallice, 30 detailed including 2 which collided on take-off
25/26	46	Berlin (Klingenburg PS, Tempelhof afd); 5 FTR
26/27	8/32	Mersburg/Leuna (oil), Leipzig/Mockau afd, Leipzig gw, Dortmund-Ems Canal
27/28	8/99 + 8	Ambes (Z158) — 6 bombed and 2 attacked Pauillac (Z161), 8 mined Lorient and off Brittany
28/29	27	Berlin (G161 Siemens & Halske works) — 15, Kiel sy, Dortmund-Ems (M25), one ditched
29/30	27	Gelsenkirchen (oil), Duisburg, Hanau, Krefeld
30/31	25	Magdeburg, Gelsenkirchen, Dortmund-Ems Canal, Krefeld
31/1.9	20	Berlin (F118 — BMW factory, Tempelhof), Magdeburg (A78), afds

September

Date	No.	Target
1/2	19	Stuttgart (Bosch factory) —P 11, Ludwigshafen (oil), Mannheim myd
2/3	21	Ludwigshafen (oil), Hamm (434) Dortmund-Ems (M25), Stuttgart (G165—Bosch factory), Lorient (U-boats) 12
3/4	18	Magdeburg, Nohra, Berlin/Charlottenburg and Tegel, Celle
4/5	25	Stettin/Politz
5/6	17	Stettin (oil), *Tirpitz* in Wilhelmshaven, Nordeney
6/7	19 + 4	Myds at Krefeld, Hamm, Mannheim, Ehrang, Dortmund; four patrol 'Yew Trees'
7/8	26	Shipping in Ostend
8/9	43/49	Hamburg (shipping), one missing over Germany
9/10	18 + 3	Hamburg, 3 mined Verdonne-Gironde area
10/11	14/21 + 3	Shipping in Calais, Ostend; 3 mine Verdonne-Gironde area
11/12	26 + 8	Bremerhaven and Hamburg shs, Harburg, Wilhelmshaven; 3 mined off Verdonne and 5 in Elbe Estuary
13/14	20	Shipping in Boulogne and Ostend
14/15	38	Myds at Mannheim, Osnabruck, shipping in Calais and Ostend
15/16	39 + 6	Myds Hamm, Osnabruck; ships in Antwerp, 6 mined Elbe Estuary
17/18	39 + 8	Shipping in Flushing, Terneuzen and Antwerp, 8 mined off Lorient
18/19	39 + 8	Shipping in Le Havre, 8 mined Elbe Estuary
19/20	37 + 8	Dortmund-Ems Canal, shipping in Flushing and Ostend; 8 mined Verdonne-Gironde area
20/21	25 + 8	Shipping in Antwerp, Boulogne, Dunkirk, Dortmund-Ems Canal; 4/8 mined off Norway
21/22	8	Ostend
22/23	29	Shipping in Le Havre, Boulogne, Ostend, Antwerp and Flushing
23/24	38 + 6	Berlin (Klingenberg ps, Charlottenburg, Moabit), 28 claimed to bomb Berlin. 6 of 14 & 16 OTUs dropped leaflets on Jersey and Guernsey
24/25	21	Shipping in Calais, Le Havre and Ostend
25/26	21	Berlin (B56 West ps, Klingenburg B57), myds at Ehrang and Osnabruck
26/27	21	Kiel docks (D4), Dortmund-Ems Canal, Calais
27/28	22	Shipping in Lorient, St Brieuc
28/29	20	Dortmund-Ems, Hamm, Mannheim (M482), Le Havre, Fecamp
29/30	18	Stuttgart (Bosch factory G165), Hamm, Gremberg, Soest, Köln Eifeltor
30/1.10	18 + 5	Berlin (H41)—5, Antwerp; 5 mined Elbe Estuary

October

Date	No.	Target
1/2	16 + 6	Köln, Goldenburg and Knapsack ps, afds; 6 mining Verdonne-Gironde area
2/3	16 + 6	Hamburg, Bremerhaven, Wilhemshaven, 6 mining Lengelens Belt
5/6	12 + 10	Hamm, Essen, Osnabruck, Soest and Gelsenkirchen; 10 mining Elbe Estuary
7/8	23	Osnabruck, Hamm, Gremberg, Lorient, Dieppe
8/9	17	*Tirpitz* and Wilhelmshaven naval base
9/10	13	Essen, afds, Ile de Groix(1)

NB: There are many variations in official records of Hampdens, the listing here being based upon Bomber Command surveys. Group and Squadron records very often conflict with this and each other. During mining operations aircraft sometimes also attacked ships and coastal targets. '14/16 + 6' = 14 of 16 proceeding claimed to bomb and 6 mined.

Hampdens used by squadrons 1 July– 15 October 1940

No. 44 Sqn, Waddington

L4070	9.1.39-FB02 19.9.40
L4085	30.1.39-EFB 1.8.40 (ditched, Cardigan Bay)
L4086	30.1.40-25.9.40
L4087	30.1.39-FTR 20.7.40 (mining)
L4154	22.4.39-11.9.40
L4178	15.4.40-27.8.40
P1322	15.4.40-1.5.41
P1324	16.2.40-15.9.40
P1338	19.3.40-FTR 11/12.9.40 (D12)
P1339	20.5.40-5.5.41
P2077	30.6.40-FTR 14/14.8.40 (F31)
P2087	21.7.40-FTR 5/6.9.40 (M101)
P2121	17.8.40-FTR 15/18.9.40 (Z11)
P2123	24.7.40-FTR 31.8/1.9.40 (ditched off Cromer, ending 8 hr 35 min flight)
P2136	15.8.40-4.9.40
P2137	16.8.40-FTR 20.10.40
P2142	13.8.40-?
P4285	31.8.40-24.12.40
P4290	15.3.40-FTR 5/6.9.40 (ditched off Lowestoft)
P4310	20.7.40-FTR 13.6.41
P4348	5.5.40-FB02 28.7.40
P4352	14.6.40-FTR 4.7.40
P4371	1.6.40-FTR 10/11.9.40 (Calais)
P4372	1.6.40-FTR 29/30.8.40 (A72)
P4373	1.6.40-12.9.40
P4374	1.6.40-EFA 2.9.40 (crashed Radlett)
P4375	16.7.40-FTR 28/29.7.40 (A10)
P4406	8.8.40-FTR 28.7.41
P4414	30.7.40-31.3.41
P4415	6.8.40-15.5.41
X2910	28.8.40-FTR 14.10.40
X2913	5.9.40-FTR 11/12.9.40 (D12)
X2916	8.9.40-3.10.40
X2917	2.9.40-EFB 6.8.41
X2918	13.8.40-FTR 10.3.41
X2959	7.9.40-16.11.40
X2965	13.9.40-FTR 1/2.10.40 (A72)
X2966	13.9.40-EFB 29.11.40
X2982	27.9.40-EFB 13.5.41
X2996	8.10.40-FTR 14.11.40
X2997	8.10.40-EFB 17.10.40 (crashed into hangar, Waddington)
X2999	11.10.40-FTR 18.4.41

No. 49 Sqn, Scampton

L4036	22.9.38-FTR 12.8.40
L4038	30.9.38-24.7.40
L4045	24.10.38-EFB 12.1.41
L4053	24.11.38-FTR 9.8.40
L4060	30.11.38-1.1.40
L4077	23.5.40-EFAO 20/21.7.40 (crashed Thornham, Norfolk; mining)
L4195	4.1.40-EFAO 17.10.40 (crashed Lenham, Kent)
P1323	29.5.40-19.8.40
P1333	11.5.40-FTR 16/17.8.40 (A77)
P1347	12.4.40-FTR 4/5.9.40(A104)
P2063	12.4.40-24.8.40
P2068	18.8.40-11.5.41
P2095	1.9.40-27.10.40
P2111	22.7.40-24.8.40
P2112	22.7.40-10.8.40
P2134	16.8.40-EFAO 29.9.40 (nr Wakefield, from CC24)
P2135	15.8.40-EFAO 31.8.40 (crashed taking off, Scampton)
P2143	13.8.40-EFAO 17.10.40 (Andreas, Isle of Man)
P2145	13.8.40-24.12.40
P2304	11.5.40-27.8.40
P4321	11.5.40-FAO2 28.11.40
P4322	11.5.40-19.12.40
P4350	18.6.40-FTR 6.9.40
P4351	23.6.40-FTR 3/4.8.40 (ditched off Skegness, D4)
P4377	22.7.40-FTR 7.8.40
P4384	28.6.40-31.7.40
P4403	7.8.40-24.8.40
P4404	7.8.40-23.8.40
P4409	9.8.40-12.12.40
P4416	6.8.40-FTR 26.8.40
X2900	16.8.40-EFA 16.10.40 (crashed Abingdon)
X2985	5.10.40-FTR 11.11.40
X3021	2.10.40-4.1.41

No. 50 Sqn, Waddington; to Lindholme 10.7.40

L4062	9.12.38-EFB 26.9.40 (crashed base; Calais)
L4075	13.1.39-14.1.41
L4076	12.1.39-4.2.41
L4078	20.1.39-FTR 3.7.40
L4079	20.1.39-31.7.40
L4097	10.2.39-FTR 10/11.9.40
L4149	15.4.40-FTR 10.11.40
L4150	10.9.40-22.11.40
L4164	25.10.39-26.4.41
P1317	16.2.40-FTR 27.8.40 (Mockau ?)
P1321	15.4.40-FTR 25/26.7.40 (A66)
P1327	10.7.40-31.12.42
P1330	5.5.40-12.12.40
P1356	8.5.40-27.8.40
P2070	16.7.40-FTR 25/26.8.40 (Berlin)
P2093	1.9.40-27.3.41
P2124	28.7.40-FTR 25/26.8.40 (ditched off Scarborough; Berlin)
P4287	8.5.40-FTR 9.9.40
P4288	8.5.40-EFAO 9.7.40 (crashed nr Waddington)
P4382	28.6.40-FTR 10.8.40
P4383	28.6.40-FTR 1.8.40
P4389	24.6.40-EFA 18.6.41

P4395	11.7.40-23.10.40
P4408	12.8.40-15.8.41
P4411	5.8.40-EFAO 1.10.40 (crashed nr Docking)
P4417	5.8.40-FTR 5/6.10.40 (M464)
X2896	27.8.40-EFB 3.10.40 (crashed SW of Dunbar; A8)
X2902	28.8.40-FTR 29.9.40 (Stuttgart)
X2907	21.8.40-FTR 6.11.40
X2908	27.8.40-EFAO 16.11.40
X2919	13.9.40-EFB 3.9.41
X2983	3.10.40-FTR 15.2.41
X2984	29.9.40-EFB 2.3.41 (crashed Wold Newton, Yorks)
X2991	5.10.40-4.9.41
X2992	5.10.40-21.4.41
X2993	5.10.40-FTR 14/15.10.40 (Berlin)
X2994	7.10.40-EFAO 8.11.40
X3000	11.10.40-EFAO 30.10.40
X3003	14.10.40-30.11.40

No. 61 Sqn, Hemswell

L4105	20.2.39-4.10.40
L4108	21.2.39-22.7.41
L4109	24.2.39-17.4.41
P2082	22.8.40-FTR 6.11.40
P2088	22.7.40-7.10.40
P2089	22.7.40-FTR 19/20.8.40 (Ambes)
P2090	22.7.40-FTR 27.9.40
P2144	16.8.40-EFB 3.6.41
P4298	17.5.40-7.7.40
P4324	31.7.40-FTR 26/27.8.40(A77)
P4335	5.5.40-FTR 13.8.40 (Salzbergen, Razzle)
P4337	5.5.40-26.7.40
P4338	5.5.40-FTR 13/14.9.40 (Boulogne)
P4339	5.5.40-EFAO 13.6.40
P4340	5.5.40-FTR 13/14.8.40 (Hamburg)
P4341	5.5.40-FTR 6.7.40 ?
P4342	5.5.40-28.3.41
P4343	5.5.40-FTR 20/21.7.40 (*Tirpitz*)
P4344	5.5.40-FTR 20/21.7.40 (*Tirpitz*)
P4357	5.6.40-EFAO 5.8.40 (ditched)
P4358	5.6.40-FTR 20/21.7.40 (*Tirpitz*)
P4379	29.6.40-FTR 13.8.40 (Salzbergen)
P4390	24.6.40-FTR 1.7.40
P4396	29.6.40-2.7.40
P4397	2.7.40-7.10.40
P4398	1.7.40-22.10.41
P4399	3.7.40-24.6.41
P4400	1.7.40-20.8.40
P4401	10.7.40-20.8.40
P4405	7.8.40-FTR 10.2.41
P4418	8.8.40-30.10.40
X2893	14.8.40-22.9.40
X2894	14.8.40-EFB 6.9.40 (crashed, Stradsett)
X2906	21.8.40-17.6.41
X2911	28.8.40-EFAO 24.9.40 (collision, Hemswell)
X2912	31.9.40-18.4.41
X2920	15.9.40-EFB (crashed nr Leeming; with mines)
X2922	7.9.40-FTR 13.9.40 ??
X2967	15.9.40-FTR 15.11.40
X2971	26.9.40-FTR 26.10.40
X2975	23.9.40-FTR 8.12.40
X2979	27.9.40-EFB 17.10.40 (crashed Swaffham)

X2980	28.9.40-30.10.40
X2981	26.9.40-EFAO 20.12.40
X2989	10.10.40-25.10.40

No. 83 Sqn, Scampton

L4049	7.40-FTR 23/24.9.40 (mining, 'Jellyfish')
L4051	5.1.40-31.8.40
L4057	30.11.38-FTR 15.11.40
L4066	2.10.39-EFAO 7/8.7.40 (crashed nr Clacton; Frankfurt)
L4070	9.1.39-FBO2 19.9.40 (often flown by Guy Gibson; CC24)
L4093	16.1.40-EFB 4.11.40 (ditched off Spurn Head)
L4094	9.2.39-FTR 26.7.40 (Dortmund-Ems, hit by AA fire)
L4095	0.2.39-FTR 9.10.40 (D2)
L4104	29.5.40-EFAO 19.10.40 (crashed W. of Malton)
L4106	11.6.40-31.10.40
P1171	15.6.40-FTR 2.7.40
P1176	16.1.40-23.3.41
P1183	30.8.40-SOC 1.10.40
P1334	11.5.40-EFB 30.8.40 (undershot Scampton)
P1355	21.4.40-16.8.40 (aircraft in which Sgt Hannah won the VC)
P2096	3.9.40-27.9.40
P2097	3.9.40-EFB 28.12.40 (crashed Abingdon)
P2125	10.9.40-EFB 27.11.40 (crashed taking off, Scampton)
P2126	10.9.40-8.7.41
P2138	14.8.40-21.9.40
P4376	11.7.40-EFAO 2.8.40 (taking off, Scampton; mining)
P4380	22.6.40-FTR 25/26.8.40 (B57)
P4381	22.6.40-EFAO 3.11.40 (crashed nr Fiskerton)
P4392	3.7.40-EFB 26.9.40 (crashed nr Lincoln; CC26)
P4402	10.7.40-16.8.40
P4410	10.8.40-FTR 12/13.8.40 (Munster lock gates)
P4412	27.7.40-13.11.40
X2897	21.8.40-EFB 28/29.8.40 (ditched off Skegness; D4)
X2898	16.8.40-1.1.41
X2899	2.8.40-FTR 7.4.41
X2901	20.8.40-EFB 15/16.10.40 (crashed, Southwold beach)
X2904	27.8.40-11.9.40
X2905	27.8.40-22.11.40
X2964	13.9.40-EFAO 10.11.40 (Scampton)
X2969	17.9.40-8.8.41
X2972	25.9.40-16.6.41
X2974	25.9.40-11.11.40
X2977	23.9.40-EFB 5.10.40 (crashed, nr Hemswell, A70)
X2978	21.9.40-EFAO 3.11.40 (Laneham, Notts)
X2990	8.10.40-FTR 27.10.40

Hampdens of 49 Squadron at Scampton. P1333:EA-F flew 11 sorties between 1 July and 16 August 1940. (IWM)

No. 106 Sqn, Finningley. Served as 5 Group training sqn until 9/10.9.40, then began operations (mining). Aircraft then and subsequently in use:

L4100	5.6.40–26.11.40
L4103	13.6.40–EFAO 7.12.40 (nr Finningley)
L4120	17.6.40–EFAO 16.12.40 (taking off, Finningley)
L4150	17.10.39–10.9.40
L4180	22.5.39–FTR 30.10.40
L4182	23.5.39–18.9.40
L4183	23.5.39–17.12.40
L4184	24.5.39–EFA 13.10.40 (taking off, Finningley)
L4189	31.5.39–EFAO 30.9.40 (crashed nr Buxton)
L4194	18.1.40–22.11.40
P1253	29.2.40–12.12.40
P1254	29.2.40–11.9.40
P1255	29.2.40–13.11.40
P1256	1.3.40–EFAO 27.9.40 (crashed nr Misson, Yorks)
P1258	1.3.40–4.2.41
P1259	1.3.40–FTR 18.9.40
P1304	1.3.40–EFAO 2.12.40
P1311	1.3.40–12.9.40
P1320	1.3.40–EFAO 25.11.40
P1337	23.4.40–4.2.41
P2083	3.9.40–4.2.41
P2098	9.10.40–FTR 28.12.40
P4413	28.7.40–18.8.41
X2914	5.9.40–EFAO 26.9.40 (Childen Polden, Somerset)
X2921	29.9.40–EFAO 7.9.41 (crashed, Waddington)
X2960	7.9.40–EFAO 18.9.40 (Cantley nr Finningley)
X2968	22.9.40–8.6.41

P1320, *a Hampden of 106 Squadron.*

L4125	15.3.39–1.10.40
L4131	22.3.39–1.4.41
L4141	7.11.39–7.5.41
L4173	13.5.39–25.10.40
P1172	26.7.39–FTR 6.9.40
P1328	4.40–13.11.40
P2063	24.8.40–31.12.41
P2079	19.8.40–EFB 9.11.40 (Hemswell)
P2080	19.8.40–18.6.41
P2081	30.8.40–7.10.40
P2094	4.9.40–3.1.41
P2117	22.7.40–2.9.40
P2122	30.7.40–29.10.40
P4291	14.7.40–FTR 16.8.40
P4347	6.5.40–27.10.40
P4359	4.6.40–15.2.41
P4360	4.6.40–FTR 22.8.40
P4361	4.6.40–FTR 4.7.40
P4362	4.6.40–FTR 5.10.40
P4364	5.6.40–9.7.40
P4365	28.5.40–FTR 17.8.40
P4366	28.5.40–FTR 11.7.40
P4367	28.5.40–FTR 21.7.40
P4368	2.6.40–FTR 10.8.40
P4369	2.6.40–9.8.40
P4370	2.6.40–FTR 2.9.40
P4378	16.7.40–EFB 5/6.9.40 (overshot West Raynham)
P4391	26.6.40–7.8.40
P4393	5.7.40–EFA 9.8.40 (Waddington; FH 360.20)
P4394	6.7.40–EFB 1.3.41 (Wainfleet)
P4407	12.8.40–EFB 30.11.40 (nr Wittering)
X2909	27.8.40–EFA 27.8.40 (nr Upwell)
X2915	5.9.40–EFB 1.11.40
X2963	7.9.40–EFB 5.10.40 (Hemswell)
X2973	24.9.40–FTR 16/17.10.40
X2976	23.9.40–25.10.40
X2988	10.10.40–EFB 17.10.40 (nr West Raynham)
X2998	10.10.40–EFB 26.10.40 (Upton, Lincs)

The Vickers-Armstrong Wellington

The most amazing thing about the Wellington is that it ever existed, the most astonishing that officialdom intended it to have folding wings allowing a squadron to fit into existing hangars. When on 31 October 1931 the Air Staff passed to the DTD the operational requirements which led to the Wellington they were told that the department was 'extremely busy', that they must expect considerable delay. At the time the nation was in dire financial trouble, the RAF at its weakest. Money problems seem ever to confront Britain — but a prime bomber whose wings fold like a butterfly's for economic reasons...?

Proposed by the Air Staff was a replacement for the Sidestrand medium day bomber with a top speed of 190 mph, ability to carry a 1,500 lb bomb load for 720 miles (1,200 with auxiliary tanks fitted) and defended by single Lewis guns in three stations. Tacit agreement at the Geneva Convention Disarmament Conference limiting the tare weight of bombers to 6,000 lb was imposing severe design restrictions.

When Specification B.9/32 emerged in September 1932 11 firms were invited to tender, seven responding and all complaining about the ridiculous weight limitation, which was later raised — to 6,500 lb. Of the designs considered at the Tender Conference of 29 May 1933, those from Vickers and Handley Page were rated ahead of the others, so recommendation was for a prototype of each design. The former's progress is outlined here; the latter became the Hampden.

With a two-year (later 21-month) delivery forecast the Vickers design utilizing Dr Barnes Wallis's unusual geodetic construction was, in the Air Staff's opinion, likely to have a maximum range of 1,250 miles, top speed of 210 mph at 15,000 ft and would weigh 6,480 lb, which all placed it well within the OR needs. Wallis's light 'criss-cross' metal structure possessed a very high strength/weight ratio, the load supported by 1 lb of structure weight being higher, than that of any stressed skin design. The entire weight of the aircraft was placed upon the fabric-covered lattice frame. Fears that producing it would be lengthy and complex proved groundless. When the covering fabric caught fire, as happened quite often during operations, the survival rate was high although draughty.

It was on 15 July 1933 that the Air Staff abandoned the idea of alternative mainplanes for a night bomber version and, to save three months' design work, folding wings. Not until September 1933 did the Chief of Air Staff inform the firm whose design had been chosen, a contract being signed on 12 December 1933 for a twin-engined Rolls-Royce Goshawk-powered Vickers B.9/32 day bomber for delivery in September 1935.

Vickers had changed their original design, mainplanes being lowered to mid-position improving the crew's view and shielding the gun positions. Then, with clearly no likelihood of the Disarmament Conference reaching full agreement on proposed bomber weight restrictions, the CAS on 21 February advised Vickers not to allow the aircraft to be inhibited by the 3 metric tonnes limitation. Needed was the best possible performance, not the lowest weight, and a further yet slight weight increase was officially approved on 1 March 1934 before, on 7 June, the Air Ministry decided to abolish the weight restriction altogether, informing Vickers a week later. That permitted a larger, longer-range aircraft, with greater load-carrying capability.

Rex Pierson, Chief Designer for Vickers, visited the USA at this time. Recalling in April 1943 the event, he said that 'on returning from America I tore up everything I'd previously done and produced a new design'. Similar, but larger, it aroused fear that the stipulated 600 yd take-off run might be exceeded. The Air Staff had, however, already been persuaded that longer runs for larger aircraft were inevitable. For sure the new design needed extra power, Vickers proposing the Bristol Pegasus or Perseus. Higher performance inevitably meant more fuel, improved defence and higher speed, which led to turreted guns.

On 21 August 1934 the Air Ministry importantly agreed to using Pegasus XVIII engines. Fearing all these changes would bring delay, the company, in October 1934, stated that the September 1935 delivery was only possible if no more major changes were required. DTD then set December 1935 as the new target date, but when on 21 November 1934 the mock-up was viewed further changes were asked for and delivery was further postponed, the Air Ministry attributing some delay to the novel form of construction being employed.

On 30 April 1935 a decision was made that both the P.27/32 (which produced the Fairey Battle) and the B.9/32 must have full night flying facilities. Surprisingly the latter was not mentioned when in May the Air Staff presented the first major rearmament plan, Scheme C, to the Cabinet.

On 15 June 1936, six months late, the Vickers prototype *K4049* — with Mutt Summers at the controls and with Barnes Wallis and Westbrook aboard — first flew, from Brooklands. Powered by 2×915 hp Pegasus X engines, its all-up weight had risen from the expected 17,000 lb to 21,000 lb, which necessitated a stronger undercarriage. Able to carry a crew of five, its bomb load was nine 250 lb or 500 lb bombs, and it had single hand traversed nose and tail guns and a retractable mid-turret. Its top speed was 250 mph at 21,000 ft. Much impressed, the Air Ministry decided to include a production variant in rearmament Scheme F in which they were expressing a need for 3,000 medium bombers to meet the German challenge. On 15 August 1936 an order for 180 Vickers bombers was placed.

A possible production variant was officially discussed on 11 September 1936, the design conference estimating emergence of a first example in June 1937 and production deliveries starting in October 1937. Armament for the aircraft was specially considered on 1 October when Vickers enquired whether the defensive armament intended for their larger

B.1/35 could also be applied to the B.9/32. That implied a Vickers K nose gun, twin-gun retractable ventral turret and two tail guns. Designing turrets was already realized to be a specialized art, particularly their gun feed systems and ammunition layouts. For a start, however, Vickers would also produce the system.

The closing weeks of 1936 found production requirements being finalized. Pegasus XVIII engines would power the bomber, but Mk XXs would be fitted until those superior engines were available. A Vickers K gun in the nose station, twin guns in the tail and a retractable mid-ships power-operated turret would defend it. The bomb load would consist of nine 250 or 500 lb HE weapons, or 2 × 2,000 lb bombs for use against warships. Full details were listed in production Specification 29/36 dated 29 January 1937.

All seemed to be going well when, very unexpectedly, K4049 was totally destroyed on 19 April 1937 in a disastrous crash attributed to total collapse of its tailplane. Until another aircraft was built and tested the precise reason for the disaster was difficult to decide. Eventually it was traced to the horn balance of the elevator which, although shielded at small angles, was much exposed at full travel. When in that latter state heavy loading had broken away the horn, causing the aircraft to invert. From its cockpit the pilot was then hurled, the flight engineer also dying in the crash.

Modifications were certainly needed, although the intended production aircraft differed much from K4049. Featuring a longer nose and deeper aft fuselage, the tailplane with altered elevators was set 6 in higher, giving the aircraft quite different aerodynamic characteristics. A major official review of the new design on 29 July 1937 showed its loaded weight had risen from an estimated 21,000 to 23,000 lb with a possible 27,000 lb being discussed. Underestimation of component weights had occurred, including that of the bomb carrying structure, extra armour and ammunition, engine, etc.

On 23 December 1937 the first example of what was now the Wellington bomber, L4212, successfully flew and on 26 April 1938 proceeded to Martlesham for trials. On 4 May its undercarriage failed and there was much criticism over the failure to order more than one B.9/32 prototype and also of continued changes of plans resulting in such a long gestation period. While the undercarriage was being repaired Pegasus XVIII engines were installed, Martlesham trials resuming on 16 May.

Now another major problem manifested itself when L4212 was found to be seriously nose-heavy in the dive, a condition again produced by the elevator arrangement. Large balance horns still causing trouble were replaced by tabs, before a new horn was tested on the second machine, L4213. Eventually — with the help of the RAE — a solution was found, but by that time 27 sets of the troublesome elevators had been produced. Too late to prevent aircraft fitted with those from entering service, it was decided to introduce them but with weight and speed restrictions.

While a suitable tailplane was devised another aspect of the aircraft occupied much consideration. This was the provision of suitable defensive armament. Already several times reviewed, it was subjected to major design conferences, on 13 January 1937 and particularly on 13 June 1938. The intention remained to fit Vickers nose and tail turrets in the first 180 Wellingtons and in a further 100 for which Gloster Aircraft had become the favoured production source. Further Wellingtons, it was suggested, should be fitted with two-gun nose and tail Frazer-Nash power-operated turrets as planned for the Vickers B.1/35 (alias Warwick). With an FN ventral turret installed the aircraft's centre of gravity state looked critical and to determine the truth one was to be installed in the first production machine.

L4212, *the first production Wellington, taking off from Weybridge.*

Despite teething troubles there was increasing belief that the Wellington would turn out to be highly successful. On 3 November 1937 Specification 33/37 was agreed, to cover production by Gloster Aircraft as outlined on 14 September 1937. Then on 29 March 1938 the desire to produce 1,500 was discussed along with the suggestion to build them at four factories. Gloster already had the task of producing all the Henley light bombers, production of which was soon lagging so badly that Wellington production there had to be abandoned. Austin Motors was a suggested producer after its Battle order was completed, but that event was 20 months away. Armstrong Whitworth did not wish to build a suggested 64 in place of its own Whitleys and B.18/38(Albermarle) and was not pressed to do so. A firm order for another 120 was, however, placed with Vickers on 3 May 1938, at which time it was reckoned 26 Mk 1s would be delivered by the end of the year, close to the actual 29. As for the remainder, approval was given on 26 October for the sub-contracting of 750 Wellingtons including 200 to Gloster — if the firm could cope. Vickers secured another order, for 100, on 5 April 1939, but by then firm plans

had been laid for two huge new shadow factories, at Blackpool and Chester, exclusively to build large batches of Wellingtons, which task continued throughout the coming hostilities.

Delivery of the Mk 1 commenced in October 1938 — five years after the design had been tendered. No. 99 Squadron at Mildenhall was first to rearm with what, among the station's Heyfords, looked to be a very advanced, streamlined aeroplane.

Excessive demands were now being placed upon aero engine manufacturers as much as airframe makers which they could none too easily meet. Bristol had huge production orders and a very extensive range of engines to develop. Luckily the production Wellington had been engineered to cope with a potential Pegasus engine shortage, its power plant pick-up points being readily adaptable for radial or inline engines. Therefore, to supplement the Pegasus version a Merlin-engined Wellington II was decided upon which initially seemed a straightforward change. It was to prove tedious and time-consuming to develop.

Air Staff thinking was that, having more power and therefore being

Basically the Wellington's shape remained the same throughout its development. L4280 *was a Mk I.*

faster, the Mk II would be better for daylight raids. *L4250* was fitted not only with Merlin X engines but also with three FN turrets, making it more than just the Mk II prototype first flown on 3 March 1939. Belief that it would be a good day bomber brought about the decision of 23 March 1939 that all IIs should have priority call on FN turrets. Since it had increased power, the aircraft's weight was allowed to rise to 32,000 lb, permitting additional fuel for a 1,400 mile range.

Once again aerodynamic problems arose, necessitating a broader chord tailplane as standard for the Mk II. *L4250* persistently swung badly to port on take-off, a problem which took considerable time to curb. Realizing that development would take some time, May 1939 saw orders given to retard Mk II production, thereby releasing intended FN turrets for use in Mk Is. On 4 October 1939 Mk II production was postponed because the aircraft was not meeting expectations. Wellingtons would have Pegasus engines for the foreseeable future although on 1 November 1939 plans were confirmed for an initial 200 Mk IIs — 'when its improvement allowed'. They eventually proceeded as 'Special Order Mk II/P1', the first

(*W5353*) being delivered on 7 October 1940 on the basis that the Mk II was more suitable for tropical operation than Mk 1 whose Pegasus engines overseas ran at borderline temperatures. Further envisaged development was to include fitting the Merlin XX engine, producing the Mk IIa redesignated Mk VII.

Release of FN turrets from the Mk II was soon followed by confirmation of their application to the Mk 1, resulting in the Mk 1a which, stressed for 28,000 lb loading, needed a stronger undercarriage. Delivery began on 1 September 1939, by which time the Mk 1a was the principal variant with 690 on order. A proviso remained, that 1as could be completed with Merlin engines if necessary, but instead of the 500 Mk IIs envisaged from the new shadow factory at Chester the latest Mk 1s would emerge. On 6 December 1939, after the trials with the FN ventral turret, orders were given to fit them to 77 Mk 1as.

On 18 October 1939 development based upon RAE Report No. 1490 was authorized for the pressure cabin Wellington Mk V. Initial belief was that carrying a crew of three and 4 × 500 lb bombs it could fly at 310 mph

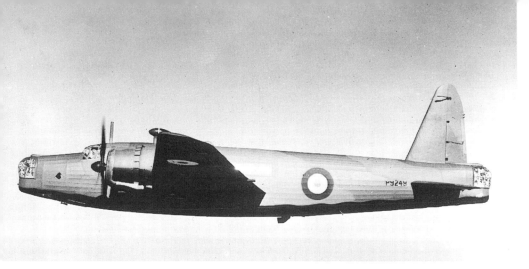

Wellington Mk 1a P9249. Improved turrets and a ventral turret were featured. (Vickers)

at 30,000 ft. Blackpool production of 30 examples approved on 22 January 1940 was sufficient for one squadron. Very little was known about high altitude flying, even less about pressure cabins. Belief was soon that with special Hercules VIII engines a top speed of 324 mph at 31,000 ft was possible, and cruise at 288 mph at 35,000 ft. Test flying proved high altitude operations very difficult to develop — and not until quite late was the question of a pressurized tail turret raised. Although the prototype *R3298* first flew from Brooklands in July 1940, test flying did not get fully underway until October by which time the aircraft was Blackpool based.

Also for the future were other versions, the most important being the Hercules powered Mk III, first flown on 19 May 1939 but which did not enter production until May 1941. Another variant was the Mk IV proposed in April 1939 and for which American Pratt & Whitney Twin Wasp engines would provide the power. Shortage of Pegasus engines in August 1940, which caused the autumn introduction of the Mk II before it was really ready for service, also resulted in an order to proceed with Mk IVs although none entered service before 1941.

The early months of the war saw Wellingtons repeatedly, and fortunately fruitlessly, searching for German shipping bringing raiding parties to our shores across the North Sea, while plans for increased Wellington production were laid. On 1 September 1939 another 300 had been ordered and on 5 December it was decided to order enough to maintain production to the end of 1941. Chester would build 1,250, Castle Bromwich 750 and on 19 December 1939 the go-ahead was given for the Blackpool factory to perform. Such was the success now of the Wellington that on 12 December 1939 it was placed ahead of the new Halifax in production priorities.

When in December 1939 Wellingtons fared badly at the hands of German fighters, orders were given that, like their German counterparts, fuel tanks must be covered with self-sealing material. So important was the task that on 7 February instructions were given to fit them even if it had to be done in the open. New aircraft were by then leaving the factory with covers fitted, and older aircraft were exchanged for these.

Destined to be the most numerous Pegasus version was the Mk 1c, a variant very similar to the Mk 1a but featuring 24-volt electrics necessary for increased equipment, along with redesigned hydraulics. Delivery began in March 1940. An order of 15 May 1940 decreed that they be built as 'Mk 1C/P1 Special', readily convertible to Mk II.

On 15 May 1940 a review of

Wellington operations during the Norwegian campaign showed that the FN ventral turret which brought such critical centre of gravity problems was of little operational value. Deletion would save 800 lb and 15 mph, therefore it was removed and replaced by two beam guns poked through the ends of the long side windows, usually blacked out or painted over for night operations. Complaints increased that Wellington 1a and 1cs were for ever losing speed and that prompted urgent fitting of the beam guns in the summer of 1940, particularly as the hoped-for FN 4 four-gun tail turrets would not be available until 1941. As an interim measure two new further aft stations were improvised, and became standard, through each of which a hand-operated gun was poked. Removal of the under turret did not meet with universal applause. Bomber Command wanted its retention for day bombers, but by mid-June agreed that no more production Wellingtons would have ventral turrets — once Boscombe Down approved the beam mountings.

After being busily engaged by day and night during the Norwegian campaign Wellingtons participated from May in night raids on Germany, France and the Low Countries. Brief detachment to France in June allowed them to mount a few sorties against northern Italy despite attempts by the French to prevent that. Then they settled to a very active night bombing campaign with daily sections of 3 Group squadrons at standby to attack enemy invasion forces at sea. During September Wellingtons attacked invasion forces in dock before switching back to the strategic air offensive.

In that they paid a major role into 1943. The great strength of the airframe and its ease of production were the Wellington's outstanding features. Its ability to accept more and more load and increased engine power

Lasting memory of Wimpey days — a geodetic frame from which the fabric has been burned away. Illustrated is the skeleton of 99 Squadron's R3170 which came down in flames near Oude Weg in Haarlem on 6/7 July 1940. (G.J. Zwanenburg)

Mildenhall's Wellingtons of 149 Squadron were, in 1940, still protected by just an old pre-war iron fence! (Bristol)

Operations

was outstanding. Little wonder that, throughout the war and into the 1950s, the RAF greatly valued the 'Wimpey'.

Any listing of 1940's Wellington raids must take into account their aim — to hit specific targets while also causing the most widespread disruption possible. Some bombing locations are no longer on record, and the accuracy of attacks varied greatly. Some crews attacked targets of opportunity such as airfields showing lights, obvious factories, searchlights and AA batteries, railway lines, etc. Targets listed here are the main ones. Where the number of crews claiming to attack those are known they precede the total of Wellingtons despatched for the night's operations. Official records of these events vary considerably, this listing being mainly based upon 3 Group returns.

Date	No. sorties completed/ despatched	Targets listed as attacked
July		
1/2	24	Ruhrort and Duisburg (8), Köln/Eifeltor (4), Deischshausen Lemwarder (8)
2/3	15/24	Osnabruck (1), Soest (2), Schwerte (2), Köln (1). Alternatives bombed: Évère (2), Dortmund (2), Rotterdam docks (1), Neuss (1), Flushing afd, Zeebrugge docks
4/5	10/24	Bremen (3), Hamm (2), Schwerte (1), Köln (1), Osnabruck (1), Wenzendorf (2), Emden (1), Stade (1), Harburg afd (1), Wesel (1)
5/6	16/20	Hamm and Gremberg myds, Hamburg and Bremen, Emden, Schipol
6/7	7	Bremen, Emden, Nordeney afd
7/8	12/20	Wilhelmshaven docks, Osnabrück, Gremburg myd
8/9	28	Hamburg sys, Hamburg oil, Wilhelmshaven, Hamm myds, Essen, Düsseldorf, Schiphol
9/10	8/27	Monheim, Soest, Hamm; force recalled—bad weather
11/12	30	Monheim (9), Bremen (9), Hamm (1), Soest (4), Osnabrück (4)
	1	Night photo recce Stettin — nullified by searchlight glare. Photo flash in second 38 Sqn aircraft exploded during loading
13/14	24/30	Bremen (9), Bremen (9), Hamm (4), Soest (4), Osnabruck (3), Duisburg (3)
14/15	24/36	Gelsenkirchen (5/8), Hamburg (6/8), Bremen (4/8), Hamm (5/6), Soest (2/3), Köln (2/3). Secondaries bombed: Stade (1), Ruhrort (1), Buer (1), Vught (1), Huntlosen (1)
17/18	7	Gelsenkirchen
18/19	13/31	Diepholtz, Bremen, Rothenburg, Hamm, Hanover
19/20	40	Bremen (7/10), Wismar (5/11), Wenzendorf 12, Essen myd 4, Schiphol & Wallhaven 2, Nordeney 1. Two Bf 109s claimed shot

228

		down over North Sea by 149 Sqn
20/21	24/38	Gelsenkirchen, Bremen, Hamm, Soest and many alternatives. Bf 109 claimed destroyed near Wesel
21/22	34	Rothenburg, Bremen, Gelsenkirchen, Gottingen
22/23	5/7	Dusseldorf, Essen
23/24	12/30	Gotha, Gelsenkirchen and many alternatives
	1	Special recce to Brest/Guipavas
	3	6 Group leaflet droppers — Rennes and Brest
25/26	27/59	Gotha, Dortmund, Enschede, Hamm, Landau, Schwerte
27/28	19/24	Hamburg
28/29	22/27	Hamburg, Homburg, Kamen, Hamm
29/30	12/26	Homberg, Monheim, Köln
30/31	11/14	Monheim, Homberg, München Gladbach

August

1/2	21/28	Köln, Homberg, Gelsenkirchen, Hamm, Essen, Mannheim
2/3	15/22	Hamburg, Emden
3/4	25/28	Gelsenkirchen, Bottrop, Homberg, Hamm, Soest
5/6	23/33	Hamm, *Gneisenau* at Kiel (7), Hamburg, Wilhelmshaven, Schiphol
6/7	26	Homberg, Emmerich, Reisholtz, Schwerte and Hamm myds (90,000 leaflets dropped too)
7/8	20	*Bismarck* at Kiel, Hamm, Soest, Homberg. (Detailed analysis showed 7 bombed primary, 2 secondaries, 1 last resort, 1 a flak post. 6 brought bombs back, 3 abandoned. Attacks claimed on Homberg (5), Soest (1), Hamm (2), Emmerich (1))
8/9	14/28	Hamburg, Hamm, Soest, Osnabrück, Köln, Ludwigshafen/Oppaù
9/10	24	Köln, Hamm, Soest
10/11	15/20	Hamm, Hamburg, Soest
11/12	22/26	Castrup Rauxel, Wanne Eickel, Hamm, Soest, forest areas SE of the Ruhr
12/13	20	Diepholz, Gotha, afds
13/14	29/34	Leuna, Frankfurt, Köln, Roermund, Krefeld, Essen, Cochem, Gelsenkirchen
14/15	8/12	Blaye oil installations
15/16	37/43	Gelsenkirchen, Leuna, Hamm & Soest myds, Leeuwarden
16/17	27/37	Bernberg, Frankfurt, Essen
17/18	41	Zeitz, Enschwege acft depot, Hamm, Soest, Schwerte, Osnabruck, Göttingen, Diepholz, Schiphol, Évère
19/20	48	*Gneisenau* in Kiel floating dock, Dortmund-Ems aqueduct, Hamm, Osnabrück, Soest
22/23	8/16	Bottrop, Mannheim, Hamm, Soest, Koblenz
23/24	6/10	Mannheim myd, Magdeburg oil target
24/25	26	Frankfurt, Köln/Knapsack ps, Dortmund-Ems old viaduct, Hamm, Soest
25/26	11/21	Berlin Siemenstadt (Siemens & Halske factory — 1/12), Hamm (3), Schwerte (1), Köln (1), Berlin force attacked alternatives in and around city
26/27	19/49	Frankfurt, Hamm, Stockum-Lippe myd, Duisberg/Ruhrort, Schwerte, Köln, Évère, Antwerp/Duerne
27/28	18	Kiel sy, *Gneisenau* in Kiel (6), Kolsterbach transformer station (4), Wilhelmshaven (1), Narrenthal afd (1)
28/29	20	Berlin/Klingenburg PS, Leipzig/Mockau act fact — 14 attacked primaries, 3 secondaries, 2 last resort, 1 early return. Leipzig (1), Berlin (13 — 2 bombed Templehof), Mercedes factory nr Enhalter Bahnhof hit, Osnabrück (1)
29/30	32	St Nazaire and Bottrop oil targets, Mannheim and Hamm myds, Évère
30/31	29	Berlin (Siemens & Halske (9), Henschel works (4), Klingenburg PS (1)), Hamm (2), Soest (1). Alternatives bombed: Berlin gw (2), Berlin myds (1), Olbrek afd (1), Schellingwoude seaplane base (1)
31/1.9	24	Berlin (Henschel works F23 and gw A385), Hamm, Soest, Osnabrück, Schwerte

September

1/2	33	Leipzig/Mockau, Bitterfeld aluminium wks, Kassel PS, Soest, Hanover oil, Soesterberg and Antwerp/Duerne afds
2/3	30	G fire Area L of Black Forest near Thuringerwald
3/4	13	Same, also Area N in Harz Mts. Used 38 × 250 lb and 618 × 25 lb incendiary bombs
4/5	32	Area L near Thuringerwald, Chartres, Duerne afd

Date	No.	Target
5/6	28	Areas L and N again, barges at Delfzil, Kiel, Wik oil depot, Soest, Hamm
6/7	24	Berlin West PS, Black Forest Area L, Brussels myd
7/8	26	Black Forest south zone, Emden docks, Köln, Krefeld myd, Mannheim, Ehrang, Hamm
	3	6 Group leaflet dropping, Channel French coast
8/9	30	Shipping in Bremen and Ostend
9/10	18	Berlin/Charlottenburg gw, Brussels myd, Krefeld, Ehrang
10/11	26	Shipping in Flushing and Ostend; Brussels, Évère, Douai
11/12	40	Hamm, Ehrang, Mannheim, Köln, Koblenz, Ostend docks
12/13	19	Emden, Ehrang, Schwerte, Brussels
13/14	15/18	Barges at Antwerp
14/15	55	Hamm, Krefeld, Brussels, Ehrang, Soest, enemy HQ in Chateau Argento (6), shipping in Antwerp (18)
15/16	36	Shipping in Calais, Soest, Krefeld, Brussels myds
17/18	42	Shipping in Calais, Ostend, Ehrang, Mannheim, Krefeld, Osnabrück, Hamm, Brussels, Soest
18/19	40	Shipping in Flushing, Le Havre (26); Osnabrück, Ehrang, Brussels
20/21	45	Shipping in Calais (20), Flushing and Ostend (14/15)
21/22	30	Shipping in Dunkirk and Calais
22/23	32	Shipping in Boulogne (6), Calais (8), Le Havre (12) and Ostend (8)
23/24	53	Berlin (Danzigerstrasse A386, Neikoln gw, Wilmersdorf PS), barges in Le Havre
	3	6 Group, leaflets on Lille, Amiens, Rouen, Brest
24/25	35	Shipping in Boulogne, Calais, Le Havre
25/26	33	Calais (15), Boulogne (12), Hamm (2), Mannheim (2), Benheim afd (1), Schwerte
26/27	16	Shipping in Le Havre
27/28	30	Shipping in Le Havre and Ostend; Hamm, Mannheim, Ehrang, Köln, Gremberg (M465), Soest
28/29	30	Hanau nickel wks L230, Soest, Köln, Frankfurt (1), Le Havre (3), Calais (1), Antwerp (1), Ostheim afd (1), Eindhoven afd (1), Köln (2), Koblenz and Bessenheim afd (1)
29/30	22	Bittefeld (L86 aluminium wks), Mannheim, Ehrang, Osnabrück
30/1.10	35	Berlin H41, Merseburg, Leuna, Mannheim, Osnabruck myd

October

Date	No.	Target
1/2	27	Berlin/Elgemeine PS, Soest, Le Havre, Gelsenkirchen
2/3	23	Bottrop, Stinnes, Hamm, Soest
5/6	4	Shipping in Rotterdam
7/8	54	Berlin (30), Le Havre in Operation Lucid (23), Eindhoven (1)

Bombing-up and refuelling a Wellington Ic at Mildenhall. (Bruce Robertson collection)

8/9	34	Hamburg, Bremen, Mannheim, Gremberg		A/R3173	16.5.40–28/29.7.40 (hit gun post on landing)
9/10	42	Köln, Grevenbroich, Ehrang, Koblenz, Flushing		L/R3220	21.6.40–FTR 17.12.40
				M/R3230	11.9.40–14.10.40
10/11	47	Grevenbroich, Hanover,		R3283	3.7.40–4.8.40 (battle damaged)
11/12	24	Magdeburg		V/R3286	26.7.40–4.7.41
12/13	25	Bittefeld L86 and L89, Berlin Area T (Chancellory and Potsdam)		P/R3296	24.6.40–FBO2 1/2.9.40 (force landed nr Manningtree)
				M/T2458	29.6.40–9.9.40
13/14	47	Kiel, Gelsenkirchen, Eindhoven afd		A/T2462	30.7.40–EFB 8.11.40
				K/T2464	12.8.40–FTR 14/15.10.40
14/15	30	Bohlen-Rotha A76, Magdeburg, Le Havre		Y/T2468	6.8.40–12.2.41
				G/T2472	17.8.40–EFB 28/29.9.40 (burnt out)

M/T2473	17.8.40–FTR 9/10.4.41
C/T2477	30.9.40–9.2.41
W/T2505	9.9.40–FTR 28/29.9.40
X/T2564	9.9.40–17.5.41
Z/T2578	11.9.40–7.1.41
J/T2579	15.8.40–10.2.41
T/T2619	4.10.40–14.3.41
G/T2620	4.10.40–FTR 9.6.41

Wellington 1a/1c used by squadrons

No. 9 Sqn, Honington/East Wretham

U/L7778	17.4.40–5.9.40
Z/L7785	25.4.40–4.9.40
X/L7786	25.4.40–11.9.40
N/L7788	25.4.40–9.9.40
Y/L7789	22.4.40–3.7.40
G/L7795	18.4.40–FTR 19/20.7.40 (Wismar)
C/L7796	11.5.40–FBO2 14/15.8.40 (landing)
D/L7799	17.5.40–FBO2 7/8.8.40 (landing, Boscombe Down)
U/L7867	11.9.40–10.12.40
L7868	11.9.40–13.9.40
U/N2744	4.9.40–FTR 12.3.41
O/N2745	4.9.40–FTR 17.4.41
O/N2898	28.9.39–?.9.40
R/N2942	18.10.39–EFA 10.10.40 (overshot Honington)

No. 37 Sqn, Feltwell/Methwold

L7779	17.4.40–15.9.40
L7780	17.4.40–17.9.40
L7781	17.4.40–3.8.40 (exploded at Feltwell when photoflash ignited, also damaging L7782 (17.4.70–8.4.40), N2937 (21.10.39–6.11.40) and N2992 (3.12.39–FTR 2.9.40, ditched)
L7782	17.4.40–15.9.40
L7790	11.4.40–EAO 24.9.40 (destroyed by bombing, Feltwell)
L7792	13.4.40–FTR 14/15.9.40
L7794	17.4.40–FBO2 26/27.7.40 (collided with another aircraft when landing)

Wellington 1a L7779:P-LF of 37 Squadron, Feltwell, has yet to have its sides painted matt black. (IWM)

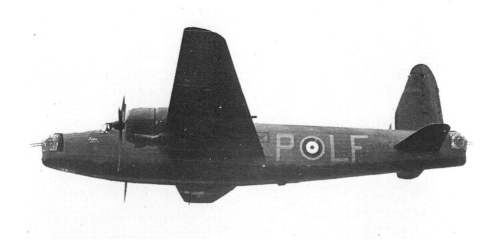

L7806	1.6.40-6.11.40
L7850	5.10.40-ME 8.11.40
L7865	11.9.40-ME 1.12.40
L7866	11.9.40-ME 1.12.40
N2757	5.10.40-ME 5.12.40
R/N2937	21.10.39-6.11.40
Q/N2938	23.10.39-23.11.40
N/N2992	3.12.39-FTR 1/2.9.40 (ditched)
P2517	9.1.40-18.11.40
P9217	25.1.40-17.9.40
R3150	27.7.40-FTR 29/30.9.40
R3195	7.5.40-6.11.40
R3210	2.6.40-FTR 20/21.7.40 (Gelsenkirchen)
R3224	29.7.40-6.11.40
R3231	17.7.40-6.11.40
R3236	21.6.40-FTR 6/7.7.40 (Hamburg)
R3275	8.7.40-6.11.40
R3281	16.7.40-FBO2 4.8.40 (overshot Benson)
R3284	21.7.40-FBO2 15/16.8.40 (Feltwell)
T2503	22.8.40-6.11.40
T2504	5.8.40-6.11.40
T2547	16.8.40-6.11.40
T2607	11.9.40-ME 22.11.40
T2609	11.9.40-22.11.40
T2812	25.9.40-ME 1.12.40

No. 38 Sqn, Marham/Barton Bendish

R/L7808	17.6.40-20.2.41
T/L7809	18.6.40-FTR 11/12.9.40
V/L7810	19.6.40-7.11.40
L7854	13.9.40-wheels-up landing 20/21.9.40
Y/N2878	30.11.39-19.11.40
F/N2995	6.12.39-3.9.40
P9207	19.6.40-25.10.40
A/P9250	13.4.40-ME 1.12.40
F/P9265	13.4.40-ME 1.12.40
X/P9287	1.4.40-damaged in combat 20/21.7.40; FTR 7/8.10.40
P/P9293	5.4.40-ME 1.12.40
E/P9294	8.4.40-EFB 22/23.8.40 (crashed nr Hessingham — fuel shortage)
X/P9299	27.7.40-7.11.40
T/R3198	19.6.40-7.11.40
R3219	12.6.40-FTR 1.10.40
R3293	28.6.40-EFB 8.8.40 (force landed Muston Rd, Filey)
T2465	24.8.40-24.11.40
T2580	27.8.40-ME 22.11.40
T2743	9.10.40-3.11.40
T2838	23.9.40-ME 5.12.40
T2839	2.10.40-ME 1.12.40

No. 75 Sqn, Feltwell/Methwold

L7784	24.4.40-23.9.40
V/L7848	27.7.40-damaged 23/24.9.40 belly landed back from Berlin; repaired, with 75 Sqn until 13.9.41
L7857	5.8.40-EFA 16/17.10.40 (fuel short, crashed nr Penrith)
N2777	3.9.40-6.11.40
N2797	11.9.40-21.9.40

P9292	11.9.40-FTR 23/24.10.40 (ditched)
R3176	22.7.40-EFB 3/4.8.40 (ditched Barton Mills, from Gelsenkirchen)
R3218	2.6.40-9.11.41
R3235	21.6.40-FTR 25/26.7.40
R3277	3.9.40-FBO2 7.11.40
R3297	29.6.40-24.3.41
T2463	28.7.40-FTR 20/21.9.40 (shot down off Ostend)
T2474	17.8.40-FTR 22.12.40 (FH 169.30)
T2550	16.8.40-EFB 9/10.1.41 (crashed nr Duxford)
T2741	26.9.40-18.11.40
T2736	17.9.40-26.2.41
T2820	25.9.40-EFB 21.10.40
T2821	25.9.40-6.11.40
T2822	7.10.40-6.11.40
T2837	23.9.40-6.11.40

No. 99 Sqn, Newmarket Heath

L7783	16.9.40-EFA 3.1.41
T/L7802	3.6.40-9.12.41
N/L7804	31.5.40-EFAO 30/31.8.40 (crashed at Widdeon, Devon, from Berlin)
Z/L7868	13.9.40-EFB 25.9.40 (port engine failed on take-off from Newmarket; exploded)
L7896	2.9.40-FTR 7.10.40
J/N2767	25.8.40-EFB 9.11.40 (ditched off Fairlight)
H/N2768	10.9.40-26.2.42
N3003	16.12.39-EFA 4.7.40 (damaged during training flight, Bassingbourn)
N3103	24.1.40-25/26.7.40 (forced landing Cantling, Norfolk — fuel short)
J/P9233	24.2.40-EFB 31.8.40 (forced landing E. of Andover — on loan to 214 Sqn)
A/P9240	19.3.40-25.9.40
B/P9242	29.2.40-FTR 18/19.9.40
E/P9243	3.3.40-FTR 13/14.10.40
K/P9274	15.3.40-EFB 25/26.7.40 (crashed by Cambridge Airport, from Dortmund)
P9275	18.3.40-FTR 25/26.7.40 from Dortmund
X/P9277	2.7.40-18/19.9.40 (damaged by night fighter, belly landed Wattisham)
R3167	23.9.40-EFB 14.11.40
R3170	27.4.40-FTR 5/6.7.40
R3197	23.6.40-heavy landing Newmarket 25/26.8.40; used until 8.12.40
R3222	7.40-belly landed 4.7.41 (FH 425.50)
R3228	1.6.40-23.8.40
R3287	27.7.40-5.9.40
R3289	27.7.40-FTR 6.11.40
T2460	31.7.40-20.8.40
T2461	31.7.40-FAO2 17.12.40
T2501	27.7.40-FAO2 31.1.41 (crashed Burgh, Suffolk)

232

T2546	18.9.40-EFB 30.10.40
T2554	15.10.40-FTR 7/8.11.41
T2611	27.8.40-damaged landing 11/12.9.40; on strength until 24.10.40
T2739	19.9.40-FBO2 3.5.41

No. 115 Sqn, Marham/Barton Bendish

S/L7798	18.5.40-damaged landing at Boscombe Down from Blaye, 14/15.8.40; held until 15.12.40
H/L7801	22.5.40-16/17.8.40 (damaged in action)
W/L7845	23.6.40-15.8.40 (crash landed Hillesden, Bicester)
N2875	17.9.39-2.7.40
I/P9224	27.5.40-18.3.41
A/P9227	22.2.40-FTR 18/19.7.40 (shot down nr Bremen)
R/P9230	22.2.40-9.9.40
G/P9235	26.6.40-9.9.40
P9236	22.2.40-FBO2 ?.7.40
U/P9283	9.7.40-EFAO 27.10.40
T/P9285	30.3.40-31.8.40
P9286	7.4.40-FTR 16.11.41
R3151	12.4.40-5.9.40 (damaged landing at Farnborough)
V/R3153	13.4.40-25.3.41
R3155	15.4.40-14/15.8.40 (forced landing at Titchwell, from Blaye)
R3232	17.7.40-21.9.40
R3237	7.40-4.41
R3276	16.7.40-EFB 22/23.8.40 (crashed Wood Dalling, Norfolk)
D/R3278	9.9.40-5.12.40
X/R3279	17.7.40-FTR 2/3.3.41
R3291	2.10.40-7.11.40
F/R3292	28.6.40-FTR 30.9/1.10.40
C/T2466	21.8.40-FTR 12.12.40
T2507	24.9.40-7.11.40
P/T2509	16.8.40-FTR 15.11.40
W/T2511	16.8.40-6.3.41
A/T2520	20.7.40-FTR 9.12.40
K/T2459	20.8.40-FTR 1.10.40
E/T2560	5.8.40-EFB 22/23.4.41 (burnt)
J/T2563	17.8.40-FBO1 20.10.40
H/T2606	10.9.40-FBO2 17.11.40
R/T2613	8.9.40-EFB 30.10.40
T2742	26.9.40-7.11.40

No. 149 Sqn, Mildenhall

L7805	1.6.40-FTR 11/12.7.40 (from Bremen)
U/L7846	21.6.40-2.1.41
W/L7855	9.9.40-12.12.40
H,A/L7858	31.8.40-FTR 14/15.3.41
N/N2769	10.9.40-FA 30.1.41
B/N2775	1.10.40-6.5.41
E/P9244	3.3.40-EFB 11/12.8.40 (hit radio mast at Mildenhall while landing from Wanne Eickel)
W/P9245	3.3.40-FTR 8/9.9.40 (in the sea off Clacton)
M/P9247	5.3.40-2.4.41
D/P9248	6.3.40-2.10, 'G' from 12.10-FTR 18.4.41 (FH 380.55)

H/P9268	11.3.40-FAO2 17.12.40 (FH 271.55)
M/P9272	15.3.40-FTR 27/28.8.40 (Kiel)
V/P9273	15.3.40-FTR 9/10.10.40 (ditched, from Heringen)
P9289	2.4.40-3.7.40
R3150	11.9.40-15.9.40
E/R3160	22.4.40-FTR 18/19.9.40 from Le Havre
O/R3161	22.4.40-2.8.40
G/R3163	25.4.40-FTR 5/6.9.40 from Black Forest
B/R3164	22.4.40-FTR 28.9.40 from Hanau
V/R3174	17.5.40-FTR 16/17.8.40
V/R3175	16.5.40-FTR 8/9.9.40
R3280	14.7.40-29.8.40
R3285	21.7.40-27.11.40
T2458	9.9.40-20.1.41
T2459	30.6.40-18.7.40
T2460	20.8.40-7/8.10.40 (damaged in combat)
J,R,A/T2737	17.9.40-FTR 14.7.41
T2740	19.9.40-23.10.40 (damaged in action)

No. 214 Sqn, Stradishall

L7773	18.8.40-13.9.40
L7774	25.1.40-8.8.40, 17.9.40-28.10.40
L7815	20.9.40-6.2.41
L7840	10.9.40-EFAO 11.10.40 (swung into Stradishall hangar on take-off, crew killed)
L7843	10.9.40-FTR 27/28.9.40 (Mannheim)
L7847	27.7.41-8.8.40
L7849	7.8.40-FTR 28.12.40 (ditched)
L7851	20.9.40-2.2.41
L7853	20.9.40-15.1.41
L7856	4.9.40-27/28.9.40 (belly landed)
L7859	3.9.40-EFA 10.10.40
N2746	10.9.40-FTR 13/14.3.41
N2747	21.9.40-7/8.10.40 (forced landing on Q Site, Horsham St Faiths)
N2776	1.9.40-EFA 6.2.41
R/N2778	1.9.40-15.7.41
N2906	?-20.7.40
N3005	22.6.40-25.9.40
N3010	16.12.39-20.9.40
N3011	16.12.39-3.8.40
P2530	14.1.40-EFA 30.8.40 (undershot Stradishall)
P9214	24.1.40-13.9.40
R3178	9.7.40-24.8.40
R3233	9.7.40-7.1.41; serviced, held until 24.12.41
T2469	20.9.40-6.2.41
T2470	24.7.40-EFB 5.11.40
T2471	24.7.40-FTR 24.11.40 (FH 147)
T2476	30.9.40-FTR 8.12.40
T2542	9.8.40-FTR 8/9.4.41
T2559	9.8.40-FTR 30/31.8.40 (Berlin)
T2562	9.8.40-5.12.40
T2612	15.9.40-6.2.41
T2708	10.9.40-18.5.41
T2709	10.9.40-12.8.41

T2738	17.9.40–6.2.41
T2819	29.9.40–EAO2 1.11.40, EFA 22.7.41
T2827	5.10.40–ME 30.10.40
T2828	5.10.40–ME 30.10.40

No. 311 Sqn, Honington/East Wretham

L7778	5.9.40–29.11.40
L7785	11.9.40–22/23.2.41 (overshot E. Wretham)
L7786	11.9.40–EFB 16/17.10.40 (crashed nr Needham Market)
L7788	9.9.40–FTR 23/24.9.40 from Berlin; captured, flown by Luftwaffe
L7841	28.9.40–13.6.41
L7842	20.10.40–FTR 6.2.41
L7844	28.9.40–FTR 16/17.10.40
L7895	1.9.40–8.9.40
N2771	28.9.40–EFA 16/17.10.40 (crashed, burnt out at HQ F/C, Bentley Priory)
N2772	28.9.40–EFA 11.10.40 (engine failure on take-off)
N2773	28.9.40–EFB 17.10.40 (crashed, Hucknall)
N2880	2.8.40–22.1.41
N3010	20.9.40–30.9.40
P9212	11.10.40–EFA 16.4.41 (FH 284.10)
R1021	28.9.40–6.2.42
R3177	9.8.40–EAO 28.10.40 (destroyed by bombing)

R3234	9.8.40–28.4.41
T2469	2.9.40–20.9.40
T2553	15.10.40–22.3.41
T2561	9.8.40–2/3.9.40 (damaged in overshoot)
T2564	9.8.40–9.9.40
T2577	9.8.40–10.9.40
T2578	1.9.40–11.9.40
T2613	1.9.40–8.9.40

Additional 3 Group organizations operating Wellingtons under 214 Sqn's overall direction were: Reserve Training Flight; New Zealand Flight (operational training for 75 Sqn using *P9206* to 22.9.40 and *P9210*).

By 15 October 1940 rearming of these No. 1 Group Fairey Battle squadrons had commenced:

No. 103, Newton: N2770 5.10, T2600 2.10, T2617 4.10, T2621 5.10

No. 150, Newton: L7870 2.10, N2758 5.10, P2523 EFA 15.10, T2475 7.10, T2510 6.10, T2618 3.10, T2622 5.10

Wellington 1a/1c used by No. 11 OTU, Bassingbourn, which had operational status: L7780, N2866, N2876, N2887 (to 15 OTU 4.9.40), N2892, N2894, N2904, N2912, N2945 (EFA — ditched off Braddu Head, IoM, 24.8.40), N2960, N2990, N2991, N3001, N3002 (EFA 1.8.40), N3005 from 25.9.40, N3014, P2528, P9216; and R3227 received 17.9.40 with R3229 and T2705.

Wellington 1cs of 149 Squadron, Mildenhall, in August 1940. P9273:OJ-N (nearest) failed to return on 9/10 October 1940. (IWM)

The Transports

When war commenced Britain had no home-based transport squadrons apart from No. 24, which was equipped with short-range passenger aircraft — Dragon Rapides, DH 86 Express air liners, Vega Gulls and other small aircraft. Not until 1942 did the assembly of a home-based strategic and offensive transport force commence. Lumbering Victoria and Valentia were to be found overseas while in Britain their long awaited replacement, the Bristol Bombay, was being produced in equally small numbers.

To provide air transport links between Britain and forces in France the Government requisitioned airliners including Ensigns, HP 42 'Hannibal' Class and Short Scylla and Syrinx large biplanes. A few Flamingos and other twin-engined civil transports also joined them. Even so, it was a small force.

During the fight for France such aircraft provided urgently needed links and carried personnel to maintain Hurricane squadrons temporarily detached from Fighter Command. To retain ease of passage over neutral territory and also operate civilian services these air liners retained civil identity letters.

There was additional to them another type of aircraft available in some numbers and whose origin lay in a bomber transport need. This was the Handley Page HP 54 Harrow bomber. At the start of the war 87 healthy Harrows were in storage, and in September 1939 began earning their keep as navigation and bombing trainers. Early in 1940 their potential as troop and light freight transports came under review and led to 15 serving such purposes.

The Harrow and the Bombay had much in common. Handley Page's HP 43 high wing two motor transport, a rugged monoplane version of the HP 42, was designed to replace the Vickers Victoria and Valentia. After updating the design it was tendered as the HP 51, and at the last minute, to meet the Air Ministry's C.26/31 specification prescribing a bomber transport with an all-up weight of 18,000 lb able to carry a 3,000 lb load 920 miles.

Bristol's Bombay won the C.26/31 order. Handley Page subsequently revised the HP 51, converting the design into an interim bomber to replace the Vickers Virginia in No. 3 (Bomber) Group until the Wellington was ready. Carrying a crew of four, and defended by nose and tail turrets and a dorsal gun position, the new HP 54 was clearly an attractive, relatively inexpensive proposition. Therefore a covering Specification 29/35 was quickly agreed, 100 Harrows were ordered in August 1935 and *K6933* (the first) flew on 10 October 1936. Due to the ease of production the next example was delivered in January 1937, the 100th being completed by the end of that year. Pegasus X engines were installed in the first 21 examples, whereas from *K6953* fitting the Pegasus XX produced the Mk II. Retrospective fitting of the superior engine was later made to the first six Harrow Mk Is. Front line service by Harrows was brief, for the Wellington entered service late 1938. Harrows soon began retiring into ASUs, the last being withdrawn in August 1939. Almost brand new, they were well worth redeployment.

As an alternative to a 3,000 lb bomb load in its belly the Harrow could carry 20 armed troops and it was this capability which was of interest by 1940.

Because of its metropolitan nature Fighter Command administered 24 Squadron, the only transport squadron. So when on 28 March 1940 No. 1680 Flight, a special transport unit, was formed at Doncaster, it was also assigned to the Command. Its siting at Doncaster might initially seem strange, but the new Flight was to operate longer-range aircraft than 24 Squadron, its main task the maintaining of links with army and naval forces in Scotland and the Isles as well as France. Thus, it was placed roughly half way between those outposts and the forces in France which it busily supported during the hectic days of May and June 1940. By then it had risen in status, becoming No. 271 Squadron on 1 May. Already it had acquired a Harrow modified for transport duty. Fitted with seats and an enlarged door it was very much a hybrid, two more examples of which arrived in May during which month 271 Squadron inherited five Bombays, three from SHQ Debden which had operated them in the support of squadron moves to France. In such a role the Bombays proved useful, but they were needed overseas, and Italy's entry into the war hastened their despatch to the Western Desert. No. 271 Squadron was only permitted three and instead it was soon relying upon Harrow transports. Support and movement of squadrons in France displayed the tactical value of such mobility. As well as supporting forces in the far north, 271 Squadron soon had a special Freight Section within its

'B' Flight, renamed on 8 September 1940 'Sparrow Flight' because Harrows hopping from place to place resembled those birds, and indeed the Harrows became commonly called 'Sparrows'. That name applied equally to aircraft retaining nose and tail turrets and others in which those were replaced by shapely fairings.

The need for rotation and replacement of fighter squadrons throughout the Battle of Britain took the 'Sparrows' of 271 Squadron to the front line and on a number of occasions they narrowly averted German bombs and fighters. Lengthy hauls and exceptionally long hours of duty characterized the squadron's work throughout the fateful months.

While Harrows and Bombays trundled between airfields throughout the Kingdom, and usually returned to Doncaster each evening, services north were in particular the task set the HP 42s which in July 1940 surrendered their civil identity upon impressment into the RAF. For company they had the rare, exotic, lone RAF Ford Trimotor, the sight of which set any lucky spotter's heart aglow. It served but briefly as *X5000* and in September 1940, by which time the Harrows had been found quite capable of lifting 6,000 lb loads — kit, starter trolleys, tool kits, etc. — or at least 31 passengers.

Very valuable was the contribution made by 271 Squadron to the winning of the Battle of Britain, as can be seen from this summary of the direct assistance it gave particularly by moving fighter squadrons in July–September 1940.

No. 271 Squadron Harrow-assisted squadron movements, 1 July–30 September 1940

Date	Aircraft	Task
July		
8	*K6998*	Base–Castle Bromwich–personnel to Aldergrove–base

Magnificent sight! Three Bombays and two Harrows of 271 Squadron photographed at Hatfield during a July 1940 mobility and defence exercise. (BAe)

9	K7010	Base–Castle Bromwich–starter trolleys to Aldergrove–base
10	K6998	Base–Hawkinge, 79 Sqn to Turnhouse
12/ 13	K6998	To Acklington–152 Sqn to Warmwell–base
17	K6998	Base–Wick–Sumburgh taking 'B' Flt 3 Sqn, then Gladiator Flt to Roborough–returned Wick
19	K6998	Returned Doncaster, loads to Exeter by two other Harrows
19	K7010	Base–Leconfield–616 Sqn to Kenley–returned Leconfield with 64 Sqn
20	K7024	Base–Wittering (sqn move cancelled)–Kirton-in-Lindsey–Turnhouse–base

August

9	K6998	Base–Catterick–Hornchurch–Catterick–base
13	K7010	Base–West Hampnett with 602 Sqn–145 Sqn to Drem–base
14	K7024	Base–Eastchurch, and flew twice to Hornchurch and back–Wittering
	K7000	Base–Eastchurch, 266 Sqn to Wittering–base
16	K7011	Base–Tangmere–West Hampnett–base
17	K7024	Base–Tangmere, 602 Sqn to West Hampnett–base
19	K7010, K6998	Base–Leconfield–616 Sqn to Kenley , 64 Sqn back to Leconfield–base
21	K7010	Base–Kirton-in-Lindsey; 264 Sqn to Hornchurch, load of 266 Sqn kit to Wittering–base
27	K6998	Base–Acklington, 79 Sqn to Biggin Hill, 32 Sqn Acklington–base
29	K6998, K7000	Base–Kirton-in-Lindsey, 222 Sqn to Hornchurch
31	K7010	Base–Duxford; sqn move cancelled–base

September

3	K7010	Bibury–Pembrey with 91 Sqn–Exeter for 87 Sqn–Bibury–base
5	K7024, K7000	Base–Catterick; 504 Sqn to Hendon–base
7	K7000	Base–Exeter–Tangmere–Exeter–base
7	K6998	Base–Drem, 605 Sqn to Croydon
8	K6998	Croydon–Base carrying 111 Sqn; then to Bicester–Tangmere for 607 Sqn to Usworth–base
	K7000	Base–Croydon–Drem
27	K7024	Base–Thorney Island to move 812 Sqn FAA
29	K7032	Base–Turnhouse–Wick–Castletown–base

The Harrows of 271 Squadron

K6943	23.4.10–1.1.45
K6951	25.10.40–25.3.44
K6962	12.10.40–23.3.44
K6986	13.10.40–SOC 15.1.45
K6987	10.10.40–2.45
K6998	28.6.40–1.1.45 (destroyed in attack on Évère)
K7000	22.7.40–29.11.40, 11.2.42–SOC 10.2.45 (after taxying accident)
K7009	12.10.40–SOC 24.4.44
K7010	29.5.40–12.4.43, 14.8.43–SOC 25.5.45
K7011	1.6.40–19.12.42 (missing over Bay of Biscay en route Gibraltar)
K7014	24.10.40–damaged 12.6.44–SOC 31.8.44
K7015	14.10.40–FAT 20.4.41 (burnt out)
K7024	3.50.40–RIW 21.5.43, 23.9.43–1.1.45 (destroyed in air raid on Évère)
K7031	13.10.40–SOC 1.1.41

Handley Page Harrows used as transports initially retained their bomber configuration thus resembling the bomber depicted. Nose turrets were usually overpainted or replaced by fairings of similar contours.

K7032 45 MU 18.6.40, to 271 Sqn
16.9.40-28.12.42, 16.7.43, to 1680 Flt
17.8.44 and via 67 MU Sidmouth
taken by ship to the Med Trng Unit;
became *4943M* in 12.44

Bristol Bombays used to assist squadron and unit moves 1 July– 30 September 1940

Date   Aircraft   Task

July

8	L5851, L5817	Base-Castle Bromwich–Aldergrove–base
12	L5817	Base-Acklington, 152 Sqn to Warmwell–base
22	L5817	Base-Lossiemouth–took spares for K7000-base
23	L5817	Base-Dyce where K7000 had force landed-base
26	L5817	Base-Gravesend–Middle Wallop–Gravesend–base

August

4	L5851	Base; 254 and 248 Sqns detachments to Aldergrove; 233 Sqn to Dyce, 248 Sqn to Sumburgh-Dyce
18	L5814	Base-Ringway for 12 parachutists-Hatston-Sumburgh, 22 men to Dyce
27	L5851	Base-Acklington, 79 Sqn to Biggin Hill, returned with 32 Sqn-base
29	L5817, L5851	Base-253 Sqn to Prestwick to Kenley, 615 Sqn to Prestwick; L5851 unable to complete return journey and force landed at Croydon — engine cowling became detached
30	L5817	Took 253 Sqn to Prestwick and moved 615 Sqn

A rare wartime sight in Britain was the Bristol Bombay. Like L5811, *production Bombays were built by Short & Harland.* (Shorts)

Ah, the memory of Imperial Airways! Thrilling, always, the sighting of a Handley Page HP 42 like G-AAXF, with 271 Squadron and calling at Hatfield in July 1940. (BAe)

September

5	*L5814*	Lifted 504 Sqn to Hendon–base, with *K7024*
7	*L5817*	Lifted 601 Sqn from Tangmere to Exeter
8	*L5817*	Lifted 601 Sqn from Tangmere to Exeter
	L5814	Base–Usworth for 607 Sqn–base — aircraft unserviceable
27	*L5851,*	Base–North Coates–Thorney Island, movement of 812 Sqn to there and Detling

The individuals

Of the 12 Bombays that saw active service in the UK only these were used during the period:

L5814	271 Sqn
L5817	271 Sqn 11.4.40–27.11.40, and 13.3.41–FAOE 1.4.41 (crashed at Ivinghoe, Bucks)
L5851	271 Sqn 14.5.40–28.2.41

Handley Page HP 42

HP 42s mostly flew passengers and light freight (usually for the Royal Navy) between Donibristle, Turnhouse, Aldergrove and the northern isles. Occasionally they assisted with RAF squadron moves, becoming an exotic and nostalgic sight in southern skies. Such occasions included these:

Date   Aircraft   Task

July

1	*G-AAUE*	To Hatfield for troop exercise at Linton-on-Ouse
2	*G-AAXF*	Base–Finningley for Harrow spares–Gosport–Farnborough––base
	G-AAUE	Participated in mock raid on Linton-on-Ouse
20	*G-AAUE*	Base–Aldergrove–Turnhouse, then took 253 Sqn to Aldergrove

August

16	*AS982*	Base–Church Fenton–took 249 Sqn to Boscombe Down–base
18	*AS982*	Pembrey–took 91 Sqn to Bibury–base
26	*AS982*	Base–Odiham–French passengers–base–Donibristle

September

1	*AS982*	Base–Digby–took 16 men of 611 Sqn to Tern Hill–Stapleford Tawney–base

The individuals

AS981/G-AAUC	'Horsa'	271	Sqn
	30.5.40–EFA		7.8.40
	(crashed NE of Whitehaven)		
AS982/G-AAUE	'Hadrian'	271	Sqn
	4.6.40–6.12.40 (destroyed in gale at Doncaster)		
AS983/G-AAXF	'Helena'	271	Sqn
	8.6.40–1.8.40 (crashed on landing, Donibristle), to RN 12.4.41, SOC 8.41		

Movements of Ford Trimotor *X5000* (ex *G-ACAE*) during September 1940

Ford Trimotor *G-ACAE* to 271 Sqn 3.5.40, assisted move of 501 Sqn to Merville 10.5.40 and made several flights to France. First flown as *X5000* on 1.9.40.

1   Base-Digby-Tern Hill-Stapleford Tawney-base (09:30-16:55 hrs)
3   Base-Shawbury-base (10:55-13:30)
10   Base-North Coates-base-Thorney Island-Abingdon
12   Abingdon-Doncaster (07:20-08:20)
13   Base-Castle Bromwich-base (15:00-16:45)
19   Base-Castletown-Belfast; flown by Plt Off Bristow and crew of 2 (17:40-19:55), force landed on Moor Farm, Ballyminetere, Co Down, crashed in ditch and SOC 25.11.40

The Americans

Something from Uncle Sam

The extent of American aircraft supplied to the RAF during the Battle of Britain in addition to British pre-war purchases is probably greater than is generally realized. Unfortunately they were mostly unsuitable for operational use. Although the British aircraft industry had drawn upon advanced innovations in America, many of the best ideas had yet to be applied to US combat aircraft. By far the most useful item Britain acquired was the .303 in Colt Browning machine-gun, its American designers being able justifiably to claim a considerable share in the winning of the fight. But most American aircraft were literally non-starters, a high proportion barely worth unpacking.

Fighters, too slow for the European war and powered by engines for low and medium altitude fighting, arrived as combat altitudes increased. By 16 October 204 P-36s were in Britain, 33 Buffaloes and 55 Tomahawks mostly residing in crates. Unpacking, erecting and testing the numbers arriving was a considerable task, whatever their value. Although many included .50 in. guns in their armoury the number was deemed insufficient. Inadequate view for the pilot surrounded by much heavy cockpit framing was another source of criticism, whereas ample creature comforts unfortunately added to weight and brought little advantage.

Another handicap to operating them was a chronic lack of spares and the great need for specialized tools. By 30 October 3,113 packages of equipment had arrived to support the 915 aircraft delivered. When the necessary maintenance manuals arrived they turned out to be massive volumes carefully prepared and needing considerable effort in interpretation.

Many of the shrouded or crated items shipped to west coast ports were survivors from undelivered Belgian, French and Norwegian orders with suitably foreign instrumentation. Much needed changing. Considerable modification programmes were needed before such aircraft could be integrated into the RAF, in particular their radio and fuel systems. Of the 200 or so Mohawks in Britain only 44 were flying by the end of 1940, by which time all were earmarked for overseas use, and it was January 1941 before any P-40 was a going concern.

Political considerations surrounding these deliveries were considerable, for Britain needed as much backing from the USA as possible, moral as well as material. That made it imperative to use what America was providing. Although P-36s had been used by the French quite satisfactorily, here was a low to medium level fighter of increasingly

241

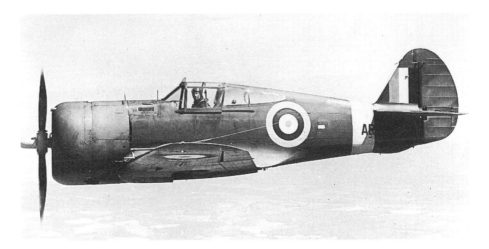

Although many Curtiss P-36s had arrived, few were flown in 1940.

little value. The dumpy barrel-like Brewster Buffalo growled a lot, was manoeuvrable but was also a low level fighter. Nevertheless on 13 September the decision was made at an ERP Committee meeting to equip 71 (Eagle) Squadron with eight Belgian Brewsters. All but 11 were being packed, for they had been promised to the Admiralty for shipment to the Middle East. Later Buffalos would replace 71 Squadron's aircraft,

although their delivery date was unknown and plans were raised for the use of Mohawks by the Eagle Squadron. Instead it switched to using Hurricanes, only ever receiving three of the planned Brewsters.

Awaited were deliveries of dive-bombers, but these were some weeks away. The 61 Northrop A-17As which were in Britain were of little value, the hope being that the newcomers would also be suitable for tactical

One of the first Douglas DB-7s to be active in Britain was AE458 tested at Boscombe Down during the summer. (IWM)

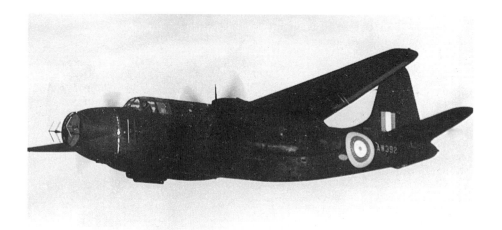

Many early DB-7s were converted into Havocs, carrying Long Aerial Mines or, like AW392, *an airborne Helmore searchlight in the nose.*

reconnaissance, allowing Lysander production to be ended. Of good potential, the DB-7, 150 of which were in Britain by mid-October, had a revolutionary nosewheel undercarriage which made it too avant garde for immediate introduction. With a 680 mile range it was of little more value than the Blenheim, and its Pratt & Whitney S3C4-Gs were none too satisfactory. Nevertheless, on 9 October Nos. 107 and 110 Squadrons at Wattisham were chosen to try out the newcomers, despite their limited range. Two days later the decision was changed to deploying re-equipped squadrons to Ulster instead of having Nos. 18 and 101 Squadrons there, then on 8 December 1940 that scheme was abandoned in favour of converting Boston Is and IIs into AI-equipped night fighters, in the hope that the DB-7A would prove to be far superior — which it was. Another use

To safeguard the Turbinlite Havocs from fighter attack they had bold white stripes painted on their upper wing surfaces. (RAF Museum)

for eight early DB-7s was with 420 Flight as aerial minelayers, for which task a few Harrows were serving, marked out only as operational trainers.

Most impressive of all the arrivals was the Glenn Martin 167F, named Maryland. Ordered by the French, 87 reached Britain by mid-October. Early tests showed the 17,800 lb 167F to be a very useful high speed reconnaissance bomber with a very long range, ideal for employment from Malta. Its top speed was 294 mph TAS at 9,000 ft, it took 12.1 minutes to reach 15,000 ft and had an estimated service ceiling of 27,250 ft. Far more useful was its range for, with 542 miles available for cruise after a climb to 10,000 ft, its endurance — if boost pressure was kept low — was rated at 10.4 hours. The dorsal turret was unimpressive and trials were undertaken with it replaced by an Anson's turret, but the additional weight cut the performance considerably.

Accordingly five 'natural' Glenn Martin Marylands were erected and flown to 22 Squadron, North Coates, there being taken on charge by 'C' Flight whose personnel practised flying them. On 26 August 1940 Flt Lt Whiteley flew one to Burtonwood, where many American aircraft were taken for erection. The Maryland was damaged in landing and during an overnight stay was further slightly harmed when incendiary bombs fell on the landing ground.

On 4 September four Marylands flew to Thorney Island and in accord with Movement Order 7/1940 three set out on 6 September for Luqa, Malta. *AR709* was left behind in reserve while *AR705* (Flt Lt E.A. Whiteley), *AR712* (Plt Off J. Foxton) and *AR707* (Sgt J.W.T. Bibby) completed their journey across Europe. On reaching Malta they left Coastal Command, became part of Mediterranean Command, joined with the personnel of No. 3 AACU, Hal Far, and on 19 September formed the basis of 431 GR Flight. Their first

Glenn Martin Maryland AR725, *one of the first to be flown in Britain, and one taken over from a French contract.*

operation had already been flown, on 14 September when *AR712* photographed Tripoli, Sicily and Pantelleria. The Flight's career was to be short for on the 26th in the hands of Flg Off Warburton the hydraulics failed, the mission was abandoned and *712* crash landed. Next day its fate was sealed by a load of Italian incendiaries. Already No. 22 Squadron had on 17 September received another Maryland to supply another crew to 431 Flight. Training was not trouble-free, for a Maryland had in the process crashed near Peterborough. Out of the 707 US aircraft which had arrived by mid-October, less than half were by then in airworthy condition.

American aircraft shipped to Britain 31 July–16 October 1940

	Total received by given date									
Type	31.7	14.8	21.8	28.8	4.9	18.9	25.9	2.10	9.10	16.10
A-17	61	61	61	61	61	61	61	61	61	61
Buffalo*		32	32/1	32/1	32	32	32	32	32	32/1
DB-7	16	39	60	83	100	128	137	137	137	139/11
Harvard II	–	–	–	–	2	8	8	16	16	16/8
Helldiver	5	5	5	5	5	5	5	5	5	5
Hudson (new contract)	70	79	87	87	87	97	97	97	97	97
Hudson II	–	–	–	–	–	9	9	16	16	16
Hudson III	–	–	–	–	–	–	–	–	–	–/11
Martlet	–	–	6	6	–	–	27	44	44	44/16
Maryland	38	40	40	48	48	74	74	87	87	87
P-36 Mohawk	32	57	69	69	83	159	175	186	193	195/9
P-40 Tomahawk	–	–	1	1	1	1	1	1	1	15/40
Total	222	313	351	369	408	552	617	682	689	707/99

To 30 October 1940 4,028 packs of spares had arrived.
From Canadian production 38 Hurricanes had arrived by 14 August, 42 by 16 October by which time the first two Canadian-built Hampdens were in Britain.
Total to 30.10.40 = 915 + 3,113 packs of spares
* all ex-Belgian contract
15/40 etc. = 15 examples in U.K./40 en route to U.K.

Appendices

Appendix 1

Summary of production, Squadron strength and write-offs, 1 July–15 October 1940

Various documents, Official and otherwise, list 1940 aircraft production and losses. Few agree! This listing in numerical order is applicable to front line use and not OTUs.

Coastal Command

Aircraft type	Total no. received		Served in squadrons 1.7.40– 15.10.40	Written off 1.7.40–15.10.40			Seriously damaged during operations (repairable)
	to 1.7.40	to 15.10.40		in/due to operational flying	other flying accidents	due to bombing	
Anson	1,415(d)	1,795(d)	158	8	2	4	2
Beaufort	252	345	123	11	6	4	3
Blenheim IV(f)	(a)	(a)	125	20	6	2	} 22****
Blenheim B/GR	(a)	(a)	81	34	–	6	
Botha	147	282	13	–	1	–	–
Fokker T-8W	8	8	8	2	–	–	–
Hudson	298	363	189	27	2	–	23
Lerwick	15	18	10	–	–	–	–
Spitfire PR	**	**	42	3	–	–	4
Stranraer	18	18	8	–	2	–	–
Sunderland	55	59	36	3	2	–	2
Whitley V	(c)	(c)	20	–	–	–	–

* includes 19 Mk I(f) also accounted for in Fighter Command tabulation
** includes 6 Mk II, and 5 Mk I used only by PDU/PRU
*** includes Mk 1(f)
**** includes Blenheim B/GR

Battles included within Bomber Command listing
(a) Blenheim I(f) and IV(f) were all converted from bombers, some leaving the works as fighters and others converted in service. Some were converted back to bombers, thus making totalling variable by date.
(c) Whitleys detached from Bomber Command not included
(d) total delivered to the RAF

Fighter Command

Aircraft type	Total no. received		Served in squadrons 1.7.40– 15.10.40	Written off 1.7.40–15.10.40			Seriously damaged during operations (repairable)
	to 1.7.40	to 15.10.40		in/due to operational flying	other flying accidents	due to bombing	
Hurricane	1,676	2,546	1,994	523	45	20	256
Spitfire	909	1,426**	1,142	363	5	11	203
Lysander	618(c)	746(c)	264	9	6	4	2
Defiant	108	266	71	18	–	–	3
Blenheim							
I(f)	(a)	(a)	194*	18	7	2	3
Beaufighter	–	40	22	–	2	2(b)	1
Gladiator	(483)	(483)	17	2	–	–	–

* includes 19 Mk I(f) of 236 Squadron
** includes 94 Spitfire Mk IIs
(a) total variable conversions
(b) during bombing of Filton
(c) total delivered to the RAF
(All Gladiators delivered pre-July 1940)

Bomber Command

Aircraft type	Total no. received		Served in squadrons 1.7.40– 15.10.40	Written off 1.7.40–15.10.40			Seriously damaged during operations (repairable)
	to 1.7.40	to 15.10.40		in/due to operational flying	other flying accidents	due to bombing	
Battle**	N/A	2,196*	277	15	7	8	1
Blenheim IV	1,059	1,437	428	133	10	1	17
Hampden	563	661	301	86	18	3	–
Wellington	648	1,031	378	46	6	1***	23
Whitley	447	543	270	60	7	8	13

* Battle production included many training aircraft, total production being 2,196
** Those used by Coastal Command are included in this table
*** on operational airfield
Production totals include aircraft diverted overseas during the period
N/A = not applicable

Appendix 2

Performance figures for RAF aircraft used by squadrons during 1940

Listed figures are those officially recorded, mainly by A&AEE or MAEE. Assessment of aircraft followed take-off at full loaded weight. Additional loading during Service use naturally reduced performance, while some modifications brought improvements. Small external additional items could reduce speeds, for example by up to 15 mph in the case of the Beaufighter. Thus, the figures can only ever present a reasonable indication of performance. Heights are in feet, maximum speed full throttle TAS mph in still air conditions. Test results do not always allow for direct comparisons to be made, and the parameters for testing often do not allow for correlation.

Principal Fighters

	Hurricane	Spitfire	Defiant	Gladiator
Powerplant	Merlin III	Merlin III	Merlin III	Mercury IX
Wing span	40 ft 0 in	32 ft 10 in	39 ft 3 in	32 ft 3 in
Length	31 ft 4 in	29 ft 11 in	35 ft 10 in	27 ft 5 in
Height (over prop disc)	12 ft 11 in	11 ft 5 in	14 ft 5 in	11 ft 9 in
Wing area	258 sq ft	242 sq ft	250 sq ft	323 sq ft
Track	7 ft 7 in	6 ft	11 ft 2.5 in	7 ft 2 in
Tare weight	4,670 lb	4,341 lb	5,868 lb	3,217 lb
Loaded weight	6,316 lb	6,050 lb	7,510 lb	4,594 lb
Petrol	107.5 gal	85 gal	159 gal	70 gal
Speed (TAS mph)/time to height (mins)				
1,000 ft	–	–	247/.7	205
2,000 ft	–	–	250.5/1.4	208
3,000 ft	–	–	254/2.1	211
5,000 ft	276/1.9	–	261/3.4	217.5
6,500 ft	–	–	266.5/4.4	222
10,000 ft	291.5/3.8	320/3.5	279/6.7	232.5
13,000 ft	301/5	–	290/8.6	–
14,500 ft	–	–	–	253
15,000 ft	307/5.85	339/5.18	297/10.1	245
16,500 ft	312/6.5	–	302/11.4	243.5
18,000 ft	316/7.3	344	300/12.8	242
18,500 ft	–	352	–	–
20,000 ft	314.5/8.35	354	295/15.1	239.5
22,000 ft	–	351	–	–
23,000 ft	310.5/10.3	–	284.5/19.5	234
25,000 ft	–	345/10.54	–	–
28,000 ft	299.5/15.25	–	–	–
30,000 ft	292.5/18.30	319.16.24	–	199.5
Service ceiling	30,500 ft	34,700 ft	29,500 ft	32,900 ft
Take-off to clear 50 ft	400 yd	370 yd	560 yd	220 yd
Landing run over 50 ft	315 yd	310 yd	870 yd	450 yd

Additional notes

Different propellers altered climb rates for the Hurricane and Spitfire, additional forward weight demanding load variations aft. A typical Hurricane L2026 (Merlin III) with three-bladed Rotol propeller at typical normal all up weight 6,316 lb had its fastest climb rate recorded as climbing at 2,645 fpm at 11,600 ft. With DH 2 pitch propeller a typical Hurricane top speed was 319 mph at 18,000 ft.

The often quoted Spitfire top speed of 362 mph at 18,500 ft reached in 8.25 min was achieved by first production aircraft (take-off weight 5,935 lb) and fitted with a Merlin II driving a two-bladed fixed pitch wooden propeller. With a Merlin III and Rotol CS propeller (take-off weight 6,050 lb) the top speed was 353 mph at 20,000 ft attained in 7.42 min.

The first Defiant Mk II had top speed of 311 mph at 20,000 ft reached in 8.3 min; service ceiling 32,800 ft, range 457 miles at TAS 220 mph at 20,000 ft.

The early Bristol Beaufighters' speeds varied much according to modification state, *R2054* (two Hercules III engines giving 1,270 bhp at 15,000 ft, 14,060 lb loaded weight) reaching only 300 mph at 14,060 ft. A Hercules X variant, engines giving 1,310 hp at 14,500 ft, had a top speed of 335 mph at 15,800 ft reached in 8.7 min.

AR643, a Curtiss Hawk 75C Mohawk 1 (Wright Cyclone GR1820-G205A) tare weight 4,850 lb, loaded weight 6,662 lb, reached its top speed of 302 mph at 14,000 ft, took off in 296 yds and landed in 485 yds. Top speed at 20,000 ft was 292 mph reached in 8.8 min. Wing span 37 ft 3 in, length 28 ft 9 in, height 11 ft 6 in, track 8 ft 1 in.

Principal Bombers

	Battle	Blenheim IV	Hampden	Wellington 1a/c	Whitley V
Powerplants	(Merlin II/III/XV)	(Mercury VIII/XVIII)	Pegasus XVIII	Pegasus XVIII	Merlin X
Wing span	54 ft	56 ft 4 in	69 ft 3 in	86 ft 2 in	84 ft
Length	42 ft 4 in	42 ft 9 in	53 ft 3 in	64 ft 7 in	72 ft 6 in
Height (top of prop disc)	15 ft	12 ft 10 in	14 ft 9 in	17 ft 6 in	15 ft
Wing area (gross)	422 sq ft	469 sq ft	718 sq ft	840 sq ft	1,232 sq ft
Tare weight	6,647 lb	9,790 lb	11,761 lb	18,213 lb	17,747 lb
Loaded weight normal	10,900 lb	14,513 lb	18,750 lb	26,641 lb	26,250 lb
Defensive armament	2 × .303 in	5 × .303 in	6 × .303 in	6 × .303 in	5 × .303 in
Fuel load	206 gal	?	423 gal	750 gal	595 gal
overload:	–	–	656 gal	1,030 gal	837 gal
Range (miles)/ associated bomb load	1,050/1,000 lb	1,460/1,000 lb	1,885/2,000 lb or 1,200/4,000 lb	2,550/1,000 lb or 1,200/4,500 lb	1,650/3,000 lb or 470/7,000 lb
Take-off run over 50 ft	725 yd	820 yd	805 yd	865 yd	890 yd
Landing over 50 ft	?	?	715 yd	460 yd	550 yd
Max Speed (mph)					
1,000 ft	–	230	–	217	–
2,000 ft	–	233.5	–	–	199
3,000 ft	–	237	239	219	202
5,000 ft	–	243.5	243	–	208
6,500 ft	–	248.5	242	221	212
10,000 ft	–	–	243	–	206
12,500 ft	–	266	–	–	–
13,000 ft	241	–	252	229.5	214.5
13,800 ft	–	275	–	–	–
15,000 ft	252	263	253.5	235	220
16,500 ft	245	260.5	252	229	224.5
18,000 ft	–	256.5	249	–	224
20,000 ft	–	266	242	–	222
Service ceiling	23,500 ft	22,000 ft	19,000 ft	18,500 ft	17,600 ft

Different loading radically altered performance, as these miscellaneous notes illustrate:
Whitley V: 4 fuselage bomb cells, 3 bomb cells in each wing for 250 lb bombs. 4 Small Bomb Containers (SBC) or 2 × 2,000 lb Armour Piercing HEs in fuselage or 4 × 250/500 lb HEs.
Wellington 1c: loaded weight (no ventral turret) 27,529 lb. *P9211* tested 2 VGO beam guns poked from amidships window position in April 1940, which were featured by many aircraft after 1940.
Blenheim IV: cruised at 225 mph TAS at 1,500 ft, possible range 1,240 miles (1,000 lb load). Camotint paint increased speed by 20 mph 10,000-15,000 ft. + 9 lb boost gave speeds of 251 mph at 1,000 ft, 254.5 at 2,000 ft.
Hampden: at 9,700 ft air miles per gal = 3.18/155 mph TAS, 2.77/200 mph, and 2.32 210 mph. Take-off run with 2 × 2,000 lb HEs — 670 yd at 22,000 lb, 1,145 yd to clear 50 ft. Possible loadings: 2 cradles of 3 × 250 lb GP, two cradles of 2 × 500 lb GP and 2 × 500 lb HE external.

Principal Coastal Command Aircraft

	Anson	Beaufort	Hudson	Lerwick	Stranraer	Sunderland
Powerplant	Cheetah IX	Taurus II/III	Wright GR1820–G102A	Hercules	Pegasus X	Pegasus XXII
Wing span	56 ft 6 in	57 ft 10 in	65 ft 6 in	80 ft 10 in	85 ft	112 ft 5.5 in
Length	42 ft 3 in	44 ft 3 in	42 ft 3 in	63 ft 7.5 in	53 ft	86 ft 6.75 in
Height	13 ft 1 in	13 ft 5 in	11 ft 10.5 in	20 ft	21 ft	30 ft 3 in
Wing area	410 sq ft	503 sq ft	551 sq ft	845 sq ft	1,457 sq ft	1,487 sq ft
Tare weight	5,558 lb	11,739 lb	11,310 lb	?	12,579 lb	29,635 lb
Loaded weight	8,001 lb	17,705 lb	17,500 lb	28,000 lb	16,080 lb	44,670 lb
Petrol	120 gal	390 gal	–	–	–	435.25 gal
Speed (mph)/ time to height (mins)						
1,000 ft	165	240/.7	–	–	–	–
2,000 ft	172/2.2	243/1.4	229	–	–	170.4
3,000 ft	–	246/2.1	–	–	136	–
5,000 ft	–	251/3.4	233/3	–	–	178/7.39
6,500 ft	182/5.4	255.5/4.4	–	214	–	–
10,000 ft	179/11.5	257/7.2	237/6.7	–	138.7	182/16.6
12,000 ft	184/16.5	254/10.5	–	–	–	–
13,000 ft	–	–	–	–	134.7	–
15,000 ft	173/20.7	250.5/13.5	206/11.8	–	131.5	171.3/36.7
Service ceiling	–	19,700 ft	24,250 ft	14,000 ft	21,800 ft	15,800 ft
Loads:						
Internal	4 × 100 lb	2,000 lb	–	2,000	8 × 20 lb	–
External	–	2 × 250 lb	–	–	1,000 lb	–
Take-off run (over 50 ft)	625 yd	440 yd	660 yd	90 secs	?	515 yd

Additional notes

Range/duration of patrol aircraft varied according to their loading and is considered too complex for listing here. Take-off by waterborne aircraft was often expressed in seconds rather than distance. Relevant data concerning patrol aircraft in some cases appears no longer to exist. N/A = not applicable.

Appendix 3

Summary of Coastal Command operations, 1 July–15 October 1940

A = Number of routine patrols/number of sorties

B = Number of offensive operations/number of sorties

C = Number of special patrols/number of sorties (for period 1 August–5 September, includes total of PR and strike sorties (RAF and FAA)

D = Number of photo-reconnaissance sorties

E = Number of convoys given special air escort

Activity over 24 hours ending 06.00 on given date

July	A	B	C	D	E
1	26/48		9/11		?
2	30/54		12/37		14
3	24/44		14/25		15
4	22/45		16/42		12
5	30/51		20/37		17
6	40/59		18/29		16
7	13/53		23/35		16
8	34/48		17/25		16
9	41/60		16/25		13
10	34/55		19/39		15
11	29/48		28/34		16
12	27/37		28/30		16
13	27/44		21/37		11
14	25/34		?		?
15	29/35		36/64		9
16	21/32		19/26		15
17	12/19		18/21		?
18	17/22		13/31		10
19	25/25		25/56		12
20	32/38		38/74		16
21	27/42		40/68		20
22	31/48		34/50		20
23	33/51		42/65		16
24	32/47		24/41		19
25	24/39		29/51		16
26	26/43		31/54		15
27	20/32		22/40		17
28	24/41		26/41		17
29	22/39		29/52		20
30	21/36		25/48		14
31	26/38		26/58		18
August					
1					
2	22/35		22/50		19
3	21/28		33/53		17
4	23/33		24/41		19
5	17/27		16/28		20
6	25/37		24/30		26
7	30/41		16/23		22
8	31/45		20/22		21
9	31/42		17/29		22
10	21/23		22/52		17
11	24/29		25/36		24
12	23/32		25/15		29
13	28/39		31/59		22
14	20/32		23/35		20
15	20/29		21/36		20
16	27/36		34/50		20
17	19/27		26/49		12
18	18/26		28/16		19
19	23/36		14/27		22
20	27/42		21/39		23
21	13/14		20/48		18
22	26/33		21/59		24
23	31/41		17/22		25
24	22/33		17/41		21

	A	B	C	D	E
25	16/24		21/35		18
26	27/38		38/91		22
27	27/38		39/59		17
28	30/41		30/50		20
29	25/34		20/50		16
30	29/40		24/42		20
31	24/31		11/23		22
September					
1	20/32		31/65		20
2	27/38		28/70		25
3	25/31		27/53		22
4	29/40	6	14/18		17
5	25/37	6	17/23		20
6	25/37	5/22	20/24		23
7	23/33	3/18	28/32		20
8	23/32	7/24	26/32		18
9	16/27	4/22	20/22		17
10	22/33	11/46	28/36		17
11	22/33	17/33	17/21	6	18
12	20/28	8/45	16/19	10	18
13	15/25	6/15	6/6	8	17
14	19/28	5/18	17/24	5	21
15	20/35	1/3	15/19	6	21
16	19/30	4/24	21/34	7	20
17	14/20	2/3	15/20	5	16
18	11/15	4/24	15/20	7	21
19	22/23	6/19	10/19	6	23
20	19/27	4/12	7/9	5	23
21	20/31	14/46	11/17	8	21
22	24/36	7/13	26/31	7	15
23	13/20	3/11	19/20	7	15
24	21/32	8/31	18/20	8	13
25	21/31	8/29	18/20	7	21
26	21/32	8/26	22/29	9	22
27	19/31	7/18	21/37	6	17
28	17/27	5/22	20/31	5	14
29	16/27	7/22	13/19	4	22
30	17/25	6/31	24/42	8	22
October					
1	20/30	7/23	27/50	6	19
2	21/32	4/12	19/24	7	20
3	16/24	8/37	20/30	5	18
4	15/24	3/12	15/15	4	13
5	10/12	8/13	5/5	5	12
6	5/5	4/9	8/10	6	14
7	15/21	8/31	16/24	8	27
8	20/29	10/24	13/24	8	23
9	9/11	4/16	16/22	6	10
10	14/18	10/36	21/30	10	19
11	16/23	7/25	15/17	8	21
12	12/19	2/6	28/42	8	21
13	19/28	5/14	16/21	7	19
14	8/13	3/5	16/26	2	17
15	14/15	5/19	21/33	6	19

Select index

252

254

256